The JFK Myths

The JFK Myths

A SCIENTIFIC INVESTIGATION OF THE
KENNEDY ASSASSINATION

Larry M. Sturdivan

First Edition 2005

Published in the United States by
Paragon House
1925 Oakcrest Avenue
St. Paul, MN 55113

Library of Congress Cataloging-in-Publication Data

Sturdivan, Larry M., 1939-
  The JFK myths : a scientific investigation of the Kennedy assassination / Larry M. Sturdivan.-- 1st ed.
    p. cm.
  ISBN 1-55778-847-2 (pbk. : alk. paper) 1. Kennedy, John F. (John Fitzgerald), 1917-1963--Assassination. 2. Firearms--United States--Identification--Case studies. 3. Forensic ballistics--United States--Case studies. I. Title.
  E842.9.S75 2005
  364.152'4'097309046--dc22
                                    2005003543

The paper used in this publication meets the minimum requirements of American National Standard for Information Sciences—Permanence of Paper for Printed Library Materials, ANSIZ39.48-1984.

Manufactured in the United States of America

10 9 8 7 6 5 4 3 2

For current information about all releases from Paragon House,
visit the web site at http://www.paragonhouse.com

"History is the present. That's why every generation writes it anew. But what most people think of as history is its end product, myth."

—*E. L. Doctorow*

To Dr. Alfred G. "Bud" Oliver, Former chief of the Biophysics Division of the Chemical Research and Development Laboratories at Edgewood Arsenal, where research was conducted for the Warren Commission, mentor, advisor, and friend; the late Victor R. "Bob" Clare, colleague, teacher, and friend; and the late Dr. Arthur Dziemian, Chief of the Biophysics Division when the JFK investigation was conducted for the Warren Commission. Without these three, the scientific investigation of the Kennedy assassination might never have been completed.

CONTENTS

LIST OF FIGURES

LIST OF TABLES

LIST OF ACRONYMS AND ABBREVIATIONS

ABA—The American Bar Association.

ABC—The American Broadcast Company.

AP—The Associated Press.

APG—Aberdeen Proving Ground (located in Maryland, on the Chesapeake Bay).

AGC—Automatic Gain Control (in a two-way radio).

BB&N—Bolt, Baranek, and Newman (the HSCA acoustic experts).

BD—Biophysics Division (of EA, where the wound ballistics tests were done).

BRL—The Ballistic Research Laboratory (at APG, where the exterior ballistics tests were done).

CBS—The Columbia Broadcasting System.

CE—Commission Exhibit (referring to the Warren Commission).

CIA—The Central Intelligence Agency

DPD—The Dallas Police Department.

DF—Degrees of Freedom (used in statistical analysis).

EA—Edgewood Arsenal (located in Maryland, on the Chesapeake Bay).

EOP—The External Occipital Protuberance (or occiput).

ER—The Emergency Room (for instance, that of Parkland Memorial Hospital, Dallas).

FBI—The Federal Bureau of Investigation.

FPP—The Forensic Pathology Panel (of the HSCA investigation).

HSCA—The House Select Committee on Assassinations (U.S. House of Representatives).

JFK—President John Fitzgerald Kennedy.

LBJ—President Lyndon Banes Johnson.

M-C—Mannlicher-Carcano (rifle manufacturer).

MS—The Mean Square (used in statistical analysis).

NAA—Neutron Activation Analysis (for trace elements, usually in a metal alloy).

NASA—The National Aeronautics and Space Administration.

NBC—The National Broadcasting Company.

Pb—Lead (the chemical symbol).

Sb—Antimony (the chemical symbol).

SD—Standard Deviation (when referring to statistical analyses).

SS—The Secret Service (Treasury Department bodyguards for the president and others).

SS—The Sum of Squares (when referring to statistical analyses).

S&W—Smith and Wesson (firearms manufacturer; also a type of caliber .38 handgun bullet).

TSBD—The Texas School Book Depository (adjacent to Dealey Plaza, Lee Oswald's employer).

WC—The Warren Commission (officially, The President's Commission on the Assassination of President Kennedy).

WCC—Western Cartridge Company (Division of Winchester).

WCC/MC—Bullets made by the WCC to fit the MC rifle.

ACKNOWLEDGEMENT

There are many to whom I owe a great debt for their help on this project. Their generous gifts of time and knowledge significantly improved the accuracy of the contents of this book. My sincere thanks to the following (in no particular order):

Mr. Roy Bexon, Defence Science and Technology Laboratory, Porton Down, Salisbury, England, long-time friend and colleague, for incisive critique of the text and appendices that helped to structure both.

Dr. Ken Rahn, Professor of Atmospheric Chemistry (retired), University of Rhode Island, more recent friend and colleague, for collaboration, advice, and comment on the manuscript.

Mr. Dale Myers, Emmy-award winning computer animator, for invaluable help on the photographs, supplying graphic illustrations, and fixing some of the more egregious errors.

Dr. Michael Carey, Professor of Neurosurgery, Louisiana State University Health Sciences Center, long-time friend and colleague, for advice on the neurodynamics and invaluable correction of errors in the text.

Mr. John Hunt, Kennedy Assassination Investigator, for supplying hard to get material from the Archives and spotting distracting errors of fact in the text.

Dr. Carroll Peters, Professor Emeritus, Mechanical and Aerospace Engineering, U. Tennessee Space Institute, Tullahoma, long-time friend and colleague, for correcting the ballistic errors in text and appendices and supplying much of the firearms information.

Dr. Robert Grossman, Chairman, Department of Neurosurgery, Baylor University, Houston, recent friend and coauthor, for his first-hand information on the wounds to the President and supplying the sketch used as figure 52.

Dr. William Hartmann, Planetary Science Institute, Tucson, for his advice and information on the startle data and his continuing encouragement in this project.

Dr. Chad Zimmermann, DC, whose collaboration in the

visit to the National Archives to see the autopsy material kept me from missing vital details.

Mr. John Canal, Kennedy assassination author, for his generous support and advice in assassination research and on the publication process.

Mr. Steve Barber, acoustics study debunker, for leading me through the arcane world of acoustics-study debate.

Dr. John Lattimer, Kennedy assassination author, for supplying advice and research material.

Mr. Todd Vaughan, Mr. Joel Grant, Ms. Patricia Lambert, and Dr. Martin Kelly, JFK investigators, for their advice and information.

The reference librarians at the New Mexico State Library.

And finally, to my family; my sons, Deryck, for his advice and help with the materials and Christopher for his invaluable work on the graphics, and, most of all, my wife Betty, without whose unending patience and advice this book would not have been possible.

FOREWORD

This is one of the most important books on the Kennedy assassination ever written. Of the 2000 or so out there, this book alone tells the clear, simple story of the assassination provided by the physical evidence. It stands in sharp contrast to the other books, articles, videotapes, and conferences, which focus on weaker evidence such as witness testimony, events before the assassination, attendant circumstances, and errors and omissions of the official investigations. These things have planted doubts and confused the country for over forty years now. It is time to tell the rest of the story.

This book is written by the person most qualified to tell it—Larry M. Sturdivan. Larry's biography is impressive enough, but it does not give the full measure of the man and why he is the person to deliver this message. In 1961, Larry graduated from Oklahoma State University with a B.S. in physics, then spent some time in graduate school and working in the family businesses. On November 22, 1963 (the day of the assassination), he received and accepted a job offer involving wound ballistics from the Aberdeen Proving Ground in Maryland. The next spring he would observe ballistic tests conducted at the Biophysics Laboratory of Edgewood Arsenal in support of the Warren Commission's investigation. Later he would receive an M.S. in statistics from the University of Delaware. In 1978, as a senior researcher, he was made the Army's contact in helping the House Select Committee on Assassinations (HSCA) as it reinvestigated the case. He testified extensively to it about the wound/ballistics involved in the assassination.

Impressive as this background is, it alone would not have been enough to shape the present book—the proper mindset is essential. Larry brings to this task a sharp, curious mind that seems to be interested in everything scientific, where "scientific" is defined in a very broad sense. But even more important, he couples these things with a big dose of common sense, perhaps reflecting his Oklahoman roots. Put these three things together and you have the recipe for this book. It has not been written before because Larry was the only one to do it. I have had the privilege of working with Larry for only three years, but it has been enough to convince me of his true capabilities.

What is so important about this book? Quite simply, it tells the opposite story from what everyone else is telling about the assassination, and it buttresses the story with facts and figures at every turn. The other 1999 books tell you that the case is so detailed, intricate, and contaminated by the long years of official mistakes—and misconduct—that it will probably never be solved. Give up hope, all ye who enter here! But *The JFK Myths* shows that just the opposite is true—that thanks to the abundance of physical evidence and its long, careful investigation by many experts, there remain remarkably few loose ends. This is good news indeed, a message that needs to be appreciated by everyone who cares about this assassination and the terrible effects that it has had on America.

There is yet another story here, and one that is still developing. *The JFK Myths* doesn't dwell on it much, so I will. It concerns the very different timelines, or progressions, of evidence for conspiracy and for nonconspiracy. Roughly speaking, the bulk of the evidence for conspiracy appeared early—some would even say in the first days and weeks after the assassination—and has remained nearly steady as four decades passed. By contrast, the evidence for nonconspiracy—roughly equatable to the physical evidence—has increased steadily throughout those decades, to the point where it is now all but irrefutable.

The last decade or so provides an interesting illustration of these disparate trends. First Oliver Stone's powerful movie *JFK,* released in late 1991, renewed the public's interest in the assassination. Its distortions of the evidence gave unjustified credence to outlandish conspiracy theories. The resulting public outcry led to the formation of the Assassination Records Review Board, which declassified millions of pages of records during its four-year existence. Although conspiracists insisted that the smoking gun would finally be found within those documents, nothing of the sort happened. When it was all over, little of substance had been added to our knowledge of the assassination, and certainly nothing that pointed the finger at anyone other than Lee Harvey Oswald.

But the physical evidence fared much better during that decade, even though few people are aware of it. Slowly and quietly beneath the surface, gaps in our understanding of this evidence were being filled, and every advance cemented the lone-assassin interpretation. *The JFK Myths* gives many such examples; I highlight only two here. First, the acoustic evidence for a second shooter (presumably on the knoll) died the death it had so richly deserved since the Dictabelt recording of the Dallas Police radio transmissions surfaced in the late 1970s. The HSCA used a one-minute portion of this recording, allegedly picked up by a motorcycle officer's stuck microphone in Dealey Plaza during the shooting, to claim that a fourth shot had been fired, from a second shooter. This meant conspiracy, to which they assigned a probability of 95 percent. Thus the American public was faced with two major governmental investigations arriving at opposite conclusions for the assassination—the Warren Commission claiming that no evidence for conspiracy could be found, and the House Committee countering that conspiracy was all but certain.

But the acoustic evidence was bogus from the beginning. One need look no further than the Dallas Police Department, which knew immediately that the sounds in question came from a three-wheeler cycle—not a two-wheeler of the type that the officers in the motorcade were riding—stationed out near the Dallas Trade Mart, some three miles from the assassination. They also knew exactly whose cycle it was, because he was "the whistler" of the department. All the later "technical" analyses supporting the extra shot are thus useless. But if you don't believe that the Dallas police can tell their two types of motorcycles apart, you can turn to a later National Research Council report on the acoustics, which demolishes the HSCA's "experts." You can also view Dale Myers's compendium of films, so brilliantly constructed during 2004, that shows that Officer H.B. McLain was not—not just could not have been—where the HSCA needed him to be in order to support their theory. I believe that the acoustic fiasco was one of the sorriest chapters in the entire history of JFK assassination "research," and I am happy to see it over and done with. Rest in peace, bogus acoustics!

A second important advance of physical evidence during the last decade was clearing up some alleged problems with the neutron activation analyses of the bullet fragments from the assassination. I had the privilege of working with Larry on this topic. The five sets of bullet-lead fragments are important because their chemistry and ballistics can potentially provide evidence on the number of bullets that struck Kennedy and Governor Connally. Two of the five had brass jackets, whose ballistic engravings tied them unambiguously to Oswald's rifle. The other three were just lead, and so had to be compared to the larger fragments chemically in order to determine their origins. On the night of the assassination, the FBI tried to do this with optical emission spectroscopy, the standard chemical technique back then, but failed because the samples were too small and too similar in composition. A few months later, they tried the newer neutron activation analysis (NAA), but again failed, this time because of a systematic error that they did not recognize.

The HSCA had Professor Vincent P. Guinn reanalyze the fragments with NAA in 1977, and he not only showed that the little fragments grouped clearly with the big fragments (meaning that only two bullets, both from Oswald's rifle, had hit the men), but also resolved the problems in the FBI's earlier analyses and found that they matched his. In the process, however, Guinn found that the chemical composition of the lead in Oswald's bullets varied enough down a single core to potentially merge the two groups into one big one and so nullify the critical finding of two bullets from one rifle.

Larry the ballistician/statistician and I the NAA analyst set about to see whether we could resolve these difficulties. We eventually were able to verify the original findings and even extend them into other areas of the assassination, confirming Larry's long belief that the NAA data were "the queen of the physical evidence" from the assassination. Our results were published in the open scientific literature in 2004, some of the very few peer-reviewed articles on the assassination.

The moral of all this is simply that the strong evidence in the JFK assassination speaks with one voice against Lee Harvey Oswald and no one else, and that the weak evidence is all over the place. This kind of result should not surprise anyone, given the nature of the two types of evidence. We should all be grateful that the full story is finally being told. The Warren Commission was right after all, and, in spite of the impressive amount of scientific expertise they assembled, the House Select Committee on Assassinations blew it big-time.

But why did it take so long for the real story to come out? I say that it didn't really take this long, that the real story was out in plain view for anyone to grasp who knew the difference between physical evidence and the weaker types. But it did take four decades for the story to be fully appreciated, and the critics must shoulder the blame for that. They beat the drum of conspiracy and cover-up ceaselessly, knowing full well that their evidence didn't support their words. In keeping a false story before the American people, they duped 80 percent of them. *The JFK Myths* lays their deeds bare for all to see.

Everyone with an interest in the JFK assassination should read and reread this book until it becomes part of them. Then they will not only understand the simplicity of the JFK assassination, but also the proper way of investigating it. By seeing what went wrong in the past and why, they may be able to prevent similar mistakes from occurring in the future. Let's hope so.

Kenneth A. Rahn
Narragansett, Rhode Island

DEALEY PLAZA -- DALLAS, TEXAS

1. TEXAS SCHOOL BOOK DEPOSITORY
2. DAL-TEX BUILDING
3. DALLAS COUNTY RECORDS BUILDING
4. DALLAS COUNTY CRIMINAL COURTS BUILDING
5. OLD COURT HOUSE
6. NEELEY BRYAN HOUSE
7. DALLAS COUNTY GOVERNMENT CENTER (UNDER CONSTRUCTION)
8. UNITED STATES POST OFFICE BUILDING
9. PERGOLAS
10. PERISTYLES AND REFLECTING POOLS
11. RAILROAD OVERPASS (TRIPLE UNDERPASS)

Commission Exhibit No. 876

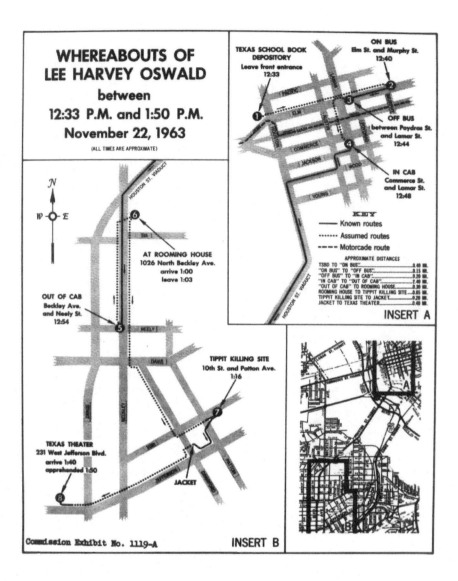

WHEREABOUTS OF LEE HARVEY OSWALD

between
12:33 P.M. and 1:50 P.M.
November 22, 1963

(ALL TIMES ARE APPROXIMATE)

TEXAS SCHOOL BOOK DEPOSITORY
Leave front entrance
12:33

ON BUS
Elm St. and Murphy St.
12:40

OFF BUS
between Poydras St. and Lamar St.
12:44

IN CAB
Commerce St. and Lamar St.
12:48

KEY
— Known routes
.... Assumed routes
- - - Motorcade route

APPROXIMATE DISTANCES
TSBD TO "ON BUS"..................................0.40 MI.
"ON BUS" TO "OFF BUS"...........................0.15 MI.
"OFF BUS" TO "IN CAB"...........................0.20 MI.
"IN CAB" TO "OUT OF CAB"......................2.40 MI.
"OUT OF CAB" TO ROOMING HOUSE........0.30 MI.
ROOMING HOUSE TO TIPPIT KILLING SITE....0.85 MI.
TIPPIT KILLING SITE TO JACKET...............0.20 MI.
JACKET TO TEXAS THEATER.....................0.40 MI.

INSERT A

AT ROOMING HOUSE
1026 North Beckley Ave.
arrive 1:00
leave 1:03

OUT OF CAB
Beckley Ave. and Neely St.
12:54

TIPPIT KILLING SITE
10th St. and Patton Ave.
1:16

TEXAS THEATER
231 West Jefferson Blvd.
arrive 1:40
apprehended 1:50

JACKET

Commission Exhibit No. 1119-A

INSERT B

INTRODUCTION

On Friday, November 22, 1963, as most older Americans vividly remember, President John F. Kennedy was shot in a motorcade in the streets of Dallas, Texas. This led to one of the greatest American murder mysteries. Lee Harvey Oswald, an intense and iconoclastic young man who worked in the building by which the motorcade was passing, was arrested and charged with the crime...and then murdered on Sunday by a bystander in the Dallas Police Station. Almost immediately, questions were raised about the whole affair. Had Oswald really pulled the trigger? Were shots fired from other directions? Was there a conspiracy? Was it the Soviets? The Cubans? The Mob? Disgruntled CIA operatives? Was there a coverup?

The Warren Commission began its probe of the affair a few days later and published a report in 1964 concluding that Oswald, some months after taking a missed shot at a prominent right-wing general, had shot the President from a sixth-floor window and had acted alone. A flood of books followed, claiming botched investigations, multiple gunmen, and conspiracies of greater or lesser magnitude. In 1967, New Orleans district attorney Jim Garrison traced tenuous connections between third-echelon CIA hangers-on, minor crime figures, private eyes, and other characters in the New Orleans demi-monde, and charged a prominent businessman with being part of a conspiracy to kill Kennedy, but the trial was something of a shambles resulting in acquittal.

In 1976-78, after public pressure, the U. S. House of Representatives formed a Select Committee on Assassinations (HSCA) and began a new review of the case. Larry Sturdivan and I, along with a number of other scientists and technical researchers, found ourselves tapped to examine various aspects of the evidence, using the latest techniques of analysis and new facts uncovered in intervening years. I entered the fray as an analyst of photographic images, thinking there was a good chance we would find evidence of multiple gunmen, but the more I learned about the evidence our team was uncovering, the more I became convinced it all pointed back to Oswald acting on his own. Sturdivan, an expert in interpreting wounds caused by bullets and other projectiles—along with others of the technical staff—moved in the same direction. Nonetheless, to our surprise, the official 1978 finding of the committee was that although Oswald fired all known shots including those that killed the President, there was a "high probability that two gunmen fired" from different directions, and that "on the basis of the evidence….Kennedy was probably assassinated as a result of a conspiracy." The report did not finger any conspirators, but could "not preclude" that individuals from the anti-Castro and/or organized crime communities might have been involved (though Oswald himself, who had defected to the Soviet Union for a while, purported to be pro-Castro).

This murky finding, of course, unleashed new books charging various far-reaching conspiratorial plots. In 1991, Oliver Stone built his widely-discussed film *JFK* (complete with Kevin Costner and a score by John Williams) around the Garrison investigation and a potpourri of conspiracy ideas—but the film was intriguing more as a rambling, noir-ish record of the American zeitgeist than as a coherent theory of the crime.

What really happened? What is the real evidence behind the morass of charges and counter-charges? This book not only shines light on the inner workings of the House Select Committee on Assassinations, but gives some sober answers based on the Committee's new findings. Some of the new evidence that impressed me during my service on the technical staff are discussed here in detail. For example, staff researchers applied the technique of neutron activation analysis, which was unavailable in the 1960s, to reveal that the recovered bullet fragments all came from the same batch of bullets—in other words, among all the fragments recovered from the President's body, the car, and Governor Connolly's stretcher, there was not the slightest evidence of any bullet from another batch or manufactured separately for a different kind of gun. In another example, the committee team recovered two new versions of the infamous backyard photos showing Oswald armed with his rifle—photos that conspiracy theorists had alleged were fakes planted in Oswald's home. One came from the possessions of Oswald friend George de Mohrenschildt, a cryptic figure with CIA ties who committed suicide on the eve of scheduled testimony to committee operatives. The circumstances showed that Oswald had acquaintances in a shadowy world of paramilitary types, but de Mohrenschildt's good-condition photo, signed by Oswald, discredited theories that the photographs examined by the Warren Commission had been faked or planted later. Work by Sturdivan (and my own discussions with forensic anthropologist Walter Birkby in Arizona) demolished the idea that you can tell the direction from which a bullet came by the direction of debris blasted out of a shattered skull; under the hydrodynamic pressure of the bullet passing through the brain material, the skull fails and blows out at a more-or-less random point of weakness unrelated to the position of the murderer. So the idea that a bullet entered the President's head from the front because brain matter ended up on the back of the car—the idea that had intrigued many students of the case, including me when I was called by the Select Committee—proved to be fallacious. My own studies of "jiggles" in the best film of the case, probably due to startle reactions, suggested an earlier shot than the Warren Commission had allowed, which relaxed the time constraints for the three shots, and gave Oswald more time to aim—as also discussed by Sturdivan in these pages.

There is an informal rule in science: If you have a theory, and item after item of new data conflict with the theory, then you better think twice about continuing to defend it! Here was a perfect example. Most of the data (at least as judged by some of us) conflicted with the idea of multiple gunmen or any serious conspiracy. It's impossible to rule out that Oswald hadn't moved in circles where someone might have advocated that "someone should get rid of the President," but one can rule out the popular scenario of a grand conspiracy where multiple gunmen shoot from different directions, with Oswald being the designated patsy. Aside from the new physical evidence that all bullets seem to have come from one gun, this scenario makes no sense if you follow it through from the viewpoint of the conspirators. If marksmen were stationed to shoot from the front and the rear (the grassy knoll and the schoolbook Depository), then the conspirators would have had to assume that wounds from front and back would be identified—so there never could have been an advance plan to have it blamed on Oswald alone.

Strangely, as chronicled here by Sturdivan, the leader the House Select Committee investigation staff, prominent Cornell University attorney Robert Blakey, chose to draw a pro-conspiracy conclusion opposite to what many of us investigators felt the new data showed! From a personal as well as a historical point of view, this is one of the most interesting aspects of this whole episode. How did it happen? In my mind, it was a collision of two, centuries-old ways of getting truth: the advocacy method and the scientific method. The advocacy method, or legal system, which dominates our society and our advertising, picks one side of an issue and then pays someone to "build a case" by presenting only that idea. Thus, a prosecuting attorney "proves" that the suspect committed the murder, and the defense attorney "proves" that doubts are overwhelming and the suspect must be found innocent. Neither side wants to spend time on evidence that does not support its case. Indeed, they may work to keep important evidence completely out of the trial! Nonetheless, the theory is that if people are paid to defend each side, the truth will emerge from their argument. One side "wins." In our case, Mr. Blakey, who already thought he had found evidence linking some of the principles to the mob, decided to "build his case" on an old audio tape purported to prove four shots were fired—a tape which, even at the time, many experts felt had too low signal-to-noise to allow any reliable interpretation, and which seems later, as Sturdivan discusses, to be embarrassingly irrelevant.

The scientific method, on the other hand, deliberately lays out all bits of relevant evidence on the table, and debates them in collegial manner. The reward is not in "winning the debate," but rather in being the one who provides the best evidence. The method is specifically not to advocate one side from the outset, but to attempt to remain neutral, to find evidence that can root out false hypotheses and to identify the one interpretation that best fits the whole body of evidence.

In my view, this collision between the advocacy method and the scientific method is a key but largely unnoticed factor in understanding our times. Larry Sturdivan shows how it played out in promoting doubts about one of the most notorious twentieth century crimes.

William K. Hartmann
Planetary Science Institute, Tucson
Fellow, American Association for the Advancement of Science

CHAPTER ONE
Nobody Can Stop It

> "…Jackie, if somebody wants to shoot me from a window with a rifle, nobody can stop it, so why worry about it."
>
> —*John F. Kennedy*[1]

The two-day trip to Texas on November 21 and 22, 1963, was primarily a political one. President John F. Kennedy's popularity had been slipping. Vice President Lyndon Johnson and Kenneth O'Donnell, special assistant to the President, had conceived the Texas trip as a method of bolstering support for the administration, as well as one that would help fill the campaign coffers. Texas Governor John B. Connally had talked the two out of multiple fundraising lunches and dinners, out of concern that the citizens would think that the only reason for coming to Texas was the money. The final agenda included the dedication of the U.S. Air Force School of Aerospace Medicine at Brooks Air Force Base in San Antonio and other public appearances, but only one fundraiser. Late in the morning of November 22, the presidential party arrived at Dallas' Love Field to begin a planned motorcade through the downtown area to the Trade Center, where the President would speak at lunch. Later that day, they planned to fly to Austin for the $100-a-plate dinner that would culminate the whirlwind trip. The sky had cleared that morning, so it was not necessary to use the weatherproof "bubble top" fitted to the presidential limousine. This transparent canopy was for weather only; it offered no real protection from bullets or explosives.

The trip was not an onerous duty for the President. He loved to travel and to work the crowds. If he was disturbed by the

---

1. Related by Jacqueline Kennedy to Kenneth O'Donnell after the assassination. Quoted in *Johnny, We Hardly Knew Ye,* O'Donnell & Powers. See Bibliography on page 311 for a list of the books and other material used as sources of data and background information.

demonstrations that marred Ambassador Adlai Stevenson's visit to Dallas the month before, he did not discuss it with the vice president when Mr. Johnson joined the party at Love Field. Nor did he mention it to the governor or Mrs. Nellie Connally, who were riding with him and Mrs. Kennedy in the limousine. Twice that morning the motorcade stopped at the request of the President, so that he could personally talk to random members of the large and enthusiastic crowd that had come downtown to participate in the well-publicized motorcade.

People had been gathering all morning along the motorcade route, among them a 45-year-old steamfitter named Howard L. Brennan, who sat on a concrete wall at the inside corner of Houston and Elm Streets while waiting for the motorcade. As he waited, he noticed a number of people appearing and disappearing at the windows of the Texas School Book Depository across the street. Among those he saw was a man who appeared "a couple of times" at the right sixth-floor corner window.[2]

Except for the police escort, the presidential limousine led the motorcade through a route that deliberately took them through the heart of Dallas. Secret Service Agent William R. Greer was driving. To his right was Roy H. Kellerman, Assistant Special Agent in Charge of the White House detail and in charge of security for this trip. The President and Mrs. Jacqueline Kennedy were riding in the back seat. This seat could be raised, but was in its lowered position that day. Each smiled and waved to the crowd on their respective sides of the car, seldom looking at each other. The Connallys were doing much the same thing from their position in the jump seats in front of, and a bit lower than the Kennedy's, the Governor at the right, in front of the President. The jump seats were also facing forward. Governor Connally had taken his hat off, perhaps to let the crowd get a better look or perhaps to be more in accord with the perennially hatless Kennedy. Whatever the reason, he was holding his hat in his right hand, letting it dangle from his fingers as he smiled and nodded to the bystanders.

The President's car was closely followed by the open-top Secret Service car with the eight agents that rounded out the President's security detail. This was followed by the vice president's car with Mrs. Claudia

---

2. For sources of quoted material, see the name of the person quoted in the Individual References section of the bibliography.

Johnson and Senator Ralph W. Yarborough to the left of Mr. Johnson. Trailing the vice-presidential Secret Service followup car were several more automobiles carrying other dignitaries and a bus with the press contingent. At the west edge of the downtown area the motorcade route left Main Street to circle the north side of Dealey Plaza via Houston and Elm Streets. As they approached the sharp left turn at the intersection of Houston and Elm, Agent Rufus Youngblood, seated in the right front seat of the vice-presidential car, glanced at the clock on top of the Texas School Book Depository, straight ahead. It was 12:30, the time scheduled for their arrival at the Trade Center. Secret Service Agent Winston Lawson, riding in the lead with Dallas Chief of Police Jesse Curry and Secret Service Agent Forrest Sorrels, radioed ahead to the Trade Center to add an estimated five minutes to their arrival time.

The closer they came to the downtown area, the larger and more enthusiastic the crowd became. The contrast with the reception given to Ambassador Stevenson was striking. As they made the turn to the southwest onto Elm Street, Mrs. Connally turned to her right and said, "Mr. President, you can't say Dallas doesn't love you." "That's obvious," he replied. They passed the Book Depository building on the right as they completed the turn and started down the slight incline toward the underpass beneath the railroad tracks. Just beyond the underpass, they would enter the ramp to the Stemmons Freeway on the route to the Trade Center. The car was moving just over 11 miles per hour. To the left was the grass of Dealey Plaza. Behind the crowd, ahead on its right, a local businessman and amateur photographer, Abraham Zapruder, was filming the presidential limousine with his 8 mm Bell and Howell movie camera from a perch on the pedestal of a depression-era concrete pergola, one of a pair flanking the slopes of Dealey Plaza. Further along that same side of the street, the last of the downtown crowd were standing in front of a grassy knoll that led up to a police car parking lot.

Suddenly, there was a loud cracking noise that Governor Connally, a hunter familiar with firearms, immediately identified as rifle fire. It seemed to him that it came from behind and to the right. He swiveled to the right to see if he could locate the source of the shot. Failing to see anything, he turned back, intending to look over his left shoulder into the back seat at the President and Mrs. Kennedy. He never made this turn. As he turned forward, he was, in his words "…knocked over, just doubled over by the force of the bullet." He immediately noticed his shirt was "drenched with blood." He shouted, "No, no, no!" then "My God, they are going to kill us all." As he was speaking, he again turned to the right far enough to bring the wounded president within his view before turning back toward the front. He never said whether he actually saw the President. Realizing that he was gravely wounded, he "more or less straightened up" just before his wife pulled him down into her lap.

In the crowd in front of the Depository building, a Book Depository employee, Virgie Rachley, thought somebody had thrown a firecracker into the street, as she noticed some sparks on the pavement near the rear of the limousine simultaneously with the first noise. James Tague, who was watching the motorcade from Main Street, near the triple railroad underpass, found a fresh smear of lead on the curb nearby. When he told Deputy Sheriff Eddy Walters about it, Walters noticed a spot of blood on his cheek. Tague then remembered that he had felt a scratch on his cheek at "the second or third shot."

Howard Brennan, thinking that the first shot was a backfire somewhere in the motorcade, glanced back up the street, and then noticed the man he had previously seen at the corner window of the Depository. The man was standing in the same place, leaning against the left side of the window with a rifle in hand "aiming for his last shot." Among several other witnesses who saw the barrel of a rifle protruding from that same window was Amos Lee Euins, a ninth-grade student who was also looking around after the first shot, which he also mistook for a backfire. In his words, "Everybody else started looking around. Then I looked up at the window, and he shot again." Euins hid behind a wall that was part of the pair of decorative structures flanking Main Street and watched the man in the corner window fire his final shot.

Three employees of the Texas School Book Depository, James Jarman, Jr., Bonnie Ray Williams, and Harold Norman, were watching the motorcade from windows on the fifth floor, two of them directly beneath the window where the gunman was seen. At first, the loud noise didn't alarm them. Like many of the onlookers, their initial impression was that it was a backfire. But before the second shot, Norman noticed that the President "slumped, or something" and said, "It is someone shooting at the President, and I believe it came from up above us." Williams said the second and third shots sounded like they were right in the building, and

"...it even shook the building, the side we were on. Cement fell on my head." Jarman noted the debris on Williams' head. Norman "...could also hear something that sounded like shell hulls hitting the floor..." above their heads.

People along the motorcade route heard gunfire that sounded like it originated from several locations around Dealey Plaza, including the triple underpass and various buildings. Some thought the shots came from the vicinity of a grassy area to the right of the advancing motorcade, perhaps the concrete "arcade" where Zapruder was standing. Of those who could identify a direction, a majority thought it came from the vicinity of the Texas School Book Depository. The number of gunshots that they heard varied from one to several.

Mrs. Connally did not identify the first shot as gunfire. Hearing a "disturbing" noise over her right shoulder, she turned to her right and looked over her shoulder to see the President clutch his neck with both hands. He said nothing, but "just sort of slumped down in the seat." She noticed that the governor had also turned to the right and heard him say "No, no, no," as he turned back. Jackie Kennedy was saying, "They have shot my husband." Nellie Connally heard a second shot and saw her husband "recoil" and slump in his seat. She pulled him into her lap "out of the line of fire." Soon thereafter, both the Connallys heard another shot. For her, it was the third shot she heard. The governor didn't actually hear the second shot, the one he knew hit him, but he also identified the final shot as the third. Immediately, they felt and saw "blood and brain tissue all over the interior of the car..." The President lunged backward into the car seat and collapsed to the left into his wife's arms. Mrs. Kennedy said, "They have killed my husband, I have his brains in my hand." Roy Kellerman shouted "Let's get out of here; we are hit!"

A picture snapped by AP photographer James Altgens shows Jackie Kennedy sprawled on the rear deck, apparently in an attempt to rescue a fragment of the President's shattered skull. The car, which had momentarily slowed as driver Bill Greer swiveled to look into the back at his passengers, lurched forward as he stepped on the accelerator, threatening to throw Mrs. Kennedy off the back of the vehicle. Secret Service Agent Clinton J. Hill, who had run forward from his position on the left running board of the followup car, leapt up on the back of the car, and is seen helping Jackie return to the passenger compartment. He remained in that position, clinging to the back of the accelerating limousine and shielding the President and Mrs. Kennedy from further gunfire.

The frantic ride to Parkland Memorial Hospital was nearly silent. Mrs. Kennedy was moaning softly, "What have they done to you." The only other sound was the repeated whisper of Mrs. Connally to her husband, "Be still, it is going to be all right." But for the man behind her it was not going to be all right. The President's head wound was immediately lethal, though it took a few minutes for his heart to stop beating from lack of oxygen and his ineffective breathing to slowly fade. At Parkland, the jarring stop brought the governor back to consciousness. He sat up in a vain attempt to get out of the car and out of the way of the people who were trying to get to the President. The exertion caused him to collapse again, whereupon the staff at Parkland swiftly placed him on a stretcher and raced him into trauma room two. It was at this point that he first felt an "excruciating pain" in his chest. Soon thereafter, the President arrived in trauma room one across the hall.

Two teams of surgeons immediately began to work on the two men. According to the report of Dr. Kemp Clark, Director of Neurological Surgery, Dr. James Carrico was the first physician to attend to the President. Noting the slow, agonal respiratory efforts, he inserted a cuffed endotracheal tube into the President's throat. While doing so, he found a "ragged wound of the trachea immediately below the larynx." He also noted the massive wound to the right side of the President's skull through which blood and brain tissue were exuding. Dr. Clark's report mentions, "Both cerebral and cerebellar tissue were extruding from the wound."[3] Shortly thereafter, attending surgeon Dr. Malcolm Perry arrived, followed by several other physicians, to participate in what each soon knew was a futile attempt at resuscitation. Evidently thinking that the blood in the President's throat from the wound in his trachea might

---

3. This wound is described differently by three of the attending physicians in their written reports, two of which give the time of the report as 1630 (4:30 p.m.) on November 22, 1963, four and a half hours after the President was declared dead. Dr. Clark described it twice, using the phrases "...occipital region..." and "... right occipitoparietal region..." Dr. Perry used the phrase "...right posterior cranium..." Dr. Jenkins said "...right side of the head (temporal and occipital)..." Dr. Ronald Jones said "...the back side of the head." The actual location shown in the autopsy photographs is predominantly parietal but extending into temporal bone and nearly to the occipital bone.

be contributing to his breathing difficulty, the team decided upon a tracheotomy, cutting a hole directly into the windpipe through which air could flow into his lungs unimpeded by clotting blood. As the wound to his trachea was at the location usually selected for a tracheotomy, Dr. Perry widened this small hole to provide for an adequate airway. This obliterated the wound. Doctors Robert McClelland, Charles Baxter, and Paul Peters inserted tubes into his chest to evacuate any blood, fluid, or air that might be compromising his breathing, while others cut down to expose veins in his left forearm and both legs. Here they inserted tubes for massive infusion of blood and fluids. As the breathing assistance was ineffective, Dr. Marion T. Jenkins hooked the President to an anesthesia machine to aid respiration. Following a few more minutes of frantic and futile activity by the physicians, the President suffered cardiac arrest. After being given last rites, he was pronounced dead at 1:00 p.m. by Kemp Clark, the neurosurgeon.

The attending physicians never turned Kennedy over, so none noted the small wound to his upper back at the base of his neck in their reports submitted a few hours later. The treatment they rendered to keep an airway open and assist with breathing must be done with the patient on his back. Though Dr. Clark did move the President's head to examine the massive wound over and behind his ear, his report does not mention a small entry wound in the back of his skull. After the President was pronounced dead, the room was quickly emptied except for Mrs. Kennedy and the personnel who had the unenviable task of removing the wires and tubes from the body. None of the attending physicians lingered to turn his body over and examine his back for entry wounds, perhaps because they felt it would have seemed only to be morbid curiosity to manipulate and inspect the body of the dead president in front of the weeping, bloodstained widow.

Meanwhile, Connally's wounds had been assessed and the life-threatening chest wound given emergency treatment. This consisted of patching the defect in the body wall left by the exiting bullet and inserting a chest tube and water trap which would pull the air out of the lung cavity and partially reinflate his collapsed right lung. He was then taken upstairs to the operating room for completion of the repair by Dr. Robert Shaw. An elongated entry wound measuring, in Shaw's words, "three cm in its longest diameter" or about 1.2 inches, was found in his back just outside the edge of his right shoulder blade.[4] The bullet had passed through the muscle at the right edge of his back, just inside his armpit, fragmented 10 centimeters of his fifth rib, and exited just below his right nipple, leaving a five-centimeter hole. The bullet had not actually penetrated the pleural cavity. The bullet plowing through the curved section of rib created secondary missiles of bone. These projectiles had ripped through the pleura, the tissue lining his lung cavity, and lacerated the middle lobe of the lung all the way down to the bronchus, the major airway on that side of the body. After exiting his chest, the bullet penetrated the top of his right forearm, near the wrist, shattering the radius, one of the two bones in the forearm. In perforating the wrist, the bullet severed a tendon and partially transected a small nerve.[5] The bullet also deposited several small bits of its lead core as it penetrated the bone. It then exited through the palmer side of the wrist. Finally the bullet struck his left thigh about one-third of its length above the knee, penetrating into the fatty layer beneath the skin but not into the muscle. X-rays showed that the bullet left a small metal fragment at the bottom of the shallow wound.

Dr. Shaw sutured the lung and repaired the body wall. The wrist wound was treated by Dr. Charles Gregory who recovered some small metal fragments from it. Dr. Tom Shires repaired the thigh wound and closed it without a drain because of its small size. He did not recover the fragment from the bottom of the wound, as he would have had to enlarge the injury to do so. Dr. Shires realized that the tiny fragment was incapable of causing a wound that large. He was puzzled by the small amount of soft tissue damage under an entry wound of that size. The surgeons speculated that one bullet might have caused all the Governor's injuries and entered the thigh nearly spent, but there was none to be found.

At approximately 1:00 p.m., the hospital's senior engineer, Darrell C. Tomlinson, was called to attend an elevator on the ground floor. The stretcher used to transport the governor to the operating room on the

---

4. When interviewed by the staff of the House Select Committee on Assassinations in 1978, he gave a different size—1.5 cm. See Chapter 3.

5. The tendon was attached to the abductor palmaris longus muscle, which pulls the hand laterally toward the thumb. The nerve was the superficial radial nerve, a small, sensory branch of the radial nerve.

second floor (two floors up) had been placed on the elevator by orderly R.J. Jimison. Tomlinson moved it to the hall adjacent to another, similar stretcher. Some time later, one of these stretchers, which was partially blocking a restroom door, was moved by one of the medical personnel to enter the door. He did not return it to its original location when he left. When Tomlinson returned the stretcher to the wall, it "bumped the wall and a spent cartridge or bullet rolled out that apparently had been lodged under the mat." He immediately gave it to the Secret Service.

Mrs. Kennedy refused to leave Parkland without the President's body. The Secret Service and the Coroner's office had a brief, but heated argument over the coroner's insistence on conducting an autopsy of the President, as required by Texas law. A short time later, the Secret Service removed Kennedy's body and transported it in a bronze casket to Air Force One at Love Field to await the flight back to Washington, D.C. This was during the height of the Cold War and the Cuban missile crisis was a recent and disturbing memory in the minds of the individuals who worked in or near the White House. The decision was made that Vice President Lyndon Johnson would be sworn in to the presidency as soon as possible. Federal Judge Sarah T. Hughes hurried to Love Field to administer the oath of office. A few minutes later, the new president, the slain president, and their wives began the flight back toward Washington. On the way back, Air Force One was in constant radio contact with the White House. Mrs. Kennedy was offered the choice of sending her husband's body to Walter Reed Army Hospital or Bethesda Naval Hospital for the autopsy. Because of his service with the Navy, she chose the latter.

Meanwhile, back in Dallas, Howard Brennan had given a policeman, probably Inspector Herbert Sawyer, a description of the man he saw at the Book Depository window earlier and saw once again as he fired the final shot at the President. Perhaps this was the source of the description broadcast on the police radio at approximately 12:45. It described the man as "…white, slender, weighting about 165 pounds, about 5 feet, 10 inches tall, and in his early thirties," a description very similar to the one Brennan gave in an official police interview later that day. Norman and Jarman, having descended from their vantage point on the fifth floor, ran out the front door of the building, saw Brennan talking to the policeman, and reported what they had seen and heard. Amos Euins found

Sergeant D. V. Harkness of the Dallas Police and reported his observations. Harkness radioed headquarters with the message, "I have a witness that says that it came from the fifth floor of the Texas Book Depository Store." He later testified that Euins correctly reported the location as the floor "under the ledge", but it was his quick count of the floors that gave rise to the incorrect fifth-floor location.

The first law enforcement official to reach the Book Depository, however, was Patrolman Marrion L. Baker of the Dallas Police Department. He was riding a motorcycle approximately 180 feet behind the President's limousine. He had rounded the corner of Main and Houston and was halfway down Houston toward Elm Street at the time of the first shot. He immediately identified it as rifle fire that came from the direction of the Depository or an adjacent building. He saw some pigeons that seemed to be flying up from the roof of the Depository, so he raced his cycle to the corner at Elm, parked it, and ran into the building. He "had in mind that the shots came from the top of…the Book Depository Building." When he shouted for the location of the elevator or stairs, Mr. Roy Truly, the building superintendent, identified himself and accompanied Baker to the elevators in the northwest corner of the building. Truly noted that both elevators were stopped at the fifth floor. The elevators did not respond to his pushing the call button, so he shouted for the people upstairs to "release the elevator." After shouting twice without being able to summon either elevator, the two men took the stairs west of the elevator, Truly in the lead. Passing the second floor lobby on his intended route to the upper floors, Patrolman Baker noticed a man who had just left the vestibule to the stairwell and elevator to enter the lunchroom. He could see the man walking away through the clear pane in the top half of the door. He entered the lunchroom with revolver drawn and called to the man walking away from him to stop and return. Truly had already gone up "two or three steps" toward the third floor when, missing Baker, he returned to find him just on the other side of the door in the lunchroom "facing Lee Harvey Oswald." The time was about 12:32.

"Do you know this man, does he work here?" asked Baker. Truly answered, "Yes." Both men noted that Oswald's hands were empty and he was not excited, though perhaps a bit startled by Baker's pointing a gun at his chest. Dismissing Oswald as a known employee of the building, the two continued up the stairs to the fifth floor where they took the elevator to the roof. They both looked around the top of the building for several minutes, finding nothing.

When he heard a police broadcast at 12:34 stating that the shooting had come from the Book Depository, Dallas Police Inspector Herbert V. Sawyer drove to that location and parked his car in front of the building. He entered the front door and took the passenger elevator to the fourth floor, as far as it would go, looked around, descended back to the lobby, then ordered the building to be sealed off. That was about 12:37. It was during this period that he was given the description of the shooter that went out in the 12:45 broadcast. He was not sure who the person was who had given him the description, but immediately after getting it, he sent the "not old, not young" man to the Sheriff's Department for an official statement. A few minutes later, Howard Brennan arrived and gave the sheriff's personnel the description that was virtually identical to the one broadcast.[6]

Presently, Roy Truly returned from the roof. Sometime around one o'clock, he noticed that Lee Oswald was not among the employees who were being interviewed by the police. After ascertaining that he was missing, he looked up Oswald's address and phone number from the employment files and gave the information to Captain J. W. Fritz, chief of the Homicide Bureau of the Dallas Police Department.

Fritz had arrived shortly before 1:00 to take charge of the investigation at the Depository, the site that the eyewitnesses had identified as that used by the gunman. He had concentrated his attention on the southeast corner of the sixth floor where Deputy Sheriff Luke Mooney found a stack of cartons and three cartridge cases on the floor in front of the corner window at approximately 1:12. Fritz had Mooney guard the area to see that nothing was moved before Lieutenant J. C. Day of the Identification Bureau arrived to take pictures and retrieve any fingerprints. In the corner of the alcove formed by the stacked boxes, they found a homemade paper sack measuring 38 inches in length. About 1:22., Dallas County Deputy Sheriff Eugene Boone and Deputy Constable Seymour Weitzman found a bolt-action rifle with a mounted telescopic sight lying on the floor among the boxes of books in the northwest

---

6. From Brennan's DPD statement of 11/22/63, "He was a white man in his early 30's, slender, nice looking, slender and would weigh about 165 to 175 pounds." (Warren Commission exhibit.)

corner of the sixth floor.[7] The rifle was photographed by Day and by newsman/photographer Tom Alyea as it was picked up by Day. Alyea was one of the few who had managed to enter the Depository before it was sealed off and the only one with a movie camera. He followed the police investigators, photographing whatever action he could get near enough to record. In spite of a couple of close calls, he managed to stay and document much of the significant physical data being recovered.

After Day determined that the stock of the gun and the bolt were devoid of fingerprints, he held the gun by the stock and Fritz ejected a live round from the firing chamber. All evidence and the area surrounding both locations were thoroughly searched for finger- and palm-prints. The evidence was marked for identification and inserted into the "chain-of-custody" that would be necessary at a trial when the gunman (or gunmen) was apprehended.

At about 12:40 Lee Oswald was recognized by Mrs. Mary Bledsoe, his former landlady, as he boarded a bus. He had stayed at Mrs. Bledsoe's boarding house for a short time while looking for work in Dallas. Meanwhile, his pregnant wife, Marina and their baby daughter were staying with Mrs. Ruth Paine in Irving, about 15 miles away. On weekends, he joined his family at Mrs. Paine's. After Bledsoe evicted him, Oswald rented a room in Mr. and Mrs. Arthur C. Johnson's rooming house on North Beckley Street. The bus he boarded followed a route that would take Oswald within seven blocks of his room at the Johnson house. He left the bus after it had gone only two blocks in three or four minutes. The bus was slowed by the traffic jam caused by the motorcade and the bedlam following the assassination. Shortly thereafter, four blocks away, a man the driver later identified as Oswald jumped in a cab, giving the driver, Mr. William Whaley, an address of 700 North Beckley, a few blocks from his residence. About 1:00, the housekeeper and manager of the rooming house, Mrs. Earlene Roberts, saw Lee rush into the house, stay in his room a few minutes, then rush out, zipping up his jacket. She spoke, but he did not reply.

---

7. The rifle was subsequently identified as a Mannlicher-Carcano. Before it was moved or could be examined closely, Weitzman, who was experienced with firearms but not familiar with the obscure Italian World War II rifle, misidentified it as a Mauser, to which it bore a superficial resemblance. This mistake was leaked to the press to become, in a short time, a source of controversy. Lt. Day's and Tom Alyea's photographs, however, are of the Mannlicher-Carcano, not a Mauser.

Several patrol cars were dispatched at approximately 12:45 to various stations around the center of the city. Patrolman J.D. Tippit, one of several who were alone in their cars, was sent to the Oak Cliff area. He reported in at about 12:54, by which time he had received several dispatches on the police radio describing the assassin as a slender, white male, about 30, weighing 165 pounds, and 5' 10" tall. About 1:15, Tippit was driving slowly past Patton Avenue, moving east on East 10th Street, when he pulled alongside a man walking in the same direction. The man walked over to Tippit's car, approaching the right side. Tippit got out of the car, started around the front, and had just reached the left front fender when the man pulled a gun and fired several times. Hit by four of the bullets, Tippit died instantly. Domingo Benavides, who was approaching from the opposite direction, heard the shots and stopped his truck on the opposite side of the road, about 25 feet from where Tippit lay in the street. He saw the gunman proceed rapidly back toward Patton, emptying his revolver of spent cartridge cases as he went. Benavides went to Tippit, saw no signs of life, and noticed that he was lying on his drawn revolver. He promptly tried to report the incident on Tippit's car radio, but was unsuccessful. Another passerby, T.F. Bowley, ultimately used Tippit's radio to contact the dispatcher. The report was received shortly after 1:18 p.m.

Standing on the corner of 10th and Patton, Helen Markham witnessed the shooting and the man's emptying his revolver. In the corner house, Mrs. Barbara Davis and Mrs. Virginia Davis, sisters-in-law, ran to the door upon hearing the shots and watched the man shaking cartridge cases out of his gun as he walked. Each lady subsequently recovered one of the cases. Mr. Benavides found two others. Another witness saw the shooting from his cab while parked on Patton a few feet from the corner. As the shooter passed his cab, William Scoggins heard the man say, "Poor dumb cop." or "Poor damn cop."

An ex-Marine named Ted Callaway was standing on the front porch of Dootch Motors sales office, where he was employed as a car salesman, when he heard "what sounded...like five pistol shots." He ran to the sidewalk on Patton in the direction from which the gunfire had come and saw a man running between his location and a taxicab parked a block north of the sales office at the corner of 10th Street. The man was holding a handgun in the "raised pistol position." He "hollered" at the man and got a reply that he did not understand. The man shrugged his shoulders and kept moving. Callaway shouted to an associate, B. D. Searcy, to "keep an eye on that guy. Follow him." Callaway ran the remainder of the block north to the scene of the shooting, saw Tippit lying on the street with what seemed to be a bullet wound to the head, and called in on Tippit's car radio to report the incident and tell them that he was sure the officer was dead. He was told that help was on the way and to stay off the radio. He waited to help load the officer's body into the ambulance. He then picked up Tippit's handgun and went back to the corner to ask the taxi driver to take him in the direction that the assailant was moving when he last saw him. They toured the area for a while and saw nothing, at which time they returned to the scene to report to the police what they had seen.

Several of the eyewitnesses to the shooting or the flight of the assailant from the scene gave the police a description of the man. They, in turn, reported the description and other information to headquarters. The police noted the similarities in the description of the gunmen in the two cases and moved into the area in force. Some officers had rushed to a library in the Oak Cliff area in response to a mistaken 'tip,' but had quickly determined that the suspect was a library employee who had just run into the library shouting the news of the assassination. Others were cruising the streets, looking for pedestrians who might be the fugitive.

On Jefferson Boulevard, one of the main thoroughfares in the Oak Cliff section and only six blocks from the Tippit shooting, Johnny Calvin Brewer, the manager of Hardy's shoe store, heard the announcement of the police shooting on his radio. As he heard the sound of a passing siren, Brewer watched a man step quickly into the entranceway to his store and stand while the police car passed. When the man left without entering the store, Brewer followed him a short distance to the Texas Theatre. There he saw the man enter the movie without purchasing a ticket. When he brought that act to her attention, the cashier, Mrs. Julia Postal, called the police. Within minutes of Mrs. Postal's call, they had sounded the alarm and the theater was surrounded. Brewer quietly pointed the man out to the police; then the manager was instructed to bring the house lights up.

Patrolman M. N. McDonald, accompanied by two other patrolmen, searched two other patrons near the front of the theater. Then as he passed the row near the back where the man was sitting, McDonald approached the man and asked him to stand. As the suspect stood and held his hands up, he was heard to say, "Well, it's all over now." He then hit McDonald in the face with his left fist and drew a gun from his waist with his right hand. McDonald grabbed the gun with his left hand and fought back with his right. McDonald, another patrolman, and a patron of the theater sitting nearby heard what they thought was the click of the hammer on the revolver, misfiring.[8] The two tumbled over the seats of the theater, while the accompanying officers scrambled to get to the gunman. Finally, they disarmed and subdued the man, but not before he had received several scratches and bruises. McDonald testified that as they left the theater, the man was "cursing a little bit and hollering 'police brutality'."

Roy Truly informed Captain Fritz that one of the 15 men who worked in the building, and was inside during the shooting, was now missing. Fritz then left the Depository with Oswald's description and address and returned to police headquarters. He started to dispatch two officers to pick up Oswald when he learned that Lee Harvey Oswald was already in the interrogation room. He had just been brought in as a suspect in the Tippit shooting following his capture in the Texas Theatre. In addition to material that identified him as Oswald, the arresting officers recovered a forged selective service card from his wallet made out in the name of Alek J. Hidell. In another twist, they soon found that Oswald had signed his registration slip at the Johnson rooming house "O. H. Lee." Like most other questions posed to him in the following 48 hours, he refused to divulge any information about either pseudonym.

At the Naval Hospital in Bethesda, Maryland, Commander James J. Humes was appointed to head the autopsy team. He chose Commander Thornton Boswell, a Navy colleague, and Lieutenant Colonel Pierre A. Finck, an Army pathologist, to assist him. The three noted the small round wound of entry on the President's upper back, which they describe in the autopsy report as: "Situated on the upper right posterior thorax just above the upper border of the scapula there is a 7 x 4 millimeter oval wound. This wound is measured to be 14 cm. from the tip of the right

---

8. The firearms expert later testified that the round in the chamber had not been struck by the hammer, so there was no misfire. The noise could have been a partial snapping of the hammer as it snagged in someone's clothing during the scuffle.

acromion process and 14 cm. below the tip of the right mastoid process."
The acromion process is the bony tip of the back of the shoulder and the
mastoid process is at the base of the skull immediately behind the ear. As
there was no obvious exit wound corresponding to this wound of entry, a
series of "roentgenograms" (x-rays) of the President's neck were taken in
hopes of locating the missile. They also noted, "The missile path through
the fascia and musculature cannot be easily probed." For the duration
of the autopsy, this remained a mystery. In the official autopsy report,
however, Humes references a telephone conversation with Dr. Malcolm
Perry after the autopsy had been completed, which explained the lack of
an exit wound. That wound was the one obliterated by the surgeons at
Parkland when they performed the tracheotomy. The report states that
the connection between the two wounds was indicated by three things:
the lack of a bullet in the x-rays of the region; the bruising of the muscles
and subcutaneous tissue around the trachea; and by the fact that the top
of the right lung and the lung cavity were extensively contused (bruised).
The pleura, the connective tissue that surrounds the lung, was intact.

The description of the entry wound in the President's skull is given
as: "Situated in the posterior scalp approximately 2.5 cm. laterally to the
right and slightly above the external occipital protuberance is a lacerated
wound measuring 15 x 6 mm. In the underlying bone is a corresponding
wound through the skull which exhibits beveling of the margins of the
bone when viewed from the inner aspect of the skull." The external occipital protuberance, also known as the occiput or EOP, is the bony knob
on the back of the skull just above where it sits on top of the neck. The
"beveling" in the second sentence is often referred to as "cratering" on the
inside surface of the skull associated with a wound of entry.[9] The report
continues by describing the massive fatal injury to the brain and the large
hole in the upper right skull that measured "approximately 13 centimeters in its greatest diameter," or about five inches. This massive defect was
above the right ear, extending from in front of the ear to behind it.

About three-quarters of the missing area of skull was found by the
Secret Service in the car or by bystanders and turned over to the Secret

---

9. A similar phenomenon is observed in the hole a BB makes in a pane of glass. The defect on
the struck side is small; about the size of the BB, or sometimes slightly smaller if the BB rebounds
without penetrating. A small cone of glass is driven out of the back side of the glass, forming the
"crater."

Service. Some pieces of the President's skull were found in the limousine. At least one was found on the street by a bystander and given to the Secret Service after the assassination. Another was found by the ubiquitous Deputy Constable Seymour Weitzman "on the south side of Elm Street about 8-12 inches from the curb." One of these skull fragments had, at its margin, a portion of a "nearly circular" exit wound measuring "approximately 2.5 to 3.0 cm. in diameter." In this instance, the cratering was in the outside surface of the bone, proving it to be a wound of exit.

X-rays of the head were developed as the autopsy was being conducted. They showed cracks throughout the skull and small metallic fragments scattered through the substance of the brain. They recovered two of the larger fragments "from the disrupted surface of the right cerebral cortex" that measured "7 x 2 mm. and 3 x 1 mm." These two fragments were "placed in the custody of Agents Francis X. O'Neill, Jr. and James W. Sibert of the Federal Bureau of Investigation (FBI), who executed a receipt therefore (attached)." The x-ray of the skull fragment in which part of the exit wound was visible showed several dense, metallic fragments embedded in the bone adjacent to the cratered exit. This likely helped to identify it as the point of exit.

The brain was removed and placed in a container with formalin, a water solution of formaldehyde, to be "fixed" or hardened so that thin slices could be removed for later microscopic examination. Navy medical photographer, John Stringer, took numerous photographs of all the above injuries, but they were not developed at Bethesda. The undeveloped film and developed x-rays were given to Agent Roy Kellerman of the Secret Service. The report also states, "The complexity of these fractures and the fragments thus produced tax satisfactory verbal description and are better appreciated in photographs and roentgenograms which are prepared."

A supplementary report submitted a few days later detailed the results of the microscopic slides of the organs. These included several sections from seven different regions of the fixed brain. The supplementary results did not require any amendment to the findings of the original report.

Within 24 hours of his arrest, the FBI had traced the Mannlicher-Carcano (M-C) rifle to Lee Harvey Oswald. The order for the weapon had been placed with Klein's, a Chicago sporting goods company, in the name of A. Hidell, the name on the forged selective service card found on Oswald when he was arrested. The company's records showed that a rifle with the serial number C-2766, the number stamped on the M-C rifle found on the 6th floor of the Depository, had been shipped to Hidell at the address given on the order form. The address printed on the order form was P. O. Box 2915, Oswald's post office box number in Dallas.

Investigators interviewed Buell Wesley Frazier, a neighbor of Ruth Paine and an employee at the Texas School Book Depository. Since Marina and the baby had moved in with Mrs. Paine, Oswald had been riding with Frazier to Mrs. Paine's house on the weekends. Oswald had no driver's license and reportedly could not drive. On Thursday, November 21, he had asked Frazier for a ride home that evening. "I'm going home to get some curtain rods…" he said, when asked about the unusual trip. The next morning another unusual occurrence was observed. Oswald was seen by Mrs. Linnie Mae Randle, Frazier's sister, placing a "heavy brown bag" in Frazier's car, before her brother finished breakfast. This was several minutes earlier than Lee's usual arrival time when returning to Dallas. As they were entering the car, Frazier asked Oswald, "What's in the package, Lee?" "Curtain rods," he answered. When interviewed later, Mrs. Gladys Johnson, Lee's landlady, stated that his room already had curtains and curtain rods.

After arriving at the worksite in Dallas, Frazier watched Oswald carry the package from the parking place toward the Depository and enter the door about 50 yards ahead of him. Both Frazier and his sister described the package as being a bit shorter than the bag found on the sixth floor of the Depository after the shooting, but Frazier disclaimed that he was paying close attention to the package. No curtain rods were found in the Depository or anywhere else Oswald had been that day. When Patrolman Baker and Roy Truly saw Oswald in the lunchroom, his hands were empty. When a Depository employee, Mrs. R. A. Reid, saw him walk through the second floor clerical office toward the door to the front stairway a short time later, Lee was carrying a full bottle of Coca-Cola, nothing else.

Among the evidence recovered from the sixth floor of the Texas School Book Depository was a palmprint on the underside of the rifle barrel in a location normally covered by the wooden stock. This indicated that it had been left there while the rifle was disassembled. Fingerprints and palmprints were found on the paper bag and the cartons in the area surrounding the sixth floor window identified by the witnesses as the position from which the shots were fired. Some of the prints on paper and cardboard were brought out by dusting with powder. This indicated that the prints were relatively fresh. The oil and perspiration from a fingerprint is absorbed into a paper surface, including cardboard, within a day or two. After absorption, they must be developed as "latent prints" through exposure to silver nitrate or other chemicals. Some of the recovered prints were latent prints. All the finger and palm prints, both fresh and latent, that were complete enough for the FBI to identify were Lee Oswald's or, in the case of the cartons, the Dallas policeman who collected them or the FBI clerk who received them. None belonged to other workmen in the building or to anybody other than these three. The homemade paper bag was made of materials identical to those readily available to the workers in the Depository. Detailed examination showed the bag contained a number of fibers from woven cloth. Other cloth fibers were recovered from the butt plate of the rifle, the part held against the shoulder when the weapon is fired.

When investigating officers went to Irving to question Marina Oswald, she took them to the site in Mrs. Paine's garage where most of the Oswalds' possessions were in storage. She thought Lee's rifle was still there, wrapped in a blanket. Though the indentations of a long heavy object were still apparent in the folds of the blanket, no weapon was found. Among the Oswalds' possessions, the officers found pictures of Lee sporting a rifle and pistol matching the appearance of those weapons that were in police custody. The negative to one of these pictures was also found. The fibers taken from the paper bag were an exact match with fibers from the blanket, though the blanket also contained fibers of a type not found in the bag. The fibers from the buttplate of the rifle were identical to fibers taken from the shirt Lee was wearing at the time of his arrest.

The FBI determined that the bullet recovered from the stretcher at Parkland was a bullet manufactured by Western Cartridge Company for use in the 6.5 mm Mannlicher-Carcano rifle.[10] It had been fired from a rifle, which leaves unique marks on the bullet, called "engraving," as the bullet passes through the barrel of the rifle. The engraving on the bullet

---

10. Warren Commission Exhibits were designated by the initials CE followed by a number. This round was labeled CE 399. Cartridges made in the United States to be used in this rifle do not contain "Mannlicher-Carcano bullets," though they are often referred to as such. Neither the bullets nor the cartridges into which they are loaded were made by the M-C Company. These rounds were made by the Western Cartridge Company. To prevent confusion, I will hereafter refer to them as WCC/MC bullets.

proved that it had been fired from the Mannlicher-Carcano rifle found near the stairwell on the sixth floor of the Texas School Book Depository. Secret Service investigators found two large bullet fragments in the front part of the limousine in which the President was killed. One, only part of a jacket, was between the seat and the right front door. The other consisted of a piece of torn jacket with part of the lead core still inside. It was on the seat between the driver and passenger positions. Although they represented two different sections of the bullet, the two fragments could not be determined conclusively to have been broken from a single bullet.

The two fragments had enough engraving on the Gilding metal (copper-alloy) jacket to unequivocally establish that they had been fired from the rifle recovered on the sixth floor of the Depository. Several fragments of lead which might have been part of the core of a bullet were recovered from the carpeted floorboards of the car. The windshield of the car showed cracks in the outer layer caused by an impact from the inside, leaving what appeared to be traces of lead adhering to the inside surface. This metallic deposit was scraped off and recovered. In addition, a second impact had dented the molding in the chrome framework at the top of the windshield. No deposits were recoverable from this impact. No further impacts or traces of bullets were found in a thorough, inch-by-inch search of the car.

The .38 caliber Smith & Wesson revolver seized from Oswald at the time of his arrest was found to have been a British military weapon rechambered to .38 Special, a modification commonly found in these revolvers. The British cartridge, commonly called the .38/200, had a cartridge case the same size as the .38 S&W, shorter than the .38 Special. Because the barrel was not changed when the cylinder was rebored, it was slightly oversize for the new ammunition. Consequently, only one of the bullets recovered from Patrolman Tippit's body could be attributed to that gun, although the condition of the other three bullets was compatible with having been fired from that weapon. The cartridge cases recovered at the scene of the Tippit murder, on the other hand, were all positively identified as having been fired in Oswald's revolver.

In all, 12 people saw Oswald shoot Tippit, watched him flee the vicinity emptying the revolver, or both. Several of these eyewitnesses independently picked Oswald out of a police lineup on the evening of November 22. Another did so on the morning of November 23. Neither

Howard Brennan nor Domingo Benavides picked Oswald out of a line-up. Brennan said he could not pick the man he saw in the window from a lineup. Benevides stated that he could not pick the assailant out of a lineup and was not shown one.[11]

Lee Harvey Oswald was charged with the murder of Officer Tippit on the evening of November 22 and the murder of John Kennedy early on November 23, 1963. Oswald was repeatedly questioned throughout the time he was in custody without yielding any substantial information about either killing, other than admitting to U.S. Post Office Inspector Harry D. Holmes that he had rented the post office box to which the rifle was sent. He denied that he had picked up a rifle sent to A. Hidell at that address. He claimed that the pictures he was shown holding the murder weapons were faked. He said that he knew how to construct composites and could prove it. He also denied both murders, stating that he was being made the "patsy" for the crimes.

Local law required that Oswald be moved to a more secure facility in the county jail within a couple of days. The move was scheduled for the morning of November 24th. The time and place of the move was not kept a particular secret, though only the press were allowed in the area—not the general public. Nevertheless, a bar owner and sometime police station hanger-on named Jack Ruby made his way into the transfer area in the basement of the city jail and shot Lee Harvey Oswald with his .38 caliber Colt Cobra revolver in front of millions of viewers watching the event on television. In an ironic replay of the events of two days earlier, the accused assassin was rushed to the emergency room of Parkland Memorial Hospital, where he died of massive blood loss. Though he only got one shot off before being subdued, Ruby's .38 Special bullet penetrated practically every major organ within Oswald's abdomen.

Before the weekend was over, the Dallas police had amassed enough evidence that J. Edgar Hoover, Director of the FBI, was convinced of

---

11. Brennan told the Warren Commission that when he saw Oswald in the lineup, he recognized him as the killer of the president. He had told the officials conducting the lineup, however, that he could not identify the shooter. When asked by the WC interrogator why he made that statement, he stated he thought it might be a Communist conspiracy and "…if it got to be a known fact that I was an eyewitness, my family or I, either one, might not be safe." Perhaps he was the first person outside the law enforcement community to modify his behavior because of the suspicion of a conspiracy in the assassination.

Oswald's guilt in the murder of John Kennedy and Officer Tippit. The bullets and cartridge cases were linked to the murder weapons and the weapons were traced to him. One of the weapons was in his possession at the time of his capture. His fingerprints and palmprints were all over the "Sniper's Nest" crime scene, including the rifle. These and dozens of other bits of physical evidence all pointed to one individual: Lee Harvey Oswald.

In response to an inquiry by Director Hoover, Assistant FBI Director Alan Belmont forwarded a memo on November 27, 1963, stating, in part, "...we are receiving literally hundreds of allegations regarding the activities of Oswald and Ruby...in the absence of being able to prove Oswald's motive and complete activities, we must check out and continue to investigate to resolve as far as possible any allegations or possibility that he was associated with others in this assassination." As in any high-profile crime, the "witnesses" were flocking in with stories that were, to a large degree, mutually contradictory. The traditional police method of sorting out the accurate and believable is to check the stories against what is already known from the physical evidence and photographs of the crime scene. The most difficult to sort out are the stories that sound plausible on the surface and agree with the facts already known. For this reason, the police usually hold back some of the details from the story given to the press. The avid publicity hound who has read everything in print before coming in with his story may still be identified and eliminated by the contradictions with the known facts not printed.

In the Kennedy case nothing was held back. 'Facts' were reported to the press, radio, and television by the Dallas police, the Parkland physicians, and hordes of reporters who were on the scene and were themselves eyewitnesses to some of the events of the day, without more than a cursory effort to check them out. Soon the FBI agents were chiming in with details of the physical evidence, nearly all pointing to Lee Harvey Oswald. Since the police and other authorities held virtually nothing in reserve, the main method of sorting out the fabrications of the publicity-seekers was either to find obvious contradictions with published facts or identify stories based on early erroneous reports. Unfortunately, the flood of allegations that the FBI was complaining about hardly decreased in intensity for years and never completely stopped.

CHAPTER TWO

An Advocate's Summing Up

> "The Report of the Warren Commission is an advocate's summing-up."
>
> —*Hugh Trevor-Roper*[12]

After Lee Harvey Oswald was gunned down by Jack Ruby, there was no possibility of a trial to settle Oswald's innocence or guilt. Because of the many rumors that immediately surfaced concerning the assassination, President Johnson appointed an unimpeachable commission to conduct a thorough investigation of the affair.

In his book *The Death of a President*, William Manchester reviews some of the early reports and rumors that emerged from Dallas on the afternoon of the assassination and over the weekend that followed. An Associated Press (AP) teletype announced that co-conspirators had killed a Secret Service agent and a Dallas policeman and that then-Vice President Lyndon Baines Johnson (LBJ) had been injured. A report went out that LBJ had entered Parkland Hospital holding his left arm—an early sign of a heart attack. The rifle found in the Texas School Book Depository was identified by Dallas police as a 7.62 mm Mauser. It was announced that a red-shirted man with black curly hair had been arrested "in the Riverside section of Fort Worth in the shooting of a Dallas policeman." A surgeon who had treated Kennedy in the emergency room at Parkland Memorial Hospital said that President Kennedy was shot in the throat from the front. The autopsy team at Bethesda was told that a bullet had been recovered from the President's stretcher at Parkland. An hour after Johnson left Love Field on Air Force One, bound for Washington, D.C., NBC broadcast that "LBJ is remaining in Dallas." Some of these reports were self-correcting. For instance, television coverage soon showed President

---

12. From the Introduction to Mark Lane's *Rush to Judgment*.

23

Johnson in Washington with no sign of having recently suffered a bullet wound or heart attack. Other rumors persisted and grew.

The Warren Commission Investigation

The investigative body appointed by President Johnson by Executive Order No. 11130 on November 29, 1963 was officially titled The President's Commission on the Assassination of President John F. Kennedy. LBJ convinced a reluctant Earl Warren, the Chief Justice of the U. S. Supreme Court, to assume the duty of Chairman. The ponderous title is usually shortened to The Warren Commission and its final report is referred to as the Warren Report. The Commission's other members were Senator Richard B. Russell, Senator John S. Cooper, Representative Hale Boggs, Representative Gerald Ford—the future President of the United States, Mr. Allen W. Dulles—former director of the Central Intelligence Agency, and John J. McCloy—a retired diplomat who had held a number of high-level positions in previous administrations.

The investigation included extensive interviews, under oath, of scores of eyewitnesses to the two shootings and other events related to the murders and the investigation. They also heard sworn testimony from the Dallas Police, Secret Service, FBI, and other experts involved in the investigation. They retrieved and examined the physical evidence collected by all those investigators, the many affidavits and interviews obtained by the Dallas police and FBI in the course of the investigation, and hundreds of documents, photographs, newspaper and magazine articles, handwritten notes, and other information. Each was carefully assigned a unique exhibit number.

The Commission attended a filmed reconstruction of the path of the limousine with actors in place of the two men who were shot. From the vantage point on the fifth floor occupied by Norman, Williams, and Jarman, they listened to the sound of cartridge cases being ejected onto the floor above. Each member could clearly distinguish the clatter of the casings falling on the floor beneath the window where the shooter was seen. They reviewed the evidence indicating the ownership of the murder weapons by Oswald and took testimony from handwriting experts explaining how their determinations were made. They called the ballistics experts from the FBI and went over the methods of determining whether a bullet was fired from a particular firearm and when such a determination was not possible.

They interviewed Marina Oswald and heard her testify that Oswald had owned weapons apparently identical to those held in evidence. She told them that Lee had taken a shot at Major General Edwin A. Walker in the spring of 1963 and that he was upset when he learned that he had missed. She also testified that she had used Lee's camera to take the pictures of Lee holding the weapons, pictures that had been widely reprinted in magazines and newspapers. They heard a photographic expert testify that the negative to one of those prints was, indeed, exposed in that camera (other negatives were not found). They patiently sat through a long, rambling, at times virtually incoherent narrative by Oswald's mother, Marguerite, in which she complained that she was getting none of the money that a sympathetic American public was sending to Marina and Officer Tippit's family. She also gave a garbled account of the conspiracy allegation being formulated by Mark Lane, a lawyer she had hired to look after the family's interests after her son had been slain, but fired shortly thereafter. Her version of the conspiracy involved Marina, Ruth Paine, two Secret Service men (one, she remembered, was Mike Howard; the other's name she could not recall), and her other son, Robert Oswald. Lee, on the other hand, was entirely innocent of both crimes, and was just the "patsy" he had claimed to be. When asked to give some detail about why she would make such a serious allegation, she said she deduced the conspiracy from the "attitude" of the two Secret Service agents.

Lane showed up at the Commission's Washington, D.C., hearing room on the day of Marguerite's testimony, but when asked who would represent her at the hearing, she chose Mr. John Doyle, the lawyer appointed by the Commission on her behalf. Though Lane no longer represented Marguerite, both Marguerite and Lane requested that Lane be allowed to participate in the investigation, side-by-side with the Commission's staff, as Lee Oswald's "defense attorney." The Commission rejected this request, stating that their inquiry was an investigation for the truth, not a trial of a specific individual. Lane was allowed to return later to testify on his own.

The Commission also asked the Army to gather some independent experimental evidence at the Ballistic Research Laboratory (BRL), located at the Aberdeen Proving Ground, and at the Biophysics Division of the Chemical Research and Development Laboratories, located at Edge-wood Arsenal. These Army facilities lay side-by-side in rural Maryland at the western edge of the Chesapeake Bay, about 60 miles from the Warren Commission (WC) offices in Washington, D.C.

Mr. Ronald Simmons was the BRL representative to the WC. He testified that BRL obtained the services of three riflemen with military experience, employed at the Proving Ground, who were qualified on the rifle range at the "Marksman" level, the top qualification that Oswald had achieved while in the Marines. They used the rifle found on the sixth floor of the Book Depository after the assassination. Simmons remarked that shims were added to adjust the scope mounted on this rifle for the BRL tests, one for the azimuth (side-to-side adjustment) and one for elevation. With shims added, the scope could be adjusted so that the crosshairs were on target at any specified range. Simmons went over the results of each man's tests showing that each of the three gunners could match the assassin's accuracy in firing three shots at three targets placed at the same distance as Kennedy was from the "sniper's nest" at the time of the three shots. One rifleman could fire all three at that accuracy in less than 5.5 seconds, the minimum estimated by the WC, with or without using the scope. This time was the minimum time allowed if the second shot was the one that missed. If it was the first shot that missed, all three riflemen were well under the Commission's estimated maximum available time. Simmons' data shows that each man's time for the three-shot, three-target set was less for the last set than for the first, showing some improvement with practice.

The Oswald rifle was then delivered to the Biophysics Division, led by Division Chief Dr. Arthur Dziemian. The principal investigator for this exercise was Dr. Alfred Olivier, Chief of the Wound Ballistics Branch. Dr. Frederick Light, Chief of the Wound Assessment Branch, acted as expert consultant. All three testified before the Warren Commission. A variety of wound ballistic tests were conducted with the Oswald rifle using cartridges manufactured by the Western Cartridge Company. The bullets were from the same production lot of Western Cartridge Company ammunition that the FBI had determined was used in the assassination.

The tests consisted of simulations of the shots to the President's neck and head and simulations of shots to the governor's torso, forearm, and thigh. It was the prior opinion of the Biophysics Division experts that a single WCC/MC bullet had sufficient penetrating power to inflict all the wounds that Connally sustained. Before starting the tests, Olivier was not certain that identical bullets, fired from the same rifle, would cause the quite different effects that were observed in the President's head injury and the shot through the governor's chest. The experiments proved that they could.

The muzzle velocity of bullets fired from the Oswald rifle averaged about 2,160 feet per second (f/s) (about 660 meters per second). Due to its relatively large weight and moderate aerodynamic drag, the WCC/MC bullet retains a residual velocity of about 1,900 f/s (580 m/s) at a range of 180 feet (55 m). The Warren Commission estimated 180 feet as the distance between the back seat of the limousine and the Depository window at the time the shot was fired that hit the President's neck.

Shots fired into blocks of 20 percent gelatin tissue simulant[13] confirmed the enormous penetrating power of the round. All of these bullets penetrated all or most of the length of two 15-inch blocks of gelatin, placed end-to-end, before exiting through the rear or side of the second block. Some of the latter missed the stack of backup blocks and penetrated into the earth backstop, too deeply to be recovered. Those which hit the backup gelatin blocks penetrated well over 30 inches of simulated tissue, more than the length of the neck wound of Kennedy and all the wounds of Connally combined. These bullets were recovered undeformed.

The Kennedy-neck penetrations were simulated with blocks of gelatin and blocks of two different kinds of animal meat. Each had shaved animal skin attached at the entry and exit points. All gave similar results, showing that the bullet had just begun to yaw at exit.[14] The yawed bullet left elongated, somewhat ragged exit wounds, in contrast to the nearly round entry wounds.

Separate rounds were fired into the ribcages of goats with an entry as close to the same location as the wound to Governor Connally's back as the difference between the two species would permit. The striking veloc-

---

13. The gelatin tissue simulant was composed of 20 percent gelatin and 80 percent water. This tissue simulant has the same density and the same water and protein content as muscle tissue, but is transparent, so that high-speed movies may be taken of the bullet during penetration. By contrast, gelatin dessert contains about 5 percent gelatin, so the tissue simulant is considerably stiffer.

14. Yaw is the term used to describe the bullet that is traveling not quite point first, but slightly skewed. It is derived from the nautical term that describes a similar motion in a ship.

ity in the trunk simulations was nearly the same velocity obtained in the simulation of the President's neck wound, though fired from a somewhat longer range. The bullet which produced the wound most similar to the governor's was flattened somewhat more than Warren Commission Exhibit CE 399, the bullet recovered from the stretcher at Parkland thought to be Connally's.

Additional rounds were fired into cadaver wrists at the same striking velocity as the torso simulations. The wounds produced by these shots were all more damaging than Connally's wrist wound, particularly the extent of fragmentation of the radius. In the governor's wrist, the exit wound was smaller than the entry wound. In the simulations, the entry wound was nearly as small as the entry wounds in the neck simulations, but the exit wound was much larger than the exit wound in Connally's wrist. The bullets in these simulations were also badly deformed.

In each case, the wrist bones were fragmented to a much greater extent than Connally's radius was. These observations indicated to the wound-ballistics experts that the governor's wrist wound was caused by a bullet traveling at a velocity much lower than 1,900 feet per second. The damage to the Governor's wrist was compatible with a bullet that had already perforated his torso before hitting his wrist. It was not compatible with a direct strike on the wrist.

Drs. Olivier and Dziemian believed that the small difference in the amount of soft tissue that the two bullets traversed in the governor and the goat before hitting the rib was insufficient to account for the difference in deformation of the two bullets. That is, they concluded that the bullet that struck the governor had lost some velocity by passing through the neck of the President before striking the governor. Dr. Light thought that the difference in deformation was too small to draw that conclusion on the basis of the anatomical findings alone, but when combined with other factors, such as the position of the two men in the car and the elongated entry wound on the Governor's back, he concluded that it was "probable that the same bullet traversed the President's neck and inflicted all the wounds on Governor Connally."

The skull simulations were conducted by firing bullets at a range of 270 feet, within five feet of the distance, estimated by the WC, between the sixth-floor corner window of the Depository and the President at the time of the fatal shot. The striking velocities for these shots were not determined. Independent test firings averaged about 1,860 feet per second at that distance. The targets were dried human skulls, obtained from a medical supply house, rehydrated by soaking in water overnight, filled with gelatin, coated on the outside with a layer of gelatin, and covered with a piece of fresh goat skin to approximate the thickness of a human scalp and subcutaneous tissue at the entry site. The simulated targets were positioned so that the entry and exit of the bullet would be approximately in the locations indicated in WC drawings of the path of the bullet.

In each case, the bullets deformed extensively on impact with the skulls. As the bullets penetrated the contents, the jackets were torn open, exposing the lead cores. Some were torn completely in two. All left numerous small fragments along the bullet's path through the gelatin inside the skull. High-speed movies were made of the shots that show the skulls to shatter in a manner very similar to the damage observed in the President's skull. More fragments of skull were separated from the experimental skulls than from the President's, as the tough scalp and connective tissue were missing.

FBI experts Robert A. Frazier and Cortlandt Cunningham and the superintendent of the Bureau of Criminal Identification and Investigation of the state of Illinois, Joseph D. Nicol, testified regarding their ballistics tests on the weapon, bullets, and cartridge cases recovered from the crime scenes and the handgun taken from Oswald when captured. They had conducted split-image comparisons of the engraving signatures of the recovered bullet fragments and a test bullet fired by the FBI from that rifle. They determined that CE 399, the bullet from Parkland, and the two bullet fragments found in the limousine, CE 567 and CE 569, had been fired from the rifle, serial number C-2766, recovered on the sixth-floor of the Depository. Likewise, the three cartridge cases found in the "sniper's nest" had unique base markings that proved they were fired from that rifle.

Markings on the cartridge cases recovered at the Tippit murder scene were traced to the revolver found in Oswald's possession at the time of his arrest in the Texas Theatre—to the exclusion of all other weapons. Three of the bullets recovered from Tippit's body could not be traced to the revolver because the revolver's slightly oversized barrel left inconsistent engraving marks. The rifling characteristics and gas erosion marks on these three, however, were consistent with having been fired in Oswald's revolver. Nicol found that the fourth bullet could be traced to

Oswald's handgun to the exclusion of all other weapons.

The firearms experts also testified regarding the inconclusiveness of the paraffin tests on Oswald's hands and right cheek, noting that many substances can be found on the hands that would produce a positive reaction to the paraffin test. On the other hand, the tight seal inherent in a bolt-action rifle often precludes a positive test for gunpowder on the hands or cheek.

The FBI lab also performed flame photometric tests on samples of the fragments recovered from Connally's and Kennedy's wounds and the interior of the limousine, as well as samples taken from the jacket and base of CE 399. Some of each test sample was consumed in these tests. Scrapings from the interior of the limousine windshield and from the curb near James Tague were shown to be lead with no traces of copper. Likewise, the fragments recovered from the two victims were nearly pure lead. Traces of copper were found on the cloth surrounding the bullet hole in the President's jacket.

In addition to the fingerprints and palmprints already discussed, a partial fingerprint was also developed by dry powder on the metal magazine housing in front of the trigger guard of the C-2766 rifle. This fingerprint possessed many of the characteristics of the fingerprint of Lee Oswald but, by FBI standards, the common features were not numerous enough for conclusive identification.

Handwriting experts Alwyn Cole and James C. Cadigan confirmed that it was Lee Harvey Oswald's handwriting on the orders for the two weapons, the money order with which the rifle was purchased, the application for the Dallas post office box at which the rifle and pistol were received, two changes of address orders filed with Dallas and Fort Worth post offices, and an application for a post office box in New Orleans at which L. H. Oswald, Marina Oswald, and A. J. Hidell were authorized to receive mail. Oswald's handwriting also appeared on the forged Alek James Hidell Selective Service notice of classification recovered on his person when arrested. In addition, a forged military Certificate of Service for Alek James Hidell, signed by Oswald, was found among his possessions. Both Hidell forgeries were determined to have been made from Lee Harvey Oswald originals. The L. H. Oswald signature on the Fair Play for Cuba Committee card was also his, but the A. J. Hidell signature on this card was found to have been written by Marina. This had already been confirmed by Marina in her earlier WC testimony.

The Warren Commission interviewed Mrs. Bledsoe about her identification of Lee Oswald on the bus and taxi driver Mr. William Whaley about the taxi ride he said Oswald took to 700 North Beckley. They interviewed Jack Ruby, the workers at the Texas School Book Depository, the Tippit crime scene witnesses, the Texas Theatre witnesses, and the law enforcement officials who had interviewed Oswald and other critical witnesses. They recreated the movements of Oswald and others, timing and photographing the events as they went to verify the feasibility of the events and times that they had heard in testimony.

The list below summarizes the Warren Commission's conclusions.

- There were three shots fired from the northeast window of the sixth floor of the Texas School Book Depository. Two of these shots caused all the wounds of President Kennedy and Governor Connally. There were no other shots fired from any other location.

- All these shots were fired by Lee Harvey Oswald from the 6.5 millimeter Mannlicher-Carcano rifle that he owned and that was in his possession at the time of the assassination.

- Officer J. D. Tippit was killed by Lee Harvey Oswald using the revolver that was in his possession at the time of his arrest.

- Lee Harvey Oswald attempted to shoot General Edwin A. Walker on April 10, 1963. This fact and the killing of Officer Tippit support the conclusion that Oswald assassinated the President.

- Lee Harvey Oswald was killed by Jack Ruby with the revolver that was in his possession at the time of his capture. Jack Ruby was not assisted by the Dallas police in any way in this crime.

- Neither Oswald nor Ruby was assisted in the planning or execution of these crimes. That is, there was no evidence of a conspiracy in either killing.

Though they did not list it with the conclusions, the Commission Report opined that the first shot struck both men and that the second shot missed.

The Commission criticized the Dallas Police Department for allowing Oswald to be subjected to harassment by reporters while in their custody, for making numerous, sometimes erroneous statements to the press, and for lack of security in Oswald's transfer to the county jail, which led to his death. They criticized the Secret Service for inadequate security and the FBI for not communicating all the information they knew regarding the threat from Oswald to the Secret Service. The criticism of the Secret Service was tempered by a comment that "...the agents most immediately responsible for the President's safety reacted promptly..." In addition, the Commission made several suggestions they thought would improve the security of future presidents of the United States.

Critics and Conspiracy Theories

The Warren Commision attempted to remain unbiased in the course of the investigation. Their report is rife with hearsay and statements known to be inaccurate. Such material would never appear in the case made by the prosecution in a criminal case. The charge by Lane and others that the Warren Report was a "prosecutors' case" was certainly untrue. Even so, the chairman, Earl Warren, made several fundamental errors that later would provide fuel for charges of a government cover-up of the evidence. Warren decided, early in the investigation, that all evidence the WC heard and saw would be made public. This decision was appreciated by most of the American public. He later decided that the autopsy photographs and x-rays would not be examined by the WC, the staff, or the expert consultants because he did not want the gory details of the autopsy exhibited in the public press. He reviewed this material alone before making that decision.

Evidently, it never occurred to Warren that making exceptions to the earlier call for total openness would be probably accepted by the public in the case of the autopsy photos (though it probably would not have been accepted by the WC critics). The three members of the autopsy team, who did not have access to these materials when preparing their official report, in a bizarre act of pushing a point to a ridiculous extreme, were again barred from examining them before testifying to the WC. This decision prevented them from adding to the report or identifying and correcting any errors in it and provided grist for the conspiracy mill for at least the next four decades.

The rumors and speculations that inspired the creation of the Commission and the Commission's terse answers to them are detailed in 32 pages of the Warren Report, as printed by the U.S. Printing Office. They occupy 17 pages of the larger-format Associated Press edition of the Warren Report, the edition most read by the American public. If the WC members thought they had dispelled these rumors, they were sadly mistaken. Many are still being repeated in books, movies, TV specials, and in conferences held annually in Dallas on the anniversary of the assassination. A summary of some of these rumors and replies are in Appendix A. In some cases, the Commission patiently investigated rumors that would have little bearing on the determination of responsibility for the assassination of the President, the murder of Officer Tippit, or the killing of Lee Oswald.

The Warren Commission's investigation hardly slowed some rumors because some skeptics were not satisfied with the Commission's explanations of the early information on the type of rifle found, or the announcement by a Parkland physician that the wound to President Kennedy's neck was a "wound of entrance," or evidence that many thought the Commission had ignored—because it was not addressed in the report. Others did not read, did not understand, or frankly did not believe the implications of the tests at BRL and Edgewood. These critics coined the term "magic bullet" to express their outright rejection of the single bullet explanation advanced by the WC regarding the bullet found on the governor's stretcher. Some, perhaps deliberately, misinterpreted the inability to match some of the bullets from Tippit's body to the Oswald handgun as proof that they were fired from a different weapon. Perhaps the major criticism, advanced by many, was that the Commission dismissed the possibility of conspirators aiding Oswald or, in the view of some, acting independently and setting Oswald up as the "patsy" for the crime, after what they thought was only a cursory look.

In the late 1960s and early 1970s, numerous books and articles appeared criticizing the Warren Commission's findings and advancing almost as many conspiracy scenarios as there were authors. Nearly all of these mix subsets of the above rumors with new interviews of witnesses to the assassination, the killing of Tippit, the shooting of Oswald, or other relevant occurrences involved in the crimes or subsequent investigation.

One of the early books was written by Mark Lane, the lawyer briefly hired by Marguerite Oswald to look after Lee's (and, at first, the family's) interests before the Commission hearings were held.

As he was not allowed to sit as Oswald's advocate during the Commission's hearings, Lane decided to conduct his own investigation, interviewing many of the same witnesses that were contacted by the WC, their staff, and the law-enforcement agencies. Lane's first book, *Rush to Judgment,* is an unabashed brief for the defense on behalf of Lee Harvey Oswald. This, he said, was necessary to counter the findings of the WC. Their investigation, he claimed, was not aimed at finding the truth, but at establishing Oswald's guilt and building a case for the prosecution. Like any such brief, its sole purpose was to cast doubt on the prosecution's case, with the WC cast in the role of prosecutor. As a stand-in for defense council, he developed a defense based partly on the assertion that the Commission's case was not proven and partly that Oswald was framed by an unnamed group of assassins, repeating Oswald's claim that he was "a patsy." His lawyer's brief claims there was a conspiracy to kill the President and that his "client" was not a part of it.

Lane used the testimony of several WC witnesses to substantiate the existence of a gunman behind the fence at the top of a grass-covered slope, subsequently termed the "grassy knoll," rising from street level to the top of a railroad overpass. The auto road beneath the railroad, usually called the "triple underpass," is the convergence of the three major highway arteries leading from downtown to the west side of the tracks and the on-ramp to the Stemmons Freeway. A witness named Julia Ann Mercer told the Commission that she had seen a white male remove an object which appeared to be a "gun case" from a green Ford pickup truck with Texas plates and "Air Conditioning" stenciled on the side and carry the object/case up the grassy hill. Lee Bowers, Jr., a railroad tower man employed by the Union Terminal Company, had the best view of the Dallas Sheriff's Office parking lot behind the fence from his 14 foot tower "behind the fence." He saw three cars pull into, then leave, the parking lot in the half hour before the motorcade's appearance. He noticed two "strangers" behind the fence before the motorcade passed and told Lane he "saw a flash of light or smoke or…something in this immediate area on the embankment" (where the two were standing), as the motorcade passed.

Several railroad employees and one or two Dallas policemen watched the motorcade from the top of the railroad overpass. The police were there to make sure that spectators who were not employees of the railroad were kept off the overpass. Railroad employee Austin Miller told the WC that, after the shooting, "I saw something which I thought was smoke or steam coming from a group of trees north of Elm off the railroad tracks." He was only one of seven men standing on the overpass who told Mark Lane that they saw "smoke" in the vicinity of the trees behind that fence at the top of the grassy knoll. Another Dealey Plaza witness, Jesse C. Price, was on the top of the roof of the Terminal Annex Building on the opposite side of the plaza from the grassy knoll. He told the police that he saw a man "about 25 years of age" whose hair was "long and dark" wearing "a white shirt, no tie and kahki [sic] colored trousers." The man was running "toward the passenger cars on the railroad siding." He continues: "He had something in his hand. I couldn't be sure but it may have been a head piece [a hat]." His statement to the DPD is contained in a WC exhibit.[15] When pressed by Lane in a March 27, 1966 interview, he admitted that the object in the man's right hand "…could have been a gun."

Several policemen and railroad employees ran to the parking lot after the shooting. One of these, S. M. Holland, an employee of the Union Terminal Company, stated that "a puff of smoke came out about 6 or 8 feet above the ground right out from under those trees." He heard four shots in all and immediately ran to the area where he had seen smoke to look for discarded shell casings. What he found was a patch of mud covered with footprints where somebody had stood for some time. There was mud on the bumper of one of the cars where that person might have rested his foot. He estimated that there might have been 12 to 15 policemen in the area while he was there. One of the police who observed the muddy footprints was Seymour Weitzman, the Deputy Constable who later found the rifle on the sixth floor of the Depository. Weitzman, one of the first on the scene, asked a railroad yardman what he had seen. "He said he saw somebody throw something through a bush." Patrolman Joe M. Smith told the WC that a woman came up to him and said, "They are shooting the President from the bushes." He ran to the area at the

---

15. Decker exhibit 5323 (multiple affidavits grouped in a single Warren exhibit).

top of the knoll and was one of several who testified that he searched the
bushes and parking lot, but found nothing. Lane reported that Smith
told reporter Ronnie Dugger that he had smelled gunpowder when he
arrived behind the wooden fence.

Lane noted the many newspaper accounts of "the entry wound
to the throat" announced by Dr. Malcolm Perry, one of the Parkland
surgeons who treated the President. A piece of the President's skull was
found by Seymour Weitzman in the street to the left of the path of the
limousine, which Lane notes is "consistent with the bullet having been
fired from the north, where the grassy knoll is located, since bone matter
tends to follow the trajectory of the bullet." He quoted the testimony of
AP photographer James Altgens. "There was flesh particles that flew…in
my direction…[which] indicated to me that the shot came out of the
left side of his head." In an FBI interview of June 5, 1964 Altgens also
stated that he observed "blood on the left side of the President's head and
face." Lane quoted Dr. McClelland's observation of a "wound of the left
temple." He stated that if the shots had hit the President from the back,
he should have been driven forward toward Governor Connally.

In addition, Lane compared the angles of passage of bullets through
the President's and Governor's bodies to angles between the street and
the window in the Book Depository to conclude that the bullets couldn't
have originated there and the same bullet could not have injured both
men. He noted the discovery of a "Mauser" on the floor from which the
shots were fired, and repeated the FBI measurements of the exact location of the holes in the President's shirt and jacket to dispute the location
of the entry wounds as stated in the autopsy report.

Lane weighed the evidence in the case: In the Depository there was
a rifle, three cartridge cases that matched the rifle found under the window where several witnesses observed a gunman firing a rifle, witnesses
who heard three cartridge cases fall to the floor as the firing took place on
the sixth floor above their heads, an eyewitness description of the shooter
that was accurate enough to prompt a policeman to stop the owner of
the rifle while walking down a street miles from the scene of the shooting 45 minutes later. In the other location, behind the fence flanking
the grassy knoll, there were some footprints, a puff of "smoke or steam,"
and a witness who saw a man leave the area with a hat in his hand and
who, when pressed, admitted that the hat might have been a gun—no

weapon, no shell casings, nobody who saw a person firing a weapon. After careful consideration of these facts, he concluded, "There is some evidence to suggest that one or more shots may have been fired from the Book Depository, as the Warren Commission maintained. It is considerably less compelling than the evidence suggesting that shots came from behind the fence."[16]

Rush to Judgment was riddled with literally hundreds of citations to eyewitness statements made to the WC, Lane, or to reporters. It set the standard for future Kennedy assassination writers on either side of the "case" by its courtroom-like, adversarial approach. Lane was doing what the "defense lawyer" always does: trying to generate reasonable doubt in the mind of the audience, in lieu of a jury.

In the course of the first few years after the assassination, other books by Harold Weisberg, Sylvia Meagher, Edward Epstein, Penn Jones, Jim Garrison, Hugh McDonald, and others repeated the rumors that the WC had tried to vanquish and reinforced them with additional eyewitness statements. Some of these were written by concerned citizens with genuine, if sometimes ill-founded, doubts. Others were merely out to make a fast buck on a concocted, sensational conspiracy story. Many of the latter bolstered claims of conspiracy by interpreting the pictures, movies, and testimony of eyewitnesses to establish the presence of other gunmen in or about Dealey Plaza. In some of these scenarios, the purported gunmen were in addition to Oswald; others, following Lane's lead, postulated gunmen in place of Oswald. A decade or more after the fact, eyewitnesses from Dealey Plaza—some of whom were provably there, others not—were changing their stories or telling them for the first time. Nearly all the changed or newly found stories were in support of one or another of the conspiracy conjectures.

Critics pointed to errors in the WC case as evidence that its investigation itself was a coverup. Two frames of the Zapruder film were reversed when reprinted in the Warren Report. Critics complained that this "error" occurred in precisely the two frames that tended to minimize the backward movement of Kennedy into the seat of the car after the

---

16. In Mr. Lane's defense, we note that the autopsy materials, including the x-rays, photographs, slides, clothing, etc. were still in the possession of Robert Kennedy or sealed in the National Archives under the family's restriction that they not be made public. If he had had access to this material, Lane could have avoided some of the more easily disproved allegations.

fatal shot. This was said to be an attempt to conceal the fact that a bullet from the front had thrown the President backward. Connally's reaction to being shot, as dramatically shown in the Zapruder film, was said to be a second or more later than the reaction of the President to the throat wound, proving that they were not hit by a single shot. Howard Brennan's statement that his eyes had been damaged by sandblasting was used to show that a man with poor eyesight could not have identified Oswald as the man in the window.[17] The description, it was alleged, came from a conspirator inside the Dallas Police Department or one feeding the information to a sympathetic officer. Critical witnesses, including J. C. Price, were "not interviewed" by the Warren Commission.

A man in the Abraham Zapruder movie flaps an umbrella up and down as the President's car passes. A lady wearing a scarf over her head is seen in several pictures holding a movie camera. The movie she took, however, has never been examined by law enforcement personnel or conspiracy researchers. These two became known as the "Umbrella Man" and the "Babushka Lady" and play a part in many conspiracy theories. Three men were rounded up by police in the railroad yard above Dealey Plaza after the assassination. Pictures of the "Three Tramps" were identified as a variety of nefarious characters in several stories. Jack Ruby, of course, continued to have a "hitman" role in the conspiracy, as a member of the mafia, a governmental assassin, a representative of the anti-Castro or pro-Castro forces, and so on.

A "mysterious deaths" allegation, used by many writers, originated in a 1973 *Sunday Times* of London article written in response to the movie *Executive Action*. It quoted an actuary's calculation of astronomical odds against 18 material witnesses in the JFK case dying in the three years following the assassination. The *Times* later apologized for the blunder.[18] The actuary had calculated the odds of a given 18 deaths, not the odds of a random 18 out of the more than 25,000 people who had been connected as closely as the 18 who had died. Ignoring the apology and explanation that the odds were not significant after all, many still use the device and have continued to add to the list, as more people have died in

---

17. The sandblast accident happened in January 1964.

18. In a letter to the House Select Committee on Assassinations, they stated, "Our piece about the odds against the deaths of the Kennedy eyewitnesses was, I regret to say, based on a careless journalistic mistake and should not have been published."

the 40 years since the assassination.

Misdeeds of the FBI and other government officials were woven into many conspiracy scenarios. Primary among these was the destruction of a note from Lee Oswald to FBI agent James Hosty. Hosty was the Dallas FBI special agent who had interviewed Marina and Ruth Paine on at least two occasions as part of his assignment to keep track of Lee Oswald as a defector returned from the Soviet Union. The existence of this unsigned, mildly threatening note, which was destroyed on the orders of a supervisor, was uncovered by a Senate Intelligence Committee probe into the performance of intelligence agencies in 1975. In a statement made on November 22, 1963, Dallas Police Lieutenant Jack Revill quoted Hosty as stating that Oswald "was capable of committing the assassination of President Kennedy." The conversation in which this statement was made was as Revill and Hosty were arriving at DPD Headquarters shortly after Oswald was brought in. Hosty denied under oath to the Warren Commission that he made the statement. Revill testified, also under oath, that he did. Literally dozens of such cover-ups appear in the best-selling conspiracy books written by Warren critics.

Probably the only one of these conspiracy advocates to do harm to a specific person was a New Orleans prosecutor named James Garrison. His conspiracy scenario mutated several times as his targets died or as incontrovertible disproof of one aspect of his current theory or another was thrust upon him. For example, he tried to charge Robert Perrin with the murder of John Kennedy until one of his staff proved that Perrin had committed suicide a year before the assassination, and then his next prime suspect, David Ferrie, also died. Finally, he settled on a live New Orleans businessman named Clay Shaw to prosecute as a conspirator in the Kennedy assassination. Garrison chose to prosecute a man at least as innocent of the charges as Garrison himself. At the conclusion of the trial, the jury returned a verdict of not guilty on the first ballot, in a mere 45 minutes, but Shaw was driven to financial ruin by the expense of defending himself. The Garrison case is laid out in his book about the conspiracy. This case was later thoroughly researched by the staff working for the House Select Committee on Assassinations for substantive evidence, but in the end they concluded that there was little they could use.

Jim Garrison gave credence to the "Oswald as spy" myth by drawing a connection among Oswald, a freelance investigator named Guy

Bannister, and Bannister's sometime associate, David Ferrie at 544 Camp Street in New Orleans. He found eyewitnesses who placed Oswald, Ferrie, and Shaw together at a voter registration drive in Clinton, Louisiana. Oswald's work at Jaggers-Chiles-Stovall, a photography analysis company in Dallas that did classified work making maps for the U.S. government, was offered as further evidence that Oswald was a spy. He was shown to be capable of making forged identification papers by the false registration card under the name of Alek Hidell in his possession at the time of his arrest. In some stories, Oswald was a CIA agent who acted under the direction of his friend and "handler" George de Mohrenschildt. De Mohrenschildt later became one of the mysterious deaths, when the official finding of "suicide" was itself used as evidence of a further government coverup.

Nearly all conspiracy researchers found much in Garrison's case to disagree with, but were quick to pick up anything that would fit their own conspiracy conjectures. Among these tidbits was the testimony of Lt. Col. Pierre Finck, the Army pathologist selected to assist his Navy colleagues with the autopsy at Bethesda. At the trial of Clay Shaw, Finck was the only one of the three who appeared. His testimony for the prosecution, though extensive, lent little support to Garrison's case, but several of his statements were found useful in support of various conspiracy stories. One was the statement that he was not allowed to dissect the neck wound by orders of "the Admiral who was in charge" of the autopsy room. Others were that the single bullet could not possibly have caused all the wounds of the two men and there was more lead in Connally's wrist than could have been missing from the core of CE 399.

Conspiracy advocates ridiculed the autopsy report issued by Humes, Boswell, and Finck. Critics included expert forensic pathologist Dr. Cyril Wecht, the medical examiner of Allegheny County, Pennsylvania. The autopsy materials remained sealed in the National Archives, however, so no refutation of the many allegations of the autopsy panel's blunders and coverups was available. The persistent allegations of the critics prompted two reexaminations of the sealed autopsy materials by panels of experts. The first was in 1968, directed by Acting Attorney General Ramsey Clark and chaired by Dr. Russell Fisher, Maryland State Medical Examiner. His panel of experts examined the 14 x-rays and 52 photographs taken at the autopsy, as well as the marks on the clothing of the two injured men, and concluded that the findings in the original autopsy report were substantially correct. The major discrepancies they identified between the documented facts and the original autopsy report were the mislocation of the entry wounds to the President's back and to the back of the head. The Clark Panel concluded that the original autopsy report placed the entry wound on the President's back about two inches too low and the head wound about 4 inches too low.

The second reexamination of the autopsy evidence was done at the request of the Rockefeller Commission in 1975. This Commission was organized, under the direction of Vice-President Rockefeller, to investigate the misdeeds of the CIA in the couple of decades since it was created. The primary focus of this investigation was on the attempted assassination of Fidel Castro by the CIA and Mafia just months before the assassination of President Kennedy. This attempt on Castro's life was unearthed by the CIA's own Inspector General, after rumors of the failed coup had leaked to the press. Rockefeller's expert forensic pathology panel agreed with the findings of the Clark Panel in every detail, endorsing their location of the entry wounds on Kennedy's back and the back of his head, the location of the exit wounds, only one bullet path through the brain, and all other relevant facts.

The findings of these two panels were almost entirely ignored by the critics who, perhaps understandably, disbelieved any findings of bodies commissioned by the government based on material still held secret from the American public.

CHAPTER THREE
The Extent of the Conspiracy

"The Committee believes, on the basis of the evidence available to it, that President John F. Kennedy was probably assassinated as a result of a conspiracy. The Committee was unable to identify the other gunmen or the extent of the conspiracy."
— *House Select Committee on Assassinations*[19]

After extensive lobbying by many citizens, the House of Representatives decided in 1976 to hold hearings on the assassinations of President Kennedy and Dr. Martin Luther King, Jr. After an aborted start and the replacement of the committee's Chairman and Chief Counsel, the House Select Committee on Assassinations (HSCA) undertook a review of the evidence in the Kennedy case, culminating in public hearings before the full committee on September 6-15, 1978. The actual investigation took nearly two years and was carried out almost exclusively by the HSCA's staff and expert consultants, some of whom gave testimony in the course of the public hearings. The HSCA's staff was headed by Chief Councel G. Robert Blakey, a prominent attorney and member of the faculty of the Law School at Cornell University. Blakey had earlier worked for the Department of Justice when Robert Kennedy was attorney general.

The review of the Kennedy assassination by the HSCA was important in two ways. It was a serious public acknowledgment that the question of conspiracy had to be given a closer look, and it represented the greatest assembly of technical experts to carefully examine all the evidence since the Warren Commission investigation a decade and a half earlier. There were several significant differences in the two investigations. The WC relied heavily on existing government agencies, such as the Dallas Police, FBI, Secret Service, and CIA, to conduct the actual criminal investigation.

19. HSCA Final Report, 1979.

They elicited the help of the Department of Defense to conduct the scientific investigation. The HSCA assembled panels of experts, most not employed by the federal government, to examine the evidence. The WC did not use the photographs and x-rays of the autopsy of President Kennedy because they decided, early on, that they would make all their findings and evidence accessible to the public. Chief Justice Warren was the only Commission official to personally examine the autopsy evidence. The HSCA obtained all these materials from the National Archives and made them available to their Forensic Pathology Panel (FPP) and other experts to use in their investigation, though most autopsy photographs were, and still are, deemed inappropriate for public release.[20]

In addition to the FPP, the HSCA organized a panel of photographic experts, handwriting experts, a firearms panel, and several individual experts to work closely with the Committee staff in the investigation. Many of the same witnesses who were interviewed by the Warren Commission or the WC staff were reinterviewed. In addition, the HSCA found and interviewed witnesses missed by the Warren investigation. They examined material supplied by those critical of the WC's findings and unearthed material that had not been discovered by the Commission or its many critics.

The several days of public hearings were carried on both radio and television by the Public Broadcasting System. The Committee's leadoff witnesses were John and Nellie Connally, who recounted the events in the presidential limousine at the time of the assassination. The story did not vary significantly from the account they gave to the WC. Mrs. Connally still maintained that the President and the Governor were hit by two different bullets before the final, fatal shot to the President's head. Mr. Connally, who recalled hearing a shot before he was hit, but not hearing the shot that hit him, still supported both his wife and the Warren Commission, in spite of the contradictions in their conclusions.

Robert Groden, a photo-optical technician and ardent Kennedy assassination researcher and book author, was one of the people instrumental in prompting the House of Representatives to create and fund the HSCA. For the benefit of the Committee members and the broadcast

---

20. This is an official formality that preserves the pretense that the Kennedy family retains control of access to this material. "Bootleg" copies of these photographs and x-rays may be downloaded from the internet and have been published in many conspiracy books. One is even published in this book, though it is merely an intact copy of a partial photograph published in the HSCA report.

audience, he reviewed the major photographic issues raised by critics of the WC's conclusions. These issues were not necessarily ones he believed in, but were ones that had been raised frequently and written about extensively. Groden's review was generally without advocacy or comment, as it was the staff's intention that these issues be addressed in the testimony of the scientific experts who were to follow.[21] The major part of this evidence was in three areas: refutation of the "single bullet theory," evidence of a shot from the front, and pictures that purported to show that Oswald was not at the sixth floor window of the Texas School Book Depository at the time of the shooting or that there was another assassin in Dealey Plaza shooting at the occupants of the limousine.

On the first point, Groden showed a drawing of an impossible zigzag course that critics of the single bullet maintain that CE 399 would have had to follow to produce the four injuries to the two men. The drawing was not made by Mr. Groden, but by another critic, based on the positions of the two men as he reconstructed it from the Zapruder movie of the shootings *(see figure 1).*

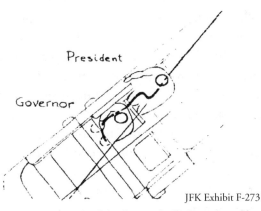

JFK Exhibit F-273

Figure 1. Sketch of the trajectory of the "magic bullet" presented by Robert Groden on the first day of public hearings by the House of Representatives. *(National Archives)*

Mr. Groden reviewed the Zapruder film with the HSCA and the television audience three times—once in the original and twice in an enhanced version that most viewers were seeing for the first time. The

---

21. Afterward he complained bitterly about being kept on a leash by the Committee's interviewing staff. He felt that other people's views were fully explored, but his own were not considered.

enhancements were effected by a technique called rotoscoping, which consists of enlarging and repositioning each individual frame so that one or more fixed landmarks would be in the same location throughout. This eliminates the shakiness and imperfect tracking of the handheld camera. In this case, the President and the Governor were consistently positioned so that they and the passenger compartment of the car would fill the frame. Mr. Groden referred to individual frames of the film by the numbers assigned by the Warren Commission, frame 1 being the first frame in which the motorcade was visible. The President first appears in frame 133 and appears last in frame 486. The rate of filming was determined by the FBI in 1963 to be approximately 18.3 frames per second, the rate consistently used by researchers.

Groden observed that President Kennedy showed evidence of the shot through the neck when he first emerged from behind a road sign at frame 225, but found that Connally did not show obvious distress from his chest wound until frame 238. At this frame, he instructed the audience, "we will see Governor Connally's right shoulder buckle sharply, his cheeks will puff out, and his hair will become immediately disheveled, all in one frame." These signs were taken as an indication that the Governor was shot between frames 237 and 238. The difference in the time at which each man exhibited a response to wounding was at least 13 frames, and probably several more while the sign concealed the President from Zapruder's view. Converting the frame count to time, he indicated that the Governor's reaction appeared a second, more or less, after the President assumed "a clutching, protective motion toward his throat." The subtle signs in the Governor's behavior were not necessarily visible in the original film, but were in his enhanced version. Some of this information was not seen by the WC when they published their conclusions 12 years earlier. It was also pointed out that if he were injured by the same shot as the President, the Governor would still be holding his hat in his right hand after his right radius would have been smashed. This is one of the critics' major arguments that Connally was not struck at the same time as the President. Groden subsequently noted at frame 274, however, that Connally was still holding his hat, almost two seconds after most critics saw evidence that he had been wounded. In this instance, it seemed that the issue was immediately resolved by the film itself.

For his second point, he showed the abrupt backward movement of the President after the fatal head shot. In this case, Groden's personal belief seemed to surface. He thought that the backward movement was produced by a bullet from the front. One HSCA member added to this evidence, refuting the WC conclusion, by observing that Mrs. Kennedy climbed on the back of the limousine to retrieve something. If it were a piece of the President's skull, his speculation was that only a shot from the front could blow a piece of skull out of the back of his head.

Groden showed photographs alleged to be human figures in various places, including the grassy knoll, fire escapes, and windows of the surrounding buildings. Conspiracy buffs could see some of these figures holding rifles and others reacting to gunshots coming from locations other than the Book Depository. The questions of some of the HSCA members indicated that they had difficulty seeing these images. He also showed pictures of Lee Oswald that were claimed by some to "prove" that there were two (or more) "Oswalds." Finally, there were pictures of the Mannlicher-Carcano rifle and Oswald holding the rifle and pistol in which some saw evidence of fakery, "proving" that there were people trying to frame Oswald for the assassination.

These issues were addressed, and for the most part discredited, in the scientific portion of the testimony that followed.

The HSCA organized the Forensic Pathology Panel soon after it was in business, wisely including Dr. Cyril Wecht, the persistent critic of the original autopsy report and ardent conspiracy supporter. The wound ballistics consultant from the Army's Biophysics Division (the author of this book) was invited to participate in two of the FPP's meetings. During several meetings, the FPP, a few members of the HSCA staff, and other consultants reviewed all the evidence from the autopsy, including the photographs, x-rays, and clothing. They also had access to material that medical examiners are usually privy to, including bullets, bullet fragments, and cartridge cases that were collected in Dallas at the time of the murders and were kept, without public access, in the National Archives.

The majority view of the FPP was expressed by its chairman, Dr. Michael Baden, in his testimony to the HSCA on September 7, 1978. Dr. Baden was, at that time, the medical examiner for the city of New York. The majority opinion was that the findings of the Clark and Rockefeller panels were correct. The original autopsy report was substantially sound. The only significant error found in the report was the inaccurate location of the President's two entry wounds. The panel confirmed that the single bullet did cause the neck wound of the President and the extensive wounds of the governor, citing the yawed entry wound in the Governor's back as conclusive evidence that it was produced by a bullet that had already hit something else before it hit the Governor. This was identical to the conclusion expressed by the Army's Biophysics Lab experts in their testimony to the WC, a finding accepted by the HSCA and included in their conclusions.

Some of the x-rays had been submitted to a computer enhancement company to see if more detail could be obtained by an increase in contrast. The quality of the original x-rays was moderate to poor, and the enhancement added substantial detail to some of the most important x-rays.

Ms. Ida Dox, a medical illustrator, was commissioned by the HSCA to illustrate portions of the photographic evidence, allowing the audience to see the details discussed by the panel without showing the actual autopsy photographs. She also drew illustrations of some of the panel's conclusions. The drawings, pictures, and x-rays that were used by the FPP to draw their joint conclusions were shown at the hearings to support them. The only vital evidence that did not appear in the pictures or x-rays was the "beveling" of the interior surface of the skull at the entry wound mentioned in the autopsy report. The picture that showed the entry wound from inside the skull was not mentioned, except to show an enlargement of a hemispherical crater on the frontal bone that was identified as a portion of the exit wound. The crater produced by a projectile penetrating bone was illustrated in a drawing.

The panel concluded that there was only one bullet wound to the head. It entered high on the back of the skull just to the right of the center line and exited high on the right front of the skull near the coronal suture. The latter was determined from the autopsy report's description of the recovered skull fragment containing the cratered exit wound mentioned in the autopsy report. The x-ray, apparently of that skull fragment, showed the unmistakable characteristics of a skull suture on an edge adjoining the crater. The passage of the bullet tore a large hole in the right side of the President's head, fragmenting the skull violently enough that it tore the scalp along some of the fracture lines, dislodging pieces of skull.

The FPP criticized the autopsy team for not dissecting completely the President's neck wound. This would have shown conclusively that the exit wound had been obliterated by the tracheotomy at Parkland. It would have settled the question of whether the passing bullet had damaged the transverse spine of the first thoracic vertebra or the connective tissue attached to it. In any case, the wound on the President's back at the base of his neck, shown in figure 2, clearly showed an "abrasion collar" characteristic of an entry wound at an angle a bit less than 90° to the skin. The drawing used to illustrate an abrasion collar is in figure 3.

Figure 2. Dox drawing of the wound at the base of President Kennedy's neck with an inserted enlargement of the actual photograph of the entry wound. *(National Archives/John Hunt)*

The FPP also concluded—based on the surgical report, the x-rays, and the holes torn in the clothing worn by Governor Connally at the time of the shooting—that a single bullet produced all three wounds inflicted on the governor. Dr. Baden stated that CE 399 probably was deformed by striking the radius in penetrating the wrist. Connally's rib, struck at an earlier point on the path was a "thin bone" that would "… not significantly deform a copper jacketed bullet."[22] Finally, they con-

---

22. This conclusion differed from the opinion of the Edgewood Arsenal experts in their testimony to the Warren Commission. Dr. Olivier, for instance, expressed the opinion that the deformation of CE 399 occurred while penetrating the Governor's rib. Baden corrected this statement in an interview with Gerald Posner, as reported in "Case Closed." In that interview, he agreed with Olivier.

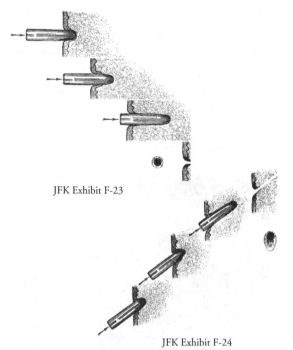

JFK Exhibit F-23

JFK Exhibit F-24

Figure 3. Drawing of the method of production and final appearance of the abrasion collar produced by normal impact (F-23) and oblique impact (F-24). *(National Archives)*

firmed the WC conclusion that a single bullet had caused the wound to the neck of the President just before striking the governor. The conclusive evidence was the elongated hole in the governor's shirt and jacket and the elongated entry wound cited in the surgical report. This proved that the bullet was "wobbling" when it struck the governor.

Dr. Humes, the Navy pathologist who headed the original autopsy team, was called to give his opinion regarding the accuracy of the conclusions of the FPP. In spite of the sometimes heated disagreements he had had with the panel, his HSCA testimony was consistent with that of Dr. Baden. He further noted that the distance between the striking point of the bullet and the external occipital protuberance was not specified in the original autopsy report and that his present conclusion was in accord with the original report, which stated that the entry was "above" the occipital protuberance. He further confirmed that there was only one entry wound in the skull and that it was on the rear. In the course of his testimony, Humes, who retired at the rank of Navy Captain in 1967, was also called upon to authenticate the photographic evidence. He stated that the photographs and x-rays he examined in the National Archives, including those on display and represented in drawings at the HSCA hearings, were the true photographic evidence taken at the time of the autopsy and catalogued by him in 1966 at the National Archives.

Photographic experts were also called to testify regarding the possibility of forgery in the evidence. The Kodak Corporation was able to reconstruct the date of manufacture of the print film from lot numbers printed on the original film negatives. This evidence was consistent with film that would have been "fresh" at the time of the autopsy. Experts in dental identification were asked to compare the x-rays to known dental x-rays of John Kennedy. All these experts expressed the opinion that the evidence was the original, unforged autopsy evidence.

A minority view of the FPP (a minority of one) was presented to the HSCA by Dr. Cyril Wecht. Dr. Wecht's view was altered somewhat from his earlier written opinions. In addition to the access that the FPP had to the autopsy photographs and x-rays, he had been granted permission to examine them in 1972. Having finally been able to examine these materials in detail, he was convinced that most of the facts reported in the original autopsy were confirmed. He also agreed with the majority's location of the entry and exit wounds, higher than the WC placement, based on the autopsy report. Dr. Wecht remained of the opinion, however, that the skull damage was too extensive to have been caused by a single bullet. He speculated that a plastic bullet could have been fired into the gaping wound in the President's head, and that bullet could have stopped in the brain without exiting, thereby avoiding creating another entry and exit wound. It was this second bullet that would have thrown the President violently backward in the car seat. Furthermore, a plastic bullet would not have shown on the x-rays. When asked why that second bullet would not have created a second wound track that would have shown on the photographs of the brain, he stated that the event would have only a remote chance of happening.

He expressed the opinion that the "single bullet theory" was impossible, showing his own version of a drawing of the two men in the car with a discontinuous bullet trajectory superimposed. He stated that this necessarily would be the path of a single bullet producing the four separate wounds to the two men. Dr. Wecht also disputed the finding that CE 399 could have caused all of the governor's wounds by referring to its minimal deformation. He showed a picture of a WCC/MC bullet that was more deformed than CE 399 after being fired by the Edgewood researchers through the carcass of a goat, grazing a rib *(see figure 4)*. The picture also includes two bullets fired from the M-C rifle found in the Depository and recovered in cotton wadding by the FBI. These bullets were deformed more than CE 399. His opinion was that a bullet that had struck Mr. Connally's "heavier" rib would have been more deformed than these three bullets, not less.

Figure 4. "Stretcher bullet," CE 399, goat-rib-shot bullet, CE 853, and two bullets recovered in cotton waste by the FBI to use as standards. *(National Archives)*

When asked if the bullet could be deformed by striking solid wood, Dr. Wecht stated that it, indeed, could. The questioner, Mr. Gary Cornwell, then dramatically dropped CE 399 onto the top of a wooden table from a height of about four feet. The bullet made a loud clatter as it bounced off the table, but it was not damaged in the demonstration, though there was a small dent left in the table. Noting the lack of damage, the questioner then asked Dr. Wecht if there was also a velocity below which the bullet could also damage bone without itself being damaged. He replied that there probably was, but he didn't know the exact velocity.[23] Finally, Dr. Wecht stated the opinion that the horizontal, elongated entry wound, corresponding to similar holes in the governor's

---

23. Mr. Cornwell had earlier asked about the risk to CE 399 in this demonstration, following our discussion of the retardation and deformation of bullets penetrating bodies. I told the HSCA staff that the bullet had been damaged on Connally's rib, not his wrist, just as Dr. Olivier had told the WC 14 years earlier. I assured Cornwell that he could not throw the bullet into a wooden surface hard enough to damage it, much less by just dropping it on a table. At the time, he gave no indication of what he had in mind.

jacket and shirt, was caused by a bullet striking at an oblique angle from the side. This shot, he claimed, could have been fired from the vicinity of the "grassy knoll."

My testimony followed Dr. Wecht. I was questioned not as an ad hoc member of the FPP, but as a professional scientist in the study of wound ballistics. The topics discussed were some of the basic concepts of the exterior ballistics and wound ballistics of supersonic rifle bullets:

- How bullets are stabilized in flight, how velocity decreases with range, and the creation of the supersonic shock wave.

- How the sound of a shock wave can deceive the listener into thinking that the shot came from a location other than the one where the rifleman is located.

- The physics of bullet behavior in soft tissue and bone in the human target.

- The impossibility of a bullet "throwing" a person around in a car.

The backward motion of the President seen in the Zapruder film, immediately after the shot that killed him, was explained as a momentary, but intense neuromuscular spasm caused by the bullet penetrating the brain. This phenomenon was illustrated in an archival Army film clip (made in 1948) of two anaesthetized goats being shot by supersonic bullets. In the movie, the live goat showed a similar neuromuscular reaction, though one electrocuted just before the shot showed no visible movement at all.

High-speed movies from the Biophysics Lab tests for the Warren Commission were shown in the same film. These were the movies of several rounds of WCC/MC bullets perforating and shattering human skulls. The movie illustrated the enormous damage that the deformed rifle bullet will cause when perforating a human skull.[24]

The Select Committee had also organized a firearms panel consisting of forensic firearms experts from several state agencies nationwide. The panel members—Monty Lutz, Donald Champagne, John Bates, and Andrew Newquist—were called to testify in the public hearings. These

---

24. These points will be reconsidered later. The format of this book allows a more complete explanation of the scientific observations than was possible during the testimony to the HSCA.

experts confirmed that it would be easy for the casual observer to mistake the Mannlicher-Carcano rifle for the more common German Mauser. They covered the same material that the FBI had done for the WC, demonstrating the link between the weapons, bullets, and cartridge cases in the Kennedy and Tippit murders. Like the FBI experts before them, they were unable to state conclusively that the bullet recovered from the wall at the home of General Walker was fired from the same rifle. They did note, however, that the bullet was almost certainly a WCC/MC bullet containing no markings that would eliminate the possibility that it was fired from that weapon. (In other words, they could neither confirm nor dispute Marina Oswald's testimony that Lee had been the person who shot at the general).

The firearms panel conducted some test firings of Oswald's rifle before they appeared at the hearings. When the bullets from these tests were compared to the FBI test bullets, they could not find a match. That is, in its current state, the rifle no longer produces the engraving signature that it did in 1963. The comparison with the FBI test bullets fired in 1963, however, clearly established that the bullets that injured the governor and killed the President were fired from Oswald's rifle. The House firearms panel politely identified the reason for the discrepancy as the neglect of the Archives in maintaining the weapon while in their care. The interior of the barrel had neither been cleaned nor given a protective coating. Propellant residue had accelerated the corrosion of the barrel in the damp basement of the Archives building.[25]

The Select Committee's staff interviewed the same eyewitnesses at the Tippit murder scene that were interviewed by the WC and confirmed that they had identified Oswald as he shot Tippit or fled the scene. The Committee found one eyewitness, Jack Ray Tatum, not interviewed by the WC or the FBI in 1963 or 1964. He says he witnessed the final moments of the Tippit killing. Not only did he recognize Oswald when he saw him on television the next day, he saw Oswald walk around the front of the police cruiser where Tippit lay on the street, felled by the earlier shots, and shoot Tippit in the head at point-blank range. This solved one mystery from the HSCA's Tippit investigation, where it noted that one bullet wound was

---

25. In fairness to the National Archives, one of the FBI experts testifying before the Warren Commission stated that so many bullets had already been fired from the rifle that it would be doubtful that it would still produce the same engraving signature that it did when they first fired and recovered standards for ballistic comparison to CE399 and the fragments recovered from the limousine.

slanted more sharply upward from front to back than the others were. The Committee was unable to draw any significant conclusion regarding the cold-blooded, "coup-de-grace" shot to the head of the dying man. Gerald Posner quotes an anonymous, high-ranking Dallas police officer who told him in an interview that another witness also came forward. The police decided not to use him because he was near the scene participating in an extramarital affair. They already had an abundance of witnesses, so they decided to save him the embarrassment of having his presence known.

At the time of the WC investigation, a technique of analysis for trace contamination, known since the mid-1930s, was just becoming practical. The test, known as neutron activation analysis or NAA, was employed by the FBI in an attempt to determine whether the small fragments of lead recovered from the President and the governor matched the lead cores of CE 399 and the large bullet fragment found in the limousine. The FBI lab determined that their NAA data, the first such that they had ever obtained, were inconclusive. No mention of the test is found in the Warren Report. In 1978, an NAA expert, Dr. Vincent P. Guinn of the University of California, Irvine, was commissioned by the HSCA to repeat the test. An additional twelve years of refinement of the technique included the incorporation of a new detector that yielded better discrimination of the trace elements in the alloy. In Guinn's hands, the new technology yielded more conclusive results.

The name of the technique (neutron activation) derives from its nondestructive method of bombarding the metal with neutrons to transmute a few of the nuclei into radioactive isotopes. Detecting the decay of those atoms allows one to determine the amount of each element originally present. Guinn showed that the bullets made by the Western Cartridge Company, to specifications for use in the Mannlicher-Carcano rifle, possessed a characteristic uncommon in modern bullets. Whereas most bullets have very homogeneous alloy in the jacket and cores throughout a production run, these bullets showed great variability in the trace elements contained in the core, from bullet to bullet in the same lot. The specific makeup of the alloy in its core allowed Dr. Guinn to match the core of the bullet found at Parkland, CE 399, to the fragment recovered in Connally's wrist. The fragments of bullets found in the car precisely matched the alloy in the small fragments recovered from Kennedy's head at autopsy. The NAA results were some of the most significant new findings to come out of the House investigation.

After a weekend recess, the House Select Committee next heard from Dr. William Hartmann. He and a colleague, Frank Scott, had performed what came to be known as a "jiggle analysis" of the Zapruder film. This analysis was invented by Prof. Louis Alvarez from the University of California, Berkeley, a recipient of the Nobel Prize in physics. His observations and procedure are explained in a 1976 article published in the *American Journal of Physics*. Alvarez had noticed that when he was attempting to track an object moving across a still background with a hand-held movie camera, there was a series of larger-than-average blurs on the film, at a rate of about three per second. He saw similar results in movies taken by others and speculated that the consistent cycle was the result of the human "neuromuscular feedback system." He proposed a study for Bell and Howell, the movie equipment maker, to develop a damper to suppress this "jitter" in hand-held cameras. This contract resulted in his successfully developing a damping system.

When *Life* magazine published frames from the Zapruder film, Alvarez noticed that some of the frames were more blurred than others. This led him to wonder if the shots in Dealey Plaza would register on the film as a "startle" reaction when Abraham Zapruder heard the loud shock waves from the bullets. After analyzing the more complete set of reprints in the Warren Report, he concluded that the characteristic three-per-second frequency "appeared in Zapruder's jitter spectrum when his neuromuscular system was set into oscillation—presumably by the sharp 'crack' of the bullets." Alvarez identified "shots" associated with "pulse trains starting about 182, 221, and 313." Numbers are associated with the WC numbering of the Zapruder film, frame by frame, as published in the Warren Report.

For their analysis, Hartmann and Scott had the original Zapruder film from which to take measurements. This offered two very significant advantages over the earlier Alvarez work. First, it eliminates the loss of detail inherent in the set reprinted in the Warren Report. Second, the Warren Report only contained frames 170 through 335, but the HSCA had the whole film to study.[26] Dr. Hartmann concluded that there were

26. The original Zapruder film had been spliced when owned by *Life* magazine, resulting in the loss of a few frames. Complete copies were made by the FBI immediately after the assassination, however, before *Life* obtained the original. These, contrary to accounts of mysterious "missing frames," show nothing of importance. After the film was returned to Zapruder, he sold it to *Life*. Hartmann was able to obtain measures from these first-generation copies to complete the series.

at least two significant "jiggle events" in the film. The largest started at frame 318, a few frames after the fatal shot (frame 312). This, he concluded, signified a startle reaction to the fatal gunshot. The second largest was a "burst" of three frames in the early 190s. Hartmann concluded that this placed the shot that hit the President and Governor at approximately frame 190. Three other large blurs were noted; one just as the President disappeared behind the street sign, one just as he emerged from behind the street sign, and one earlier at frames 158 and 159.

The Select Committee organized a panel of photographic experts to consider the evidence, primarily from the Zapruder movie, to reconstruct the sequence in which the events that accompanied the assassination occurred. Mr. Calvin McCamy reported the results of that panel in his testimony to the Committee. After a review of the photographic evidence and a discussion of particular points, the panel opinion was obtained by voting. Not all experts were present for all sessions, so any vote represented only the views of those attending that particular session. The panel split 12 to 5 on the point of whether the President showed signs of distress just before disappearing behind the road sign at Zapruder frame 207. The better than 2 to 1 majority thought that he did show distress. The panel voted 15 to 1 that, at that time, the alignment of the two men was consistent with a single bullet striking both men.

McCamy reported that the actions that Governor Connally described making in response to hearing the first bullet were seen clearly in Groden's rotoscoped copy of the Zapruder film. Mr. Connally swiveled sharply to the right in what was described as two separate "jerks," turning 60° in a ninth of a second between frames 162 to 164 and then another 30° between frames 166 to 167. The panel concluded that the first bullet from the Depository was fired just prior to frame 160 and missed both the limousine and its occupants (just as Governor Connally maintained all along). This placed the occurrence of the first shot several seconds before Mr. Kennedy showed any form of distress. In fact, Mr. Kennedy was still smiling and waving at the crowd at the time that his wife and Mr. Connally were both turning to the right to look over their shoulder.

They determined that the second bullet was fired just prior to frame 207 and struck both men, and the third bullet struck the President's head between frames 312 and 313. The latter frame is the one showing the President's head exploding. The occurrence of a shot at approximately frame 160 of the Zapruder film, they said, coincides with a brief gap in the foliage of the oak tree through which the limousine would be visible from the window of the Book Depository.[27]

Making no assumption on the location of the shooter, Mr. Thomas Canning, a NASA engineer, and members of the Committee staff projected three bullet trajectories backward from the entry and exit points of the wounds on the Governor and President. The Zapruder movie was augmented by other movies and still pictures to establish the positions of the two men in three-dimensional space at the time of each shot. They also calculated the car's position relative to the Depository and street. Estimated errors at each stage of the process were combined to provide a circle of probable error in the projections. Of the three trajectories they reconstructed, the one based on the entry wound in Connally's back and the exit wound in Kennedy's throat, had the smallest error circle. This is because that projection was based on the distance between the two men, as opposed to the distance between the entry and exit points of a single wound to an individual. The "single bullet" trajectory puts the position of a rifle in the hands of a person firing from the upper half of the corner window on the sixth floor within the circle of probable error. That window is the only site from which a bullet could be fired that appears in all three circles of probable error.[28]

The Committee considered the claims of fakery in the two photographs of Lee Oswald holding a rifle similar to the one found on the sixth floor of the Book Depository and traced to Oswald's post office box. We recall that the two pictures, one with the original negative, were found in the cardboard box among the Oswald's possessions in Mrs. Ruth Paine's garage by Detective Guy Rose. Sergeant Cecil W. Kirk, with 17 years experience in the Identification Branch of the Metropolitan District of Columbia Police Department, used the Oswald camera to expose several test frames. He compared the negative found by Detective Rose to the test frames, using characteristics such as irregularities in the border and

---

27. This differs from the WC conclusion that Mr. Kennedy would disappear behind the foliage at about frame 161.

28. These backward projections, especially the "circle of probable error," have little validity. At worst, however, they indicate that the shots came from behind. The single bullet trajectory indicates that the shot originated well above street level. See Chapter 6.

scratch marks on the film made when the film was pulled over the guide rails. All visible markings on the two were identical. In a repeat performance of the WC photo expert, he was able to spot sufficient identical characteristics to establish conclusively that the negative (CE 133-B) was exposed in the Oswald camera.

Mr. Calvin McCamy of the photographic panel testified that there was no difference in the grain pattern of the images of Oswald's head, his body, and the background of either picture. A difference in grain pattern is conclusive evidence of tampering, and a specific grain pattern is extremely difficult to duplicate. In addition, he used a stereoscopic view of the two pictures to attempt to find traces of tampering. As the two pictures were exposed from slightly different positions, this would put a slightly different perspective on the two views, similar to the difference obtained with two eyes in natural human vision. If such a pair is viewed with the proper equipment so that one eye views one picture while the other eye views the other, a three-dimensional view will be created. When viewed in this manner, any modification made by tampering would stand out as a "ghost" image, when seen by one eye but not the other. If the modification was made to both pictures, however, the modification would stand out as an image "floating" in front of the background or "submerged" within it, unless the fabricator took the stereoscopic principle into account and was somehow able to align the modifications perfectly. The two images of Oswald, of course, were different in the two views. Other than these images, no ghosts or floaters were visible in McCamy's stereo analysis.

He also examined the proportion of Oswald's head and body in the two pictures and found them to be within the normal variation due to posture and facial expression, accounting for the ability of the person to stand erect or slumped, leaning toward or away from the camera versus normal to the view, and with teeth closed or parted. He demonstrated how the shadow of facial features change not only with posture but with the three-dimensional interaction of posture and sun angle, so that two consecutive photographs, taken a few seconds apart, can show nearly identical facial shadow patterns even though the person was photographed in two different poses. They examined the "transplanted" chin pattern and found nothing unusual in these pictures, compared to other pictures of Oswald used by Groden in his presentation to the Committee.

The differences were entirely attributable to the difference in lighting by strong, overhead sunlight and the more uniform lighting one sees with snapshots and portraits taken indoors.

The panel of photographic experts also examined the picture of the front of the Depository building that was taken at the time of the assassination. It contains a figure that resembles Lee Oswald. Warren critics have maintained that Oswald could not be in front of the building and on the sixth floor at the same time. The WC staff identified the person in question as Billy Lovelady and confirmed that finding with Lovelady as well as several of his coworkers at the Depository. Contrary to a common claim by critics, the Commission did interview Mr. Lovelady about his being the person in the picture. The HSCA Photography Panel, working with forensic anthropologists, found from anthropometric data on the two that the photograph resembles the features of Lovelady more closely than those of Oswald. In addition, the clothing matches the description of what Lovelady was wearing at the time, not what Oswald was known to be wearing. Committee investigators interviewed Billy Lovelady about the photograph and he again confirmed that he was the man in the picture.

The Select Committee obtained two photographs that the Warren Commission did not see—or at least did not mention having examined. One was an original print of one of the pictures taken by Marina that Oswald had given to his friend George de Mohrenschildt. During the course of the Committee's investigation, but before they had a chance to interview him, de Mohrenschildt committed suicide. The Committee subpoenaed his personal papers and discovered the print as well as written reference to it in the manuscript of an unpublished book written by de Mohrenschildt. The picture, reproduced in Figure 5, has an inscription on the back, "To my friend George from Lee Oswald." It also has a date, 5/ IV / 63.[29] The Committee's handwriting expert, Mr. Joseph P. McNally, examined Oswald's signature on the back of the picture and found it to match the signature on the fingerprint cards and other Oswald signatures and handwriting.

29. Either the fourth of May or the fifth of April, if written European style with the day before the month. The substitution of a Roman numeral for the month seems more likely and may have been a personal peculiarity acquired while living in the Soviet Union. In this case, the date would have been April 5, 1963.

Figure 5. Front and back of the "backyard" photograph that Lee Oswald gave to his friend George de Mohrenschildt, dated April 5 or May 4, 1963. *(National Archives)*

The de Mohrenschildt picture also has a handwritten inscription on the back, "Killer of Fascists, ha, ha, ha." The inscription and date are in Russian (Cyrillic) script that appeared to be in pencil that had been retraced, again in pencil. Marina was not sure who had written the original inscription, but thought it might have been herself. Mr. McNally was unable to determine who had written the inscription or whether the original writer had retraced the letters. He did observe that the retracing mostly obliterated the original and was done slowly and painstakingly, which tends not to resemble a person's normal handwriting.

The second new photograph was a third pose of the backyard photograph turned over to the Committee by Roscoe White, a retired Dallas police officer. Curiously, the pose in this photograph was a third view that was used in the WC reconstruction of the backyard photography session in 1964, but not seen in the two photographs published as part of the Warren Report. It is surprising that this pose goes not only unprinted, but unmentioned in the Warren Report. When questioned by the House Committee, Marina was no better at remembering the exact number of photographs she took in the backyard than she was when questioned by the WC. She did confirm again that it was she who had taken the photographs—with Lee's camera. The panel examined these pictures, along with the two found in the Oswalds' possessions in 1963. They found no trace of alteration in any of the four prints.[30]

Responding to reports that the rifle found in the Depository was first identified as a German 7.65 mm Mauser and subsequent claims that the rifle in various photographs, including the backyard photos of Oswald, depicted several different weapons, the photographic panel compared a series of photographs of the rifle found in the Depository to the rifle in these backyard photographs and to each other. These pictures were taken by police photographers, newspaper photographers, and others at all stages from the first discovery of the weapon—before it was even touched—to putting it into the National Archives repository. After painstakingly noting the relative lengths of components, a unique wear spot, and other identifying features, they found all these pictures of the weapon, including those in Oswald's hands in the backyard photographs, to be the same weapon to the exclusion of all other, similar weapons.

The Committee had obtained the money order sent to Klein's Sporting Goods Co. of Chicago to pay for the Mannlicher-Carcano rifle, serial number C-2766. They also had signed fingerprint cards from Oswald's Marine enlistment record and from his arrest in New Orleans for disturbing the peace. They obtained the fingerprint card from his arrest in Dallas after the killing of Tippit, but in this case he refused to sign it. Fingerprint experts examined the fingerprints on all three cards, finding them to be identical.

Oswald had admitted that he had rented the post office box to which the rifle was sent while being questioned by a postal inspector on November 23, 1963. In addition, the Committee's handwriting panel examined the signature and handwriting on the application card for the post office box and the money order used to pay for the rifle and found them to be identical to those on Oswald's fingerprint cards. The panel

---

30. Priscilla McMillan reports that Marina admits that she and Marguerite Oswald destroyed all the copies of these photographs that she knew about so they would not be found by the police. It is likely that she knew exactly how many photos she took that day as Lee posed in the backyard, but only admitted taking as many as she had been shown at the time. In the USSR, covering up a crime was almost as serious an offense as committing the crime itself. Refusing to testify, even against one's spouse, was also a crime. This young woman, who spoke very little English at the time of her Warren testimony, probably did not know that U.S. law was quite different. Had she known, she might have said nothing at all.

also attempted to compare the handwriting on the order form for the rifle and envelope in which it was sent, but the only record of the order that the company kept were microfilm copies. In a break with the conclusions of the WC's photographic experts, they found microfilm copies unacceptable for definitive handwriting identification.

After almost two years of negotiating with the CIA, a Soviet KGB agent named Yuri Nosenko defected to the United States in January, 1964. He almost immediately became the center of one of the CIA's greatest controversies. The CIA was split down the middle. Half believed him to be a bona fide defector and the other half a KGB purveyor of disinformation. Mr. Nosenko stated that he had been assigned in 1959 and 1963 to the American tourist section and, as such, had free access to Oswald's KGB file. He declared that there was no connection between the KGB and Oswald. In Nosenko's story, the KGB regarded Oswald as so unstable as to be useless to them and equally unlikely to be a CIA or FBI agent. The Committee spent considerable time on the Nosenko case. One of the people that they heard testimony from was the CIA's representative to the Select Committee, detailed specifically for the Nosenko case. John Hart made it clear from the outset that he was an employee of the CIA, not a "career agent," a title that has a special meaning within the CIA. He expressed the current (1978) CIA view that Nosenko probably was a bona fide defector, but plagued with a poor memory. Hart stated that the CIA no longer questioned Nosenko's credibility, but he didn't think that Nosenko was close enough to the Oswald case to have useful knowledge. He recommended that the Committee ignore Nosenko remarks on Oswald, not because he believed Nosenko to be lying, but because he was not knowledgeable. After much testimony and deliberation, the Committee found itself unable to draw any useful conclusion based on the Nosenko statements.

Next the Committee dealt with the question of whether Oswald had gone to the Cuban consulate in Mexico City, as claimed by the Warren Commission, in an attempt to obtain a visa for a visit to Cuba. The House Committee heard testimony from Señor Alfredo Mirabal Diaz, the consul at the Cuban consulate in Mexico City in September 1963, during the time that Oswald was said to have been there. He remembered Oswald well, as did his secretary, Señora Sylvia Tirado Duran (later Sylvia Tirado Bazan). In ordinary circumstances, Ms. Duran would have been the only one at the Consulate to have talked to a person who came in to fill out an application for a visa. But Oswald was very demanding. Sr. Mirabal stated that it was his impression that Oswald wanted to create a disturbance. He appeared at the Consulate on two occasions and started a loud argument on both, demanding to be issued a visa on the spot rather than having to wait for approval from Havana. Sr. Mirabal, however, did not speak English, so it was the consul he had replaced, Sr. Eusebio Azcue Lopez, who rebuffed Oswald's demands. Sr. Azcue was held over at the consulate for a time, as was the custom, to ease the transition. Azcue, unlike the other two witnesses, repeatedly denied that the person who had twice visited the consulate was the Lee Harvey Oswald he had seen on television, accused of assassinating the President, and being killed by Jack Ruby. Azcue thought that the visitor was taller and slimmer and did not resemble the Oswald on television.

McNally, the Committee's handwriting expert, effectively settled the disagreement between Azcue and the other two witnesses in favor of the visitor actually being Lee Oswald. The Cuban government required two original copies of a visa application. The Cuban government forwarded both originals to the Committee for their study. McNally and his expert panel examined the two independent original signatures and confirmed that the application forms were both signed by Lee Harvey Oswald. Each also had Oswald's original passport-style photograph stapled to it. The panel could find no evidence that either picture had been unstapled and replaced.

Congressmen Preyer, Dodd, and Committee Chairman Stokes actually went to Cuba with members of the Committee staff to interview President Fidel Castro. Castro, of course, denied any involvement in the assassination, even though it was known that the CIA had attempted to have him assassinated. Blakey supported that denial with a variety of documents and statements from highly-placed government officials in the Kennedy administration that indicated that Castro had nothing to gain from an attempt on Kennedy's life.

In addition, the staff obtained surveillance photographs of the Soviet embassy in Mexico City during the period that Oswald was in town, but he did not appear in any of them. This did not prove or disprove an attempt on the part of Oswald to visit the Soviet embassy, as the coverage was not continuous and there were embassy entrances not covered.

The Committee heard testimony from Jack Ruby's friend Lewis

McWillie, a Mafia employee who was in Dallas for a time and then was sent to Cuba to manage the Tropicana Hotel in Havana for its owner, Martin Fox. This was just before Castro came to power and closed down the Mafia operations in the early 1960s. They found that Ruby had visited McWillie in Havana at least twice, and possibly three times, in August and September of 1959. McWillie recalled only one visit lasting six days and professed to remember little else about the visit. A Mafia chieftain, Santos Trafficante was in Trescornia prison in Havana during that period. There was speculation that Ruby went to Trescornia to meet with Trafficante on one of these trips, based on a story circulated by a British businessman named John Wilson, or John Wilson-Hutson, who was in the same low-security lockup for a brief time while Trafficante was there. The Committee tried to contact the British source of the story. He was reportedly deceased by 1978. Trafficante and McWillie both denied under oath that any such meeting ever took place.

Tony Zoppi, an entertainment reporter for the *Dallas Morning News,* knew Jack Ruby as well as anybody in Dallas. Ruby was constantly pestering Zoppi for favorable reviews of the acts in Ruby's club in his column and was a frequent visitor to Zoppi's office. In his statement to the Committee, Mr. Zoppi expressed doubts about any meeting between Ruby and Trafficante, stating that they were "…not in the same league." In any case, there could not have been any plot to assassinate Kennedy hatched in Trescornia in 1959, a year before Kennedy was elected. The only purpose in investigating the alleged meeting was to explore Ruby's possible mob connections.

In a polygraphed interview for the Warren Commission by Special Agent Bell P. Herndon, an experienced polygraph operator for the FBI, Ruby stated that the trips to Havana were "solely for pleasure." The Commission regarded the test as controversial because of Ruby's mental state. Dr. William R. Beavers, the WC psychiatrist who interviewed Ruby before the polygraph test and observed the administration of the entire test, diagnosed Ruby as a psychotic depressive. After the test, he testified, "In the greater proportion of the time that he answered the questions, I felt that he was aware of the questions and that he was giving answers based on an appreciation of reality." In other words, he told the truth as he perceived it. The House Committee decided to disregard the polygraph results, not because of Ruby's "psychotic depression," but because of procedural errors in its administration.

Throughout 1963 Ruby held a running battle with the union representing the entertainers in his club, the American Guild of Variety Artists (AGVA). This problem was the major contributor to a large increase in his long-distance phone bills. The Committee staff uncovered evidence that Ruby made several phone calls to known Mafia associates in September, October, and November 1963, and that these calls were not clearly connected to his problems with AGVA. One call was to Irwin Weiner, a bail bondsman in Chicago who dealt with anybody, including the Mafia. The second was to Nofio Pecora, a Carlos Marcello lieutenant who ran a trailer park in New Orleans. The last three were to Robert Baker, an aide to Teamster boss Jimmy Hoffa, a known Kennedy-hater. The last of these phone calls was made on November 8. Ruby told the police that the Weiner and Baker calls were related to the AGVA problem and the call to the trailer park was to leave a message for his friend Harold Tannenbaum, a fellow night-club owner, to call him back.

In March 1977, Committee Staff Investigator Gaeton Fonzi interviewed José Aleman about a *Washington Post* article in which he stated that Santos Trafficante had said in September 1962 that John Kennedy was going to be "hit." In the course of the interview, Aleman repeatedly referred to a "hit." At one point in the interview he stated that he got the impression that it was Jimmy Hoffa who was going to make the hit. But when the Committee had him under oath, Aleman recanted everything, stating that Trafficante was only expressing an opinion that Kennedy would not be reelected. No further coherent testimony was obtained from Aleman.

The staff for the House Committee also delved into a plot hatched by the CIA and the Mafia and uncovered in 1967 by the Inspector General of the CIA, to kill Fidel Castro. The Committee reviewed a report of a staff interview of a former CIA official who preferred to remain unidentified. This individual stated that he had been Chief of the Operational Support Division, Office of Security. In September of 1960 he was told by his supervisor, Colonel Sheffield Edwards, of an operation to assassinate Cuban leader Fidel Castro. Robert Maheu, a private investigator, was approached by the CIA to assist in the operation. Maheu recruited John Roselli, who brought in Sam Giancana and Santos Trafficante, two Mafia chieftains. Though Giancana and Trafficante went by aliases, the

CIA officials knew who they were. The unidentified former CIA official served as liaison with these two men. Giancana argued vehemently against assassination by gunfire, as nobody could be recruited to carry out such an act with any hope of survival. He convinced them to go with poison pills. Trafficante, who had many contacts among former employees still in Cuba, was to arrange to get the poison pills into Cuba and to recruit highly placed government officials to introduce the pills into Castro's food or drink. The CIA witness stated that Trafficante fulfilled his end of the bargain. He recruited a Cuban-Exile leader and a disaffected Cuban official with access to Castro to serve as the actual assassins. Trafficante passed the pills to them. The Cuban official, however, got cold feet and returned the pills to Trafficante. These details were confirmed in the 1967 report by the inspector general.

The Mafia had good reason to want to kill Castro. When he drove the Mafia out of their casinos in Havana and seized the property in the early 1960s, it cost the Florida family millions in lost property and even more in lucrative gambling profits. Santos Trafficante was called as a witness by the Committee. While he admitted participating as an "interpreter" in the assassination scheme, he denied that he had an active role in it. He denied passing the pills to anybody, receiving any money, or passing any money to the assassins. He thought that using poison pills was the idea of Roselli or Maheu.

Mr. Trafficante was read some excerpts from a column in the September 7, 1976 *Washington Post* by Jack Anderson and Les Whitten. The article stated that after the Cuban underworld elements recruited by Roselli and Trafficante had failed in the attempt to assassinate Castro, they were "turned" by Castro and recruited to assassinate John Kennedy. The article states:

> Before he died, Roselli hinted to associates that he knew who had arranged President Kennedy's murder....According to Roselli, Castro enlisted the same underworld elements whom he had caught plotting against him. They supposedly were Cubans from the old Trafficante organization. Working with Cuban intelligence, they allegedly lined up an ex-Marine sharpshooter, Lee Harvey Oswald, who had been active in the pro-Castro movement.

According to Roselli's version, Oswald may have shot
Kennedy or may have acted as a decoy while others am-
bushed him from closer range. When Oswald was picked
up, Roselli suggested the underworld conspirators feared
he would crack and disclose information that might lead to
them. This almost certainly would have brought a massive
U.S. crackdown of the Mafia.

So Jack Ruby was ordered to eliminate Oswald, making
it appear as an act of reprisal against the President's killer. At
least this is how Roselli explained the tragedy in Dallas.

Trafficante was asked by the Committee if he had any knowledge of
the topic of the article or how Anderson had come by the information.
He said "No." He was asked whether he had any prior knowledge of a
plan to assassinate the President or had heard the name of Lee Harvey
Oswald or Jack Ruby prior to the assassination. He denied any such
knowledge. He denied discussing with Roselli any retaliatory action by
Castro. He stated that his interest in participating in the scheme to assassinate Castro was purely a patriotic gesture of cooperation with the CIA
and had nothing to do with losses of property and business in Cuba.
He admitted that he had visited Madrid, Spain for ten days in 1966 or
1967, at the invitation of Mr. Bango, the Cuban attorney who represented him while he was in Trescornia prison. While he had encountered
a number of short-time inmates at Trescornia, he did not remember the
name John Wilson-Hutson. He denied even knowing Jack Ruby, much
less being visited by him in Trescornia. José Aleman he knew. Trafficante
had arranged for him to get a loan, presumably from the Teamsters, as
he referred Aleman to Frank Gargano, an attorney for Jimmy Hoffa. He
denied ever telling Aleman that Kennedy would be "hit." He said that he
spoke fluent Spanish and Aleman's English was poor, so all conversations
with Aleman were in Spanish. The implication is that the Spanish word
for "hit" would not arise in the conversation, as it doesn't have the same
connotation that it has in English.

The Committee also found a connection between Lee Oswald and
La Cosa Nostra,[31] albeit a tenuous one. Lee's uncle, Charles "Dutz" Mur-
ret was discovered to have been an associate of several members of the
Marcello family in New Orleans. While most of this association seems to

have been in the 1940s and 1950s, it is clear that Oswald and his mother, Marguerite, were familiar with them. Oswald had discussed the matter with Marina. Marguerite, herself, was personally acquainted with some of these same underworld figures. At least one such acquaintance of Dutz and Marguerite reportedly was, at one time, a driver for Marcello. David W. Ferrie, one of the people indicted by New Orleans District Attorney Jim Garrison, was a self-proclaimed associate of Marcello. It was noted that he stated that he was with Marcello in a New Orleans courthouse on the morning of the assassination. Marcello, on the other hand, stated that Ferrie had worked for his (Marcello's) lawyer, G. Wray Gill, as a private investigator, but had never worked for him, nor was their relationship close.

The association between Oswald and David Ferrie apparently began when Oswald was a teenager in a Civil Air Patrol unit for which Ferrie was an instructor. Later, it was found that Ferrie had worked part-time out of private investigator Guy Banister's office at 534 Lafayette Street. This office is in the same building as offices entering 544 Camp Street, the address that Oswald had printed on his "Fair Play for Cuba Committee" pamphlets that he had handed out during his stay in New Orleans in early 1963.[32] The WC, however, found that neither Oswald nor the Fair Play for Cuba Committee ever had an office at that address.

The HSCA staff went over all the evidence and interviewed all the witnesses that Jim Garrison had used in his effort to establish links among Ferrie, Clay Shaw, and Oswald in Clinton, Louisiana. The HSCA report approvingly declares "that the Clinton witnesses were credible and significant." However, when one compares their original interviews and affidavits, there were as many Clinton stories as there were Clinton witnesses. Garrison and his staff had essentially coached the witnesses into a consistent story for the trial. Ultimately, molding the Clinton connection

---

31. Also sometimes referred to as Cosa Nostra, La Causa Nostra, the Mafia, or the Syndicate. This is an organized crime group, dating from the late-nineteenth century in the United States and much earlier in Sicily. In the U.S., the group is made up mostly of Italian and Sicilian immigrants or their descendants.

32. There was, however, no way to get from one set of offices to the other without going outside, around the corner, and entering from the other street. The only establishment that had entryways from both streets was Mancuso's restaurant. A similar "connection" was purported in that the Cuban Revolutionary Council, an anti-Castro organization, had had an office at 544 Camp St., but it was determined that the CRC had vacated that office a full year before Oswald moved to New Orleans.

into a Mafia-based conspiracy proved impossible. The Committee report states, "From the evidence available to the committee, the nature of the Oswald-Ferrie association remained largely a mystery."

The Committee's staff consultant on La Cosa Nostra was Mr. Ralph Salerno, a retired New York Police Department organized crime investigator. In his report for the Committee and in his testimony, he outlined the organization of La Cosa Nostra, defined the terms used by the investigators and the criminal organization itself, and went over the methods used in the traditional Mafia—or Cosa Nostra—hit. The killing is ordered by the "approver," a member high enough in the organization to authorize an execution. The "expediter" is a lieutenant who could be trusted to carry out the order. The expediter could do the job himself but, as Salerno reports,

> The most likely thing is that he will pass the contract on to others.... They will be recruited, if possible, from felons who have demonstrated some successful ability in the past.... Persons who will be doing their first hit will more than likely be part of the team where there are some more experienced members....you will find that there is usually more than one executioner; most likely two....they will decide whether they are going to act simultaneously in their gunfire or one may be the covering backup man for the other....the record shows very clearly that the imported, out-of-town killers is overwhelmingly the exception rather than the rule.

He continues, stating that the recruitment is usually through a string of associates, lower in the organization, that provides a buffer between the top two and the crime. Generally the "hit men" do not know the authorizer; often not even the expediter.

The decline in gangland "war" after repeal of Prohibition reflected the ability of top Mafia leadership to discipline the organization to limit violence in general and murder in particular to an act of "last resort." They learned in the Prohibition era that the threat of violence is often as effective and brings much less troublesome repercussions than the actual use of violence. In most cases, when the last resort is employed, there is no attempt to disguise the fact that the hit is a gangland-style execution. In the words of the Committee's final report: "Indeed, an intrinsic characteristic of the typical mob execution is that it serves as a self-apparent message, with the authorities and the public readily perceiving the nature of the crime as well as the general identity of the group or gang that carried it out."

While the Kennedy assassination did not fit the pattern of the traditional gangland "execution," Salerno recounted the details of three known organized crime "hits" that did not fit that pattern either. These included the blinding of investigative reporter Victor Riesel in April 1956. The mob recruited an apparently unreliable petty thief and burglar, who was also a known drug user, for the act. A few weeks later, Riesel's attacker was himself killed by those who had recruited him. The second case was the shooting of Sol Landie, a Kansas City, Missouri, businessman in 1970. Landie was a witness in a Federal gambling case against Kansas City crime boss Nicholas Civella. He was killed by four young black men who did not know who had ordered the "hit" and were not members of the Cosa Nostra organization. They were told by their recruiters to make it appear that robbery was the motive for the crime. All the assailants and two of the intermediaries were convicted. The third case was the shooting of Joseph Columbo, the New York Cosa Nostra leader, in 1971. This hit was carried out by a petty criminal, not part of the syndicate, who had been recruited through a series of intermediaries. The gunman himself was shot and killed immediately after the shooting. Columbo lingered in a coma for 7 years before dying in 1978. This murder is still listed as unsolved.

These cases have several things in common. In each case, the hit man was a petty criminal not associated with the mob. All three would have been considered unreliable by La Cosa Nostra standards. Finally, two of the three were themselves eliminated in a short time by those who had recruited them. These three cases were used to show that a Cosa Nostra hit does not always fit the mold. The Kennedy assassination has some traits in common with these three cases. The conclusion of Salerno's report, however, is that La Cosa Nostra was probably not involved in the assassination as an organization. Some of the elements that would have served to protect the organization, such as a getaway car, were absent. The similarities to the above cases, on the other hand, indicated to him that individual members might have been involved.

In 1977, Gary Mack, program director of KFJZ-FM, a popular music station in Dallas-Fort Worth,[33] informed the Committee of the existence of a recording of the radio transmission from a police motor-cycle radio whose broadcast button had been stuck in the open position throughout the time that the motorcade had been in Dealey Plaza. On the Dictaphone belt recording of the motorcycle radio in question, there seemed to be a number of sharp noises that did not belong. Mack thought that the motorcycle with the stuck button was probably in Dealey Plaza, where most of the DPD cycles were located at the time. The Committee obtained the November 22, 1963 police dispatch tapes and the Dicta-phone belts on which the returning transmissions were recorded. The Committee hired the Cambridge, Massachusetts firm of Bolt, Baranek, and Newman (BB&N) to do an acoustical analysis of these sounds to determine if they were identifiable as gunshots and if they were recorded at the site of the assassination. Dr. James E. Barger, chief scientist at BB&N, presented the results of his company's acoustic analysis to the Committee on September 11, 1978.

The recording from the Dictaphone belt was of very poor qual-ity, partly because of the recording instrument, but mostly because of the cheap microphone on the motorcycle radio. The system had what is called an "automatic gain control" (AGC) circuit that automatically adjusts to the volume of the input sound. This allows the mike to pick up low-level sound but prevents an overload from very loud noises. One must bear in mind that the system was intended to transmit legible voice communication and keep a record of these communications. For this purpose, it was adequate, but the AGC plus a relatively low frequency re-sponse would not allow a high-fidelity reproduction of the half-millisec-ond, high-intensity shock wave from a bullet or weapon. The shock wave signal would be transformed from a sharp rise and fall (an N-wave, in Dr. Barger's terminology) to a series of oscillations. In truth, one cannot hear the sounds of gunshots on the recording. There are only what Dr. Barger identified as "impulses" that might have been created by shock waves from a supersonic bullet or the detonation of a firearm. He stated that the poor quality of the recording on the Dictaphone belt did not affect the ability to identify the echo patterns. Therefore, they could be

---

33. Mr. Mack later became the Archivist of the Sixth Floor Museum, located in the former Texas School Book Depository. He is now Curator of the Museum.

compared to the patterns he obtained from the sophisticated equipment they installed around Dealey Plaza for the test.

A team from BB&N went to Dallas on August 20, 1978 to gather acoustic data. With the cooperation of the Dallas police, BB&N made numerous recordings of gunshots from several weapons fired at several sites around Dealey Plaza. The Dallas police not only roped off the Plaza for extensive periods of time for these experiments, but also provided firearms experts to do the shooting. The reason for the numerous recordings that were taken was to obtain the echo signature of different weapons, fired from different locations and recorded at each of several different positions, to compare to those on the Dictaphone belt.

Dr. Barger showed the Committee how the various paths of reflected and scattered shock waves from bullets and weapon reports would arrive at different microphone positions at different times. The shock waves from both sources are well reflected by solid surfaces, including brick and glass of buildings or concrete and steel of structures such as overpasses. As each of these primary and reflected shock waves would reach different locations at different times, each point in Dealey Plaza would have a signature, a different pattern of impulses. Each point, in turn, would have a different signature for each firing location. Each echo pattern could have a duration as long as a second, the time it would take for the sound to travel the most distant reflected path back and forth across the plaza. This gives each position in Dealey Plaza a unique echo signature for each type weapon fired from each of several locations, including the sixth floor of the Texas School Book Depository, the triple underpass, and the grassy knoll.

Because it was not possible to put microphones at every point in the plaza, the microphones were evenly spaced a few feet apart, at locations on the paths that motorcycles could have traveled. Of course, if the motorcycle with the stuck button were part of the motorcade, its position would have been continuously changing as time passed. Whenever a shot was fired, it would not have been precisely at the position that a microphone would be located in the test 14 years later. The distance between microphones was calculated to be small enough that the signature would still be well correlated with at least one microphone location. Out of the extensive comparison of echo patterns, four one-second time slots were found that had high correlations with echo patterns from the Dictaphone belt. Most of the correlations were with shots from the Book Depository, but three of the high correlations were with shots from the grassy knoll. Each of these high correlations was correlated with a recording from a specific microphone position in Dealey Plaza.

Matching these positions and times with the known position of the limousine and the rate at which it was moving, Dr. Barger reconstructed the position of a motorcycle accompanying the car. The Committee interviewed Dallas policeman Hollis B. McLain, who was riding motorcycle escort some 180 feet behind the President's car. McLain said that the switch on his motorcycle radio sometimes stuck in the open position. The Committee concluded that it probably was McLain's radio that broadcast the signal being analyzed. Barger found two impulses at the times Hartmann's jiggle analysis indicated there were gunshots. Based on this time/position correlation, he found two additional gunshots that correlated with a possible position of McLain's motorcycle. Dr. Barger's chart, summarizing his findings, appears as figure 6.

Barger's conclusion was that there were four shots with a spacing of 1.6 seconds between the first and second, 5.9 seconds between the second and third, and 0.5 seconds between the third and fourth. By correlating the last of these with the shot that everybody agreed was the final shot—to the President's head, these shots would have occurred at frames 166, 196, 296, and 312 of the Zapruder movie. In the HSCA final report, Blakey pointed out that Governor Connally was turning in response to the first shot approximately three frames before the acoustic evidence indicated that it was fired. This apparent discrepancy of one-sixth of a second in the acoustic and photographic evidence, he said, reflected the inaccuracies in the ability to determine the exact filming rate of the Zapruder camera and the exact recording rate of the Dictaphone equipment, both of which were recorded 14 years earlier.

The half-second spacing between the third and fourth shots would preclude both being fired by Oswald. Thus, the conspiracy advocates had their 'smoking gun'—necessarily in the hands of a second gunman. Barger was a bit equivocal about the certainty of this conclusion, so a second team of acoustic experts, Professors Mark Weiss and Ernest Aschkenasy of Queens College, New York City, were asked to review the acoustic evidence. Near the end of the Committee's deliberations, Weiss and Aschkenasy were asked to testify. Their conclusion was that, with 95 percent

**List of All 15 Correlations Between Impulse Patterns
Occurring in 6 Segments of the DPD Record and Echo Patterns
from 432 Test Shots (2592 Separate Correlations)
Having a Correlation Coefficient Higher than 0.5**

Beginning Time of First Impulse on Tape Segment	Microphone Array and (Channel Number)	Rifle Location	Target Location	Correlation Coefficient**
136.20 sec	No Correlations Higher Than			0.5
137.70 sec	2 (5)	TSBD*	1	0.8
"	2 (5)	TSBD*	3	0.7
"	2 (6)	TSBD	3	0.8
"	2 (6)	KNOLL	4	0.7
139.27 sec	2 (6)	TSBD*	3	0.8
"	2 (6)	TSBD	3	0.6
"	2 (10)	TSBD	3	0.6
140.32 sec	2 (11)	TSBD*	3	0.6
139.27 sec	3 (5)	KNOLL	2	0.6
145.15 sec	3 (4)	KNOLL	3	0.8
"	3 (7)	TSBD*	2	0.7
"	3 (8)	TSBD	3	0.7
145.61 sec	3 (5)	TSBD	3	0.8
"	3 (6)	TSBD	4	0.8
"	3 (8)	TSBD*	2	0.7
146.30 sec	No Correlations Higher Than			0.5

*Indicates Muzzle Withdrawn 2 ft from Plane of Window.

$$**\text{Correlation Coefficient} = \frac{\text{Number of Echoes Matched with Impulses}}{\sqrt{\text{Number of Echoes X Number of Impulses}}} \leq 1.0$$

F-367

Figure 6. Echo correlation table with Dr. Barger's handwritten numbers showing the four, one-second time intervals. The third was linked to a shot from the "Grassy Knoll." *(National Archives)*

probability, there was a fourth gunshot emanating from the area of the grassy knoll. Dr. Barger was recalled to comment and agreed with the 95 percent probability figure.

A second panel participated in the tests in Dealey Plaza at the time Dr. Barger and the other acoustic experts were making their comparison tapes. This might be called the "ear-witness" panel, headed by Dr. David Green, Chairman of the National Research Council Committee on Hearing, Bioacoustics, and Biomechanics. Dr. William Hartmann was included on this panel. Green and his associates positioned themselves at various points around the route of the motorcade to hear the shock waves made by the bullets and firearms as the Dallas police firearms squad discharged the weapons from the different locations. In his House testimony, Dr. Green reiterated the deceptive nature of trying to localize the source of gunfire by listening to the shock waves from bullets. He did, however, state that it was "comparatively easy to localize knoll shots."

The final report of the HSCA begins with their conclusions and recommendations. A summary of the major conclusions regarding the assassination of President Kennedy:

- Lee Harvey Oswald fired three shots from the Mannlicher-Carcano rifle he owned from the sixth floor southeast corner window of the Texas School Book Depository building. The second and third shots hit President John F. Kennedy, the latter killing him.

- Acoustical evidence establishes a high probability that two gunmen fired at the President. Other scientific evidence does not preclude the possibility of two gunmen firing at the President, but does negate some specific conspiracy allegations.

- The Committee believes, on the basis of the evidence available to it, that President John F. Kennedy was probably assassinated as a result of a conspiracy. The Committee is unable to identify the other gunman or the extent of the conspiracy.

- The conspiracy did not involve the Secret Service, the Federal Bureau of Investigation, the Central Intelligence Agency, the Soviet government, the Cuban government, anti-Castro Cuban groups, or organized crime groups. The available evidence does not preclude the participation of individuals from the anti-Castro groups or organized crime groups in the conspiracy.

- Agencies and departments of the U.S. Government performed their duties with varying degrees of competency. President Kennedy did not receive adequate protection. The investigation of the responsibility of Lee Harvey Oswald was thorough and reliable. The investigation into the possibility of a conspiracy was not. The Warren Commission arrived at its conclusions in good faith on the basis of the evidence available to it, but it presented its findings in a fashion that was too definitive.

The HSCA also presented conclusions regarding conspiracy in the assassination of Dr. Martin Luther King, Jr. and recommended revising the policies for protecting high-ranking government officials and for investigating future assassination attempts. In addition to the final report, the HSCA compiled and published 12 volumes of testimony, depositions, expert reports, pictures, and drawings related to the two cases.

After the public hearings of the HSCA in 1978 and the publication of their report in 1979, the conspiracy advocates were elated. Here was a high-level government investigation that found "hard, scientific evidence" that there was, indeed, a conspiracy behind the assassination of President Kennedy. But, while the conclusion was cheered, the physical evidence established or reconfirmed during the hearings was mostly ignored. New books immediately appeared on the newsstands that trotted out all the same old myths of the 1960s and 1970s. Most of these concluded that President Kennedy was shot from the front by an assassin from the grassy knoll. In some accounts, he was hit by more than two bullets, reviving the "entrance" wound to the front of his neck as well as a bullet from the front hitting his head and "throwing him into the back of the car." Heavily retouched copies of the Oswald photographs were again obtained from the newspapers and magazines of the 1960s and displayed as proof that the "backyard" photographs were fakes. More pictures were "found" of gunmen lurking in the bushes on the grassy knoll, on the triple underpass, or in one of the buildings facing Dealey Plaza.

Then tragedy struck that some thought would shake the conspiracy community to its roots. The acoustic evidence that was the sole objective, scientific support for the existence of a conspiracy in the HSCA investigation was debunked. And it wasn't a highly paid acoustic expert who did it with the aid of expensive scientific instruments. Rather, the debunker was an accomplished drummer/percussionist from Ohio named Steve Barber, who used even better equipment—his trained musician's ear. Barber had purchased a copy of *Gallery* magazine in July 1979 that contained a plastic record with the Dallas Police Dictabelt recording transcribed on it. He immediately played it, trying to hear the gunshots. What he heard instead sounded like static and a few faint words that he couldn't quite identify. About a year later, he decided to try again to make out the mysterious words. He played the record over several times, and was able to reconstruct the phrase "Hold everything secure until the homicide and other investigators get there." This was the voice of Dallas County Sheriff Bill Decker talking on the second police channel from the front of the motorcade. He was instructing the other units what to do in Dealey Plaza, nearly a minute after the assassination.

There was a different recording system for each of the two police channels recorded and preserved from the day of the assassination. A trace of cross-talk from the second channel was recorded on the Dictaphone track of channel one, made famous by the HSCA's acoustic panel. Barber's insightful observation was followed up by an FBI review of the evidence and conclusion. The FBI review was not well accepted by a skeptical public because of a perception that the FBI was not an unbiased party, so the government requested a review by the National Academy of Sciences. The NAS study was headed by a Harvard University acoustics expert, Professor Norman Ramsey. The so-called Ramsey Panel found the original study by Bolt, Baranek, and Newman, as well as the review by Weiss and Aschkenasy, to be seriously flawed.

In addition, Dallas policeman H. B. McLain, the motorcycle officer the HSCA decided had owned the cycle whose microphone switch was stuck, first heard the complete Dictabelt recording some time after his testimony to the HSCA. After hearing the recording, he denied that the cycle was his or even that the cycle with a stuck switch was present in Dealey Plaza that day.[34] McLain was one of the several motorcycle escorts to the presidential motorcade. He was riding with the press camera cars, paired with Marrion Baker, some distance behind the President's and vice-president's cars. At the time of the shots, McLain was on Houston Street about half way between Main and Elm. He looked "through an opening in the decorative wall behind the fountain and pond in Dealey Plaza" and saw Agent Clint Hill jump on the back of the limousine. He then heard Chief Curry's instruction over his radio to provide police escort to the limousine on its way to Parkland hospital, so he raced forward and caught up with the front portion of the motorcade on the Stemmons Freeway before it reached Parkland.

---

34. It was well known among Dallas motorcycle officers that the cycle with a stuck microphone switch was a three-wheeler, not a two-wheeler like McLain was riding. They even knew whose cycle it was. McLain's statement, as well as those of others providing escort to the motorcade that day, are in Dallas County Sheriff James Bowles' article posted on Dave Reitzes' website (see references).

While an idling cycle engine is clearly heard throughout the five minutes or so that the switch was stuck, there is no siren, crowd noise, nor racing cycle engine in the part that followed the final "shot." Instead we hear only the occasional stirrings and idle whistling of police personnel or passers-by and a faint, but clear note that resembles a bell tone. The motorcycle continued to run at low speed for some two minutes after the "final shot" on the tape. An idling motorcycle and whistling of a casual passerby contrasts sharply with the shouts, screams, and sobs described by the witnesses in Dealey Plaza following the assassination. The absence of the sounds of a crowd, a siren, and a racing motorcycle engine is incompatible with McLain's recollection of his movements, verified by independent sources. Photographs clearly show him in the position he said he was in—with the motorcade at Dealey Plaza. Witnesses place him at Parkland Hospital a short time later. Dale Myers'[35] careful reconstruction of his locations alongside the motorcade are quite different from those used by BB&N in their acoustic study. Myers shows that neither McLain nor any other motorcycle policeman is at the Acoustic Panel's purported locations at the time they assert the echo patterns were recorded. Finally, had his microphone switch been stuck, he could not have heard the instruction from Chief Curry to accompany the motorcade.

The Dallas police have long maintained that the cycle with a stuck microphone switch and an idling engine belonged to one of the many police guards stationed at the Trade Mart to help the Secret Service maintain security at that facility from early morning through the luncheon. Reports of the "bell sound" on the recording were later determined to be the result of a momentary feedback in the radio or recording circuit. It is heard on the other channel at the same time and actually doesn't sound like a bell. A bell produces a loud sound that rapidly diminishes in volume and gradually fades to inaudibility. The sound on the recording is a momentary pure note at a steady volume which cuts off as abruptly as it begins. Gary Mack, Curator at the Sixth Floor Museum, disputes the feedback explanation and continues to search for a bell. A carillon was recovered which once played from the bell tower of the Old Court House, adjacent to Dealey Plaza, but it was found to have no note which matched the frequency of the bell on the Dallas Dictabelt containing the "acoustic evidence."

---

35. Emmy-award winning computer animator. See also Chapter 6.

While disputes over the details continue, the authenticity of the HSCA acoustic evidence had taken a seemingly fatal blow. But the resiliency of those conspiracy researchers whose stories relied on the acoustic study was gravely underestimated. Some attempted to revive the acoustic evidence through counterattacks on the credibility of the National Academy of Sciences study or by trying to prove that the Dictabelt obtained by the HSCA staff was not the original, but a copy— with the cross talk and bell sound presumably deliberately introduced on the chance that somebody would eventually notice them. Others pointed out that proving one piece of evidence to be bogus does not prove the absence of a conspiracy. Then they went about the task of finding more evidence.

The release since 1989 of thousands of documents from the sealed Kennedy file in the National Archives provides a gold mine for digging out new nuggets of proof. Virtually all these new nuggets were fool's gold, however, as the HSCA staff had mined that file of classified and unclassified material, documents since-released and not-yet-released. Every scrap that might have been of value in substantiating a conspiracy had already been thoroughly studied by one of their expert panels and put on public display in the hearings or mentioned in the 12 volumes of their report—or both.

After the House hearings in 1978, Anthony Summers, David Lifton, David Scheim, Jim Marrs, Henry Hurt, Robert Groden, Charles Crenshaw, and dozens of others, including several of the earlier authors, published new conspiracy books on the heels of the new interest stirred by the hearings. The 1981 book by Robert Blakey repeats very few of the allegations used by the others to support conspiracy but, not surprisingly, finds a conspiracy similar to that found in the HSCA investigation he guided. The only traditional conspiracy allegations he relies on are a shot from the grassy knoll (that admittedly didn't hit anything) and the Oswald-Mafia connection. Few conspiracy writers are as cautious as Blakey who, after all, was confronted with a large influx of scientific evidence in the years he ran the HSCA's staff.

Oliver Stone's 1991 movie, *JFK,* drew heavily on the Garrison investigation and the books by Garrison and Marrs. The best comment on the movie was the one Stone made himself. He stated that the movie was a counter-myth, an alternative to the myth put forth by the Warren

Commission. Very little of the movie, aside from the contemporary movies and still pictures cleverly woven into the context of the film, is accurate. Even the words in Garrison's speeches at the trial bear virtually no resemblance to what Garrison actually said at the time. Many of the phrases were never used by Garrison at all, but were taken from books written by others.

Some were able to sell books by including 'bootleg' copies of the graphic photos taken at the autopsy of the late president, confirming Robert Kennedy's worst fears when he reluctantly returned all the material that had been in his possession to the National Archives. Perhaps it was best that the President's brain, pickled in formalin, the slides, and other human remains were not among the material he returned.[36] But the majority of neoconspiracy authors just picked up where their predecessors had left off, ignoring the physical evidence, ignoring the findings of the experts for the Warren Commission and HSCA, and repeating the same, well-worn conspiracy stories supported by new pictures and supplemented by recently "recalled" experiences and events that were said to have occurred in the early 1960s. By this time, those memories were approaching 20 years of age.

The American Bar Association (ABA) put on a mock trial of Oswald at their annual meeting in 1992, complete with prosecution, defense, jury, and witnesses. The defense case hinged on the supposition that Oswald would have had a better shot while the motorcade was coming up Houston Street, and that the President could have been shot by a glycerin bullet from the grassy knoll; a bullet that wouldn't have exited the President's skull nor shown on an x-ray. In support of the glycerin-bullet hypothesis, a Bay City company named Failure Analysis Associated (FAA) fired glycerin bullets into plastic bottles filled with water to prove that the bullets stopped inside the bottle.

This novel defense tactic ultimately resulted in a hung jury at the ABA trial, but the important outcome was really the new processing of old material evidence. FAA did considerable lab work for both sides of

---

36. The receipt, signed by President Kennedy's former personal secretary, who was working at the Archives at the time, lists the container that would have contained the brain, but that container almost certainly was not actually returned by Robert Kennedy. The container was never located by the HSCA. They could not confirm that it was reburied with the body when it was moved to its present location in Arlington National Cemetery, Virginia.

the "case." Their enhancement of the Zapruder film, along with later, even better versions, clearly shows Governor Connally's suit bulging out at frame 224, a phenomenon they dubbed the "lapel flip."[37] This is the right side of the coat that shows the bullet hole. Two frames later, just as the President is emerging from behind the road sign, his arms are rising in response to the neck injury. The fatal shot to the President's head was just prior to frame 313. Their reconstruction of the first shot, the one that missed, places it in the vicinity of frames 160 to 166. This timing is close to that of the House Committee's Photographic Panel, who arrived at their timing of all three shots based on the reactions of the victims, without the benefit of observing the definitive suit bulge. Thus, FAA confirmed the sequence of shots determined by the HSCA: the first shot missed, the second shot hit both the President and the Governor, and the third shot was the fatal one to the President's head. The sequence, as timed by the Zapruder film, gives the assassin a liberal eight seconds to get off three rounds with a slightly shorter time between the first and second than between the second and third.

FAA also reconstructed the path of the bullet that struck the President and Governor in a manner similar to the method utilized by the House Committee's NASA consultant and staff. This method establishes a projected trajectory backward from the known paths of the bullet through the victims and the position of the men in the car without making any assumptions about the origin of the gunfire. Their projection at frame 224 was similar to the House Committee's at frame 190.

In 1993, Gerald Posner relieved David Belin as the foremost advocate of the lone-assassin argument with his publication of *Case Closed*. His 'case' seemed to be the answer to the conspiracy debate: Lee Harvey Oswald was the lone assassin; no conspiracy existed. Posner exhaustively dealt with the critics' points of disagreement with the Warren Commission's findings. He pointed out the facts established, as well as mistakes made by the WC, the HSCA, and the major conspiracy authors, dealing with each by copious expert opinion, physical evidence, and credible eyewitness accounts to straighten out the record. His conclusion was that Oswald was the unassisted, lone assassin. He quoted

---

37. The "lapel flip" is actually a pushing out of the front of his coat by the momentum deposited by the penetrating bullet. The suit bulge was first observed in April 1975 by Robert P. Smith of Pittsburgh. It was rediscovered by FAA 17 years later. See Robert P. Smith in the bibliography.

experts from the HSCA investigation panels that the "magic bullet" did not have to be magic to do the damage that it did. Nor did the backward movement of the President have to result from the impact of a bullet from the front. Like the Warren Commission and HSCA, Posner dealt extensively with Oswald's sojourn in the Soviet Union. He found additional witnesses to dispute many of the witnesses found by the conspiracy theorists to support their cases. His book seemed to vanquish the vast majority of credible support for the existence of a conspiracy in the Kennedy assassination.

The conspiracy theorists, however, were not routed. Unfortunately, in his efforts to refute the conspiracy allegations, Posner makes up a few myths of his own and repeats a few more made up by anti-conspiracy experts. The opposition regrouped, found errors in the Posner book (some real, some not) and, in a tactic similar to the attack on the Warren Report, conclude that those errors invalidate his whole case. The conspiracy books published since the appearance of *Case Closed* generally make at least a token effort to refute Posner's findings on those points that affect their case, generally with a quote from another expert that contradicts Posner's expert. The debate resembles a legal battle in a high-profile court case. Each side makes the rounds of the talk shows and conducts interviews for newspapers and magazines, doing their best to try the case in the media. They leave the reading public wondering which expert to believe.

If the "prosecution's case" is that Oswald was the lone assassin, it must be complete and consistent to be airtight. For the "defense," consistency and believability are not necessary. All they have to do is raise reasonable doubt. Those who believe that there was a conspiracy in the death of President Kennedy are by no means a monolithic group. Mary LaFontaine's locating the arrest records of the three 'tramps' hauled off from Dealey Plaza by the police shortly after the assassination disproved several conspiracy stories involving a variety of public-figure assassins, including Howard Hunt and Charles Harrelson (father of actor Woody Harrelson), disguised as tramps. Robert Groden finds unbelievable David Lifton's story of a body being kidnapped and surgically altered to fool the autopsy team into thinking he was shot from the rear. He notes that those close to the President never left the body unattended for a moment, even during the swearing-in of Lyndon Johnson on Air Force One. It is Groden's contention that the evidence of the "shot from the Grassy Knoll" cannot be found in the autopsy evidence because all the autopsy photographs and x-rays are forgeries.

Other myths, however, are merely rhetorical sleight-of-hand that creates the illusion of refutation of the Warren Report. Some writers mention the "suspicious" unidentified man who pointed out Oswald to the police in the Texas Theatre. This was parlayed from the WC testimony of the policeman who had temporarily forgotten the name of Johnny Calvin Brewer, the shoe store operator who had followed Oswald into the theater, located him before the police arrived, and pointed out his location to the officers before the lights were turned on. "Prior warnings" are featured by many conspiracy writers, ignoring the well-known fact that such warnings come in to FBI and various police departments with such regularity that anything that happens to a high elected official in any country at any time will be preceded by several.

Another myth derives from the fact that some photographs of the assassination rifle taken after it was recovered in the Depository show it without a clip. The writer then makes the statement that the bolt could not be operated without a clip present, concluding that this was not the assassination weapon. There are two false assumptions in this myth. First, the rifle can be fired by manually inserting one cartridge at a time into the firing chamber. Second, the clip is usually ejected when the last cartridge is chambered, but this weapon had the common problem of the clip "hanging" occasionally. It was still present, but empty, when the last bullet was removed from the chamber by Captain Fritz and when he carried it out of the Depository. It was removed sometime thereafter and bagged for evidence so that any latent prints would not be destroyed by handling. Pictures of that clip, one loaded with six cartridges and another taken while empty, were given exhibit numbers CE 574 and CE 575.

Many of the mistakes made by the conspiracy writers are no more malicious than the mistakes made in the two government investigations of the case. Others are not errors of fact but errors of judgment on the part of the writer that merely seem slightly silly: the multiple 'Oswalds' seen at various locations in Dallas doing things that would seem to have no bearing on the case—or a 'bulletproof' top that wasn't bulletproof being left off to doom a clueless president. Does anybody believe that the assassin selected by a nefarious group capable of bringing down the President of the United States would need a man standing near the parade route to flap an umbrella up and down to tell him when to shoot? Some have used Oswald's trip to Mexico City as proof that there was a conspiracy while others try to debunk the Mexico trip to prove that there was a conspiracy. Would a side trip to Mexico, in an attempt to get into Cuba, make Oswald more likely or less likely to continue the trend started by taking a potshot at General Walker?

Nevertheless, there are a large number of well-informed, rational people who believe that there was a conspiracy to kill the President. It has been claimed that the majority of Americans who have an opinion think that there was some sort of conspiracy in the assassination of John Kennedy. The assertion is probably true. Conspiracy books, movies, and television specials have done a credible job of raising doubt. In spite of their best efforts, however, this probably wouldn't be the case if it weren't for a number of well-established facts for which a ready scientific explanation is not immediately apparent. The most important of these are:

In spite of their back-pedaling in testimony to the WC, several of the Parkland physicians initially thought that the bullet hole in Kennedy's throat was an entry wound. The Parkland and Bethesda physicians all thought that the large wound in the right rear of the President's head was an exit wound, and most said so in writing. Several witnesses saw smoke in the vicinity of the parking lot behind the grassy knoll, at least one saw a person in that parking lot, and there were muddy footprints to back up his testimony. After the lethal gunshot the President did move rapidly backward into the seat of the car. Several witnesses swear to this day that they heard gunshots from places distinctly not in the direction of the Book Depository. The HSCA investigation concludes that they were right. One of the three shots from the "sniper's nest" missed, not only the President, but also the whole car—a target several times the President's size. The timing of the shots by each group of HSCA experts—the photography panel, the acoustic panel, and Hartmann's jiggle analysis—differs from each other, the Warren Commission's, and John Connally's estimate of when he was hit.[38]

---

38. The estimates of the Zapruder frame at which Governor Connally was hit are as follows: HSCA Photo Panel, frame 207; Robert Groden, frame 237; Acoustic Panel, frame 196; Hartmann, before frame 190; WC, frames 210-225; John Connally, frames 231-234; HSCA Final Report, frame 190.

Serious JFK researchers still doubt the single bullet scenario; some because of lack of deformation, others because of their reconstructed zigzag trajectory. There is still argument about the location of JFK entry wounds. Was the first hit to JFK a neck wound or a back wound? Was the entry wound on the President's head really as high as the various pathology panels place it? Does it matter? Was the large hole in the right rear of Kennedy's head an entry or exit? These and other questions really do have a sound scientific explanation, but the format of the government's inquiries tends to touch on disconnected fragments without completing the investigation of any. It also allows inordinate distractions into irrelevancies—even more so than in the courtroom. It's like a jigsaw puzzle, partially assembled, with pieces missing and pieces of different puzzles deliberately thrown in by detractors.[39]

There have been hundreds of books and articles written about a Kennedy assassination "conspiracy." The reader would not tolerate a point-by-point refutation of all the allegations they contain. As I have no desire to try the patience of the reader, most must be ignored. The task would be pointless, at best. There are those on both sides of the conspiracy issue who will never deviate from their currently held conclusions, regardless of the evidence or refutation. Instead, the approach herein is to review and add to the science that provides the foundation of any unbiased inquiry into this crime. My only goal will be to establish what is true—not the interminable task of countering all that is false.

The Scientific Approach: A Better Way

The scientific investigation is one that has served humanity for several hundred years, leading to amazing technological progress that has improved our lives and health in countless ways. In science, evidence is judged by standards of truth and consistency with known scientific laws and facts that are established on the basis of objective physical data and the results obtained from it. Evidence isn't judged on the validity of a search warrant, a breach in the chain-of-custody, or admissibility based on the court's opinion of the expertise of the witness. In the courtroom,

---

39. The more credible myths, along with a few others, I describe by a familiar, mythic phrase associated with each myth. I use these phrases in the Table of Contents to describe specific chapters.

the eyewitness is king and the emotions of the jurors are a significant factor, due in part to the long history of English common law that formed the basis of our legal system a little over 200 years ago.[40] In the establishment of generally accepted scientific fact, conclusions drawn by inexpert eyewitnesses usually do not have significant weight. It makes no difference how many eyewitnesses are willing to swear that they saw a perpetual motion machine in action. The scientist usually doesn't waste time considering—or debunking—the claim (unless a close relative is considering investing his life savings in it).

As with any criminal investigation, there are a few facts that cannot be fully explained by science. In this case, there are amazingly few loose ends, thanks to dozens of people who were merely photographing a presidential motorcade and ended up documenting the assassination, as well as a substantial amount of physical evidence that has had an unprecedented amount of time devoted to its analysis. In terms of the time spent on it, the John Kennedy murder is likely the best investigated murder case in history.

With the rules of best scientific evidence in mind, let us look beyond the mistakes, misinterpretations, misrepresentations, and outright fabrications and see what a careful reassessment of the scientific data tell us about the events of November 22, 1963.

---

40. Once a lawyer friend stated a maxim of the profession that went something like "it's better to have a sympathetic client than sympathetic law." A case that strikes sufficiently sympathetic feelings in the jury can sometimes cause them to ignore expert opinion, physical evidence, and even the written law.

CHAPTER FOUR

Crude, Dangerous, and Inaccurate

"The Mannlicher-Carcano rifle…is crudely made, poorly designed, dangerous and inaccurate."
—*Mechanix Illustrated*[41]

People who denigrate the Marine Corps' combat training, including proficiency training with the rifle, are obviously people who never went through it. The Marine Corps in 1960 was one of the world's premier fighting forces of all time. Whenever the United States has needed to project its force—from the Tripolitan War in North Africa (1800-1812) to the recent ousting of Saddam Hussein in Iraq—the Marines have always been among the first to land. Their heroism, the stuff of legends, is due in no small part to superb training.

While Lee Oswald's proficiency as a "Marksman" with his weapon would only have made him an average Marine, the shooting skill of the average Marine is head and shoulders above that of the average person, including those who downplay his skill for the sake of a conspiracy story. His military training was with the M-1 rifle, the .30 calibre military weapon used in World War Two (WWII) and the Korean War. His marksmanship with that weapon was documented several times in official qualification tests. Hits on man-size targets in these tests were more numerous and taken at a greater distance than the shooting in Dallas. It is not known whether Oswald had any experience with the Mannlicher-Carcano rifle before he ordered one through the mail. Unlike Mark Lane, however, he probably knew the difference between "obsolete," which the Mannlicher-Carcano was, and "crude, dangerous, and inaccurate" which it most certainly was not.

At the end of the nineteenth century, typical military ammunition was a long, heavy bullet, propelled at just under mach 2—just

---

41. The October 1964 issue of *Mechanix Illustrated,* quoted by Mark Lane in *Rush to Judgment,* page 103.

less than twice the speed of sound. These bullets had enormous penetrating power, but the size of the wounds they produced was very inconsistent. The magnitude of the injury depended on whether they penetrated only soft tissue, making a small, clean, through-and-through wound, or whether they struck bone near the entry point and badly deformed, creating a very nasty wound from that point on. The intent of the Hague and Geneva Conventions was to prevent such nasty wounds by requiring fully-jacketed bullets for all weapons used in war. As with many man-made laws, however, the underlying assumptions were faulty. Outlawing open-point bullets was not sufficient to prevent deformation of bullets when they strike bone at the velocities associated with practical ranges. It was this myth of the nondeforming, "full-patch," solid-point bullets created by the promoters of these conventions that led to accusations of one or both sides' using illegal, hollow- or soft-point bullets in every war between the Hague Convention of 1899 and WWII. This fiction is still repeated in the JFK conspiracy literature and, to a lesser extent, in the general medical literature today. The 6.5 mm Mannlicher-Carcano weapon, though manufactured and used through WWII, was of the earlier, late-nineteenth century design. The bullets it fired had all the characteristics of that obsolete design.

Ronald Simmons, who reported the results of the tests at the Ballistics Research Laboratory (BRL) to the Warren Commission, described the measurement of the inherent accuracy of CE 139, the rifle found in the Depository. He expressed the analysis of the test results in technical terms that mean little to those who are not experts in the field. The ballistic data were obtained by firing the weapon while mounted in a machine rest—that is, by clamping it to an immovable platform that removes the shooter's aiming error from consideration. His conclusion, however, is very clear. The rifle had an accuracy that was equivalent to modern military weapons. At some time before the rifle was delivered for the ballistic tests, the inexpensive scope had either been damaged or removed from the Oswald rifle and replaced without the shims necessary to align it.[42] An FBI report states that some damage was done to the lens end of the scope, probably when the rifle was hurriedly tossed between the book cartons where it was found by Weitzman and Boone. Neither the BRL

42. The scope was made in Japan and imported by Ordnance Optics, Inc, Hollywood, California. It was and is standard practice among gun dealers to use shims when mounting 'universal' scopes on a variety of different rifles to properly align it with the barrel. This allows the user to

nor experts at the Biophysics Division laboratory at Edgewood Arsenal mention observing any obvious damage to the scope that degraded its performance in the tests conducted with the weapon. There is a hint in WC testimony that the FBI or the Dallas police may have removed the scope in the exploration for fingerprints. In this case, they may have replaced it without shims. Whatever the cause, its built-in reticle adjustment did not have sufficient range to center the crosshairs on the target. Simmons remarked that shims were added to adjust the scope for the BRL tests, one for the azimuth and one for elevation.

Warren critics take advantage of the fact that most people do not understand the accuracy data obtained by BRL in the machine rest. In fact, some imply that clamping the weapon in a machine rest might cause damage or was done to mislead the public by eliminating the aiming error of the rifleman. The Biophysics Laboratory tests offer a more understandable measure.

Nothing distinguishes the obsolete from the inaccurate better than the tests of Oswald's Mannlicher-Carcano rifle conducted by the wound ballistics researchers at Edgewood Arsenal for the WC. The Division lab gunner added a third shim under the scope's mount to assist in his adjusting it to his own aiming preference. Thereafter, he hand-fired all tests with the Oswald rifle, using the scope. The gunner for these tests, Mr. Donald Smith, is seen firing the rifle for one of the Biophysics Division lab tests in figure 7. A close-up of the scope appears in figure 8.

Dr. Olivier, the director of the tests, confirms that he had no trouble acquiring an ample supply of ammunition from the same lot as the one used in the assassination and the unfired cartridge left in the chamber of the weapon when it was found. This was not "left-over" WWII ammunition, but one made by Western Cartridge Company, a Winchester Arms subsidiary, in 1954. The bulk of the four lots they made were supplied to the Department of Defense. The remainder was marketed to supply ammunition for the imported military surplus rifles. Olivier phoned his contacts at

---

use the built-in reticle adjustment screws to set the crosshairs to his particular taste and to readjust for different ranges. It would be surprising if this particular rifle, sold with the scope attached, did not have shims required to fit the scope to that type weapon. They are not "welded on" as claimed by some, including Mark Lane. They are merely slipped under the mount at one end before the screws are tightened to adjust the scope to that particular weapon. Even if the scope wasn't originally mounted properly, it wasn't beyond the skill of Lee Oswald to loosen a screw and insert a spacer to adjust the scope or to remove it and use the iron sights. The iron sights provided a perfectly acceptable aiming system at the distance from the Depository window to the assassination site on Elm Street and could be used even with the scope mounted.

Winchester and Remington and got several boxes of that lot of ammunition from both within days at no cost. Some of that ammunition was left over after the test; it was later sent to the National Archives for preservation.

Figure 7.   Gunner Donald Smith firing the Oswald rifle in the Biophysics Division tests at Edgewood Arsenal in May 1964. *(Biophysics Division, EA/L. M. Sturdivan)*

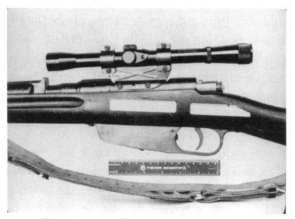

Figure 8.   Close-up of the Oswald rifle and 4-power scope, showing no apparent damage to the scope. *(Biophysics Division, EA/L. M. Sturdivan)*

Anesthetized goats were used to simulate the governor's torso wound. The goats were Texas Angora withers that had aged beyond their prime so that their hair was too coarse to be of value. They were cheap because they were rescued from being processed for dog food—or from a similar fate on mink farms. But they were large, just smaller than the average man, so that scaling the size of wounds was not a problem.[43] These tests were conducted by firing from a "bench rest" (resting on a stable platform) at the same distance that Governor Connally was from the sixth floor Depository window at the time he was hit, a little over 200 feet, or about 70 yards. Smith fired 18 shots at body walls and had no trouble putting several bullets through the body wall of a goat, tangentially, so that they did not enter the pleural cavity. Five shots that were slightly too high and missed were used to establish the striking velocity at that range. Three shots skimmed the pleural cavity, just touching the lung. Ten shots, more than half, passed through the body wall only, where one-half inch too low would have penetrated the lung and one-half inch too high would have missed altogether. Seven shots struck a rib directly and two passed between the ribs, also fracturing ribs by their passage. One of the shots just grazed the rib in a manner similar to that which produced Governor Connally's wound, shattering the rib and sending secondary missiles of bone into the lung. This was the bullet, CE 853, used by Dr. Wecht in his HSCA presentation. It was flattened somewhat more than the stretcher bullet, CE 399.

At the longer range (90 yards) used for the skull shots, all of Smith's shots hit within an inch of the aim point on the skull. One such skull is shown in figure 9, a picture taken before the shot. The reader might note that the aim point was well below the impact point described by the HSCA Pathology Panel and shown in Miss Dox's drawings of the autopsy photographs. The entry and exit points were not inadvertently misplaced in these tests. They were the locations specified by the Warren Commission. Their entry point was just above the occipital protuberance, about three inches below the entry wound in the President's skull established by the House Pathology Panel and two previous expert reviews. The exit location indicated by the WC was at the right supraorbital ridge, several centimeters from the exit location mentioned in the autopsy report, but close to the notch identified by the HSCA's Panel as the exit wound.

This kind of marksmanship is world-class: better than Oswald was, but better than Oswald needed to be. The point is that even a world-class marksman cannot get this kind of performance out of a weapon that is

---

43. They were killed humanely, by the way, without ever recovering from the anesthesia, in a manner similar to the way tens of thousands of discarded pets are euthanized every year in animal shelters.

"crude, dangerous, and inaccurate." The war-surplus weapon was cheap, partly because of its obsolete design, but just as indicated by Ronald Simmons, it was capable of accuracy that matches or exceeds that of a modern military rifle.

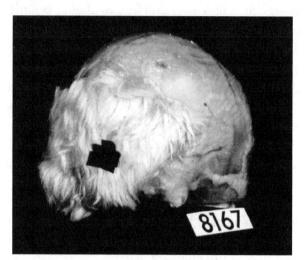

Figure 9. Pre-shot photograph of skull from biophysics tests, showing the aim point given by the Warren Commission as the entrance location. *(Biophysics Division, EA/L. M. Sturdivan)*

Conspiracy writers are still repeating the story that the marksmen at the Aberdeen Proving Ground (APG) could not fire the Mannlicher-Carcano rifle in the 5.6-second interval that the WC said was the minimum time that Oswald had for the three shots. This would allow only 2.8 seconds between shots. They choose to ignore the HSCA conclusion that it was the first shot that missed and that the assassin had four seconds or more between each shot, close to the maximum time estimates of the Warren Commission. This amount of time is a liberal amount of time to operate the bolt and re-aim the rifle, especially from a makeshift bench rest (the box). He should have been able to hold the position of the rifle while operating the bolt. With a bit of practice with this method, a shooter can hold the rifle within inches of his target while chambering the next round. The limousine carrying the President was moving away and slightly downhill, so the target's position changed very little in the two seconds, more or less, that it took to operate the bolt. For the shooter, re-aiming was not difficult.

The APG riflemen—Hendrix, Staley, and Miller—were asked to fire at each of three human-size targets from an elevated platform. The targets were located at the same distance as the President was from the "sniper's nest" in the southeast corner of the sixth-floor of the Depository at the time the Commission had reconstructed for the three shots.[44] The tallest available tower was lower than the sixth-floor window, at 30 feet, but the distance was set to that specified by the WC. Each was to reload, re-aim, and fire as quickly as they could accurately do so. The first shot was to be at the nearest target, the second at the middle target, and the last at the most distant. All three of the test firers conducted two complete sets, using the telescopic sight. Miller fired a third set, using the iron sights, which were still visible and usable if one merely sighted beneath the scope.

Hendrix fired the set in 8.25 seconds for the first and 7.00 seconds for the second. Staley's times were 6.75 and 6.45 seconds. Miller's times with the scope were 4.6 and 5.15 seconds. Using the iron sights, Miller fired the set of three shots in 4.45 seconds. In the seven sets, there were two misses on the third target, four on the second, and none on the first. A majority of misses on the second target (four out of seven) may have sub-consciously swayed the WC to believe that the assassin's second shot was the one that missed. Miller did not adjust the iron sights before he fired his third set (the phrase was "not zeroed for him"). In this last set, his hits on the first two targets were high and the third went just above the target's 'head,' constituting one of the two misses on the third target.

Because of the time constraints put on the test, the riflemen had no practice firing, and only two to three minutes practice learning to operate the "difficult" bolt. This is the bolt that Marina told the WC Lee had spent considerable time operating over and over while sitting on the back porch of their New Orleans apartment. The practice at APG did not include pulling the trigger without a cartridge in the chamber for fear of damaging the firing pin by "dry firing."[45] The gunners were

---

44. Based on the assumption that the first and third shots had hit and the second missed.

45. Contrary to the implications of WC critics, the hazard of firing pin damage in dry firing is neither unique to the Mannlicher-Carcano nor that rare in military rifles. The BRL experts probably were aware of the existence of "snap caps," empty cartridge cases with a cushioned pad in place of the primer. They evidently felt that there was not sufficient time to acquire or manu-facture them to fit the M-C rifle. If they had allowed the trigger pulls in rehearsal without this type of protection and the firing pin had been damaged, the Army would have been open to the charge of negligence in their treatment of this vital piece of evidence.

slightly surprised by the two-stage trigger pull that they first encountered in the live tests. The trigger pulled easily at first, then gave significantly more resistance just before firing. With one exception, the time for the second set was lower than the first set. The exception, however, was for Miller, whose second set was longer than the first, but whose third set was the shortest time of all. All three protested that they could have done better in both time and accuracy with some practice. Without firing a single shot in practice, the BRL shooters, qualified at the same level as Oswald was, all fired the rifle within the eight seconds that the HSCA determined that it took between the first and third shots.

The "Mauser" argument was thoroughly debunked by the House Photographic Panel. But the fact that the murder weapon wasn't a

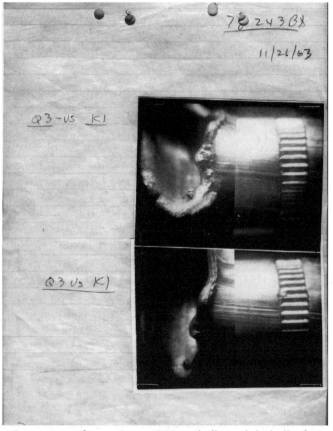

Figure 10. Comparison of engraving on FBI test bullet and the bullet fragment CE 569 (FBI designation is Q3), found in the front seat and front floorboard of the President's limousine. *(National Archives/John Hunt)*

Mauser doesn't depend only on the photo panel's determination; it was established that the fatal bullet was fired from the Mannlicher-Carcano found in the Depository. This determination was made soon after the gun was recovered and well before Oswald was, himself, slain. The firearms experts for the WC—Robert A. Frazier, Cortlandt Cunningham, and Joseph D. Nicol—testified that CE 399, the bullet from Parkland, and the two bullet fragments found in the limousine, CE 567 and 569, were fired from the M-C rifle, serial number C-2766, recovered on the sixth-floor of the Depository. This rifle was given the exhibit number CE 139. Figure 10 shows the microscopic, split-image comparison of the engraving signatures of one of the bullet fragments recovered in the car and a test bullet fired by the FBI from that rifle. Figure 11 shows a similar split-image comparison of the FBI test bullet and CE 399.[46] The three cartridge cases found in the "sniper's nest" had unique markings that proved they were fired from that rifle. Two of these comparisons are shown in figure 12. These markings were made on the base of the cartridge case at the time the bullet was fired, then ejected from the firing chamber when the bolt was pulled back. The upper image shows a split-view comparison of the firing pin marks on the primer of one of these cartridges and the same marks from an FBI test cartridge fired from CE

Figure 11. Comparison of engraving on FBI test bullet and bullet CE 399, found after falling from a stretcher in Parkland Hospital. *(National Archives/ John Hunt)*

46. These two figures are from FBI firearms expert, Robert Fraziers' work notes made shortly after the assassination, not from WC or HSCA exhibits. Researcher John Hunt supplied high-resolution copies of these notes, now held in the National Archives at College Park.

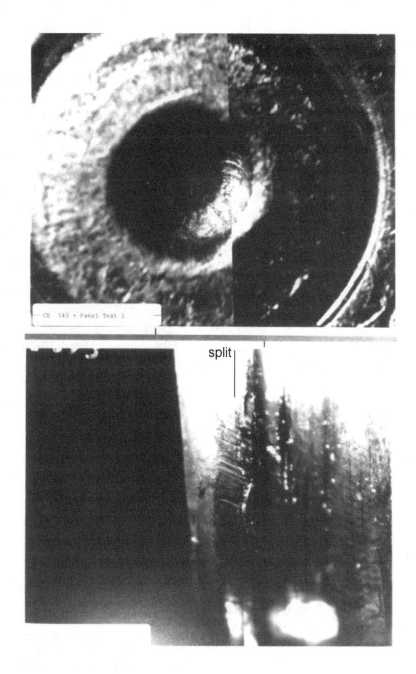

split

Figure 12. Comparison of base markings on FBI test cartridge and one of the three M-C cartridges found on the floor of the "sniper's nest" on the sixth floor of the book Depository building. *(National Archives)*

139. The lower image is a split-view comparison of the extractor marks on one of the recovered cartridge cases to those on a test cartridge. In the lower view, the location of the split is hard to see, so an indicating mark was added. These are only representative samples of dozens of similar comparisons made by the FBI that indisputably link Oswald's rifle to the bullets that injured the two men and the cartridge cases recovered in the sniper's nest.

Controversy has been raised about one of the cartridge cases being "dented" when recovered, but it is hard to understand how the dent leads one to the conclusion that the cases were "planted." Wouldn't the conspirator trying to frame Oswald have planted undented cases? How the dent came to be is very easy to understand, however. There are two possibilities: If a shooter is trying to operate the bolt quickly to rechamber another round and he shoves the bolt forward before the expended case being ejected is quite clear, he can jam the case against the front of the ejection port and dent the edge. On the other hand, the FBI observed a number of dented cases resulting from their testing of the weapon. Evidently, the lip of the case struck the edge of the ejection port or the scope following vigorous operation of the bolt to eject the empty case and chamber another round.

Many writers have noted that the method of serially marking the M-C rifles did not preclude two rifles having the same serial number, so that there might be another one with the serial number C-2766 out there somewhere. Again this is irrelevant. That other rifle would not have the distinguishing marks that the photo panel found on the Oswald rifle. The serial number is not visible in any of the controversial pictures and was not one of the distinguishing marks used. Nor would that other rifle leave the same engraving marks on the bullets fired from it, or the unique marks on the cartridge cases fired within it. It would make no difference if several rifles had that serial number. The significance of the serial number is that Lee Oswald was shipped a rifle with that number stamped on it under the name Alek Hidell. This was proven by both the WC and by the HSCA's handwriting experts.

Some have speculated that the WCC/MC bullet could have been fired from a "better" rifle by means of a sabot. The word "sabot" is from

---

47. The word root also appears in the French word "sabotage." The latter derives from a tactic by the Dutch resistance of throwing a wooden shoe in the industrial works of occupied factories during one of their many occupations by enemy forces, perhaps even during French occupation.

the French word for the wooden shoes used by the Dutch.[47] In the ballistic vernacular, the term sabot applies to a wooden or (more recently) plastic device that will hold a bullet or other projectile and provide a gas seal that allows the missile to be launched from a weapon that has a larger caliber than the projectile. It is most often used to fire missiles that do not have a circular cross-section, like cubes, irregular fragments, or fin-stabilized projectiles. Typically, the conspiracy writer speculates that bullets recovered from Oswald's rifle were fired by means of a sabot from another weapon, perhaps from the grassy knoll, perhaps from "the 7.65 mm Mauser found in the Depository" or from a 30-06. This assertion allows the conspiracy theorist to accept the fact that the bullets that struck the two men, killing one, had engraving marks from Oswald's rifle. No details are given as to how the conspirators recovered the bullets after firing them from Oswald's rifle or how they recovered them undeformed. This is not a trivial problem. The FBI found that firing the bullets into the customary cotton wadding deformed them more than CE 399. These are the other two bullets shown in figure 4, along with CE 399 and CE 853.

The "saboted" bullet story has other problems. The first is that any rifle that could have been used with a saboted WCC/MC bullet could only be marginally better in the sense of rapid firing, in a firing sequence that was not too rapid for an M-C rifle in the first place. Second, no "other rifle" would be justified on the basis of accuracy. As we have seen, the M-C rifle is as accurate as any rifle of modern design and firing a saboted bullet would necessarily degrade the inherent accuracy of that other rifle. The third is that it would be very difficult to design such a sabot. The difference in diameter would require a sabot too thin to be made of wood or plastic, so a major design problem would have to be researched and solved to develop new technology. Even if that were done, it is unlikely that a sabot of any design could grip a heavy bullet such as the WCC/MC with force enough to impart a stabilizing spin on it. This is the main problem with the use of sabots in the laboratory to launch any smooth, spin-stabilized projectile. Without an extensive design and testing effort to insure sufficient spin, the resulting unstable bullet, gyrating through the air, wouldn't fly accurately enough to hit an automobile at the distance the assassin was from the President, much less a human skull.

Fourth, the value of the saboted-bullet allegation is predicated on the bullet being fired from a location other than the sniper's nest. But the trajectory of the bullets, reconstructed multiple times by researchers working independently of each other, indicates that the bullets came from the general direction of the upper southwest corner of the Depository (see chapter six). The firing of a saboted WCC/MC bullet from the sniper's nest, or anywhere near that window, would not only be superfluous; because of the degradation in accuracy, it would be foolhardy. Anybody with the required access to Oswald's weapon would not need a sabot; he could just have used Oswald's rifle. Then, of course, there would be the problem of making his way to the upper floors of the book Depository and back out after the shooting without being noticed by the Depository employees.

Firing from another location in that general direction, such as the upper part of the Dal-Tex building, would have been a much longer shot. This would have been much more difficult with an ordinary rifle and its usual ammunition. If the shooter were using a saboted bullet, the shot would have been virtually impossible.

WC critics have consistently maintained that the paper bag seen by Wesley Frazier and his sister, Linnie Mae Randle, was too short to have contained the M-C rifle, even broken down. This betrays another problem with eyewitness reconstruction of events that, in Frazier's words, they "didn't pay much attention" to in the first place. People are actually quite good at remembering faces, but notoriously poor at estimating exact lengths of objects by memory alone. Frazier unhesitatingly identified Billy Lovelady as the man on the steps in front of the Depository from the picture the questioner showed him. But his memory of Oswald carrying a package tucked in his armpit as Frazier described it was a very odd method of carrying a long heavy package, even if it had contained the alleged curtain rods. If anything, the length that Frazier likely reconstructed by memory would probably be closer to the length of a collapsed curtain rod than to a disassembled gun. This is an object he was familiar with and was told was in the package at the time he saw it. We tend to believe what people tell us; otherwise, con artists would be out of business.

Similarly, the lack of visible oil stains in the paper bag is found suspicious by critics who note that the gun was described as being "well oiled." The phrase doesn't mean that the gun had oil all over the outside. It means that the operating mechanism was lubricated on the inside of the gun. It isn't necessary to use so much oil that it will leak out and stain the container. Any traces of oil left on the outside during sloppy maintenance would probably have been absorbed in the blanket from which it was removed the morning of the assassination. Nor is it necessary to oil the parts of the gun that would be exposed when disassembled.

In short, the rifle that Lee Oswald obtained from Klein's Sporting Goods for $21.95 was accurate, lethal, and well suited for the job. There was no "better weapon" available and no possibility that another weapon could have been used to re-fire bullets somehow recovered from Oswald's Mannlicher-Carcano (presumably without his knowledge).

CHAPTER FIVE

A Sound All Over

> "I have no way of determining what direction the bullet was going...there was too much reverberation. There was an echo which gave me a sound all over."
> —*Abraham Zapruder*[48]

A few years ago, my wife and I were driving through downtown Baltimore late in the evening of June 14. We arrived just in time to witness the Flag Day fireworks high over Baltimore harbor. The flashes of light from the exploding fireworks lit up the sky over the harbor, but the sharp cracks and deep booms of the fireworks were reaching us multiple times from every direction of the compass as the shock waves created by the explosions echoed down the brick and steel canyons of the city. Strangely enough, none of the noise seemed to come from the direction of the harbor, as there was always a large building between us and the explosion to reflect the shock waves and sound waves away.

Given the fact that shock waves, like ordinary sound waves, are readily reflected by brick, concrete, glass, and other hard surfaces, it is no wonder that people in Dealey Plaza heard the sound of "shots" coming from many directions. Secret Service agent Roy Kellerman, assistant special agent in charge of the White House detail who was riding in the right front seat of the presidential limousine, told the Warren Commission that he heard a "flurry of shots" within five seconds of the first "noise." Reflected shock waves, however, provide only part of the explanation for the many locations from which the gunfire seemed to originate in Dealey Plaza that day. Most were fooled by the misleading sound of a supersonic bullet.

---

48. From his Warren Commission testimony Volume VII, p. 572, in response to Mr. Liebeler's question concerning his opinion on which direction the shots came from "by the sound."

The study of the behavior of bullets and other projectiles as they fly through the air is called exterior ballistics. One of the important factors in the science of exterior ballistics is the velocity of sound—the "sound barrier" of supersonic aircraft fame. Sound waves travel almost the length of four football fields in a single second. Most rifle bullets are supersonic, including the bullets fired from a Mannlicher-Carcano rifle like the one used by Lee Harvey Oswald. With a muzzle velocity averaging about 2160 feet per second (660 meters/second), the WCC/MC bullets fired from Oswald's rifle traveled at nearly double the speed of sound. By contrast, the muzzle velocity of bullets fired from the modern U.S. M-16 rifle is nearly three times the speed of sound.

Supersonic rifle fire is one of the major hazards faced on the battlefield. Combat troops are taught the "crack-thump" method of locating the enemy rifleman. They ignore the deceptive crack of the supersonic bullet and listen for the duller, more distant "thump"—the muzzle blast of the rifle. The weapon's characteristic thump is created when the bullet leaves the muzzle of the rifle. It is like the pop made by uncorking a champagne bottle. The high-pressure combustion gas that pushes the bullet down the gun barrel rushes out when the bullet emerges. The emerging gas is also supersonic, so it also creates a shock wave—the "muzzle blast." More important is the fact that it is created all at once, like a firecracker.

Most shock waves are followed and overtaken by an expansion wave (below atmospheric pressure). This was described by Dr. Barger of BB&N, as an N-wave, for its shape that resembles the letter. As the expansion wave overtakes the shock wave, it weakens the shock and converts it to an ordinary sound wave that is not as loud. As it spreads and slows to the speed of sound, the sharp peaks of the N are rounded into a sine wave. The key difference is the distance between the observer and the source. When this distance is a few feet, the person will hear a loud crack—the shock wave. At a greater distance, the shock will have become an ordinary sound wave that sounds like a "thump" and is not as loud. This allows the observer to distinguish between the crack of the bullet and the thump of the muzzle blast from the more distant weapon.

A subsonic bullet, most commonly fired from a handgun, gives the air in front a preliminary push that travels through the intervening air at the speed of sound. The air has time to move aside, so that the bullet slips past more easily and quietly. Since the supersonic bullet moves faster than a pressure wave can move through the air, the air cannot be nudged aside before the bullet arrives. A molecule of air is sitting motionless at one instant and at the next it is jammed into a mass of super-compressed air on the nose of the bullet. This dense layer of air streams off as a shock wave like that photographed in figure 13.[49]

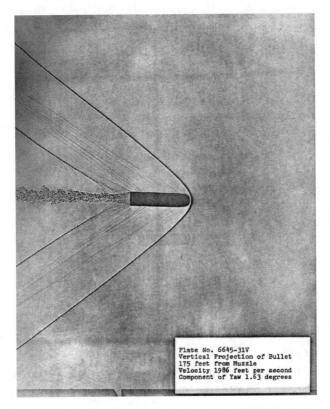

Plate No. 6645-31V
Vertical Projection of Bullet
175 feet from Muzzle
Velocity 1986 feet per second
Component of Yaw 1.63 degrees

Figure 13.   Spark shadowgraph of a Western Cartridge Company bullet, made for the Mannlicher-Carcano Rifle, showing the shock wave. *(National Archives/Modified)*

49. This is similar to the spark shadowgraph that I showed the HSCA in testimony given September 7, 1978. To obtain a picture of the shock wave, one fires a supersonic bullet in a darkened range in front of sensitive photographic plates. An ultra-fast timing mechanism triggers a microsecond (one-millionth of a second) spark just as the bullet passes the plate. The spark casts a shadow of the bullet and the shock wave on the plate, which is then developed just like any photograph. The shock wave casts a shadow because the dense, compressed air forms a "lens" that bends the light from the spark, like the ripples above a hot blacktop road on a sunny day.

The characteristic of the shock wave that is important to the situation in Dealey Plaza is the direction from which it seems to originate. The human ear senses the direction of movement of a shock wave much as it would an ordinary sound. An exploding firecracker creates a shock wave that travels outward as a sphere, expanding at a velocity just over the speed of sound. When that spherical shock wave passes over a person, it sounds to that person like the noise is coming from center of the sphere—the location of the explosion. Note that this is a direction perpendicular to the "surface" of the spherical shock front. A person hearing the firecracker would usually point back toward the center of the sphere as the location of the explosion. So far, all is as expected.

In the case of the supersonic bullet (or aircraft), the shock wave isn't created in a single instant like the pop of a firecracker. As long as the bullet is moving faster than the speed of sound, the shock wave is created continuously along its path (a line source, in contrast to the firecracker or muzzle blast of the weapon, which are point sources). The shock front travels away from the path of the bullet in the shape of a cone, a three dimensional surface like the surface of an ice cream cone. In figure 13, the two dimensional shadow of this cone on a photographic plate appears to be a V originating at the nose of the bullet. Like all shock waves, the walls of this cone move outward at or just above the speed of sound. The angle of the cone depends on the speed of the bullet relative to the speed of sound. The faster the bullet, the narrower the angle of the cone is.

A study conducted by Mr. Georges Garinther at the Human Engineering Lab at Aberdeen Proving Ground was brought to the attention of the HSCA's staff. Mr. Garinther ran an experiment in which a group of U. S. Army volunteers was asked to identify the source of supersonic gunfire when the rifle was fired out of visual range and muffled so that the report of the weapon was inaudible. When the v-shaped shock front passed his "ear-witnesses," they heard a loud crack that seemed to most of them to come from the center of the cone (the path of the bullet). This is, as with the firecracker, a direction perpendicular to the surface of the shock front as it passes over the person. A significant number, about 25 percent, pointed in the opposite direction.

Dr. David Green, the chairman of the Earwitness Panel that attended the gunshot reenactment in Dealey Plaza for the Acoustic Panel, gave testimony to the HSCA in which he explained the perceived direction of the sound of the bullet's shock wave and the "front-back" confusion. In a recent phone conversation, Mr. Garinther pointed out that this phenomenon is not particular to shock waves. The front-back confusion applies to sounds in general. Though we are good at guessing direction from the modifications to the sound waves induced by complex reflections from our cup-shaped exterior ear (the pinna), our directional perception isn't perfect. A person wearing a coat with a heavy hood over his head with an opening only for his face will hear almost all sounds as though they were coming from the front.

Garinther drew a sketch of this phenomenon for the HSCA. His sketch was redrawn and used by Dr. Green in his testimony to the Committee. It appears as figure 14. To the person's ear, the sound seems to come from the place where the nose of the bullet was when the shock wave he hears was created. By the time that sound reaches the ear, how-

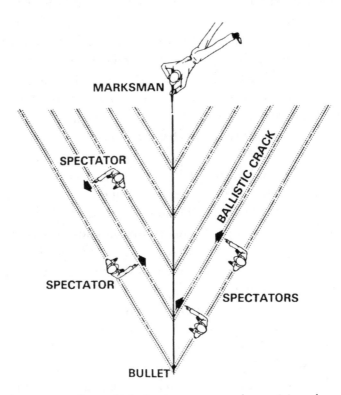

Figure 14. Direction from which the shot appears to have originated, as detected by hearing the shock wave from a supersonic bullet. *(National Archives/ Modified)*

ever, the bullet is far down-range. As in trying to locate a fast-moving aircraft by the sound it makes, a person hears the sound as coming from a point far behind the bullet's actual location at the time one hears it. Imagine a supersonic bullet fired down the center of a street with people standing on both sides. As the shock wave moves past the people, they each point in the direction that seems to them that the sound comes from, indicated by the arrows in figure 14 (note the figure pointing in the exact opposite direction from the majority). People on opposite sides of the path point in nearly opposite directions, and none, even those suffering from front-back confusion, would point toward the gun. Trying to locate the gun from the sound of the shockwave of a supersonic bullet is like trying to use the sound of the aircraft to locate the airport from which it took off.

Because the bullet is traveling much faster than the speed of sound, the crack of a passing bullet reaches the downrange listener before the thump of the muzzle blast does. If the shooter is some distance away from the observer, the delay between the two sounds might be an appreciable fraction of a second. This is enough time for a person to distinguish the two sounds from each other. In this case, the weapon's thump allows the listener to get a good sense of the direction in which the shooter is located. John Connally, an experienced hunter, identified the direction of the weapon on the very first shot as behind him and to his right.[50]

After the bullet emerges from the muzzle, the hot, light propellant gasses accelerate around the bullet and get ahead of it, forming a bubble around the gun muzzle and bullet. But the light gas rapidly decelerates to a velocity less than the bullet. As the bullet passes through this bubble of hot gas and makes the transition into normal air a few inches in front of the gun muzzle, the conical shock wave of the supersonic bullet begins. At the base of the cone, the shock wave of the bullet joins the spherical shock wave from the muzzle.

Figure 15 shows the relationship between these two waves: the spherical one growing at or near the speed of sound and the conical one being created at double the speed of sound—that is, at the speed of the bullet. If the two shock waves reach the ear with less than a couple of milliseconds separating them, a person hears them as a single sound. This

50. Hunters, like soldiers, are not necessarily well versed in the physics of shock waves. They learn to distinguish the two sounds by experiencing them.

position is indicated by the letter S in figure 15. In this instance, the perception of the direction of the origin of the sound comes from the thump of the rifle, the last sound to reach the ear. In addition, anyone standing well off to the side of the bullet's path, at the position of the letter M, will not get a shockwave from the bullet at all, but only the sound of the muzzle blast. Thus, those out of range of the shockwave of the bullet will hear only one sound, properly identified as coming from the direction of the gun. This is why the people who were standing adjacent to the Book Depository (but not immediately in front of it) or along Houston Street almost universally identified the sound as coming from its actual source. Most of those who identified other locations as the source of the gunfire were standing near the path of the bullet as it went down Elm toward the presidential limousine, indicated by the letter B. For these people, the shock wave of the bullet was the loudest sound they heard.

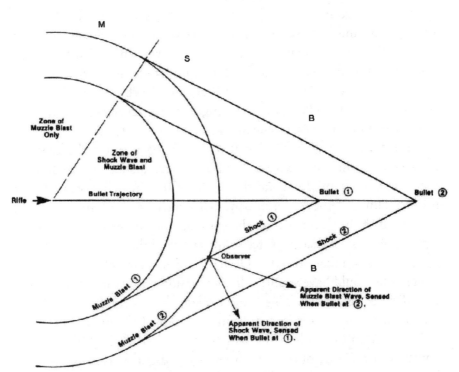

LOCI OF MUZZLE BLAST AND SHOCK WAVES AT TWO TIMES AFTER FIRING OF BULLET.

Figure 15. Directional perception from the shock wave of the bullet and the blast wave from the weapon (notation added). *(National Archives)*

After the muzzle blast of the rifle expanded enough to reach them Patrolman Baker and others in the back of the motorcade, a block away from the Depository, they were close to the position indicated in figure 15 by the letter M. The crack of the bullet never reached them, but the report of the rifle did. This is the reason that Baker and half a dozen others, including Mrs. Earle Cabell, the wife of the mayor, newspaper photographer Bob Jackson, and reporter Malcolm Couch, in the middle of the motorcade, had no difficulty in locating the general location from which the shots were fired. Like Brennan and Euins, who were nearby and off to the side of the path of the bullet near the position marked S, each of these three immediately looked up and saw the barrel of a weapon protruding from the sixth-floor window. Officer Baker did not see the gun sticking out from the window, only the pigeons flying up from the top, so he assumed the gunman was on top of the building.

We considered the fact that as the shock wave propagates, it gradually becomes a sound wave. This is why a supersonic aircraft, traveling at four to five miles above the earth, makes what is described as a "sonic boom" rather than a sharp crack. A shock wave reflected off a rough surface like a brick wall is modulated in a similar manner. As parts of the wave are reflected from the peaks of that rough surface and other parts are reflected off the valleys, the wavelength is broadened and the conversion to a sound wave is accelerated.

People standing in Dealey Plaza could have heard the primary shock coming directly from the bullet, a reflected shock with modulation from a brick building, and the report of the rifle, all separated a bit in time. Think of these as a nearby sharp crack, a more distant boom, and a loud thump, all reaching the ear from different directions. If the distances were such that the three sounds reached the listener at different times (a situation that existed in Dealey Plaza at a few isolated locations), a single shot could have sounded like three different weapons fired from three different locations. This could explain the "flurry of shots" Agent Kellerman heard from his position in the front of the presidential limousine, close to the path of the bullets. Nevertheless, the House found that the vast majority of the ear-witnesses heard gunshots from only one direction, no matter which direction they identified. For a collection of people mostly unfamiliar with the sound of rifle fire, it was a remarkable feat to distinguish between primary and reflected shock waves, though many were confused by the directional information.

Dr. Green added that the situation was even more confusing to the ear-witnesses when the source of the shock wave was nearly overhead. When members of his panel stood in front of the Texas School Book Depository while supersonic rifle bullets were fired from the sixth-floor window, the direction was very difficult to pinpoint. Several of the panel, in fact, identified the direction as being whatever direction they were looking at the time the gun was fired. Some witnesses to the assassination in 1963, who were standing directly in front of the Depository and on the sidewalk between the corner of the Depository and the limousine, were confused by what Dr. Green called the "overhead" phenomenon. For people in these locations, the bullets passed almost directly above and, unless they were a considerable distance from the building, the shock from the bullet and the weapon were amalgamated into a single shock front. These witnesses heard the initial shock wave as it passed from overhead toward their feet. Then a few milliseconds later they heard the shock wave going back up after it was reflected from the concrete sidewalk. This may have been long enough for some people to distinguish two separate sounds, but most would have heard it as two oscillations of a single noise. In either case, the directional perception is confused by the shock fronts passing twice in opposite directions.

Two Depository employees, Mrs. Robert A. Reid and Depository Vice President O. V. Campbell, were standing side-by-side on the sidewalk down Elm Street a bit from the Depository at a place about where the first bullet would have passed directly above them. According to Mrs. Reid's testimony to the WC, after the shots were fired she turned to Campbell and said, "Oh my goodness, I'm afraid those came from our building." She added that it was "because it seemed like they came just so directly over my head." Campbell, she reports, replied, "Oh, Mrs. Reid, no, it came from the grassy area down this way." Billy Lovelady, standing on the steps of the Depository, thought that the shots came from the concrete "arcade," sometimes referred to as the "pergola" where Abraham Zapruder was standing (at the end of the pergola farthest from the Depository) while filming the motorcade. Danny Arce was standing on the grass triangle between Elm and the street immediately in front of the Depository. He heard three shots and said, "I thought they came from the railroad tracks west of the Texas School Book Depository." William Shelley, another Depository supervisor standing in front of the building, also heard shots from the "west," but De-lores Kounas, an employee of McGraw-Hill, whose offices were located on the third floor of the building, heard three shots "coming from the triple overpass." She was standing on Elm at the corner of the intersection with Houston about 100 feet south of the Depository. All these people likely heard only the amalgamated muzzle blast and the shock wave of the bullet coming from nearly overhead.

A classic example of the deceptive shock wave of the bullet was the experience of Officer Bobby Hargis of the Dallas police, who was riding in the motorcycle just to the left rear of the presidential limousine. When asked about the source of the shots by the WC, he stated; "Well, at the time it sounded like the shots were right next to me." No wonder. He was very close to the path of the bullets. Those shock waves produced by the three supersonic bullets would have been by far the loudest noises he heard, and they were created "right next to" him. Similarly, an example of front-back confusion was provided by William Eugene Newman, who was standing on the sidewalk on Elm, on the opposite side of the motorcade from Officer Hargis. When he heard the shock wave from the bullets, they sounded like they were coming from behind him, in the direction of the grassy knoll. From his position, the shockwave of the bullet was louder than the report of the rifle which arrived a few milliseconds later, and the loud shock of the bullet sounded to him like it was going from back to front, rather than the actual front to back direction. In view of his perceived impression that people were shooting from behind his back, is not surprising that he did "...not recall looking toward the Texas School Book Depository."[51]

Like many witnesses, Abraham Zapruder heard "...too much rever-beration. There was an echo which gave me a sound all over." He had thought perhaps the shooter was behind him, but that, he made clear, was because the "motorcycle cops" had left their motorcycles, with the en-gines still running, and had dashed up the grassy knoll. (Actually there was only one policeman who had left his motorcycle idling while he ran up the knoll; it was Officer Hargis.) When pressed for his own auditory im-pression, Zapruder's candid statement was, "I have no way of determining what direction the bullet was going." Zapruder is only one of many that conspiracy writers count as hearing shots from the "grassy knoll." Even the

---

51. The latter is from his November 22, 1963 affidavit to the Sheriff's Department.

HSCA report lists Zapruder as a "grassy-knoll" witness.

The HSCA staff did a careful survey of the WC witnesses, including those who gave affidavits to the Commission staff and the Dallas police, who commented on how many shots they heard and where they seemed to come from. These results are included in Table I. The largest group (78 out of 178, or 44 percent) said they could not distinguish where the shots originated. More than twice as many identified the Depository (28 percent) as picked the grassy knoll (12 percent). But on the number of shots, they were much more definitive. Nearly three-quarters of the earwitnesses declared they heard three shots (132 out of 178). If those, like John Connally, who heard fewer, are included, more than 88 percent stated that they heard no more than three shots. The equivocal "Other" and "Don't know" categories did include some who heard one shot and some who did not count them but did not think there were more than three. Note that the largest single group in the table, over one-third of the witnesses (61), heard exactly three shots, but had no idea where they came from.

Table I. Number of Shots Reported

Number ->	2	2 or 3	3	4	Other*	Don't Know	Total
Location							
TSBD	3	2	38	2	3	1	49
Knoll	5	2	11	0	1	2	30
Other	2	1	22	3	1	1	30
Don't Know	7	2	61	1	2	5	76
Total	17	7	132	6	7	9	178

* The seven other witnesses report 1, 4-5, 5, 6, or 8 shots.

Though the skeptic suspects that the HSCA counted Zapruder among the grassy-knoll witnesses in order to inflate that number as much as possible, the HSCA is not in the same league as those less-inhibited writers who solemnly declare that a large majority of witnesses identified the grassy knoll as the source of the shots.

The HSCA, ignoring the testimony of scientific witnesses Sturdivan and Green, regarding the deceptive sound of shock waves that could make people hear reflected shocks as separate gunshots and their own count of 90 percent hearing no more than three shots, found that there was a fourth gunshot emanating from the area of the fence behind the grassy knoll. Though the HSCA's staff were predisposed to find a gunman on the grassy knoll, the witnesses claiming to have seen gunmen there were not found to be credible by the expert consultants or the HSCA's staff. Their "case" rests on the (later discredited) acoustic study, a carefully selected sample of people who heard shots from the vicinity of the grassy knoll, and Mark Lane's standby: people who saw "smoke" in that area.

CHAPTER SIX

The Magic Bullet

"For the single-bullet theory to stand, a lone bullet must be credited with feats that are bewildering in scope. One must accept that in wounding President Kennedy and Governor Connally, this remarkable bullet traversed seven layers of skin, pierced through muscle tissue, and smashed bones. The bullet then emerged practically unscathed."

—Henry Hurt[52]

Everyone would agree that flesh and bone are firmer than water, but anybody ever bruised by a bad dive off the high board would agree that, if you are moving fast enough, water can feel as hard as a rock. Given sufficient impact velocity, the force of resistance of water can do serious injury. Indeed, many people who have fallen from a considerable height have broken bones when they hit the surface of the water. Fatalities from such falls often result from injuries received upon impact with the water—not from drowning.

Whenever an object moves through some material, it generates a resistance, whether that substance is air, water, or a solid. As a bullet flies through air, the air pushes back and slows it. The retarding force is like the pressure you feel when you stick your hand out of a car window at highway speeds. The faster the car is moving, the higher the force is. Because the bullet is moving many times faster than the car, the pressure on the bullet is much greater than it is on your hand. The force is also a function of the density of the material. Wave your hand through the air and you can feel the air. Wave your hand at the same velocity in a swimming pool and the force that resists the movement is much greater. In fact, it is directly related to the density of the two.

---

52. *Reasonable Doubt,* page 61.

The density of water is about 800 times greater than that of air, making the force of resistance 800 times as great at the same velocity. Soft tissue, such as muscle, is only a bit denser than water and, therefore, has about the same (density-related) resistance to penetration. Water offers more resistance than air and bone offers more resistance than water. Bone is about twice as dense as water or soft tissue, so the retarding force in bone is roughly twice what it is in soft tissue.[53]

The velocity at which the bullet penetrates the body is even more important than density is. The force on the bullet is roughly proportional to the square of the velocity. Double the density and you double the force; double the velocity and you quadruple the force. It is difficult to extrapolate from the resistance one feels in pulling one's hand through the water in a swimming pool to the pressure on a rapidly falling body when it hits the water; it is even more difficult to extrapolate to the pressure on a bullet penetrating a target, because the velocity involved is so great.

The "magic" bullet is the derisive term coined by the WC critics, almost before the ink was dry on the Warren Report, to describe the bullet labeled WC Exhibit No. 399. They use the term "magic" because they do not understand the roles the velocity of the bullet and the density of the tissues play in the bullet's deformation—or lack of it. The tests conducted for the Warren Commission at the Biophysics Division of Edgewood Arsenal showed conclusively that the bullets manufactured by the Western Cartridge Company to be fired from the M-C rifle will deform on the skull but can penetrate a great distance through soft tissue without deformation.

To understand this fully, we must figuratively take the bullet apart. The bullet is like a metallic egg, hard on the outside and soft in the center. A picture of the WCC/MC bullet and a newer military rifle bullet appear in figure 16. The harder jacket is made of gilding metal, an alloy of copper and zinc. The softer core is either pure lead or a hardened alloy of lead. The egg analogy can't be carried too far, though, because the bullet is still about four times as strong as dense bone. This means that the bullet is still capable of smashing a bone while remaining intact. It is not uncommon to recover a low-velocity handgun bullet undamaged, after penetrating a human body

---

53. The resistance to penetration due to the strength of the bone or soft tissue is not negligible as the bullet slows. For the WCC/MC bullet, traveling at or near muzzle velocity, the resistance due to strength will be considered small compared to the resistance due to density of the target.

and penetrating or breaking a heavy bone. Dr. Michael Baden, the spokesman for the panel of forensic pathologists at the HSCA hearings, reported that virtually all the panelists had observed bullets like this.

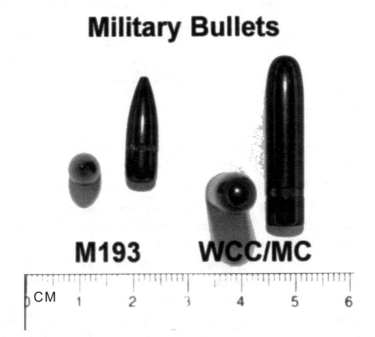

Figure 16. Photograph of the Western Cartridge Company bullet, made for the Mannlicher-Carcano Rifle, with the U.S. 5.56 mm M193 bullet for comparison. *(Larry M. Sturdivan)*

Whatever the density of the liquid or solid material a bullet penetrates, however, there is a velocity high enough that the force will permanently deform the bullet. In Appendix B, a "tissue" drag law is used to approximate the force on the bullet while it is penetrating tissue and bone.[54] Comparing these forces to the yield strength[55] of the WCC/MC bullet and bone, we obtain threshold velocities—that is, higher velocities will cause the bullets to deform upon impact. The approximate threshold velocities appear in Table II.

---

54. Appendix B contains details on the construction, penetration, and deformation of bullets. See the references listed in Appendix B for the full story on penetration and material strength.

55. Yield strength is the pressure (force per unit area) at which a material will begin to undergo permanent deformation. Bone deforms by brittle fracture, rather than the plastic deformation of metals and other ductile materials. Yield strength is not defined for an elastic tissue like muscle.

Table II. Approximate Velocities At Which WCC/MC Bullets and Bones Deform

Orientation of the bullet	Velocity at which the bullet will shatter bone	Velocity at which bone will deform the bullet	Velocity at which soft tissue will deform bullet	Muzzle Velocity
Point First	120 m/s (400 f/s)*	520 m/s (1700 f/s)	730 m/s (2400 f/s)	660 m/s (2160 f/s)
Sideways	135 m/s (450 f/s)	425 m/s (1400 f/s)	610 m/s (2000 f/s)	n/a**

* m/s = meters per second; f/s = feet per second
** not applicable

The velocity required to deform the WCC/MC bullet on normal, point-first impact with soft tissue is higher than its muzzle velocity. Under ordinary circumstances the bullet would not deform in soft tissue. That is, one would have to increase its velocity by overloading the cartridge with gunpowder, strip the jacket from the nose of the bullet to expose the softer lead core, or fire the bullet sideways to cause it to deform in soft tissue. Bone is another story. The velocity at which the bullet will be deformed in penetrating bone is well within the velocity expected from the WCC/MC bullet out to several hundred yards. On approximately half of the possible paths through the human body, a bullet would encounter bone somewhere along the path. If the WCC/MC bullet still had a velocity greater than 520 meters/second (1700 f/s) at the moment it strikes bone, then the bullet will deform.

When flying through the air, the bullet has gyroscopic stability, just like a spinning toy top, that keeps it moving point first. When it hits a human body, it loses stability and will gradually turn sideways, then backward (if it stays inside the tissue long enough). The angle that the bullet makes with its line of flight, the yaw angle, is shown in figure 17. If the bullet were moving sideways when striking bone, it would undergo even greater deformation than if moving point first.[56] If the first part of the path of the bullet included enough soft tissue, the bullet might be slowed to less than 425 meters/second (1400 f/s) before striking bone. Once the bullet's velocity drops below that threshold, it will still smash bone, but the bullet will not be deformed in doing so. The yield strength of soft tissue—the tearing

---

56. The bullet's jacket is stronger if the force is on its nose than if the force is on its side. To see this, step on the top of a tin can and it will usually hold your weight. Lay it on its side and step on it and it will collapse.

of muscle, skin, or internal organs—is much lower than the yield strength of bone. This accounts for the fact that a bullet will still penetrate soft tissue at a velocity too low for it to penetrate bone.

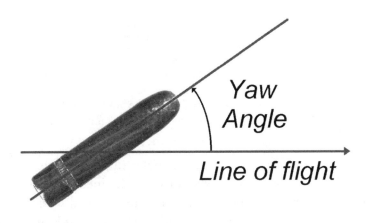

Figure 17. Representation of the yaw angle of a bullet. *(Larry M. Sturdivan)*

There is one more consideration. If the bullet strikes bone at a velocity just above its deformation velocity, the bullet will have just started to deform when its velocity drops below the threshold. At that point, the deformation will stop, leaving the bullet only slightly damaged. The result would be a bullet like CE 399. The higher the velocity, the greater the force, and the more rapidly the bullet will deform. Its deformation increases its presented area and drag coefficient which, in turn, increases the deforming forces. At high-striking velocity, it also takes more time for the bullet's velocity to drop below the deformation threshold, so the time during which it is being deformed lasts longer. If the bullet strikes bone at a higher velocity—550 to 600 meters/second (1800 f/s or more) for instance—it will be broken in two. Once the jacket is torn, exposing the softer lead core, the bullet will deform at much lower velocities, and will continue to deform even in soft tissue.

The result is similar to the bullet that struck the President's skull, a bullet broken into at least two major pieces plus many smaller fragments. Figure 18 is a schematic representation of Table II for a WCC/MC bullet moving point-first. It indicates the increased deformation of the bullet and tissue with increased velocity.

After making theoretical calculations such as those in Table II, the

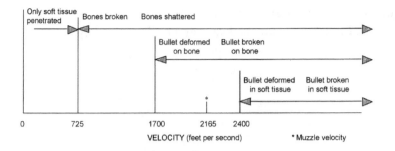

Figure 18. Bullet and bone deformation regions for the bullet made for the Mannlicher-Carcano Rifle by the Western Cartridge Company. *(Larry M. Sturdivan)*

scientist likes to conduct some experimental verification of the predicted result, particularly when the predictions are obtained from simple approximations, as these are. In this case, the experimental work was completed in 1964 when the Army's Biophysics Laboratory at Edgewood Arsenal did the tests for the Warren Commission that were first mentioned in chapter two.

The researchers at Edgewood's Biophysics Lab conducted simulations of each wound inflicted on the two men. They also fired some shots into a gelatin tissue simulant at short range. As predicted, none of the bullets showed the slightest deformation if fired only into soft tissue (animal meat, simulating the President's neck) or gelatin tissue simulant. Figure 19 contains a picture of CE 399 beside one of these recovered bullets. Except for the engraving from the rifle barrel, the bullet is just as it was when loaded into the cartridge. Some authors call CE 399 "pristine" without giving a precise definition of the word. If the word pristine may be applied to a bullet that has been fired through a weapon, it would apply to the undeformed bullet in figure 19—not to CE 399.

Conspiracy writers like Crenshaw want to have their cake and eat it too. He calls CE 399 "pristine" but then he comments, "There were no residues of blood or tissue on the bullet and it was obviously a 'plant'." While the bullet was significantly deformed, it still has a very smooth surface, with no convolutions or holes in which tissue or blood could easily be deposited. A bullet that is not broken up during penetration usually emerges without detectable amounts of blood or tissue clinging to it. As it penetrates, the bullet is moving so rapidly that its primary effect on tissue is to push it aside, creating a temporary cavity, not pick it up.

Bullet Recovered from Gelatin

CE 853 (from Goat Shot)

Figure 19. The "stretcher" bullet, CE 399, compared to the goat bullet, CE 853, and a WCC/MC bullet recovered from a gelatin block. *(National Archives and Biophysics Division, EA and Larry M. Sturdivan)*

The distance from which the bullets were fired at the gelatin-filled skulls in the Biophysics tests was the same as the distance between the President and the Depository window at the time of the fatal shot. At this distance the bullet's velocity on impact with the skull averaged about 1826 feet/second (557 m/s), well above the threshold of 520 meters/second for deformation of the bullet on bone. The force is 15 percent higher at 557 meters/second than it is at 520 meters/second, high enough to rip the bullet's jacket and sometimes to tear the bullet in two. All test bullets were badly mangled when they hit the skulls, just as predicted. Figure

20 is a picture of two of these bullets "soft recovered" in gelatin blocks placed behind the skull to minimize any further damage.

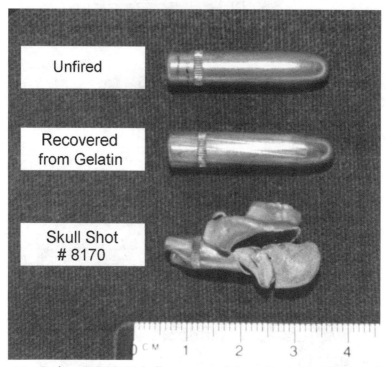

Figure 20.   Broken WCC/MC bullets recovered from Biophysics Division skull shots, compared to WCC/MC bullet from gelatin test and an unfired bullet. *(Biophysics Division, EA and Larry M. Sturdivan)*

Though each of the bullets shot into a test skull deformed in a unique manner, all are deformed to an extent similar to the bullet in figure 20. The bullet fragments recovered by the Secret Service from the front seat area of the presidential limousine after the assassination, labeled CE 567 and CE 569, are in figure 21. CE 567, a portion of the nose, consisting of jacket and lead core, was found on the front seat beside the driver's position. CE 569, a portion of a jacket only, from the base of a bullet, was found on the floor to the right of the front seat. The fragments found in the limousine show greater damage than the bullets in the simulated skull shots. This is primarily because the fragments struck hard parts of the car after exiting the President's skull, but a small part of the added deformation might be attributed to the fact that a live skull is a bit denser than the dried skulls used in the simulation. The skull of the robust President may also have been thicker than the skulls from medical supply sources. These were often obtained from unclaimed bodies that have suffered varying degrees of malnutrition. The mangled surface of the bullet fragments recovered in the limousine did have cavities containing traces of tissue and blood.

CE569   CE567

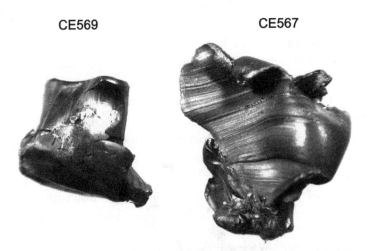

Figure 21. Bullet fragments recovered from front seat and front floorboard of the president's limousine. *(National Archives/John Hunt)*

The nose portion, CE 567, struck the limousine's windshield (but did not perforate the glass as claimed by some). We know this by the smear of lead left on the windshield.[57] The recovered base fragment, CE 569, consisting of jacket only, may have separated and struck the chrome molding at the top of the windshield frame or it may have separated when the two hit the windshield. Both of these defects in the car are too slight to have been caused by intact bullets, even at handgun velocity. The defects are compatible with the extent of damage that would be caused by bullet fragments, after having been broken apart and slowed by penetration through a human head.

The picture of figure 22 shows the WC reenactment of the view of the limousine from the Depository window. Even though the actor

---

57. There is some controversy over whether the chrome damage may have been caused before the motorcade (See Josiah Thompson's *Six Seconds in Dallas*). There is also evidence that the two pieces separated when the bullet exited Kennedy's skull (see Chapter 10).

playing the President is slightly misplaced—laterally—in the car, it is seen that an emerging bullet fragment has a high probability of impacting the windshield. Of course, either fragment could have bounced out of the car after the impact, as they did not have sufficient energy to penetrate and lodge in the glass or metal frame, but they did not. These two major fragments and the many tiny fragments left in President Kennedy's skull, plus the few recovered from the interior of the limousine, total less than half the mass of a complete WCC/MC bullet.[58] Some fragments obviously did leave the car. If a large core fragment cleared the windshield and trim, it could have been the source of the lead smear on the curb near James Tague and the small cut on his face. A straight line from the Depository through the President's position at the final shot passes close to the location of Tague and the curb smear at the time of the third shot. As we will see shortly, the path does not have to be perfectly straight, as the bullet fragment must have been deflected a bit as it passed through the President's head.

Conspiracy authors frequently cite the Tague wounding as making it necessary to "create" the single bullet theory, as it was necessary to have

DISTANCE TO STATION C	181.9 FT.
DISTANCE TO RIFLE IN WINDOW	218.0 FT.
ANGLE TO RIFLE IN WINDOW	18°03′
DISTANCE TO OVERPASS	307.1 FT.
ANGLE TO OVERPASS	0°44′

PHOTOGRAPH THROUGH RIFLE SCOPE

COMMISSION EXHIBIT NO. 902: Photo made through rifle scope in reenactment of the assassination.

Figure 22. Picture from the Warren Commission reenactment of the assassination scene. *(National Archives)*

---

58. The fragment of jacket and core had a mass of 2.89 g (44.6 grains), the jacket fragment 1.36 g (21 grains) and the small fragments from the car and Kennedy's head totaled 0.265 g (4.1 grains). If a few milligrams are added for fragments too small to recover and flushed from the wound by the flow of blood, the total recovered mass is about 4.6 g (71 grains). Whole WCC/MC bullets average about 10.45 g (160 grains).

a "missed bullet" to hit the curb near him. But the Warren Commission expressed the opinion that it was a fragment from the head shot that hit the curb near Tague and that a fragment from that impact or another fragment from the head shot was the one which cut his cheek. The investigating authorities never thought that it was a direct strike of a complete, jacketed rifle bullet that hit the curb. There was no copper in the scrapings, only lead, so there was no jacket on the impacting fragment. Also the damage to the curb was too slight to be compatible with the impact of an intact bullet, unless somebody were attempting the assassination with a low-velocity, pure lead .22 rimfire round fired from a handgun. The curb was not chipped, as some have claimed. It only had a smear of lead on it.

If the WCC/MC bullet were propelled at a velocity higher than the "soft tissue deformation" velocity in Table II (considerably higher than its normal muzzle velocity), it would deform on impact with soft tissue. Overloaded cartridges that would propel WCC/MC bullets at that velocity could have damaged the rifle and were considered dangerous to the shooter, so no such shots were attempted during the Biophysics Division Lab tests. So we must be satisfied with an alternate illustration of "soft" materials damaging bullets. Figure 23 is a picture of a gelatin block struck by a U.S. M80 bullet fired from the M14 rifle. The multiple tracks in the gelatin were produced by fragments of the bullet as it broke apart in the tissue simulant. This is a more modern fully-jacketed military bullet with a muzzle velocity 25 percent greater than the velocity of the WCC/MC bullet, a velocity sufficient to deform and break it apart. An M80 bullet recovered after having broken apart in gelatin is shown in figure 24. Both pieces contain parts of the jacket and lead core. The broken bullet leaves a trail of small fragments through the gelatin tissue simulant similar to the trail of fragments along the wound track deposited by the WCC/MC bullet broken on impact with the President's skull.

Table II points to the source of the errors made by Drs. Baden and Wecht in their testimony to the HSCA. Both men indicated that the deformation of the bullet that struck Connally was more likely to have happened on the radius, the bone in his wrist, than on his rib.[59] The rationale was that the "heavier" radius would have exerted more force than the "lighter" rib. As the drag law indicates, the force actually depends

---

59. It was earlier noted that Dr. Baden corrected the error. It is not known whether Dr. Wecht has changed his opinion since he testified before the HSCA in 1978. The mistake does not reflect on the professional competence of either man. Neither claims to be an expert in the physical sciences.

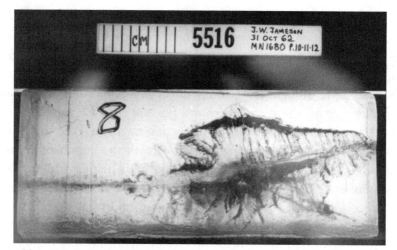

Figure 23.   Gelatin block with a permanent track from a 7.62 mm M80 bullet, which deforms and breaks up; 10 meters range. *(Biophysics Division, EA)*

Figure 24.   7.62 mm military bullet (M80), deformed and broken in gelatin tissue stimulant at 100 meters range. *(Larry M. Sturdivan)*

more on the velocity than the density; the density is actually about the same for the two bones. Though the rib is, indeed, thinner, the bullet didn't penetrate its thin dimension. It traveled along the rib, penetrating rib for a much greater distance than wrist bone. And it did so at higher velocity. The deformation could only have occurred while the bullet was penetrating the governor's rib. Any reasonable reconstruction of the velocity lost in penetrating his trunk leaves the bullet with too little velocity to deform when impacting the radius.

The yield strength of the soft lead core is about the same as that of bone, so the deformation velocity of the two is comparable. The lead that was sticking out of the base of the bullet was easily scraped off as the bullet penetrated the radius. This observation also indicates that, by this time, the bullet had penetrated enough tissue that it was moving nearly backward. Otherwise the slight bulge of lead core at the base of the bullet would not have contacted the bone and could not have been scraped off. No fragments were found in Connally's ribcage by the surgeon or by the House Pathology Panel on the x-rays of his trunk. Nor was the nose of CE 399 dented; the bullet was flattened side-to-side. These facts, in addition to the great destruction of the governor's fifth rib, are compatible with a WCC/MC bullet moving sideways—neither point first nor backward. It is likely that CE 399 would have been deformed to a greater extent if it had not been slowed and yawed by passing through the President's neck before hitting the governor.

This point was not missed by Dr. Olivier, the supervisor of the wound ballistic tests at the Biophysics Division laboratory. During his WC testimony, he showed pictures of the bullets fired into goat ribcages, then "soft recovered" in gelatin backup blocks. One of these was the one used by Dr. Wecht (figure 4). It was the one that just grazed the goat's rib in a manner similar to the one that perforated Connally's chest. But the difference in size of goat and human ribs is not great and there is no reason to believe there would be a difference in the density or strength of the hard outer (cortical) layer. The telling factor is the velocity at which it struck. If the bullet that struck Connally was deformed less, it was because it struck the rib at lower velocity. Not only did it strike Connally's back with lower velocity, but it would penetrate a larger amount of muscle in man, because of the anatomical differences between humans and goats. Also, the greater presented area of a yawed bullet produces a corresponding increase in the drag force, resulting in an even lower velocity when it reached the rib. This fact is entirely consistent with CE 399 having injured both men and being deformed less than CE 853.

Bullets are designed to fly point-first and straight through the air, but when they enter the body, or something equally dense, they not only yaw, but the yawed penetration causes them to take a curved path.[60] The curved path cannot be seen in opaque tissue, but it can be seen in high-speed movies of bullet penetration through gelatin tissue simulant. The track of the WCC/MC bullet that strikes at near zero yaw is about as straight as any bullet can go. Because of its length and weight, it has a large inertia and yaws slowly. This track is shown in the top picture of figure 25. The second picture is that of a backup gelatin block penetrated by an WCC/MC bullet after exiting from one of the neck simulation shots. This bullet struck at high yaw, like the yaw CE 399 had when it struck Mr. Connally. Higher yaw produces more curvature in the bullet's trajectory.

Jim Marrs presumably is alluding to the work done at the Biophysics lab for the Warren Commission when he states that the "Commission attempted to duplicate the feat of CE 399…but with no success." No such attempt was made. The curved trajectory of the yawed WCC/MC bullet through tissue (or a tissue simulant) as in the second view in figure 25, makes this nearly impossible. If the various pieces of simulated body parts had been placed in a straight line, the last pieces, the simulated wrist and thigh, would have been missed by the curving trajectory of the bullet. But placing the simulated pieces on a curved line would have been equally fruitless, as the direction and amount of curvature are random, depending on the depth the bullet penetrates before beginning to yaw and the direction in which it yaws; both random variables. Even the trajectory of a bullet striking the Connally simulation at small yaw (eliminating the simulated neck) would likely have too much curvature for such an experiment to be successful.

The next best thing is to simulate the governor's torso and use an array of wrist bones, embedded in gelatin tissue simulant to stand in place of

---

60. If a bullet is yawed by hitting something before striking the body, the yaw will just continue to grow in the same direction. It will reach a sideways orientation sooner than the bullet that strikes in normal, low-yaw flight. As the bullet yaws, it develops a lift, like an airplane wing. If it yaws in air, it will degrade the accuracy of the round. In tissue, the lift forces are greater than in air due to the greater density of the material being penetrated and the unstable bullet will yaw to a larger angle. Thus, undeformed bullets describe a curved trajectory through soft tissue.

his wrist. With this technique, one of the bones is likely to be hit, whatever the curvature of the bullet track. This approach was used by Dr. John Lattimer and colleagues in 1994, and in 2004 by an Australian company hired by the Discovery Channel to repeat Lattimer's test. In each case, the bullet hit a simulated rib, was deformed, and exited to hit a simulated wrist bone, creating damage similar to that caused to Connally's radius. In Lattimer's test, the bullet was deformed in a manner similar to CE 399 when it hit the rib. In the Discovery Channel special, first aired on November 14, 2004, the bullet was a direct strike on the rib and was deformed to a greater extent than Lattimer's bullet, CE 399, or CE 853, the Biophysics Division bullet that grazed the goat rib in a manner similar to CE 399's grazing strike on Connally's rib. The Discovery Channel's bullet resembled the bullets that made direct strikes on ribs in the Biophysics tests.

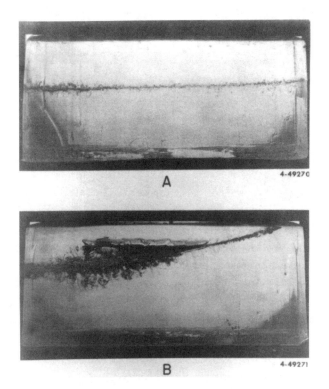

Figure 25. Permanent tracks of the WCC/MC bullet fired directly into gelatin block A (near zero yaw) and into block B after having passed through a simulated "neck" (with large striking yaw). *(Biophysics Division, EA)*

The development of a similar simulation technique was infeasible under severe time and funding constriants on the wound ballistic tests at the Biophysics Division.[61] Thus, Dr. Olivier chose to follow the other alternative: to fire the bullets into wrist bones at full velocity. Some of these struck the cortical (hard) bone on the shaft of the radius and were torn open. Others hit the cancellous (spongy) bone near the joint and were less extensively damaged. The greater damage to the bullets, greater destruction of the wrists, and lack of lead fragments left in the wrist simulations proved that the bullets in the simulations were traveling at a much higher velocity than the bullet that struck Connally's wrist. Conversely, a low-velocity bullet striking Connally's wrist base-first proves that CE 399 had already perforated his trunk. These differences are shown in Figures 26 and 27.

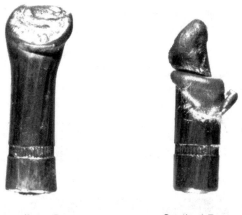

Cancellous Bone   Cortical Bone

Figure 26.   M-C bullets recovered from Biophysics Division wrist simulation firings into two types of wrist bone, using the Oswald rifle. (Biophysics Division, EA)

Earlier, the FBI inadvertently proved that cotton waste, when compressed as it builds up on a penetrating bullet, is denser than soft tissue. They did this by firing WCC/MC bullets from the Oswald rifle into cotton waste at muzzle velocity. They were trying to recover undeformed

---

61. The Biophysics lab, under one name or another, conducted over 45 years of ground-breaking research in wound ballistics before the mission diminished and was terminated in the early 1990s. The duration of the experimental investigation for the Warren Commission was less than two weeks in late-April and early-May 1964.

bullets fired from the Oswald rifle. Such bullets were needed as ballistic standards with which to compare CE 399 and the fragments recovered from the floor of the limousine to determine whether they were fired from Oswald's weapon. The bullets they recovered in this manner were suitable as standards, but were deformed to a greater extent than CE 399. This point was missed entirely by Dr. Wecht in his HSCA testimony when he used the picture reproduced as figure 4 that contains those bullets. He claimed that the deformation in cotton waste proved that CE 399 did not smash the governor's wrist since it would have been deformed more in the "hard bone." He considered the effect of strength and, perhaps, density of the target on deformation—but not the much greater effect of velocity.

The Biophysics Lab tests established that Connally was injured by a single bullet that entered his back and ended up in his thigh. The distance that the bullet traveled between those two points is characteristic of

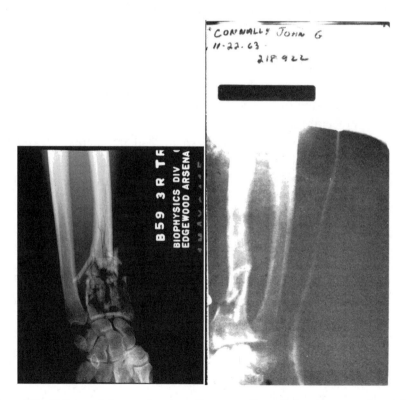

Figure 27. X-Rays of shattered wrists, Governor Connally's versus experimental shots from the Biophysics tests. *(Biophysics Division, EA/Dale Myers)*

a WCC/MC bullet, but it is characteristic of many other heavy, nearly-cylindrical rifle bullets, as well. No magic is required to get that amount of penetration with little or no deformation from a nineteenth-century-design rifle bullet. Consider the shallow entrance wound in his thigh, with no exit wound and no bullet present on the x-rays of the thigh, or found by the surgeons while cleaning and suturing the wound. Some conspiracy writers express the opinion that the tiny fragment at the bottom of the thigh wound created it, but Dr. Shires, the surgeon who repaired the wound, was not misled. The only explanation is that the missing bullet was expelled from Connally's thigh by the movement of his leg muscles somewhere between Dealey Plaza and the hospital,[62] perhaps even when he stood and attempted to exit the car upon arriving at the hospital.

This phenomenon is occasionally seen in combat wounds. Shallow wounds are found devoid of the projectile that produced them, the projectile having been ejected by the intermittent tensing and relaxing of surrounding muscle. That there was a "missing bullet" and one was found on his recently vacated stretcher,[63] however, do not prove that it was CE 399 that was dislodged from Connally's thigh. How do we know that CE 399, or any other bullet from a Mannlicher-Carcano rifle, was the bullet that injured Connally? The proof comes from the fragment of lead core that was recovered during the surgical repair of his wrist.

Dr. Vincent Guinn's work for the HSCA was briefly discussed in chapter three. He compared the small lead fragments recovered at surgery from both the Governor and President to the cores of CE 399 and the fragment of a WCC/MC bullet recovered from the floor of the

---

62. The WC critics who claim that CE 399 was a "plant" never mention the bullet that was missing from Connally's thigh. Given the thoroughness of the investigation of a presidential assassination or the attempted assassination of a governor in his home state, it was inevitable that the bullet that worked its way out of the governor's thigh would be found. The only danger of its being lost was that the finder might pocket it as a souvenir. This also raises another interesting question: How did the purported "planter" of CE 399 know that there was a bullet dislodged from Connally's thigh? If another bullet had actually produced the injuries, but remained lodged in his thigh, a bullet planted on his stretcher would have been puzzling, but hardly deceptive. If, on the other hand, the "other" bullet had completely perforated Connally's thigh, or missed it altogether, CE 399 should have been planted in the car, not on the stretcher. The "planter" not only had to know about the dislodged bullet, he had to recover it before planting CE 399, not in the place where he found the real bullet but - in the usual conspiracy scenario - on the "wrong" stretcher.

63. I assume it was from Connally's stretcher, because it would make no sense that a bullet with engraving from Oswald's rifle would be found on a stretcher belonging to anybody other than a passenger in the presidential limousine.

limousine. He pointed out that his results were similar to those obtained by the FBI in 1964.[64] Critics note Guinn's statement that one of the vials identified as scrapings from the windshield was empty, other vials did not contain the mass of lead that was recorded on the outside, and an admission that he had to trust the National Archives to give him the vials containing the actual recovered fragments. A portion of some of the recovered fragments had been consumed in early FBI flame spectrometer tests (apparently, all the mass of the windshield scraping and the lead scraped from the curb impact near James Tague). Guinn also noted that the FBI had evidently not returned the small pieces of lead that they had cut from the recovered bullet fragments for their own NAA analyses to their containers. Evidently, they were misplaced or discarded. Detractors parley portions of these statements, taken out of context, into an "admission" by Dr. Guinn that he had tested the wrong fragments. Guinn said no such thing.

Guinn had already done some work with WCC/MC bullets from the four lots, of a million rounds each, manufactured for the U.S. Army in 1954 by the Western Cartridge Company. A Kennedy researcher, Dr. John Nichols, discovered the FBI letter to the WC in the National Archives in 1973. After considerable effort, Nichols got the FBI's test results through a Freedom of Information Act request. As Nichols was not an NAA expert, he sought Guinn's help in assessing those results.

In 1964, the FBI researcher, Mr. John F. (Jack) Gallagher, conducted four NAA runs on the recovered bullet evidence in the case, after the emission spectrography tests had yielded no conclusive results. These NAA tests were conducted at the Oak Ridge National Laboratory in Tennessee, as the FBI did not acquire its own NAA laboratory until 1966. NAA causes no detectable change in the small samples being tested, some cut from the larger bullets or bullet fragments. Therefore, Gallagher could repeat the test using the same samples for all four runs. His four different runs, however, resulted in widely differing levels of the trace metal content from run to run. This unexpected problem was the

---

64. Carl Oglesby reprints the entire letter from FBI Director J. Edgar Hoover to the Warren Commission declaring the results of the neutron activation tests to be "inconclusive," but ignores Dr. Guinn's 1978 report and testimony to the HSCA. Oglesby's book was published in 1992, and he frequently refers to the HSCA report in which Guinn's complete results are printed. The only conclusion that one can draw is that the omission was a deliberate attempt to deceive the reader by omitting physical evidence that refutes his conspiracy allegation.

primary reason that the results were labeled inconclusive.

But Guinn immediately recognized the unusually wide variance in antimony within the samples. This showed up in all four runs, independent of the difference in levels between runs. From late 1973 to early 1975, he conducted NAA tests for trace metals in fourteen WCC/MC bullets, representing all four lots, that Dr. Nichols supplied. Guinn's tests on these random samples of unfired WCC/MC bullets, using a refined technique and a gamma-ray detector with better discrimination between peaks from the metals in the alloy, showed an even greater variability in the antimony content than was seen in the FBI tests on the recovered bullet evidence. This raised the possibility that one could, indeed, trace recovered bullet fragments to a single source and distinguish them from fragments of a different bullet.

In his HSCA testimony, Dr. Guinn was faced with a dilemma. His tests with random unfired WCC/MC bullets had shown a large variance in antimony from bullet to bullet and a smaller variance within bullets, determined by analyzing samples from different quarters of the same bullet. Thus, he had to walk a fine line in declaring that the fragment recovered from Connally's wrist probably came from CE 399 and that the fragments from the car and Kennedy's head were all from the same bullet. His statement to Mr. Jim Wolf, the HSCA's staff member conducting the interrogation:

> *Mr. Wolf:* "You can, however, today state for the first time scientifically that CE-399 did cause the injuries to Governor Connally's wrist?"
>
> *Dr. Guinn:* "Yes sir, those two match so closely that I would say that such was the case."
>
> *Mr. Wolf:* "What is the degree of confidence and certainty with which you can state this conclusion?"
>
> *Dr. Guinn:* "I wish that I could put a number on it, as we often can do, that is, calculate a probability, but we really don't have the background information to make a numerical calculation in this case. One can only show what information we do have, and that is that you simply do not find a wide variation in composition within individual Mannlicher-Carcano bullets, but you do find wide

composition differences from bullet to bullet for this kind of bullet lead. Thus, when you find two specimens that agree this closely, you can say it looks indeed like they are pieces from the same bullet."

Mr. Wolf [trying again]: "Would you state that your conclusion is more probable than not, highly probable, or what is the degree of certainty of your conclusion?"

Dr. Guinn: "I would say highly probable, yes. I would not want to say how high, whether it was 99 percent or 90 percent or 99.9 percent. I can't make a calculation like that."

Not to worry. Appendix C contains those probability calculations. Guinn's dilemma arises from the idea that the variability in antimony concentration within the core of a single bullet would influence the probability calculation. But the planting of a bullet or bullet fragments to frame Oswald would necessarily involve different bullets than the ones used to shoot the two men. So the variability in antimony concentration among different bullets is the relevant factor to be used in the statistical tests.

There are, of course, a number of different conspiracy scenarios to examine. The most common is that of multiple shooters scattered over Dealey Plaza inflicting several separate wounds on the two men with the "magic" bullet and bullet fragments "planted" to frame Oswald for the crime. In this case, all the recovered fragments would have a different origin. Even if all conspirators were using M-C rifles and the same ammunition as that found in the Depository, the statistical analysis shows that this theory has odds greater than ten-thousand-to-one against it. If the other conspirators were using "better" weapons than the M-C rifle (a frequent theme), the odds increase to something on the order of a-million-to-one.

There are simpler conspiracy stories possible, involving Oswald as the main assassin, but involving the planting of even one bullet or fragment, which would constitute a conspiracy. These themes are less popular, probably because they are less spectacular (perhaps reducing the book sales), but they have better odds than the multiple shooter scenario. The probability that a planted CE 399 would match the fragment from Connally's wrist is a bit less than two percent. Of course, the fragments with engraving from his rifle, CE 567 and CE 569 (jacket only, none of the lead core), might have been planted in the car. This one has better chance: a bit over three percent. To separate Oswald from the bullets completely would require planting CE 399 and the car fragments. The probability of "planted" bullet fragments, CE 399 and CE 567, both matching the fragments recovered from the two men is 0.00059, or less than one-in-a-thousand. Add the necessity to plant the matching small fragments in the upholstery and recover any fragments from the "actual" lethal bullet and we are back to the range of one-in-ten-thousand to one-in-a-million odds.

As Vincent Guinn noted: in retrospect the FBI's NAA demonstrates the same result as his test did 13 years later. The only problem is the systematic error that crept into the FBI results. Appendix C also has statistical calculations based on the fourth FBI NAA run. This analysis takes a different approach than the one done on Guinn's data. It doesn't depend on the entire WCC/MC bullet population, but only on the repeated measurements for each sample. This second type of analysis shows that the probability that the five recovered samples of WCC/MC bullet cores would fall, by chance alone, into the two groups found meaningful by the Warren Commission is on the order of one-in-a-hundred-thousand.

These probabilities are the best that a completely knowledgeable co-conspirator could do. The second person would have to use another M-C rifle to do the shooting and recover any pieces of jacket that might be traced to his own weapon. Then he would have to plant bullets or fragments fired from Oswald's rifle and recovered in a manner that would not obscure the rifling marks, as happened in the bullet fired at General Walker. If the co-conspirator had used a different type of rifle and bullet to do the shooting, the probability of a random match is effectively zero.

Compared to the whole population of WCC/MC bullets, the two involved in the shooting are actually fairly close in antimony concentration. Only one out of seven randomly-selected pairs would match this closely. Of course, the associated probability of 14.5 percent isn't close to being statistically significant, but is small enough to prompt Guinn to characterize the two as being in the "unusual" range.

Some conspiracy writers maintain that there are chain-of-custody problems in the recovered bullet evidence, usually noting the change of weight caused by the FBI's taking samples for testing and either destroying the sample in testing or failing to return it to the container. In spite of their obfuscation on the issue, none of the critics offers any credible evidence that the chain of custody of these fragments was compromised. Guinn's work, on the other hand, completely verifies the chain of custody.

Dr. Guinn's NAA, along with the earlier FBI test, unequivocally connects the fragments recovered from the two men to WCC/MC bullets that were fired from Oswald's rifle. Thus, we know to a better than 98 percent probability that Connally's wrist wound was caused by CE 399. We know from the results of the Edgewood Arsenal tests that the wrist wound could not have been a direct strike without causing more damage to his wrist and more damage to the bullet than CE 399 exhibited. Thus, we must conclude that CE 399 was slowed by producing the trunk wound before striking the wrist. To create such a shallow thigh wound, the bullet striking the thigh had to be nearly spent. This proves that the bullet penetrated several inches of tissue prior to hitting the thigh, an amount consistent with one bullet causing all of Connally's wounds. Furthermore, if the bullet had exited his chest or wrist without striking another body part, it would have been found in the upholstery or the floor of the limousine where he was sitting.

Although they insist that the Warren Commission should have explained every known detail, conspiracy writers make no attempt to explain the absence of bullet holes in the car. Multiple bullets exiting the two men would have had a velocity that would necessarily have damaged or perforated the seats, carpets, or car body, like the bullet fragments from the head shot that marked the windshield and dented the trim. But there were no bullets or bullet holes found in the area where Connally was sitting. In the pictures taken immediately after the President showed signs of the neck injury, the Governor was still turned a bit to his right, after having looked over his right shoulder. He was holding his hat in his right hand with his arm in front of his chest and over his left thigh. In this position, Governor Connally's wounds all line up.

The critics would counter that the lack of bullet holes probably is definitive for connecting all of Connally's wounds, but the President was sitting higher in the car and no fragments were found in his neck wound to be connected, via NAA, to CE 399. If he were leaning only slightly backward in the seat at the time the road sign shielded him from the

Zapruder film and was shot from street level, a bullet could have passed over the windshield after it exited his neck. Aside from the number of reconstructed trajectories that line up Kennedy's and Connally's wounds, is there other physical evidence that the same bullet did injure both men?

Indeed, there is. It is the entrance wound in Connally's back, as described by the surgeon who repaired it, as well as the elongated holes that may still be seen in his shirt and jacket. We have already observed that the WCC/MC bullet in normal flight possesses nearly zero yaw. When a bullet traveling with little or no yaw hits a target perpendicular to its surface, it makes a perfectly round hole. A bullet striking at a small angle relative to the surface, as the trajectory through Connally's chest indicates it did, it will produce a hole that is only slightly elliptical. This entry was shown in the drawing of figure 3.

A WCC/MC bullet striking at a large angle of yaw, however, will make a distinctly elongated hole in the target. In his hospital report, Dr. Shaw gave the length of the entry wound as three centimeters (1.2 inches), but in his testimony to the House FPP he said that it was actually 1.5 cm. In either case, the horizontal hole in Connally's back was so long that it could only have been made by a bullet at significant yaw, far too large for any WCC/MC bullet in normal flight. The yawed entry is shown in figure 28.[65] There is no controversy about the wound in Connally's back being an entry wound. Not only was it identified by the surgeon as an entry wound, but if a bullet had passed through Connally from chest to back, it would have to be fired from a weapon between the Governor and the seat immediately in front of him—a clear impossibility.

In his HSCA testimony, Dr. Wecht maintained that the elongation of the entry wound was caused by a bullet striking at an oblique angle to the governor's back. He claimed that its horizontal orientation was due to the shooter's standing off to the side, perhaps on the grassy knoll. Even if Connally had turned to his left far enough that the entry location on his back had been exposed to a shot from the knoll (he did not), the bullet did not penetrate Connally from right to left; it went from back to front. To do what Wecht would have it do, the bullet would have to take an

---

65. This figure is reproduced from the HSCA drawing. It shows an exaggerated "tumbling" motion before strike that is somewhat misleading. The yaw grew from a few degrees when it left Kennedy's neck to a bit more than 20° (the 1.5 cm hole), when it struck Connally's back. The yaw, like the hole, was nearly horizontal, not vertical like that in the figure.

abrupt turn as it entered his back. Bullets that abruptly change direction, such as a bullet deflected by a piece of armor plate, are shattered into a hail of small fragments (see Appendix B). Only the milder acceleration produced by a gradually curving trajectory would leave the bullet intact. The bullet was badly yawed when it hit the Governor's back, though not quite as near sideways as the one drawn in figure 28.

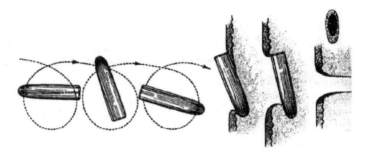

Drawing of a typical entry wound, displaying an asymmetrical abrasion collar resulting from a distant rifle shot with a trajectory at an acute angle to the skin surface.

Figure 28. Abrasion collar produced by a yawing bullet with an exaggerated illustration of the bullet's yawing motion. *(National Archives)*

A WCC/MC bullet striking with 20° or more yaw would have to have been tipped by hitting something just before it struck Connally's back. There were two possibilities for the intervening object: an oak tree, still full of dull green leaves, and the President's neck. Even if the shooter had tried to take advantage of small gaps in the foliage and lucky enough to hit somebody by doing so,[66] the oak tree is ruled out by the position of the car when both Kennedy and Connally reacted to the shooting; a fact well-documented in the photographic evidence, including the Zapruder film. This leaves only Kennedy's neck.

---

66. We have already noted that the wood in the tree, which is less dense than tissue or water, could not deform or appreciably deflect the bullet that accidentally struck it. Penetration of a substantial amount of wood, on the other hand, would induce yaw. Shooting through a piece of heavy paper (wood fiber) will produce a measurable increase in yaw. Considerably greater thickness would be required to induce a significant yaw in the WCC/MC bullet. The required thickness would be comparable to the thickness of the president's neck. Though stronger than soft tissue, wood is less dense. Whether the bullet would be yawed more or less in wood than in the same amount of tissue depends on the velocity at which it strikes.

The tracks through the simulated "necks" in the Biophysics Lab tests show that the WCC/MC bullet would only just begin to yaw in its passage through the President's neck but, because the bullet is long and heavy, this yaw would reflect a considerable amount of transverse (sideways, as opposed to rotational) angular momentum. This angular momentum might be thought of as the persistence with which the bullet overturns. This would have caused the yaw to continue to grow while the bullet was in the air between the President and Governor, accounting for the yawed entry wound on Connally's back.

Conspiracy writers criticize the Warren Commission for using the Secret Service's Cadillac convertible in the assassination reenactment, then use the positions of the two stand-ins in that reconstruction to establish a jagged trajectory for CE 399. They also combine these inaccurate positions with flawed geometry to dispute the HSCA's reconstruction of the trajectories that led back to the sniper's nest window. This tack was initiated by Mark Lane. He used the angle between the Depository window and the car's direction on the street and the angle the bullets were said to have made with the body to assert that the bullet could not have originated from Oswald's position in the Depository window. Like many others, he neglected two other relevant angles: the angle the President's body made with the long axis of the car and the lateral angle from the car to the corner of the building. If the President had been stooped over tying his shoelace, changing the angle of his neck with respect to the car, Lane's method would have led to the conclusion that the assassin had shot from a helicopter hovering over Dealey Plaza.

When those who are adept at three-dimensional geometry reconstruct the path of the bullet, going backward from its entry in Connally's back to its exit from Kennedy's neck, it lines up the wounds of the two men and points back in the direction of the sniper's nest in the sixth-floor Depository window. The HSCA's expert, Mr. Thomas Canning, an engineer with NASA, did this in 1978, with the assistance of members of the HSCA staff. Failure Analysis Associates (FAA) also made trajectory projections for the mock trial of Oswald at the American Bar Association's annual meeting in 1992. FAA worked with their own enhancement of the Zapruder film and projected a three-dimensional mockup of the positions of the two men in the car.

An impressive computer simulation of the bullet trajectory through the two men was also prepared by computer animator Dale Myers for ABC's fortieth anniversary special on the JFK assassination, hosted by Peter Jennings.[67] This painstaking computer reconstruction was based on virtually every available movie and still picture taken as the motorcade passed around the corner of Main onto Houston until the limousine passed under the underpass on Elm. The quality of this reconstruction won Myers the Emmy award for Outstanding Individual Achievement in Graphic and Artistic Design in September 2004. In the ABC special, Myers showed how the improper positioning of the men in the car was what led to the discontinuous trajectories one sees in conspiracy books. Myers' is the definitive effort in this regard. His reconstruction of the position of the two men is more detailed and accurate than earlier efforts and the timing of the shot is nearer to the actual time of the second shot; much nearer than the HSCA's.

The sequence shown on the ABC special is only part of the animation Mr. Myers did for his documentary, "Secrets of a Homicide: The JFK Assassination." The documentary also shows the backward projection of the trajectory from the entry point on Connally's back through the exit point on the President's neck. The circle of probable error of Canning's trajectory, based on a shot at Zapruder frame 190, nearly misses the sniper's nest window. Failure Analysis' trajectory, based on frame 224, is somewhat better, but Myers' more accurate reconstruction at 223 is centered precisely on the area at the top of the boxes in the sixth-floor window of the school book Depository, the "bench rest" for the sniper's nest. Myers' probable error includes this location only during frames 217 to 224 and the center trajectory is centered almost precisely on the alleged firing position, at the top of the box sitting in the window, at frames 221–223. A frame from Myers' animation sequence that shows this trajectory at frame 223 is in figure 29.

Calculated circles of probable error—based on a baseline along the distance between the President and the Governor and the exit wound in Kennedy's neck and the entrance wound in Connally's back—pinpoint the shooter's location. On the other hand, relatively small circles of probable error, based on the very short baselines of the President's isolated neck and head wounds, as promoted by the HSCA, are a bit too good

---

67. This special has since been shown on cable networks, such as the History Channel.

to be true. Because it was neither deformed nor badly yawed as it passed through the President's neck, CE 399 deviated very little from a straight line between the Depository and its entrance on Connally's back. The very short baseline upon which it is based, however, would amplify any positional errors to very large circles as it was projected a large distance backward. Extrapolating backward from the head shot is much worse. It involves a number of false assumptions, including the assumption that yawed and deformed bullets travel in nearly straight trajectories through human bodies.

Figure 29. Circle of probable error on the sniper's nest window in the Texas School Book Depository building, from Dale Myers' backward extrapolation of the shot through the two men. *(© 1995–2004 Dale K. Myers. All Rights Reserved.)*

Projection of the trajectory of CE 399 in the relatively short distance it traveled as it passed through the two men is even more realistic than the backward extrapolation of that bullet to the Depository window. FAA's version of this projection was shown at the ABA's mock trial. The trajectory shows a "deflection" of the bullet off Connally's rib. A sudden deflection of the magnitude shown in the drawing would not only violate the laws of physics, it would contradict the surgeon's observation that the bullet shattered ten centimeters (four inches) of the governor's fifth rib. A bullet's remaining in grazing contact with a rib for four inches would hardly be described as a "deflection." The change in direction is actually accounted for by the curved trajectory that a yawing bullet will take through a target as thick as Connally's trunk, including the part where it was in contact with the rib. A more accurate rendition of the curved trajectory that the yawed bullet took is in Dale Myers' documentary "Secrets of a Homicide." A still from that animation is reproduced in figure 30. It is informative that FAA found the curve through Connally's trunk required by physical phenomena that they did not anticipate. Objective physical evidence is always consistent with the truth, often when we least expect it, and even if we can't properly explain it.

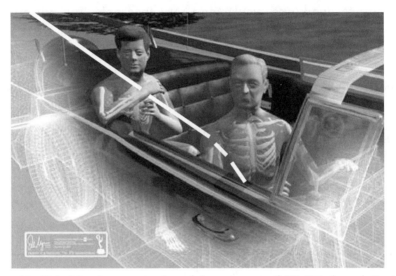

Figure 30. Dale Myers' reconstruction of the trajectory of CE 399 through President Kennedy and Governor Connally. *(© 1995–2004 Dale K. Myers. All Rights Reserved.)*

A summary of the reconstructed velocities of the WCC/MC bullet that injured both men is in Table III. The calculation of these estimates is included in Appendix B.[68] At the time of this shot, the President was about 57 meters (188 feet) from the sniper's nest window of the Texas School Book Depository.

---

68. These differ from the estimates given to the HSCA in 1978, as they were redone for this book. The reader is cautioned that both sets are only rough approximations. The striking yaw and yaw growth of the bullet, exact amount of muscle and bone encountered in Connally's chest, and the models used to calculate the results are all inexact.

Upon exiting President Kennedy's neck, the bullet had a velocity of about 560 meters/second. In the short distance traveled in the air between the two men, it would have lost practically no velocity, so the striking velocity on Connally would have been about the same. By the time it exited the governor's chest, the path through the rib and several inches of soft tissue had slowed the bullet considerably.

The Edgewood Arsenal tests showed that some of the bullets fired through goat ribcages lost about 300 feet/second (91 m/s). The much greater thickness of the Governor's trunk, approximately 25 to 30 cm, and the fact that the bullet was traveling sideways through a good portion of the wound, was calculated to have quadrupled this velocity loss. Thus, the exit velocity from his chest, equaling the striking velocity on his wrist, would have been around 150 meters/second.

Table III.   Probable Velocity and Orientation of CE 399 at Various Points Along Its Trajectory

Muzzle Velocity	At Impact on Kennedy's Neck	At Impact on Connally's Back	Penetrating Connally's Rib	At Impact on Connally's Wrist	At Impact on Connally's Thigh
660 m/s ± 10 m/s	615 m/s ± 10 m/s	560 m/s ± 15 m/s	440–244 m/s ± 30 m/s	150 m/s ± 30 m/s	40 m/s ± 6 m/s
(2160 f/s ± 30 f/s)	(2015 f/s ± 30 f/s)	(1830 f/s ± 50 f/s)	(1450–800 f/s ± 100 f/s)	(500 f/s ± 100 f/s)	(135 f/s ± 20 f/s)
Orientation:	Nose-first	About 60°	Sideways	Nearly Backward	Backward

The side-to-side flattening of CE 399 indicates that the bullet was moving nearly sideways when it grazed the Governor's rib. Reference to Table II indicates that the bullet must have struck the Governor's rib at a velocity of nearly 425 meters/second in order for it to receive the deformation it shows. The rough estimate of the velocity at impact on the Governor's rib (440 m/s) is consistent with this estimate. The impact velocity on the radius bone in his wrist is too low to cause deformation of the jacket of the bullet, but is more than enough velocity to shatter about two centimeters (less than an inch) of radius bone. It is also enough velocity to deform that part of the core of the bullet that was extruded from the base, allowing a few fragments to be scraped off on the bone as it penetrated.

Some conspiracy writers quote Dr. Finck's statement in the Clay Shaw trial to the effect that there is more mass in the wrist fragments than was lost from CE 399. But the fragments recovered from Connally's wrist, which appear significant on x-rays, really contain very little mass. In the words of Dr. Gregory, the surgeon who repaired his wrist, "I would judge that they were…flat, rather thin, and that their greatest dimension would probably not exceed one-eighth of an inch." The thigh fragment, not recovered by Dr. Shires was, he judged, "a very small 1 mm bullet fragment…" Gregory thought at the time that the fragment was embedded in the femur, because it appears in the center of the femur on the anterior x-ray. But the lateral x-ray, particularly the enhanced version produced for the HSCA, shows the fragment to be at the bottom of a very shallow wound. At the speed with which it occurs, the transfer of lead from the bulge at the base of CE 399 onto bone is comparable to applying lipstick. Though the surface area may seem substantial, the coating is very thin and represents very little loss of mass.

Josiah Thompson debunked the too-much-lost-mass myth in his book, *Six Seconds in Dallas* in 1967. He added the estimated and measured weights of the fragments to the weight of CE 399 and found that the sum would fall inside the range of initial weights of bullets from that lot. Biophysics Division's average of WCC/MC bullets was 10.45 grams (161 grains), CE 399 weighed 10.277 grams (158.6 grains). In a paper for the journal *International Surgery,* published in 1968, Dr. John Lattimer and his son Jon describe deforming an WCC/MC bullet to about the extent of CE 399 and slicing off 2.1 grains (136 mg) of the core extruded from the base. They then sliced this 2.1-grain piece of lead into 41 thin slices that matched the description of the smaller fragments in Connally's wrist and thigh. Even the fragment recovered from his wrist, the largest of the three, weighed only 32 milligrams (less than half a grain). This is a typical technique used in making a case for conspiracy. Rely on the Parkland doctors' opinion in the medical examiners' area of expertise, based on incomplete information (wounds they never saw), then rely on the opinion of one of the autopsy team, the Clay Shaw trial testimony of Pierre Finck regarding fragments he never saw, recovered from a patient he never saw. Then employ these relatively uninformed impressions in questioning the judgment of experts who do have first-hand knowledge upon which to base their opinion.

The exit velocity from Connally's wrist, equaling the striking velocity on his thigh, is estimated to have been about 40 meters/second, a velocity barely above that required for skin penetration. The fragment at the bottom of the wound indicated it was moving backward as it penetrated. If the bullet had been turned sideways when it hit his leg, its presented area would have been several times as great, and it might not have penetrated the Governor's thigh at all.

CHAPTER SEVEN

No Signs of Distress

> "From the left at frame 225, this is the first frame
> where we see the President reemerging from behind
> the road sign. His left hand is clutching his lapel, his
> right hand is starting up toward his neck, toward his
> throat. Governor Connally appears to show no signs
> of distress at this point."
>
> —*Robert Groden*[69]

During the Vietnam war, the Army had a team of military specialists, called the Wound Data and Munitions Effectiveness Team, which collected data on those wounded and killed by weapons of all types, including bullets, fragments from exploding grenades and bombs, and nonmilitary weapons, such as "punji sticks." In more than 7,000 cases studied, there are numerous instances of people being wounded by high-velocity missiles and not being aware of it until minutes or hours later. Even when they were immediately aware of being hit, soldiers injured in combat often describe the feeling of an impact of a bullet or fragment as a "tug" on the body part without any associated pain. The pain, sometimes overwhelming, comes later. Scientists (including me) at the former Biophysics Lab have attributed this lack of immediate pain as resulting from the instantaneous stretching of the tissue surrounding the path of the projectile. This could cause minor damage to the pain receptors and nerves and temporarily disable them out to some distance from the path of the projectile, so that no signal gets through to the brain to produce the sensation of pain.[70] Movement of the tissue beyond this numbed region would only feel

---

69. When reviewing the enhanced Zapruder film with the HSCA on the afternoon of the first day of the open hearings, September 6, 1978.

70. The tensile stress on the nerves and receptors might stimulate an impulse that would travel up the nerve as a single spike, but it would not *(continued on next page)*

like the "tug," as the tissue distortion at that location would not exceed the pain threshold of the intrinsic receptors. Dr. Michael Carey,[71] a military neurosurgeon in Vietnam and the first Gulf War, observed a similar phenomenon in soldiers with traumatic amputations.

If the President and Governor were hit with the same bullet, the apparent delay in the Governor's reaction to being shot must be considered. Mr. Connally was not thrown into the back of the car seat in front of him by the force of the bullet (see next chapter), so we cannot use that event to determine when he was shot. The claim that "immediate excruciating pain" would make it impossible for the governor not to have known he was wounded for the better part of a second is contradicted by Connally's own testimony. He first felt pain in his chest after arriving at Parkland Hospital and was not aware that he had wounds in his wrist and thigh until he woke up the next morning.

Both Robert Groden and the House Photographic Panel observed, in the Zapruder film, that frames in the late 230s, the governor's cheeks puff just before he begins to speak, about frame 240. This is nearly a second after they see a reaction in the President. In his sworn testimony, the governor said that when he turned back from looking over his right shoulder, he felt a blow between his shoulder blades and noticed his chest was "drenched with blood." He shouted out, "No, no, no,"[72] then "My God, they're going to kill us all." After speaking, he "straightened"—then slumped.

As the bullet exited from his chest, it would not have taken enough blood with it to drench his shirt. Blood does not pool under the skin in anticipation of a bullet about to exit there. The bullet would only have taken a small amount of tissue with it, along with the normal amount of blood within that tissue at the time (see the exit spray from the skull in figure 33 in the next chapter). This would produce a small spot of tissue and blood on his shirt surrounding the bullet hole. Unlike the passage

---

(continued from previous page) elicit a pain response. Accidental discharges occur frequently among the body's millions of sensory nerves, so the brain's pain center requires the redundancy of a series of such impulses from the high-threshold receptors before taking it seriously.

71. After Vietnam, Dr. Carey became Professor of Neurosurgery at the Louisiana State University Health Sciences Center in New Orleans, LA, with a return to active military duty during the Gulf War.

72. In his testimony before the House Committee, Mr. Connally was a bit equivocal about when he said "No, no, no!" The Photo Panel's conclusion from their study of the Zapruder film was that it was after he was shot. Modern enhancements show that he first shouted before being shot.

of a bullet, the body's reactions cannot be considered instantaneous, nor even simultaneous. If a blood vessel is severed, the blood will not immediately drain from the body. It took a heartbeat or two to pump enough blood from the severed vessels in his chest wall to drench Connally's shirt before he realized he was hit. Even though his heart rate probably increased as soon as he heard the first rifle shot, a couple of heartbeats would still take a second or more. The governor said the impact of the bullet "knocked" him over, but the Zapruder film shows that he didn't go over until his wife pulled him into her lap.

Another study of the film was done for the HSCA by Francis Corbett and colleagues at the Itek Corporation of Lexington, Massachusetts. One of the conclusions in their report, on file in the National Archives, is "Governor Connally begins a rapid and seemingly involuntary change in physical appearance at about Zapruder frame 225. Part of this change (hand and arm movement) is similar to President Kennedy's voluntary reaction (hand and arm movement) to a wound, which reaction is first observable at frame 224. Governor Connally's hand movement lags President Kennedy's by about two frames or about 1/9th of a second."[73]

This movement, however, was not similar to the dramatic reaction of the President. Critics have said that people move their hands all the time. There is no way of determining that this was not a voluntary movement. Like FAA's 'lapel flip' that could have been caused by a gust of wind, we have to put this movement in the context of all other evidence to see if it fits.

Some critics have said that Connally could not have shouted after he was shot because, with a collapsed lung, one cannot shout and can barely breathe. This assertion assumes an instantaneously collapsed lung. Just as it takes time for a substantial fraction of a person's blood supply to be pumped out, it also takes a finite time for the air to flow out of a punctured lung. The deflation of a lung, causing it to collapse, takes time—probably a few minutes in Connally's case.

If the lung and body wall are punctured, leaving holes enough to leak air, a sequence of events is started that leads to the collapse of the lung on that side. The action of the respiratory system to pump the air out of the punctured lung has different effects in the two phases of a

---

73. I believe they meant "President Kennedy's involuntary reaction," as this is the beginning of his awkward, elbows-raised posture.

single breath. In the inspiration phase—to breathe in—a person's chest muscles either hold the chest rigid or pull it into a slightly expanded volume while the main power to pull air in is provided by the diaphragm. The diaphragm is a large dome-shaped sheet of muscle that separates the pleural space (containing the lungs) from the contents of the abdomen. To pull air in, the diaphragm tenses and flattens, pushing the abdominal contents down while at the same time opening up the volume of the chest. This lowers the pressure inside the lung, creating a partial vacuum. We speak of this action as "pulling" the air in, but in reality the presence of the partial vacuum allows the normal atmospheric pressure to "push" the air in. In this phase, if there is a hole through the chest wall, air flows through the hole into the pleural cavity between the chest wall and the lung, rather than (or, perhaps, in addition to) through the normal airway into the lung itself.

Dr. Shaw stated that the governor's lung was lacerated down to the major airway by the secondary missiles of bone from his shattered rib. As in this case, if there is a hole in the lung that communicates to its outer surface, some inspired air is also diverted through that hole into the space between the body wall and lung at the same time. There is a slight elasticity to the substance of the lung that causes it to have a resistance to being inflated, like a "weak" toy balloon. Air is not pushed into the pleural cavity containing the other lung, as the two lungs are contained in two different cavities on opposite sides of the chest.

As the lung collapses, the body signals that it is not getting enough oxygen. To compensate, a strong inspiration cycle is triggered. The chest heaves and the diaphragm pulls down in an unusually strong contraction that normally would result in fully inflated lungs. The air in the side of the collapsed lung is at atmospheric pressure, but the heaving chest and diaphragm create an unusually strong partial vacuum on the other side. The pressure difference pushes the mediastinum, the compartment that separates the two pleural cavities, toward the uncollapsed side. The mediastinum contains the heart, which is attached at the top to the aorta, Vena Cava, and the pulmonary artery and vein, the body's largest blood vessels. The mediastinal shift has two serious consequences. It compresses the uncollapsed lung, cutting the respiratory capacity even further, and it bends the major vessels, partially occluding them (like a bent garden hose) and reducing the flow of blood to and from the body and lungs.

This combination can be fatal in a matter of minutes.

The governor describes what he assumes is the bullet knocking him over as: "At the time I was hit, strangely enough, I felt no sharp pain. It was as if someone had come up behind me with a doubled up fist and just hit me in the back right between the shoulder blades." But the bullet entered outside his right shoulder blade, nearly under his armpit. It is likely that the "blow" he felt in the center of his back was the shifting of his rib as ten centimeters of it were being fragmented by the impact of the bullet. The rib articulates with the spinal column "right between the shoulder blades." The force that would shatter the rib and send shards slicing into the lung would have been transmitted down its shaft to feel like a blow to his spine, obviously not hard enough to be painful, but enough to be felt. In another few minutes, the Governor collapsed and lost consciousness from lack of oxygen and diminished blood supply. These injuries could have been lethal had he not received emergency medical treatment to reinflate his lung and restore his circulation to normal a short time later at Parkland Memorial.

Mrs. Connally testifies that she heard three shots. After the first, she said she turned and saw President Kennedy clutch his neck with both hands. At the sound of a second shot, she saw her husband "recoil" and slump. But the HSCA's photography panel concluded that it was the first shot that missed the limousine. They see governor Connally turning to look over his right shoulder, just as he said he did, in reaction to the first shot. In addition, Dr. Hartmann's jiggle analysis shows a smear consistent with that earlier shot. The Photographic Panel determined from the Zapruder film that Mrs. Connally did not turn to see the President until after the second shot, an observation confirmed by many, including Dale Myers, and one that the reader can see for himself in one of the better copies of the Zapruder film available on CD or DVD. The "reaction" she saw in her husband was probably the "straightening" he described and the "opening the mouth...and puffing of the cheeks" reaction described by Groden as he and the HSCA viewed the enhanced film.

Dr. Charles Gregory, one of the surgeons attending to Connally at Parkland, described the reaction in an interview with Gerald Posner as the bullet's compressing the chest, producing an involuntary expulsion of air as much as a half a second after the shot. This is insightful medical speculation, but poor physics. First of all, the impact of the bullet would not compress the chest. The major force was tangential, not lateral, and would have lasted too short a time to move the chest wall in either case. The temporary cavity that forms after the projectile penetrates solid tissue does not form as well in the air-filled lung, as the air is compressible. Secondly, if the force from the fragments of bone that became secondary missiles and lacerated the lung had combined with the small temporary cavity to produce an involuntary expulsion of air, it would have been within a time much shorter than half a second. It does not take half a second to blow out a candle, and that's a voluntary motion with all the neural delays in the loop. The action that the above descriptions probably allude to, perhaps a second or two after he was hit, may have been a strong inspiration that followed the decreased oxygen transfer from his injured right lung.

The slight misalignment in Mrs. Connally's memory of the sequence of sounds and sights probably resulted from attempting to reconcile the difference in times she observed in the reaction of the two men. She knew that the President was hit when she saw him raise his arms up to his throat, but she did not know that her husband was hit until she saw his "reaction" the better part of a second later. She was likely thinking that he would have to react immediately to a serious chest wound, so she automatically associated the reaction with a separate shot. The sights, sounds, and sensations of the third and final shot were unmistakable, so she associated the other memories with the first two shots.

John Connally, on the other hand, was always quite clear in his testimony. There were several seconds between the first and second shots and he was certain that he was not hit by the first.[74] Careful examination of the enhanced Zapruder film proves that he was right all along. He was not sure why he didn't hear the second shot. There certainly isn't any physical or physiological reason for it. The purported "shock" of being hit by a supersonic bullet has no basis in fact and was long ago discredited by the international wound ballistics community, though the myth is

---

74. Critics claim that Connally insists that he and the President were hit by "different" shots. But there is no way he could have known which shot hit Kennedy. As the Zapruder film confirms, he only managed to turn around far enough to bring the President into his line of sight after he was wounded by the second shot. His wife insisted that Kennedy was hit by the first bullet and he was too much of a gentleman to flatly contradict her. Nevertheless, he did support the WC conclusions and ignored the implied contradiction with his wife's opinion. What he consistently did claim was that he was hit by the second shot.

still repeated in trauma journals and "gun lore" publications. Dr. Charles Baxter, who, with Dr. Malcolm Perry, performed the tracheotomy on the President spoke of the rifle bullet in his WC testimony, "…first its speed would create a shock wave which would damage a larger number of tissues." A bullet cannot produce a shock wave as it penetrates tissue, like the shock wave in air shown in figure 13. Though the bullet is supersonic in air, it is not supersonic in tissue, where the speed of sound is nearly 1500 meters per second (5,000 feet per second—higher than the fastest rifle bullets).[75] The auditory nerve and the rest of the hearing mechanism in the brain cannot be damaged by a bullet except for the one that strikes it or passes nearby. But if a bullet passes through the head near the auditory nerve, there is a more profound reason that the victim does not hear it.

The governor's testimony seems to indicate that he thought the reason was expressed by the old WW II story that "you never hear the bullet that kills you." There is some truth to this claim. A bullet reaches the person before he could hear its shock wave, so if the victim is instantly killed, he could not hear the bullet or the report of the weapon. Mr. Connally heard the supersonic 'crack' of the first bullet that missed, but the shock wave of the second was cut off when it hit the President, so it only reached him by going around the President's neck, becoming greatly muffled in the process. By the time it reached Connally, the "thump" of the rifle wasn't nearly as loud as the sound of the first bullet and the weapon noise arrived about one fifth of a second after the bullet did. That sound reached him just before he observed that he was "drenched with blood." Perhaps the sound had not yet registered in his memory when the much more urgent and disturbing realization that he was fatally wounded (so he thought) simply dominated both his immediate attention and his memory of the event.

Some still claim that the governor could not have held his hat after the injury to his wrist. But he did not know he was not supposed to be holding his hat, since he did not know his wrist was injured until the next day. Although the radius was shattered, the other bone in his forearm, the ulna, was intact, stabilizing his wrist and hand. All the tendons, muscles, and motor nerves that powered his fingers and thumb were also undamaged. It is sometimes claimed that there was an injury to

---

75. A small shock wave is created at impact, but it passes harmlessly through the tissues at a velocity of about 1500 meters per second, well ahead of the bullet.

the radial nerve, but it was actually to a small branch of the radial nerve, well below the muscles of the forearm, which could not have affected his grip. That nerve is sensory only, not affecting any movement. The one severed tendon would only have disabled the abduction of his hand at the wrist (lateral movement of the hand in the direction of the thumb). The smashing of the radius disabled the rotation of his forearm, a loss he never completely regained. Physically, however, he was as capable of gripping a hat immediately after the injury as he was before the shot. The bullet's passing through his wrist would not have moved his wrist and hand enough to dislodge his hat.

The enhanced Zapruder film shows a "flutter" in Connally's hat immediately after his suit coat momentarily puffed out. The time span is just about the time it would take for the small amount of momentum the bullet deposited in his arm to have pushed his arm down and his stretch reflex to have prompted his muscles to return his arm, overshooting its original position and waving his hat in the air. This could happen without the governor's being aware of it and, by his own testimony, it did. Actually, the discussion is moot, as pictures show him holding his hat while Mrs. Connally was pulling him down into her lap. This is well after the time when even the multiple-bullet advocates recognize indications in the Zapruder film that Governor Connally knew he was hit.

The governor was not the only witness whose testimony is consistent with the first shot being earlier than the one that hit the President in the back at the base of his neck. In his notes, handwritten on the plane ride back to Washington and later given to the Warren Commission, Secret Service Agent Glenn Bennett states, "At this point I heard a noise that…reminded me of a firecracker. I immediately…looked at the Boss's Car. At this exact time I saw a shot that hit the Boss about 4 inches down from the right shoulder; a second shoot [sic] followed immediately and hit the right rear high of the Boss's head."

But why did the President react more quickly than the governor did to that shot that hit them both? Even if the delay was only one ninth of a second, as suggested by Itek, it is nonetheless significant (and may well have been longer than their estimate, though shorter than the delay usually seen by the conspiracy theorist). The clue to the difference is in the way Kennedy responds. Many have noted that the movement that Mrs. Connally described as the President's clutching his throat is not a clutching at all. In the Zapruder movie, and other movies and still pictures, his hands are not shown grasping his throat, they are clinched into fists that are nearly touching his chin, and his forearms are elevated to a nearly horizontal position. This does not resemble the classic 'choking' position seen in posters illustrating the Heimlich maneuver. In the more 'natural' position, the upper arms are near the chest, the forearms are more nearly vertical than horizontal and the hands are overlapping, grasping the throat.

The autopsy photographs and x-rays prompted the HSCA Pathology Panel to conclude that the first shot to hit the President struck at the base of his neck, to the right of the last, or seventh cervical vertebra (C-7) near the upturned transverse spine of the first thoracic vertebra (T-1). The bullet then passed close by the body of C-7 and exited through the right side of the trachea just below the larynx. The straight-line path between the entry wound and the exit wound in the suprasternal notch is diagrammed in figure 31.

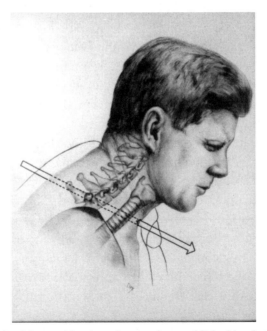

Figure 31.   Track of the president's neck wound as established by the House Forensic Pathology Panel. *(National Archives)*

The seventh cervical nerve emerges from an intervertebral space (called a foramen) between C-6 and C-7 and the eighth cervical nerve between C-7 and T-1. The path of the spinal nerves may be traced through the brachial plexus, a complex tangle of nerves on each side of the upper back where the spinal nerves are resorted into major nerve trunks that supply the arms and upper trunk. A careful tracing of the individual fibers shows that the control of the deltoid muscle of the upper shoulder and the biceps and brachialis anterior muscles in the arm comes through higher nerves, the fifth and sixth cervical nerves. These muscles raise the arm, bend the elbow, and flex the fingers. The pectorals, the muscles of the chest that pull the arm forward, also derive from the same cervical nerve roots. The nerves that control the triceps, the muscles at the back of the arm that straighten the arm at the elbow, as well as the muscles that straighten the fingers, originate from the two cervical nerves closest to the bullet's path, the seventh and eighth. These two nerve roots also provide the primary input to the latissimus dorsi, the muscle below the shoulder that would normally lower the arm and, if the pectorals are relaxed, pull it backward

If a person sustains damage to the spinal cord at C-7, the seventh and eighth cervical nerve and everything below will be disabled. This would disrupt the signal to the muscles below the shoulder and back of the arm. With these muscles disabled, the normal muscle tonus of the deltoid, biceps, and flexors of the forearm would be unopposed. The arm would then be pulled up and slightly forward and bent at the elbow. The fingers would be flexed into a loose fist. Without neural control over the affected muscles, the person has no ability to straighten his arm or fingers or lower his arm. With long-term spinal injury, the arms will stay in this position until the unopposed muscles are relaxed. This malady is known as Thorburn's position. A similar posturing could be caused by minimal, transient damage to the spinal cord at that level. The posture was obviously not caused by damage to just the two nerve roots on the right, as the bullet passed between them. The injury affected both arms. Only spinal damage at this level would have caused the left arm to duplicate the posture of the right.

As a bullet penetrates the body, it pushes the tissue away from its path like a ship plowing through water. A similar effect is shown in the sequence of pictures in figure 32. These are frames from a high-speed movie of a bullet penetrating a block of gelatin tissue simulant. A high radial velocity (outward from the path of the bullet) is imparted to the gelatin. This radial motion continues to carry the tissue outward long after the bullet has passed, creating the cavity that is shown on the film as a dark shadow. A similar cavity[76] is formed when a bullet penetrates a human body (or any other animal tissue, live or dead). As the tissue is incompressible, the radial movement pushes out the surface of the body in synchrony with the growth of the temporary cavity. Outward motion continues until the elasticity of the tissue absorbs all the radial kinetic energy, then the elastic tissue snaps back, collapsing the temporary cavity.

Figure 32. Temporary cavity from a high-speed movie of a 5.56 mm M193 military bullet penetrating gelatin tissue simulant. *(Biophysics Division, EA)*

The tissue set in motion by the bullet can exert enormous pressure. When it pushes against a rigid bone, however, the bone resists bending. Three things can happen: the whole bone can be displaced, the bone will break, or the soft tissue will be compressed against the bone and damaged by the resulting shear stress. When the moving soft tissue pushed against the President's spinal column, it encountered considerable resistance, as the vertebrae are all tied together with strong ligaments that

---

76. This cavity, referred to as a "temporary cavity" is not filled with air; it is a partial vacuum. After the cavity opens, air will immediately begin to move into the vacuous cavity, carrying with it anything dislodged by the impact of the bullet, such as bits of clothing, dirt, or buttons. This explains the presence of such contaminants deep in the wounds. Contrary to what is often found in combat and civilian medical literature, such objects are not "carried into the wound" by the bullet. It is moving too fast. These objects would be penetrated or pushed aside by the bullet, just like the gelatin, flesh, or bone is. Before the air has had time to completely fill it (in milliseconds), the cavity will collapse under the forces of atmospheric pressure and the elasticity of the tissue. Most of the air will be driven back out in the collapse, but some of the heavier materials may have too much inertia to reverse their course in that short span of time, so they will be trapped inside. Dr. Carl Herget, a past Chief of the Biophysics Lab at Edgewood Arsenal, used to like to entertain visiting VIPs with a high speed movie of a .30 cal. bullet penetrating a gelatin block. As the shutter opens, a fly is seen sitting on the face of the block adjacent to the aim point of the bullet. When the bullet penetrates and the vacuous cavity fills with air, the fly is sucked into the cavity. As the cavity collapses, the fly is blown back out—apparently none the worse for the experience.

prevent one vertebra from moving relative to its neighbor. The result is that the spine was undamaged, compressing the soft tissue against it. The pressure was transmitted through the openings from which the spinal nerves and blood vessels emerge (the intervertebral foramina). This pressure inside the spinal canal may have actually been amplified by the conical shape of the foramina, like the pressure of sound waves is amplified at the eardrum.

The Thorburn-like posture can only be caused by damage to the spinal column at this level. After this injury, the President would be unable to resist raising his arms into that awkward position.[77] If the bullet had taken any other path than that shown in the autopsy photographs, the President would not have assumed this particular involuntary posture.

Movement caused by the sudden interruption of the signal from the spinal nerves below the cord injury would have appeared much faster than a startle reflex, probably even faster than a spinal reflex, like jerking one's hand from a hot stove. In a spinal reflex, a nerve impulse travels from the hand to the spine and back down to the muscles without having to go through the brain. This typically takes less than one-quarter of a second, or about four frames in the Zapruder film. In a direct reaction to a spinal injury, the uninterrupted impulse only has to make the 'outward' path to initiate the movement of the arm. This would probably take little more than half the time of a spinal reflex.[78] Connally had no such direct disruption of his nervous system. His reaction, though equally involuntary, was entirely the result of sensory input to his spinal cord. Thus, the President's response to that shot precedes the governor's by a time equivalent to a few frames of Zapruder's movie.

---

77. Gerald Posner has been criticized for employing the term "Thorburn's position," slightly erroneously, to describe the phenomenon. Contrary to critics' claims, Posner's several minor errors do not detract significantly from the truth of this observation or others that he makes.

78. One-eighth of a second, or less, is about two frames of the Zapruder film.

CHAPTER EIGHT

The Laws of Physics Vacated

> "…the laws of physics vacated in this instance, for the President did not fall forward."
>
> —*Mark Lane*[79]

Back in Vaudeville days, when stage magicians weren't as sophisticated as they are today, one of their favorite tricks was to set up a dinner table on the stage, complete with tablecloth, dishes and cutlery. After this elaborate preparation, the magician would suddenly whip the tablecloth from under the table full of dishes, leaving everything in place. The only evidence that the tablecloth had disappeared was a slight rattling of spoons and teacups. The stage magician takes advantage of the fact that he can move the cloth fast enough that the coefficient of friction is low and little momentum is transferred to the dishes. The small amount of momentum is quickly transferred to the table by friction.

Bullets that throw people backward—preferably in slow motion through a plate glass window—are a popular Hollywood cinematographer's fiction. It looks believable, because anything that can blow a hole through a person would seem capable of bowling them over as well. The actual effect of the penetrating bullet resembles the tablecloth trick. The momentum of the bullet is so small that its contribution to the motion of a target as massive as a human body is negligible. The reality goes against our intuition because the velocities involved are entirely out of the range of our visual experience. One cannot "watch" a bullet penetrate a target. Even the Zapruder film, with a framing rate that produces no visible flicker to human vision, missed the passage of the bullet. If the bullet struck while his camera's shutter was closed between frames and the film was advancing to the next stop, the bullet would have penetrated the President's skull, fragmented, and exited in pieces—two of which struck the

---

79. *Rush to Judgment* page 45.

windshield and windshield trim, and come to rest on the floor of the limousine before the shutter opened again.[80]

Dr. Crenshaw repeats a common myth that the Zapruder film shows "the President's head and upper body being thrown toward the rear of the limousine at a speed estimated at 80 to 100 feet per second. This violent movement is consistent with a shot from the wooden fence to his right front—not the Book Depository—to his right rear." Of all the conspiracy writers, only Hugh McDonald, a retired law enforcement officer with a background in military intelligence, indicates that he understands the physics involved. In *Appointment in Dallas* (page 183), he says, "A high velocity rifle bullet penetrates with such speed that there would not necessarily be movement in any direction." The writers that use the device of the President being "thrown violently" into the back seat by a bullet to the head are seemingly unconcerned that the bullet that passed through the President's neck and through the governor's thorax did not produce any visible motion in either man.[81]

The autopsy photos and x-rays confirm the autopsy statement that only one shot hit the President's head. It created only one track through the brain. It entered the back of the head, just to the right of center, and exited the upper right front (see chapter ten). The momentum deposited by this bullet contributed to the small forward movement of the President's head, which may be seen between frame 312 and 313 in the enhanced Zapruder film.[82]

Up to now, I have used the word 'momentum' without being very specific about what it means. Now we need to be a little more specific.

---

80. Actually, we cannot be sure that all this did not take place while the shutter was still open on frame 312. The bullet would have passed across the field of view so fast that it could not have registered on the film. President Kennedy had a thick head of hair that would have concealed the early stages of skull fracture, so it probably took a few hundredths of a second for the effects to become visible. The shutter would have closed in that amount of time.

81. Some writers appeal to "Newton's Laws of Physics" without actually having the slightest idea what they mean. Others do not have that excuse. It is inconceivable that those who understand the law of conservation of momentum would not have done the math, if only to satisfy their own curiosity about the magnitude of the velocity one should expect.

82. In his article, Professor Alvarez pointed out the fact that the limousine was decelerating at that time. Other occupants of the car also show forward movement between those two frames, though not quite as much as the President. The Itek study for the HSCA concluded that JFK's head moved about 2.3 inches between frames 312 - 313. This is a mean velocity of about 3.5 feet per second (1 m/s), only part of which can be attributed to the deceleration of the car.

Momentum is the product of mass (grams or kilograms, for instance) and velocity (meters/second), usually abbreviated as MV. Compare an automobile and a freight train, both moving at the same velocity. The freight train is thousands of times more massive than the auto, so it has thousands of times the momentum. MV is a vector, meaning it has direction, the same direction as the velocity part of the product. If two billiard balls are moving in opposite direction at the same speed, the resulting momentum vectors are not equal. Pick one to be the positive vector and the other would be a negative vector. Assume the two balls were made of putty, so that they would not bounce off each other, but instead stick together. In a direct impact, these two vectors in opposite directions would cancel each other. The resulting single blob of putty would have no motion at all.

Energy, on the other hand, is not restricted to motion and is not a vector. The energy of motion is called kinetic energy, but some forms of energy (chemical energy, for instance) have no motion and, therefore, no direction associated with them. (A quantity without an associated direction is referred to as a scalar.) When it penetrates a target, the kinetic energy of a bullet is nearly all converted into other forms of energy. After the impact, the kinetic energy contained in the target and the bullet is not equal to the kinetic energy of the bullet just before impact; it usually is only a small fraction of that original energy, the bulk having been converted to damage and elastic potential, with a small amount of heat caused by the friction. The energy stored as elastic potential (stretching of the soft tissue) is also quickly converted to heat. What we are most concerned with is the kinetic energy that is converted to tissue damage.

The bullet contains a large amount of energy because of its high velocity, but its momentum is small because of its very small mass, compared to the mass of a person, or even a human head. The liberated kinetic energy may do a lot of damage, but results in very little movement to the body. Appendix D contains the calculations of momentum that would have been deposited in the President's head by the passage of the bullet. The resulting motion of his head would result in a velocity of less than a meter per second (two to three feet/second). The momentum of the bullet fragments and Kennedy's head after the impact would have to equal the momentum of the bullet before impact. By the time the momentum was transferred from his head to Kennedy's 77-kilogram

(170-pound) body, he would have had a velocity of about a centimeter/second (two inches/second). One gets a larger dose of momentum when jostled in a crowd. The calculations show that no bullet of reasonable size can possibly throw a person in any direction. So, if the laws of physics prove that a bullet could not have "thrown" him, why did he move backward into the car seat just after the shot that killed him?

Louis Alvarez' *American Journal of Physics* article presents one possible explanation. In his introduction, he supports the Warren Commission conclusion that the backward movement could not have been caused by the momentum deposited by a bullet (he did the calculations). His explanation for the backward motion of Kennedy was a "jet" or "rocket" effect of the material ejected from Kennedy's head by the final shot. Conspiracy writer Carl Oglesby ignores the bullet momentum comment and rejects the Alvarez' jet effect theory with the statement, "This novel explanation suffers unfairly from the painfulness of explaining it, but its main problem is that the technical premise has never been demonstrated outside its creator's backyard." One wonders if his rejection is because it is too "painful" or because he just did not understand it. In either case, we cannot dismiss the argument merely because it is complex or because Alvarez' did not demonstrate it in a human subject.

There are situations in which the jet effect produces a great deal of movement. The best example is a modern aircraft. The jet engine forces a very large mass of gas rearward at very high velocity. This produces an equal force in the opposite direction that pushes the aircraft forward (the correct expression of Newton's third law). The question is: Did the gunshot produce enough force in expelling the material from Kennedy's head to throw his body backward into the limousine? Based on the high-speed movies of the skull shot simulations at the Biophysics Laboratory (see chapter two), the answer is no. Recall that the skulls were dried human skulls that were rehydrated and filled with gelatin gel to simulate natural contents.

Figure 33 shows a sequence of views of one of the Biophysics Division skull shots that the HSCA saw as a movie during the Sturdivan testimony in 1978. The bullet has already exited as the series begins. This movie was taken at a framing rate of 4,000 frames/second, over 200 times faster than the Zapruder film. While it is more dramatic when seen as a movie, the series of still shots are adequate to show that the skull

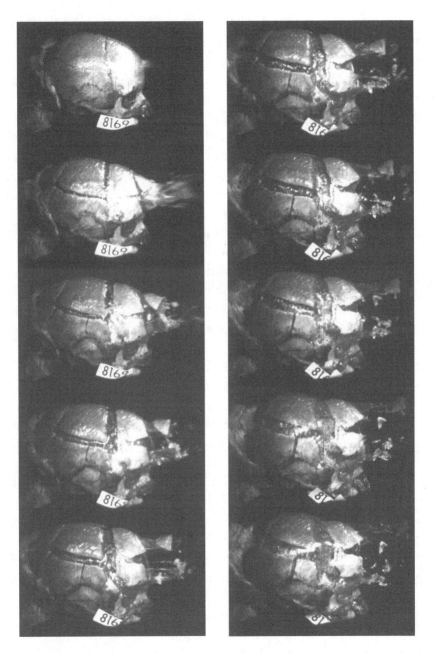

Figure 33. Sequence from the high-speed movie of one of the Biophysics Division skull Shots, using the Oswald Rifle. *(Biophysics Division, EA)*

does, indeed, produce a jet of gelatin and bone fragments from the front of the skull as the bullet exits and more afterward as the skull explodes from the internal pressure caused by the bullet.

In these films, the skull jumps up from the table, moves forward at approximately 3 feet/second (90 cm/s), just as it must from the momentum deposited by the bullet, and rotates slowly to the left, due to the subsequent explosion of the skull that sends fragments of gelatin and bone off to the right. Again the sum of all the momentum, that of bullet fragments, skull, and expelled bone fragments and gelatin, must equal the momentum of the bullet before impact. When the skulls fall back to the table in the movies, the direction that they go is determined by how the irregular skulls impact when they hit the table. Those that rolled off the table did so in different random directions. The major movement was the skull jumping into the air, as the force of the bullet expanded and shattered the skull, causing it to push hard against the table.

Dr. Ken Rahn has used the position of the back of Kennedy's head as plotted in Josiah Thompson's book to calculate the velocity and acceleration of the head after the explosion at Zapruder frame 313. Kennedy's head is accelerated rapidly forward (the momentum of the bullet), then rapidly backward, nearly to its original position. The motion is far too soon to be a neuromuscular response. It had to be from the physics. Dr. John Lattimer conducted some skull shots that resembled the Biophysics Division's simulations, but for which the skulls were filled with animal brain tissue. In his shots, all skulls fell back from the table in the direction of the shooter. Evidently, the lack of a jet effect from the stiff gelatin in the Biophysics Lab's simulation was a bit misleading and there was enough of a jet effect to move Kennedy's head back after its forward surge. The momentum of that return 'head snap,' however was not sufficient to move the President's torso backward into the seat of the car. This whole-body motion is shown in the longer backward movement in Thompson's plot. The jet effect, though real, is not enough to throw the President's body into the back of the car.[83]

The true cause of the backward movement was shown to the HSCA a bit later in the same movie. Archival film clips, taken by the Army in 1948, show two goats being shot to prove that the penetration of a

---

83. The entire article may be found on Dr. Rahn's web site, at the address given in the Individual Reference section of the bibliography.

bullet did not produce movement of the goat's entire body.[84] Each goat was deeply anaesthetized (all reflexes, including the 'eye blink' caused by touching the eyeball, were suppressed). They were then suspended in a sling from a metal rack so that it could swing freely. The first goat was shot through the skull by a .30 caliber military bullet. The results are shown in the sequence of pictures in figure 34. This sequence was taken at a framing rate of about 2,400 pictures/second, over 100 times faster than the Zapruder film. About one-tenth of a second after the shot, the goat goes into what one Biophysics Lab colleague, Bob Clare, described as a 'swan dive,' which results in his leaping out of the back part of the sling. His back arches, his head is thrown up and back, and his legs straighten and stiffen for an instant before he collapses back into his previous flaccid state, dangling from the front portion of the sling. The second goat was electrocuted just before being shot. This goat showed no visible movement, even though the movie continued for some time after the shot. The only way to determine the frame in which the shot occurred is by a small puff of hair as the bullet exited the skull.

The explanation for the mechanical disruption of nerves was given in the last chapter. But inside the skull, the motion of the tissue is a bit more complicated. If the brain were free to move like the gelatin in figure 32, it too would develop a large temporary cavity. The brain, however, is enclosed in a rigid container—the skull—so instead of moving outward, away from the bullet, the substance of the brain is forced to flow around the interior of the skull, creating only a very small temporary cavity that closes rapidly behind the bullet. The substance of the brain is relatively free to slide over the inner surface of the skull except at points where it is connected by blood vessels, fibrous sheaths that run between certain lobes, and the emerging nerves. One of the places where the brain is most solidly anchored is at its attachment to the spinal cord.

The spinal cord is the brain's major nervous link to the rest of the body, receiving messages from heat, cold, pain, and position sensors and

---

84. An earlier demonstration that proved that Newton's law of conservation of momentum also applied to human bodies was carried out circa 1916-1918. War stories, derived from WW I experiences, related that the .45 caliber handgun, introduced in 1914, had the ability to knock a charging Moro warrior over backward. This assertion was checked by shooting .45 bullets into cadavers suspended by ropes from the rafters. The cadavers showed no perceptible movement. It is likely that this gory experiment has been repeated, in different forms, ever since the invention of firearms in the Middle Ages.

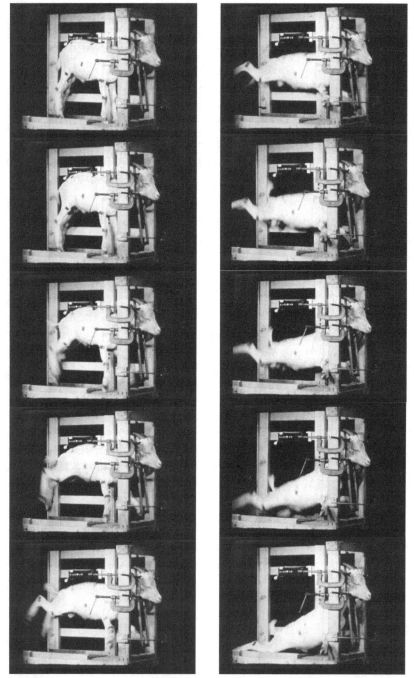

Figure 34. Sequence from a high-speed movie of a shot to the head of an anesthetized goat, showing an intense neuromuscular spasm similar to the
president's. *(Biophysics Division, EA)*

sending messages that move muscles, time the heart beat, stimulate secretions from glands, and a myriad of other physical and physiological controls. The cord descends from the bottom of the brain through a hole in the skull called the Foramen Magnum to travel the length of the spine through the spinal canal down to the lumbar region. Beyond that, a bundle of nerves, called the Cauda Equina, runs through the remaining spinal canal. The spinal canal passes through the hard bone at the center of each vertebra in the vertebral column and forms a protective path just a bit larger than the cord. Between the vertebrae, the cord sends pairs of spinal nerves off each side that form the connection with the rest of the body. The enervation of muscles of the upper arm and shoulder was discussed earlier. A similar function attends every pair of spinal nerves. The cord and nerves that arise from it are the stimulus of all the body's movement.

Ordinarily, a nerve impulse is stimulated in one nerve fiber by the chemical release from another fiber across a junction called a synapse. The impulse then travels along the nerve fiber to the center of the cell where it is routed out to one or more synapses with other nerve fiber endplates, muscle fiber junctions, and such. The impulse is a form of electrical discharge that travels rapidly along the nerve fiber as a wave. After an impulse passes down a nerve, the nerve cell quickly pumps ions across the cellular membrane to reestablish electrical charges of opposite polarity inside and outside the cell membrane. This primes the nerve for the next impulse. When a nerve's cell wall is damaged, by stretching for instance, the damaged area can lose its ability to hold the electrical charge. This can initiate a depolarization wave that travels down the nerve just like the ordinary nerve impulse.

Where the cord descends into the Foramen Magnum, the disruption of the brain by the bullet caused a shear strain on the nerves, the fibers that make up the spinal cord. It is as if one grabbed a bundle of fibers emerging from a conduit and attempted to tear it off by pulling one's fist across the top of the conduit. This violent, wrenching motion momentarily stretches every nerve fiber in the cord, "stimulating" them all at once. The distance from the bullet that passed through Kennedy's skull to the Foramen Magnum is larger than the distance from the bullet that passed through his neck to the cervical nerves; but the confinement of the skull prevents the surface from moving outward, limiting the growth of the temporary cavity to that allowed by the elasticity of the bony skull. This forces the contents to quickly fill the space behind the bullet, increasing the shear in the soft tissue. The shear force on the spinal cord was large enough to produce transitory damage, but not enough to break nerve fibers.

When the nerve is connected to a muscle fiber, the arrival of a nerve impulse stimulates the muscle fiber to perform a single 'twitch' that momentarily shortens the fiber. The muscle fiber exists in only two states: relaxed or shortened. After it is stimulated to twitch, it remains shortened for a fraction of a second, then relaxes. By contrast, a steady pull by a muscle requires the brain to send a continuous series of pulses down the bundle of nerve fibers that stimulates fibers throughout the whole muscle. The series of pulses alternates among the individual nerve fibers, so that the stimulation of different muscle fibers is staggered, resulting in a steady force.

When the passing bullet disrupted the brain tissue, the shear force developed at the Foramen Magnum stretched the live goat's spinal cord. The mechanically induced neural impulse descended down nearly every nerve fiber in the cord. Almost every muscle fiber in the body was simultaneously commanded to twitch. For an instant, every muscle in the body pulled with near maximum force. The result was that the more powerful muscles overpowered the weaker ones. The heavy muscles in his back overpowered the smaller abdominal muscles, so the back arched. The heavy, "running" muscles that pull his back legs to the rear overpowered the flexors that bring the legs closer to the body, so the goat's back legs were extended rigidly behind him. This battle was repeated in every pair of opposing muscles in the body, forcing the goat into the "swan dive" position seen in the movie.

The anatomy and the relative strength of the muscles of a man are not very different from the goat. A similar reaction may be seen in the famous Robert Capa picture of a Spanish Loyalist as he is shot in the head during the Spanish Civil War in 1936. This picture, figure 35, gives us a single snapshot of the ongoing event. At the moment this picture was taken, the neuromuscular spasm has already descended down the spine. The nervous impulse reached the neck and arms first, as those are the shortest nerves. The neck and back are arched backward and the arms are shown fully extended and angled slightly backward as the more-powerful triceps and back muscles predominate over the biceps and the muscles of the abdomen and chest. The rifle stayed clutched in his hand as his arm straightened, as the gripping muscles are stronger than those that open the hand. The back is almost fully arched. The unfortunate victim was evidently sitting or squatting with his thighs flexed when shot. The thighs are lagging a bit behind the arms in the process of violent extension that leaves the legs of his pants trailing and lifts him bodily off the ground. His knees remain flexed, the more powerful movement, in spite of the force of his upper legs pushing them toward the ground. The spasm is actually already completed and the muscles have already relaxed. The hand can be seen losing its grip on the rifle, which will be flung outward and backward, continuing the motion that the victim has given it. He will fall in a limp heap to the ground.

Figure 35.   Robert Capa Picture of a Casualty in the Spanish Civil War, 1936.
  (Robert Capa/Magnum Photos)

The results may be seen in the reaction of the President, a bit less clearly because he is partly concealed within the car. Within a tenth of a second of the shot that exploded his skull, the unseen straightening of his thighs and the visible arching of his back throw his upper body violently into the back of the car. The arching of his neck causes him to seem to be looking toward the sky. The strong nerve impulse has unlocked his arms from that peculiar posture and they are extended from his body. The momentary spasm is over before he hits the seat. Some writers deny the existence of the neuromuscular spasm because Kennedy seems to hit the seat "like a rag doll." But a single muscle twitch lasts less than one tenth of a second. By the time Kennedy was in motion from the spasm, it was all over. He hit the seat like a rag doll because that was the last signal most of his muscles ever got from his destroyed brain.

It would seem that we are asking two different bullets to do two quite different things in the President's neck injury and head injury. But this is not the case. The injury to the spinal cord in either instance would cause depolarization and a sudden massive nerve impulse down the length of the affected nerves. It is quite likely that his arms did suffer a momentary spasm from that shot through his neck before they began to rise. The strong nerve impulse down the seventh and eighth cervical nerves would have tended to straighten his arm at the elbow and pull it down to his side. This would have happened while the President was behind the sign in Zapruder's movie. In fact, there is a slight indication of the President's right and left hands moving downward as he emerges from behind the sign between frames 223 and 224 in his movie. This has been pointed out by many observers over the years. The massive head injury stimulated virtually every motor nerve in his body. For most of those nerves, it was the final stimulus.

As Michael Carey has pointed out, the neuromuscular spasm bore a striking resemblance to a momentary "decerebrate posture" (aka "decorticate posture" or "decerebrate rigidity").[85] This posture may be induced by severing the brainstem above the level of the vestibular nuclei, which effectively removes the control of the cerebral cortex over the efferent nerve fibers going directly to the spinal cord from that lower region. The neuromuscular reaction was over in a fraction of a second, as the President's body was limp when he hit the back of the seat. In the Parkland emergency room, the physicians noted that he was making some unsuccessful attempts to breathe (the "agonal respiration" mentioned in their reports). This shows that some signal was still passing down the spine.

There have been 40 years of bickering among researchers, pro- and anti-conspiracy, as to whether the large hole in Kennedy's head was more

---

85. When asked about this possibility in 1978 by the Forensic Pathology Panel, I disagreed, thinking that the decerebrate reaction must last much longer, as it usually does. Dr. Carey points out that if the disruption is momentary; the posture is also. The decerebrate reaction preferentially affects the extensors, which are usually the stronger muscles. This makes momentary decerebrate rigidity virtually indistinguishable from a massive stimulation of all nerves at once. Just which it was—or whether it was a combination of both—is indeterminable.

to the side or back. Groden, Crenshaw, Lifton, and many others go into great detail in bending the Parkland physician's statements to indicate that the gaping hole was in the back of the President's head, "proving" that there was a shot from the front. In addition, many others, including bystanders, physicians at Parkland, the autopsy team, and conspiracy writers, interpreted the hole in the right side of the President's head as an "exit" wound above (and sometimes behind) his ear. Dr. McClelland evidently had this thought in mind when he jumped to the conclusion that there was an entrance wound in the "left temple." No other Parkland physician reported this nonexistent entrance wound and McClelland himself corrected the error in an interview published in the *Journal of the American Medical Association.*

The argument is predicated on the assumption that the injury was an exit. It was not. The reader might already have noted that figure 33 shows what actually happened. The bullet entered the back of the skull and exited in a small spray at the front in the space of one frame of the high-speed movie. Only after the bullet was far down-range did the internal pressure generated by its passage split open the skull and relieve the pressure inside by spewing the contents through the cracks. A similar explosion would have taken place if the bullet had gone through in the opposite direction. The only way to distinguish the direction of travel of the bullet is to examine the cratering effect on the inside of the skull at entrance and on the outside of the skull at exit. Thus, whether the explosion was more to the side or back is completely irrelevant.

Like the simulations at Edgewood Arsenal, the center of the blown-out area of the President's skull was at the midpoint of the trajectory—not at the exit point. The midpoint is the point at which the bullet has fully deformed and is giving up energy at the maximum rate—that is, pushing outward with the maximum force. At its actual point of exit toward the front of his head, the fragmented bullet had lost half its velocity and a small amount of mass (more than three-quarters of its energy). His forehead was not torn open. The pressure inside the skull at the bullet's exit location was not high enough to cause the front portion of the skull and scalp to rupture, but the x-rays do show that throughout the President's skull the individual bony plates were separated at the suture lines and fractured between sutures almost as extensively as those in the simulations. The pieces of bone were only held in place by the skin and connective tissue. A still picture of one of the experimental skulls is shown in figure 36 after the "flaps" were removed, but the gelatin still in place inside the skull. The entry was at the back, near the occiput, and the exit of the bullet was at the front edge of the blown-out area. After this picture was taken, the gelatin was melted away with hot water and the fragments of skull recovered. The fragments of another skull are in figure 37. A comparison of an x-ray of one of the experimental skulls to the President's x-ray is given in figure 38.

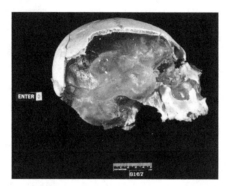

Figure 36. Still photograph of an experimental skull after being struck by the bullet from the Oswald rifle, after loose flaps of bone and gelatin "scalp" were removed. *(Biophysics Division, EA/Dale Myers)*

Figure 37. All fragments of an experimental skull, with the gelatin melted away by hot water. *(Biophysics Division, EA/Dale Myers)*

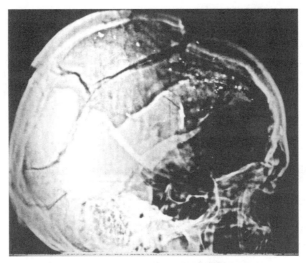

John Kennedy X-ray, lateral view

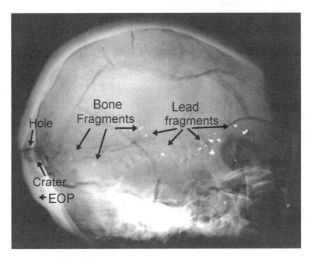

Biophysics Division Test Skull X-ray

Figure 38. X-rays comparing JFK skull (top) to experimental skull. (Note lead fragments deposited after the jacket ruptured.) *(Biophysics Division, EA/Dale Myers & National Archives/John Hunt)*

Some bystanders interpreted the blown-out portion of skull as an entrance wound, evidently interpreting the explosive effect in the skull as a "backsplash" like that of a stone thrown into the water. Bill Newman, standing on the north side of the street, told an FBI interviewer, "...he was hit on the right side of the head." Later he told author Jim Marrs, "...a shot took the right side of his head off. His ear flew off."

(Actually a hinge of skull and scalp covered his ear, creating that illusion.) It may have been this interpretation, as much as the deceptive shock wave from the bullet, which led him to conclude that the shots came from the direction of the grassy knoll behind him. Few people who saw that gaping hole in the President's head were aware that the massive wound was neither entrance nor exit of the projectile. The pathologists on the autopsy team were among them.

At the site of the explosive rupture, the President's scalp and connective tissue were torn along the lines of skull fracture. Some of the pieces were completely torn loose; others clung by a "hinge" of connective tissue and scalp along one edge. In some cases, the skull clung to the hinge and in others it had enough kinetic energy to be torn loose and fly off in the direction of the hinging motion. Pieces of skull flew in many directions, much later than the passage of the bullet and completely independent of the direction the bullet was moving.

It may have been one of these fragments—near the back of the blown-out portion of skull that momentarily hinged toward the rear then tore loose from the scalp—that Mrs. Kennedy was pursuing on the rear deck of the limousine. According to some witnesses, she still had the fragment in her hand when she walked into Parkland Hospital. Mrs. Kennedy, however, did not remember retrieving a skull fragment or, indeed, even climbing onto the trunk of the limousine. The Secret Service found skull fragments in the rear seat of the limousine, however, so even if it was a skull fragment she was pursuing as she climbed out onto the rear deck of the car, it is impossible to say whether she carried it into the emergency room. Memory as well as perception is distorted in times of extreme stress. That is why the memories of well-meaning witnesses to such disasters so often prove to be unreliable.

Groden and Livingston claimed that a "dark" area at the back of Kennedy's head as he hits the seat is an exit wound from a second shot. But a bullet carries very little material with it as it exits. The small exit spray is visible on the laboratory movie in figure 33 because of strong lighting, a close-up view, and (especially) a very high framing rate that captures the rapidly moving spray. Even this high-speed movie, at over 200 times the framing speed of the Zapruder movie, does not freeze the motion. It would take a microsecond exposure, like the spark shadowgraph of figure 13, to do so. Unlike gunshots in the movies, where copious quantities of fake blood and tissue are splashed around by the special effects crew, an exit spray, front or back, could not be visible on the Zapruder movie. It is not an exit spray from the WCC/MC bullet leaving the front of Kennedy's head that is visible in frame 313; it is the spray of blood and brain from the explosion above his ear, an explosion that took place about the time fragments of the bullet were coming to rest inside the car.

Notice that this spray appears to be directed upward and only slightly forward in the movie. If we could see it in three-dimensions, the spray from each tear in the scalp would be seen to be emerging nearly perpendicular to the skull at that point. Since the tears were so extensive, the spray went in all directions, just like the skull fragments did. The dark area that Groden and Livingston see in the Zapruder movie at the back of the President's head is the shadow of Jackie's elbow as she reaches up to grab her husband to pull him into her lap.

The autopsy photographs of the brain show a massive "gutter" wound of the right cerebral hemisphere that leads from the entry wound on the back of the skull to the exit wound at the front edge of the blown-out area of skull. This is in the Dox drawing, copied from that photograph, in figure 39. It is true that there would not be another cratered entry wound in the skull if a second bullet had entered the explosive hole on the right side of the head, as in Dr. Wecht's scenario. But the explosion was lateral to the track of the bullet, not at its point of emergence. Even a plastic or glycerin bullet subsequently entering through that hole would have produced a second wound track through the brain at a large angle to the first; one which is obviously not there in the photographs and could not have been missed by the pathologists, particularly after they removed the brain for a careful examination. A non-metallic bullet is of value only in supporting the existence of a conspiracy—not in establishing an alternate killer—as President Kennedy was already dead the instant the bullet hit the back of his head. Nor would that second bullet have the potential to throw the President into the back of the car.

Frangible[86] and soft-nosed bullets are proposed by some writers who do not believe that the fully-jacketed WCC/MC bullet was capable

---

86. A frangible bullet is one made to rapidly and completely disintegrate on impact with a solid surface, to prevent accidental injury from ricochets or fragments. They are made by suspending metal powder in a polymeric matrix, shaped to the desired bullet configuration. They are used, mainly by the military, as practice rounds to minimize the hazard to nearby personnel. In times past, they were also used in traveling shooting galleries in carnivals and circus side-shows.

of creating the massive explosion of the President's head. Soft-nose and hollow-point bullets expand to create larger wounds than fully-jacketed bullets usually do, but these do not usually shed small fragments. The

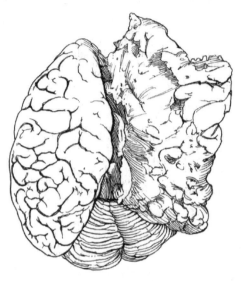

JFK Exhibit F-302

Figure 39.   Dox drawing of brain wound from photograph, showing nearly intact cerebellum and severely injured right cerebrum. Gutter wound extends from tip of occipital lobe to tip of frontal lobe. *(National Archives)*

cores deform, but almost always stay in one piece. If they hit a bone, a large fragment will sometimes break off, but these are not the pinhead-sized pieces of lead seen in the Kennedy x-rays.

Hugh McDonald's "Saul" was a self-confessed assassin who claimed to have shot JFK from a location in the Dal-Tex building, located on the other side of the street from the Book Depository. Saul said he used a "disintegrating type of bullet" that would only disintegrate when it struck bone. This, McDonald says, explains how Saul's first bullet penetrated the President's neck without disintegrating, but created the severe chest injury in Governor Connally's chest when it struck his rib. Saul knew about the bullet's momentum, but evidently did not know about the role of velocity in bullet deformation. A "disintegrating" bullet would have fragmented much worse on impact with the skull than the normal WCC/MC bullet. In this case, the fragments would be much more numerous than shown on the President's x-rays and they would be clustered around the entry point. The x-ray of the President's head taken before the brain was removed was shown in figure 38. Lead fragments are scattered within the skull, reaching to the frontal bone (where two were recovered at autopsy), not clustered at the entry point. Frangible bullets would disintegrate very quickly, producing a dense cloud of fragments at the entry site and no further wound track at all.

The usual reason for the unusual type of bullet is to "prove" that another weapon was used in the fatal head shot. This assumes that the shooter could not obtain or fabricate such bullets to fire from the M-C rifle. Soft- or hollow-point bullets would, of course, be more readily available for the typical hunting rifle, but frangible bullets would be as difficult to procure for any other weapon and no more difficult to fabricate for the M-C than for any other rifle. The observed wound and extent of fragmentation of the bullet is characteristic of that of a fully jacketed military bullet that deformed and broke apart upon impact with the skull, penetrated several centimeters of soft tissue, and scattered fragments along its path before exiting. The wound was very similar to the damage done to the skulls in the Biophysics Lab tests. It is not that of a frangible, soft-nosed, or hollow-point bullet.

The President could not have been thrown backward into the car seat by the force of a bullet. He moved by means of the force that usually moves a person, his own muscles. All the controversy about whether the hole in the side of Kennedy's head was more to the side or the back and debate over whether it was an entry or an exit wound are irrelevant. The debates are based on simplistic assumptions that are demonstrably false.

After the side of President Kennedy's head exploded, relieving the internal pressure, disruption of the contents ceased and the muscles relaxed from their powerful surge. Even though nearly all of the sequelae recorded on frame 313 of the Zapruder film took place after the bullet came to rest in the floor of the car, they all happened in less time than it takes to blink an eye. The violent spasm, pushing Kennedy's body backward into the seat, occupies the next several frames. A few seconds later, the President's limousine was racing to the hospital, the assassin was quickly leaving the sniper's nest, and the sequence of events that would lead to two more deaths had begun. Unfortunately, the next victim had no way of knowing what those events were going to be.

CHAPTER NINE
Poor Damn Cop

"I heard him mutter something like, "poor damn cop,"
or "poor dumb cop." He said that over twice…"
                                    —*William Scoggins*[87]

If you read the explanation of why there was not enough time for
Oswald to have done all the things that the Warren Commission
credited him with doing between the time he entered the bus
near the Depository and shooting Tippit, you would conclude
that all the witnesses in the case had assembled on the morning
of November 22 to synchronize their watches and take a pledge
to check them at crucial moments as the day's events unfolded.
The reality is that, like the spring-driven clocks in most people's
houses in 1963, what would have been the crucial clocks and
watches probably varied in the time they showed by several minutes. And the people involved probably had better things to do,
as the events happened before their eyes, than to check the clock
to see what time it was so that they could accurately report the
time that the event took place in their testimony to the WC. The
truth is, Oswald had sufficient time to effect those movements
and was seen by credible witnesses at both locations.

Conspiracy writers have a valuable ally in the person of Dallas County Deputy Sheriff Roger Craig. He was standing in front
of the Sheriff's office on Main Street, about 20 feet from the corner at Houston, watching the last of the motorcade pass, when
he heard three shots. He ran through the plaza, picking up information from police officers as he went. He rounded up witnesses,
including a young couple who probably were Arnold Rowland
and his wife, and took them to an associate, Mr. Lummy Lewis,
so that Lewis could get names and addresses. He searched along

---

87. Testimony to the Warren Commission by Scoggins, the taxi driver who was parked
at the corner of 10th and Patton at the time of the Tippit shooting. Heard as Oswald
walked quickly past his cab.

Elm in front of the Depository to look for bullet ricochet marks on the street ending up on the south side of the street. He heard a shrill whistle and looked up to see "a white male running down the hill from the direction of the Texas School Book Depository Building." He then saw "a light colored Rambler station wagon with [a] luggage rack on top" driven by "a dark complexioned white male." He saw the car "pull over to the curb and the subject who had come running down the mall get into this car." He tried to cross Elm to stop the car, but "the traffic was so heavy I could not make it." Craig makes a very credible witness when he later identified Lee Harvey Oswald as the "same person I saw running down the hill and get into this station wagon and leave the scene." The car, he stated, "headed toward the Dallas-Fort Worth Turnpike." This incident would have taken place about the same time as Mrs. Bledsoe, Oswald's former landlady, said she saw Oswald leave the bus.

This is the typical contradiction in eyewitness testimony that plagues criminal investigations. Of course, Mrs. Bledsoe knew Oswald, while Mr. Craig did not. But we don't have to rely only on the word of the eyewitnesses. Sometimes their accounts are backed up with ample physical evidence. For instance, when a witness says she saw Oswald on the bus, finding a bus transfer from that bus with a time stamp on it in his pocket is good verification. Likewise, when three witnesses say they saw a man unload a revolver and toss the empty shells as he crossed a lawn belonging to one of the witnesses, it increases their credibility enormously when they hand over the cartridge cases they picked up from the lawn and out of the shrubbery. It further aids credibility when the person they pick out of a lineup as the man who discarded the cases is found a bit later in possession of the gun in which the shells were fired. Figure 40 illustrates that the markings on the cartridge cases recovered at the Tippit murder scene were traced to the revolver found in Lee Oswald's possession at the time of his arrest in the Texas Theatre—to the exclusion of all other weapons. This figure and several others were used by the FBI in testimony to the WC and were reexamined by the House Firearms Panel. They reconfirmed the original conclusion of the Commission.

Critics seldom assert that the revolver found in Oswald's possession at the time of his arrest was unsuitable for the killing of Tippit. They usually state, simply, that the bullets in Tippit's body could not be traced to that weapon, neglecting to mention that one of them was and why the others could not be. The FBI explained in their WC testimony why three of the bullets recovered from Tippit's body could not be traced to the revolver. Conspiracy theorists usually attempt to discredit the cartridge cases with "breaks in chain-of-custody" arguments and implications that they were "planted." There is no credible evidence that the chain-of-custody would not have met contemporary court standards, however, in spite of the fact that chain-of-custody questions became moot when Oswald was killed by Ruby.

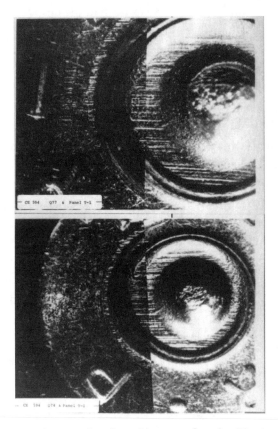

Figure 40. Split-view photographs of cartridge cases found at Tippit murder scene, compared to test cartridges fired by the FBI from the handgun in Oswald's possession at the time of his arrest. *(National Archives)*

The frequent argument that revolvers do not eject expended cartridge cases could only be used by somebody who had never read the eyewitness accounts in the Warren Report (or hoped that the reader would not). The most credible argument against the cartridge cases being genuine is that there was a mismatch between the types of cases recovered and the bullets recovered from Tippit's body on autopsy. As far as I know, it has never been determined where Oswald acquired the bullets for either gun or what he did with the remainder, or if he had owned more than the number in evidence. There was no reloading equipment found with which he could have reloaded his own handgun bullets (one explanation for the mismatch), but it is possible that he had acquired a handful of .38 Special cartridges from a person who did his own reloading.

Another possibility is that Oswald had an empty cartridge in the chamber under the hammer. This strategy was touted in the gun literature of the day as a safety feature, if a person is going to conceal a handgun in his clothing. The strategy derives from the belief that the hammer of a revolver can be caught in one's clothing when a person is in a hurry to extract it and snap back when released with enough force to detonate the primer.[88] Oswald was well-read, if not well-informed, and may well have been aware of this particular myth. This would assume that he kept one empty shell when he emptied the expended cartridges with the intention of doing the same thing again. When captured, however, he had six unfired rounds in the gun, so he would have had to change his mind and dispose of the extra shell casing somewhere between the property where the other empty cases were found and the Texas Theatre.

The Warren Commission noted that a six-shot revolver holds more than the four shells that were recovered and that one of the shells was found by Mrs. Virginia Davis after the police had searched the scene and left. It is possible that one of the shells was never found—or was pocketed by a souvenir hunter. A rumor to this effect still circulates. This also assumes that there were five shots fired, with one of the bullets missing the target and being lost. This is one argument that conspiracy writers never use: that Oswald was such a good shot that he could not possibly have missed one shot out of five with a cheap handgun. This may be one of those loose ends that are never explained with any certainty, but as evidence of a conspiracy, it is not particularly convincing.

If a 'conspirator' shot Tippit with the intention of framing Oswald for it by planting cartridge cases from Oswald's gun, he certainly went out of his way to make it difficult for himself by shooting Tippit with different brands of bullets. This blunder made it necessary to 'plant' the right

---

88. Dr. Carroll Peters points out that this has not been true of any S&W revolver built since the early 1900s, but the myth persists.

assortment of expended cartridge cases. Then the conspirator that was brilliant enough to induce Oswald to assist in his own frame-up by carrying his handgun into the theater was dumb enough to lose count. Perhaps, you think, it was necessary because he knew that Oswald would be carrying both kinds of bullets when captured. If he did, then how did he come by that knowledge? How did he know that Oswald would not load his gun with one kind and dispose of the rest? He had sufficient numbers of bullets in his possession when captured to have done so. And Oswald did dispose of any other ammunition that he might have possessed, without leaving a trace. No more .38 Special or 6.5 WCC/MC cartridges were ever found in any place he lived, worked, or was known to have visited. And why would the conspirator have to use both kinds, even if he could somehow know that Oswald would have both in his pocket? After the fact, it would make just as much sense to assume that Oswald loaded the weapon with one brand, then put some of the others in his pocket to have what he considered to be a sufficient number of spares.

On the other hand, if those four shells were all the conspirator could obtain, then why not just make sure he killed Tippit with three shots, using Western cartridges, then plant the three Western cases? Surely, the purported conspirators would not have sent somebody who could not do the job at point-blank range with three shots, even using a rechambered .38 identical to Oswald's. This particular loose end is very difficult to work into a credible 'proof' of conspiracy.

In fact, the amount of physical evidence, especially with what was easily proved to be the murder weapon being in his possession, and the number of eyewitnesses who picked Oswald out of a lineup, makes this one of those cases that would have been assigned to the member of the prosecutor's staff with the least experience to give him the court time. The reader might wonder why any time was spent refuting the myths that have grown up around the Tippit killing, but they are very common and, with selective omission of most of the physical and eyewitness evidence, might seem plausible. The conspiracy theorist who wants to make Oswald the innocent "patsy" he claimed to be has to try to refute his guilt in the Tippit murder, as it makes his guilt in the assassination of President Kennedy much more plausible.

CHAPTER TEN

Bungled Autopsy

"Where bungled autopsies are concerned, President Kennedy's is the exemplar."

—*Michael Baden*[89]

A n official at the Army's helicopter flight school once told me that they prefer to train pilots who do not have experience flying fixed-wing aircraft. It seems that under combat conditions fixed-wing pilots sometimes revert to their earlier training and try to fly the helicopter like a fixed-wing plane. Because the method of flying the two types of craft is so different, this can cause the helicopter to become unstable and crash. When the adrenaline level is high, it seems that the only reaction one can depend on is that which is uncluttered with any conflicting training and so well-rehearsed that the performance is almost automatic. In combat, when life and death hangs on split-second decisions, the mind is so overloaded with sensory input that clear thinking seems impossible. The same phenomenon seems to affect all people, whatever their profession, in emotionally charged emergencies. It happens whether they are called upon to act or merely to witness the events. Jackie Kennedy, the one most immediately involved in the wrenching tragedy, remembered little of what went on between the time her husband was first injured and the ordeal of waiting, alternately outside and inside the door of the emergency room (ER), for her husband to be declared dead.

If you compare the medical reports of the surgeons who treated President Kennedy at Parkland, you will find the emotion-driven inconsistencies typical of eyewitnesses to a terrible event. Experienced trauma surgeons remembered wounds that were not there; others had trouble reconstructing the location of wounds that were. The description of the gaping wound in the right side of the President's head varied considerably. As usual,

---

89. *Unnatural Death,* page 5.

the "average" description is better than any individual description of the wound. Among the descriptions, the occipital, temporal, and parietal bones were mentioned. All except the occipital were involved, though it was more predominantly parietal than a summary of all descriptions would indicate.

Dr. Jenkins stated that "…the cerebellum had protruded from the wound." Some of the others wrote or made similar statements. The autopsy photos show a nearly intact cerebellum. There was so much blood and detached cerebral tissue dripping from the skull and lying on the ER table that some of the surgeons misidentified the origin of the brain tissue exuding from the wound. One of the few memories Mrs. Kennedy had of the post-assassination ride to Parkland was trying to hold the wound in her husband's head closed. While she may have been partly successful in the car, autopsy pictures show the wound gaping open while he was on his back on the table, as it might have in the ER.

Contrary to frequent claims, the description of the explosive wound by Parkland and Bethesda are not so different. Much of the controversy is created by the erroneous assumption that the wound was caused by the entrance or exit of a bullet. Even the autopsy pathologists were confused by this massive wound. The report states, "A portion of the projectile made its exit through the parietal bone on the right carrying with it portions of cerebrum, skull, and scalp." The other "portion of the projectile" deposited the trail of fragments from back to front. They thought there were two "exit" wounds of the skull produced by different pieces of the bullet. Given the opportunity to examine blocks of gelatin tissue simulant after being shot by deforming bullets, you would see that it is not uncommon for two major pieces of the bullet to exit at different locations, generally not too far apart. In other words, it is possible that there were two exit locations at the right front of the head. But the explosive rupture of the side of the President's head over his ear was not caused by an exiting bullet fragment.

The explosive rupture of a skull in the Biophysics Lab simulation is shown in figure 33. This 'wound' was very extensive and surrounded by loose flaps of skull and simulated skin. The extent of the damage to one of the skulls is apparent in figure 36, after the loose skull and gelatin (simulated skin) were removed. A similar massive injury on the right side of the President's head extended from in front of his ear to the posterior part of the right side. In terms of bony plates that make up the skull, it extended across the right side of his head from the rear of the frontal bone nearly to the occipital. Between these, the bulk of the right parietal and the upper edge of the temporal were broken and parts were missing. Measuring the extent of such a wound is difficult and its appearance would vary widely depending on the position of the head. As the President was on his back the entire time he was being treated, the forward flaps of bone and scalp would tend to remain closed but the ones toward the back of the wound would hinge open and nearly reach the table. This could explain the impression left with some of the Parkland staff that the wound they mistook for an exit wound was nearer the back of his head.

Even the members of the autopsy team were not immune from stress-induced lapses of attention. They either forgot to make measurements of some critical dimensions (how high "slightly above" the external occipital protuberance [EOP] really meant) or forgot to record them in their notes. In addition, they recorded the position of the wound in the neck from a moveable landmark, the mastoid process (at the base of the skull behind the ear). Because the skull can be tilted in all directions relative to the trunk, this landmark does not pinpoint the location of the entry wound in the back at the base of the neck. Of course, they had no way of knowing that the photographs and x-rays would not be available to allow a precise location to be established until years later. But even this inaccurate method comes closer to indicating the true entry point of the wound in the back at the base of the neck than does a circle sketched on the autopsy drawing, so those who wish to claim a much lower entry wound ignore the more accurate measurement and rely on the circle instead.

Standard practice in writing up an autopsy report is to indicate a rough location of the finding on a drawing and pinpoint the exact location by recording measurements from fixed landmarks. If there is more than one significant observation in the vicinity, a brief description of the finding is also written on the drawing. The measurements are usually given to the nearest millimeter, which is accurate enough for most purposes, including trial evidence. Descriptions and measurements of wounds and other significant findings are generally repeated in the narrative portion of the report.

In spite of the emotional overlay on this particular job, those involved with the treatment and investigation carried through on their most fundamental training. The surgeons behaved like surgeons, trying to establish an airway and administering cardiac massage to a failing heart, and the pathologists behaved like pathologists, measuring, photographing, and x-raying the President's wounds. As Commander Humes wrote in his report and later testified, it is the photographs and x-rays that provide the best documentation of any autopsy.

It is a trauma surgeon's job to save lives and they made every effort to do so, even though they knew that it was a futile effort. They did not turn the dying President over to observe the wounds on his back because the attempt to save his life did not require it. After it was obvious that their job was over, none wanted to hang around the ER to be reminded of the failed attempt. At that point, none turned the dead President over to see the wounds. It was not part of their job.[90]

Critics dwell on the discrepancies among the many reports filed subsequent to the assassination, quoting Secret Service agents, law enforcement personnel, and bystanders at Dallas and Bethesda, as well as the Parkland physicians, who saw entrance and exit wounds at many locations. Virtually none of these people recognized the large hole above the President's ear that extended nearly from the front to the back of his head for what it was. The autopsy team identified a portion of an exit wound on one of the pieces that was dislodged in the explosion, but the team did not actually locate where it thought the exit wound would be. Team members spoke of the hole in the side of Kennedy's head as the "exit wound." A portion of an exit wound was given a physical location by the HSCA pathology panel, represented by Dr. Baden in testimony at the open hearings, in the frontal bone at the front margin of this hole. It was on one of the autopsy photographs, the only one that showed an interior view. In the report of the open hearings (Vol. I), the exit 'notch' is only shown on a blowup of a portion of that photograph. Though Dr. Baden identified this exit as being at the coronal suture, it is actually lower in the frontal bone.[91]

The full extent of bone damage can only be seen on the x-rays and,

90. After seeing the autopsy photographs and x-rays, all the Parkland physicians who were interviewed by the HSCA's staff agreed with the findings of the House Forensic Pathology Panel and the earlier studies concerning the location of entrance and exit wounds.

91. In the Forensic Pathology Panel's written report, the notch indicated by Dr. Baden is not as definitively identified as an exit as it was in his testimony at the open hearings. The written report placed the exit at the coronal suture in the right side of the skull (see figure 47).

thus, could not be observed or commented on by the Parkland surgeons. To expect that a physician can see everything of relevance in an external examination is to misunderstand why medical facilities are equipped with x-ray machines. Fractures and dense missiles often cannot be detected any other way. As usual, the autopsy revealed much that otherwise would have been missed. This was the pathologists' job, and they did reasonably well under the circumstances.

Dark patches in the temporal bones show above and behind the eye on the autopsy x-rays, which are misinterpreted by critics as "missing" bone not mentioned in the reports by the Parkland surgeons. What they fail to mention is that similar dark patches show on the 'from life' x-rays of the President's head. The darkness at this location is merely a reflection of the fact that thinner bone casts less of a pale 'shadow' on the x-ray negatives.

None of the autopsy team did post-mortem examinations on a day-to-day basis, but each was a board-certified pathologist, familiar with the procedure. The unique circumstances surrounding the assassination of the President of the United States, however, dictated that this was not going to be an ordinary autopsy. Autopsies are conducted in the isolation of the laboratory of the medical examiner, while the family is grieving at home. A postmortem exam supplying critical evidence in a murder case may take more than a day to carry out in a thorough and competent manner. It is never conducted while the widow and brother of the victim are waiting nearby for it to be completed—except when the widow is the First Lady and the brother is the Attorney General of the United States. Who was going to request that they go home and let the pathologists do their job? Who would demand it? The team had the authority to conduct a complete autopsy, but they chose not to.[92] The resulting failure to completely dissect the President's neck wound to demonstrate that the entry wound to the base of the neck communicated with the tracheostomy in front provided fuel for future controversy.

---

92. Dr. Finck testified at the Clay Shaw trial that "an Admiral" had ordered a truncated autopsy, which is why they did not dissect the wound through the neck. Cdr. Humes, in his testimony to the HSCA, denied that anyone had given such an order. He again stated that it was his decision not to perform a complete autopsy. Finck's impression could have arisen from the relaying of Jackie and Robert's question "When will it be finished?" by one of the senior military staff who entered and left the room at various times during the autopsy. Whatever he was thinking at the time of his New Orleans testimony, Finck denied that any such orders affected the conduct of the autopsy. Finck expressed this view in an interview conducted by Dennis Breo for the *Journal of the American Medical Association,* in an article published in October 1992.

One major blunder that the team is accused of in this "botched autopsy" is misplacing the entrance wound to the back of the skull by ten centimeters (four inches). Three panels of experts examined the autopsy photos: the Clark Panel in 1968, the Rockefeller Commission in 1975, and the HSCA Forensic Pathology Panel (FPP) in 1978. Each of these panels examined the various reports, autopsy photographs, and x-rays at length, and each gave considerable weight to the same features mentioned by the FPP. In each case, the conclusion was the same: the entry wound on the back of President Kennedy's head was shown by a hole in his scalp (see the Dox drawing of figure 41) to be a full four inches above the EOP that the autopsy team had used as a landmark to locate the entry wound. Figure 42 shows a sketch of the Forensic Pathology Panel's entry and exit wounds with a straight bullet trajectory between them.

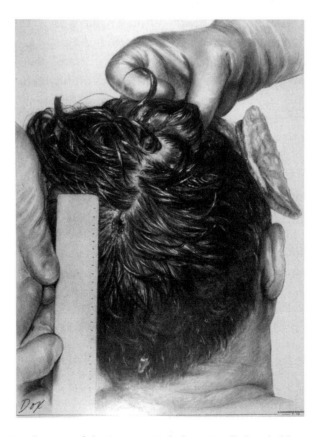

Figure 41.   Dox drawing of the Forensic Pathology Panel's "cowlick" entry wound
to the back of the president's head. *(National Archives/John Hunt)*

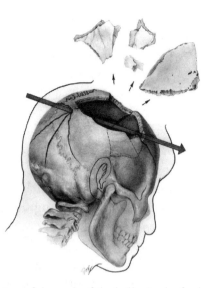

Figure 42. Dox drawing of the path of the bullet in the fatal skull shot, established by the FPP, representing the explosive post-shot rupture. *(National Archives/John Hunt)*

The location of a penetrating wound to the cranium is usually pinpointed by the cratered hole in the skull, like that mentioned in the autopsy report. A scalp is ordinarily somewhat mobile. Most people's scalps can be moved back and forth a half inch or so. Virtually all the bones of the President's skull were separated at suture lines and many of the plates further broken by the internal pressure. Due to the stretching and deformation, his scalp was probably loosened and considerably more mobile than the usual undamaged scalp. A hole in a highly mobile scalp is not the best means of pinpointing the location of the entry or exit wound. These panels seem to be making the same mistake they criticize the autopsy team for making: using a movable body part to locate the entrance.

Notice that a hand is seen holding the scalp in place in figure 41. As other autopsy pictures show, this was necessary, as the scalp and bone flaps draped over the back of the skull when the body was on its back, hanging down to the tabletop. To get a picture of the back of the head, the scalp had to be draped back over the remaining skull toward the front. Even if "slightly above" meant an inch above the center of the EOP, a full three inches of displacement of the scalp by the tugging hand would seem to be extreme. Whether that scalp defect is, indeed, the bullet entry wound is open to question.

There is another feature that the panels used to locate the higher entry point. The frontal x-ray of the head, especially the enhanced version printed in the HSCA report, shows a nearly circular density near their higher entry site that the panel identified as a bullet fragment deposited on the skull at entry. It appears to be a disk of something as dense as metal, with a small circular "bite" taken out of the lower edge. This object is indicated by the arrow on the copy of that x-ray reprinted as figure 43. This second bit of evidence was discussed several times during the meetings of the FPP and is mentioned by Dr. Baden as a "relatively large metal fragment" in his majority report in the open hearings. It is interesting that it was phrased that way, ducking the obvious fact that it cannot be a bullet fragment and is not that near to their proposed entry site. A fully-jacketed WCC/MC bullet will deform as it penetrates bone, but will not fragment on the outside of the skull. In the Biophysics Lab tests, most of the test bullets' jackets ruptured about midway through the skulls.

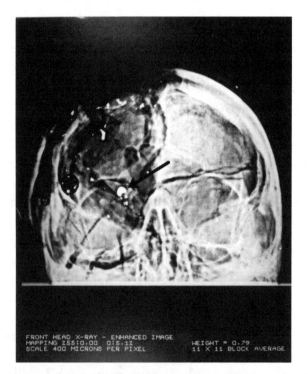

Figure 43. Autopsy x-ray of JFK skull, front-to-back view, with disk-like object indicated. *(National Archives/John Hunt)*

The projectile would only break into disks if a person were shot by something like a roll of coins. When they break up in the target, real bullets break into irregular pieces of jacket, sometimes complete enough to contain pieces of the lead core, and a varying number of irregular chunks of lead core. It cannot break into circular slices, especially one with a circular bite out of the edge. As radiologist David Mantik points out in the book edited by Fetzer, there is no corresponding density on the lateral x-ray. The slightly lighter area indicated by the FPP as the lateral view of this object is not nearly light enough to be a metal disk seen edge-on. As bright as it is seen flat in the frontal x-ray, it should be even brighter when seen edge-on in the lateral. If an object is present in only one x-ray view, it could not have been embedded in the President's skull or scalp.

A metal fragment that cannot be a bullet fragment and appears on only one view of the x-ray would ordinarily be dismissed as an accidental artifact that somehow found its way to the top of the x-ray cassette for that single exposure. It isn't unusual to see things fall out of the clothing or hair, especially on the tables in the Medical Examiner's Laboratory. Objects such as metal buttons would easily cast a shadow on an x-ray. However, the appearance of this artifact adjacent to the location of the purported cowlick entry wound is interpreted by some, including researcher/authors John Canal and David Mantik, as a deliberately introduced artifact. The point of introducing a piece of metal that cannot be related to the bullet and appears on only one view, however, is hard to explain. The fact that a pathologist reviewing the photographs might accept it as evidence of an entry location would seem to be too uncertain to justify such an act. If one were going to plant evidence, it would seem more appropriate to plant something that could actually be mistaken for a bullet fragment and to plant it on both the lateral and frontal x-rays.

In early 1994, I was approved by the Kennedy family representative to view the restricted autopsy photographs and x-rays of the President, from the autopsy in Bethesda. On September 23, 2004, I made the approved visit, in the company of Dr. Chad Zimmermann, who had received a similar approval. After the visit, the apparently metallic fragment on this x-ray and the enhanced version prepared for the House Forensic Pathology Panel was still just as mysterious as when we went in. The greater detail visible, especially on the enhanced version, was of little help. The disk was not as nearly circular as it appears on the frontal view printed in the HSCA report. The edges are irregular, with the "bite" being merely the largest indentation in the irregular, jagged margin. The object it most resembles is the flattened piece of the jacket from the nose of the WCC/MC bullet that has accidentally hit one of the pieces of armor plate set in front of equipment on the firing range to keep it from being hit by the stray bullet. When the bullet hits the armor at high velocity, the tip flattens, then the jacket ruptures circumferentially around the tip, as the lead core pushes out and finally splashes off the armor in pieces. I am not proposing that this is what the artifact is, as there is no reasonable explanation for how such a fragment would have gotten onto the back of Kennedy's head.

The object on the outside of the skull in the lateral view that was identified by the FPP as the disk seen in the frontal view is, as Dr. Mantik says, far too faint to be the metal disk seen edge-on. It seems more the density of bone and is probably a bone chip spalled off the outside of the skull as it cracked at that location in the explosion of Kennedy's skull on the right. This is similar to the small spall fragments from the crack in a glass that one sweeps up after the breakage. The object I take to be a bone chip is on the outside of the skull and appears to be under the scalp.

According to the autopsy team, they saw the entry wound in the scalp, but they did not make the mistake of describing the entry only by referring to a hole in the mobile scalp. They further described the cratered entry wound as being visible on the inside of the skull after the brain was removed. With numerous photographs taken of the autopsy, it would seem very strange that none show this cratered entry hole. In fact, one view does.

One of the series of near-duplicate autopsy photographs that were taken of the inside of the skull was used by Dr. Michael Baden for his presentation of the majority position of the HSCA Panel at the public hearings before the Committee on September 8, 1978. Only a portion of this photo was isolated and enlarged to show the lower half of a cratered "exit wound" on the frontal bone to pinpoint an exit location for the fatal bullet. Baden's testimony referring to the enlarged portion of the photograph labeled JFK Exhibit F-60 was:

Mr. Klein: Doctor, do you recognize that photograph and that blowup?

Dr. Baden: Yes; this is a detail of one of the autopsy photographs, in fact the only photograph that shows any internal structures of the President at the time of autopsy as opposed to all of the other photographs which are outside of the body. This photograph shows the bullet exit area on the right side of the head and is seen in better detail and sharper on the photograph than in the blowup.

So why not show the sharper image? The HSCA, audience, and the reader of the HSCA report are left to presume that it would be improper to show photographs of the interior of the President's skull, whereas showing the picture of the broken frontal bone was acceptable. And why not mention the fact that the picture shows the entry wound? There were drawings of other wounds, so if it was improper to show the photograph, why not a drawing showing the entry wound on this one? An enlargement, similar to Baden's JFK F-60, but a bit sharper, is included as figure 44.

Figure 44. The lower portion of the exit wound in the frontal bone (at the arrow), as identified by the HSCA Forensic Pathology Panel. (From an enlargement of a section of one of the autopsy photographs.) *(Web/John Hunt)*

Dr. Baden's testimony also included a discussion of the "cratering" of the entry wound, mentioned in the autopsy report and touched on in earlier chapters. The drawing he used to illustrate this phenomenon is included as figure 45. It shows, schematically, how the entry hole widens as the missile penetrates the second 'table' of the skull. The inner and outer 'tables' are the hard, dense surfaces of the skull, made primarily of nonliving mineral containing few living cells. Sandwiched between the two tables is a less dense bone with bigger and more numerous voids, filled with living cells.

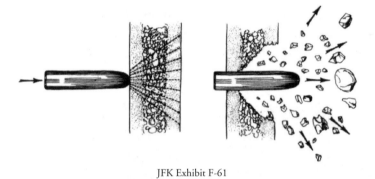

JFK Exhibit F-61

Figure 45. The "cratering" of the back surface of a skull or other brittle material when struck by a projectile (WCC/MC Bullet Pictured). *(National Archives)*

When Dr. Pierre Finck was interviewed by the FPP, he was adamant that the entry wound was located in the occipital bone, as specified in the autopsy report. He was asked to mark the area of the entry wound on the inside of a skull that the FPP supplied for the purpose. This was obviously an autopsy specimen that was donated or from an unclaimed body that had been autopsied. The conventional "skullcap" was cut out so that the brain could be removed. A photograph of the skull, with Finck's dot marking the location of the entry crater on the inside of the occipital bone at the back of the skull is in figure 46. Some notations were added to the picture to aid in identifying some of the important landmarks.

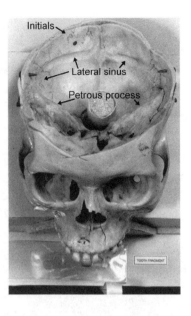

Figure 46.

Photograph of a skull with the location of the entry crater in the president's skull marked by Dr. Pierre Finck with his initials for the HSCA Forensic Pathology Panel. *(National Archives/John Hunt)*

The entire photograph mentioned by Dr. Baden, when he discussed the blowup in figure 44, is reproduced as figure 47.[93] The upper arrow indicates the bullet hole in the dura mater, the tough connective tissue sheath that lines the inside of the skull. The dura is uplifted and torn from a bullet punching through from the outside. In the autopsy report and in subsequent testimony by Commander Humes we learn that the wound on the back of the President's skull was cratered on the inside surface, showing that the wound to the back of the head was a wound of entry. At the bottom right of the entry hole in Figure 47, a hint of the cratering of the skull may show (or not, as it is not clear because of the shadow that fills the space under the uplifted dura in this copy of the photograph). The San Jose Medical Examiner, Dr. Richard Mason, points out that the dura should have been stripped off to reveal clearly the crater in the bone to pinpoint the entry location. Like dissection of the neck wound, it just was not done. It is possible that they suspected that the dura was critical to holding the fractured skull together. It is more likely that they just did not want to take the time.

---

93. This is not a picture that can be obtained from the National Archives. It is part of the collection that is still restricted by the family. This is a poorly reproduced version from the "bootleg" autopsy photos that circulate on the internet. The originals are of much higher quality, particularly one of the color prints.

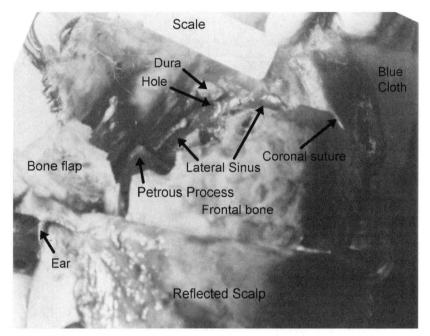

Figure 47. Complete copy of the only interior view in the autopsy photographs, showing the entry wound in the inner table of the skull. (Annotations added). *(Web/John Hunt)*

The House Forensic Pathology Panel reconstructed the exit wound from the shattered pieces of skull that appear on the autopsy x-rays. They were assisted in this task by anthropologist Dr. Lawrence Angel of the Smithsonian Institution. The reconstructed hole incorporated the fragment that the autopsy team had determined showed a crater on the outer surface of the skull. The x-ray of this fragment shows the two groups of lead fragments embedded in the surface of the bone next to the portion of the crater, but one cannot determine which surface the crater is in from the x-ray. Dr. Baden stated in the public hearings that a portion of this exit is shown in figure 44. Cratering or beveling to the exterior would seem characteristic of a wound of exit. However, it seems too low on the forehead to be near the coronal suture. Also, neither the autopsy report nor the interviews of the team members mention any crater in the intact skull. They only mention a portion of an exit crater on a recovered fragment of skull. It seems unlikely that they would overlook such an obvious feature. In spite of identifying this notch as an exit, the FPP placed the exit at the coronal suture, as in figure 42.

As the features in the photograph of figure 47 are not immediately apparent, the features are identified. The view is nearly face-on, but elevated so that the camera is peering over the broken bone at the top of the forehead down into the empty vault of the skull.[94] Notice the height of the broken edge of the skull at the back, beneath the gloved hand holding the ruler. It seems quite high, given that the entry was supposed to be high up on the back of the head.

As is the usual procedure in a case where photographic documentation is critical, the autopsy photographs were taken as multiples. As a precaution against the possibility that a photograph might not turn out, the photographer will snap a picture, advance the film, and immediately take another, with or without minor adjustments in shutter speed or f-stop to bracket the proper exposure. In addition, photographs were taken using both black and white print film and color slide film. There were six views taken in the autopsy photographs, but 27 exposures. The number of exposures taken of each view varied from two to seven.

In Chapter 3, it was noted that this routine act usually produces a stereo pair. Unless the camera is mounted on a tripod and left in position between shots, it is impossible for the photographer to avoid changing his position slightly between exposures, just as the House Photography Panel observed in the "backyard" photographs that Marina took of Lee and the murder weapons. While this stereo pair is inadvertently created, it is almost impossible to alter without detection. Subtle differences in grain pattern, shadows, and a dozen other features are easy to spot but extremely difficult to eliminate. In addition, any slight misplacement of an added feature in one of the pair will cause its image to float above its intended location or be sunken into another feature. As they did with the "backyard photographs" of Oswald, the experts on the House photographic panel did such a stereo examination of duplicates from the autopsy, examination of the grain pattern by microscope, and other tests for alteration. They found no evidence of alteration in any autopsy photograph.

When we visited the National Archives, Dr. Zimmermann had the foresight to bring a stereo viewer with which to examine the autopsy pictures. With this device one lays near duplicate photographs side-by-

---

94. The photograph was almost certainly taken with the photographer standing 'above' the president's head as he was lying on the table. However, it seems more natural to rotate it a half turn, so that we are looking at the head face-on, but elevated.

side and looks through the binocular viewer, where one picture is seen with each eye. There were two, near-duplicate color autopsy photographs of the interior of the empty skull in the Archives collection, designated #44 and #45. Photo #44 was much better, as #45 was moderately over-exposed. When viewed as a stereo pair, however, the three-dimensional view was as clear as a view of the inside of the skull. The frontal bone was out-of-focus in the foreground, while the back of the inside of the skull was in focus. The stretched 'hood' of dura overlying the entry wound was clearly extending into the hollow of the skull, while what is marked as the transverse sinus on Figure 47 was a groove across the back of the head, filled with a shiny red substance. If Dr. Finck's drawing was accurate, this is where the transverse sinus should be, if the tentorium were removed by slicing around the inside periphery of the skull, exposing the sinus.

The entry crater was filled with what seemed to be clotted blood with a dark hole through it. On the poorer view, #45, there was a blue highlight on the side of this hole. All other highlights in the picture (presumably reflections from the lighting source) were white. The shade of blue on this one highlight, however, was the same shade as the blue cloth lying behind the head. We took this as an indication that the hole through the clot extended all the way through the skull and the highlight was reflected light from the underlying cloth.

While the perspective is different in figures 46 and 47, features common to the two provide other landmarks that one can use to identify structures in the autopsy photo of figure 47. For instance, the lateral sinus runs around the periphery of the skull until it approaches the petrous portion of the temporal bone. This sinus dives down just behind this extension of the temporal bone and passes through a foramen into the internal jugular vein. In the autopsy photo, the groove labeled "lateral sinus" does disappear behind a structure identified as the petrous bone, which is broken at the top.

Finally, the enhanced lateral view of the autopsy x-ray of the head is cut off on the back and the bottom in the version printed in the HSCA report (figure 38). As a result, the dentition is not available to help determine the orientation of the x-ray. More importantly, a few millimeters of the skull has been cut off at the back, precisely in the location that the autopsy report says that there is an entry hole through the skull. In the complete, enhanced lateral x-ray, these features are quite clear. The skull is complete, including jaw and teeth. The skull has a dark streak, indicating an entrance hole at the location specified by the autopsy report as the site of the entry wound near the external occipital protuberance. There are also faint outlines of bone chips just inside this location and a few small metallic fragments, starting about halfway from back to front. All these features are similar to those in the x-ray of the test skull in figure 38. The lead fragments in the test skull show a clearer path of the bullet, as they stayed in place after the shot.

Many of the fragments deposited in the President's brain were flushed out, along with the brain tissue, as the large amount of blood flowed out of the explosive wound in the side of his head, in the car and in Parkland. It is evidently some of these that were deposited on the bone flaps by clotting blood that show as a "trail" of fragments near the top of the lateral view. This "trail" does not show on the frontal view, and is much higher than the FPP's reconstructed trajectory. In fact, at the apparent location of these fragments there was no brain matter in which the fragments could be embedded (see figure 39).

Figure 48 shows a picture of a human skull with spots pasted on the rear in the positions approximately of the autopsy entry near the external occipital protuberance and the FPP entry at the "cowlick." I then took a properly scaled cutout of the entry hole in figure 47 and placed it on the skull at the correct distance above the scalp fold at eyebrow line and properly situated left to right. Using the cutout as a guide, I then took pictures of the skull with the entry wound projected (as though the top of the skull were missing) on the back of the skull at the two claimed entry points. To aid in positioning, I placed the corner of a cardboard rectangle at the center of each spot for the two pictures.

Figure 49 shows the resulting picture for the autopsy entry location: about an inch above and to the right of the center of the EOP. This will be called the 'low' entry. The lower half of figure 49 shows the autopsy photograph of figure 46 superimposed in 'transparent' mode on the skull photograph. The upper broken part of the President's skull is a bit lower than the profile of the intact skull. Given the inexact location of the entry point in the autopsy report, the differences in the proportions of different human skulls, and my inability to position the camera perfectly, the result is a possible match.

Figure 50 shows the autopsy photograph positioned on the skull

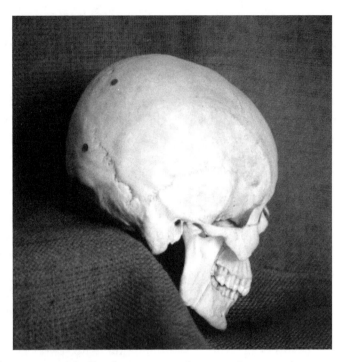

Figure 48. Picture of skull with approximate location of purported impact points marked: HSCA entry (upper) and autopsy entry (lower). *(Larry M. Sturdivan)*

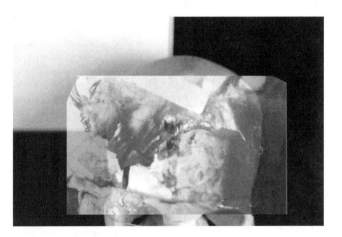

Figure 49. Autopsy photograph superimposed on the skull with the entry wound projected to the "autopsy" location near the external occipital protuberance. *(Larry M. Sturdivan/Christopher Sturdivan)*

so that the entry hole would project back to the "cowlick" entry location specified by the FPP in figure 42. In the superimposed view, the upper edge of the President's broken skull extends well above the profile of the intact skull. Again, the scalp is presumed to be folded just over the eyebrow line. If the fold in the scalp were assumed to be low enough to allow the top of the broken bone to match the profile of the sample skull for the FPP entry location, the eyes would show over the top of the fold and Dr. Baden's "exit" notch would be within the right orbit. This mismatch is well outside the possible errors of positioning. The profile of skull above the FPP trajectory, with entry and exit both high on the skull, is much too shallow to allow the high profile of broken bone seen in the autopsy photograph.

All three review panels note the extensive fracturing of the skull

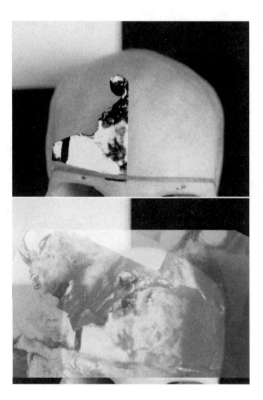

Figure 50. Autopsy photograph superimposed on a human skull with the entry projected to the Forensic Pathology Panel's "cowlick" location. *(Larry M. Sturdivan/Christopher Sturdivan)*

mentioned by the autopsy team and shown in the x-rays. In fact, the cracks that extend down from the "cowlick" entry location were cited as part of the evidence of an entry at that location. However, the Biophysics Lab test skulls do not show extensive cracking from the entry holes, even though the dried skulls used in the tests were more brittle than live bone (indicated by more extensive fragmentation at the site of the explosive post-shot rupture). Figure 51 is a typical entry hole from this series. Some had a small crack that descended to the groove that contains the lateral sinus, then followed that groove around the base of the skull. Others had a small crack through the body of the occipital plate similar to this one. Each had, at most, a single crack that ran across the entry hole. None had multiple, displaced cracks radiating from the entry hole.

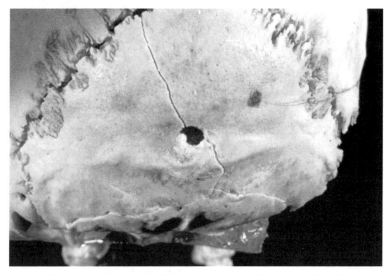

Figure 51.   Bullet entry on one of the skulls in the Biophysics Lab Tests. Pencil spot indicates aim point. *(Biophysics Division, EA)*

The large metal fragment seen near the 'cowlick' was another piece of 'entry' evidence. However, when the bullet is fully jacketed, no metal fragments will be found at the entry location. The tough gilding metal jacket is deformed on entry, but not fractured. No lead core would be exposed to be scraped off on the bone. The skull simulations showed that the jacket ruptured well inside the skull. The x-ray of one of these skulls in figure 38 shows that the scattering of small lead fragments began about midway through the skull. Even though the jacket was extensively torn and deformed, no gilding metal was found in any of the skulls. The autopsy team recovered no jacket fragments from the President's skull, because none were left to be recovered.

The President's parietal bone was extensively fractured all the way back to the occipital. The autopsy team said they removed loose pieces of broken bone instead of cutting out the usual "skullcap" to remove the brain. But if they removed enough of the parietal to remove the brain, the pieces containing the 'higher' entry wound would have to have been among the pieces removed. If the entry wound had been lying on the autopsy table, how could it have been clearly shown in the photograph of the interior of the skull shown in figure 47?

One hesitates to disagree with the opinions expressed by three panels of expert pathologists who had the autopsy pictures and x-rays to study. It is equally difficult, however, to believe that three pathologists who actually saw the body, and who could identify the lacerations to the various structures within the brain and skull, did not know the difference between occipital and parietal bones. But the three autopsy pathologists are not the only ones who saw the entry wound. An expert witness at Parkland and two others at Bethesda also saw the entry wound near the EOP.

Dr. Robert Grossman was the Chief Resident in Neurosurgery at Parkland at the time of the assassination. He and his immediate supervisor, Dr. Kemp Clark, Chief of Neurosurgery, arrived at the ER about the same time, a few minutes after the President was placed there. They immediately turned their attention to the head wound. As Dr. Clark lifted and turned the head to examine the large wound on the right side, Dr. Grossman got a clear view of the entry wound in the back of the President's head. In the November 2003 issue of *Neurosurgery,* Dr. Grossman describes the location of the entry wound—a location nearly identical to that in the autopsy report. The article also contains a sketch of this entry wound, reprinted here as figure 52.

The fifth witness is Chester H. Boyers, Jr. Boyers was the Navy officer in charge of removing the President's body from the casket and placing it on the autopsy table at Bethesda. As he removed and unwrapped the body, he saw the head wound and recalls its position very well. He wrote the following statement for author John Canal in November 2003. "As I recall the entrance wound which entered President Kennedy's head was located approximately one inch to the right and approximately one half of an inch above the occipital protuberance and exited on the right side of the head above the right eyebrow and towards the rear."

The sixth is John Stringer, the Navy photographer who took the autopsy photographs. Stringer was not only a competent medical pho-

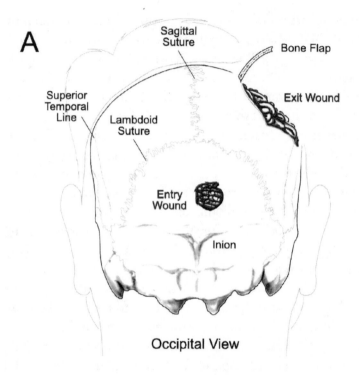

Figure 52. Dr. Robert Grossman's sketch of the JFK entry wound. *(Reprinted, by permission, from* Neurosurgery, *November 2003)*

tographer; he later gained the reputation of being one of the best in the world and taught classes in the technology at Bethesda. He is now retired from the Navy at the rank of Commander. When John Canal recently showed Stringer a copy of his graphic, similar to figure 49, he agreed with the perspective shown and added a notation on the figure, stating that the "entry wound was 2.5 cm to right and slightly above EOP."

No member of the WC staff or any of the three pathology panels talked to Dr. Grossman to get his input, so he was not among the Parkland physicians who agreed with the HSCA's location of the President's entry and exit wounds. The HSCA did interview Boyers, but evidently decided to disregard his description of the location of the wound. His original statement contains a description much the same as that in the last paragraph, but the "official" affidavit to the HSCA merely contains the fact that he "saw the entry wounds." Surprisingly, Canal found both the original and revised versions of the affidavit in the HSCA file in the National Archives.

Why would three expert panels ignore the autopsy report, the recollections of other first-hand witnesses, and the high profile of intact bone above the entry on the photograph to rely instead on a blemish on the highly mobile scalp which might or might not be a bullet hole and the position of a "relatively large metal fragment" that cannot be a piece of a bullet? John Canal believes it is because a straight line drawn backward through the correct entrance and exit locations would not line up with the upper floors of the Texas School Book Depository.[95] In fact, depending on how high "slightly above" the EOP is, that trajectory might point to street level. He also points out that the drawing used by the WC to illustrate the head shot trajectory, CE 388 (reproduced as figure 53), has the President's head tilted much too sharply to match the actual position seen in the Zapruder film. If the head in this drawing were rotated into the correct position, the bullet trajectory would be nearly horizontal.

Dr. Robert Artwohl, in a 1993 article for the *Journal of the American Medical Association*, says, "…for a bullet to enter just above the EOP

Figure 53.
Warren Commission drawing, CE 388, made to illustrate the fatal JFK head injury. *(National Archives/John Hunt)*

95. Now here is a sentence that is sure to be picked up and quoted out of context.

and exit the right frontotemporoparietal area, it would have had to travel in an upward direction, fired from inside the limousine's trunk." In his view, the situation is even worse, as he accepts the autopsy team's assumption that the bullet's exit location was at the center of the explosive hole in the President's head over the ear.

It seems likely that these three panels allowed the idea of a straight-line trajectory to influence the conclusion that there was a high entry point. But if an "impossible," street-level trajectory was the reason for ignoring the autopsy report and failing to acknowledge the existence of the best photograph of the entry wound, it was completely unnecessary.

The HSCA's expert consultant, Tom Canning, reconstructed a trajectory from points near the Forensic Pathology Panel's entry and exit locations on the skull and projected it in a straight line back to a point "with a circle of probable error" that overlapped the sniper's nest window. Researcher John Hunt points out that Canning's and the FPP's entry locations are actually slightly different. Had he used the FPP points, the circle of probable error would have missed the window. But the difference is irrelevant and the trajectory meaningless. The path of a deformed bullet through a body is never straight. Like the yawed bullet already discussed, the odd-shaped piece of a bullet is inevitably unstable and will develop some degree of lift that will curve its trajectory in tissue. Both the sharpness of the curvature and its direction will depend on the shape and orientation of the fragment, but all will curve to a greater or lesser extent. Of the thousands of examples of yawed, deformed, and broken rifle bullets fired into gelatin tissue simulant at the Biophysics Division lab and other similar facilities, none had a perfectly straight trajectory. Few are even close.

Though all the Biophysics Lab test shots were aimed so that the WC's specified entry and exit locations would lie on a straight trajectory, none of the bullets penetrated the front of the skull at the "intended" exit location. One even punched out through the right orbit (eye socket) near the nose. Nor were the researchers surprised by the fact that all those fragmented bullets exited from an obviously curved path. All were quite familiar with the trajectories of bullets and bullet fragments through tissue simulant. The curved path of 7.62 mm bullet fragments was shown in figure 24.

Like the Acoustic Panel and the Forensic Pathology Panel, Canning became a bit overzealous in his support of the case being made by the

HSCA staff in his "reconstruction" of a backward trajectory from the head wound. Because of the indeterminate direction and extent of curvature of the trajectory of the deformed bullet, the entry and exit locations of the head wound are of no value in reconstructing a backward trajectory. What can be concluded is that the bullet approached from the rear. The true connection between that shot and the Oswald rifle is provided, to a high degree of statistical certainty, by the engraving on the recovered jacket fragments and the Neutron Activation Analysis, which connects the lead core in one of those recovered pieces to the lead fragments recovered from the President's head.

Likewise, the wound locations have no value in reconstructing the exit trajectory of a yawed or deformed bullet or bullet fragments. Though it probably is not noticed by most, if the exit trajectory of the HSCA path shown in Figure 42 were correct, the bullet fragments would have gone into Governor Connally's back or the back of the car seat in front of him, not up to the windshield, as they actually did. The President was no longer sitting nearly erect by frame 312 of Zapruder's film.[96] At the time of the final shot, he was leaning forward and to his left. Figure 54 shows a drawing of the President at frame 312 with an entry trajectory from the sixth-floor window of the Depository and an exit trajectory that leads to the known impact points on and just above the windshield.[97] This curvature shown in this drawing is about the amount of curvature to be expected in the trajectory of a badly deformed or broken bullet. Because the amount and direction of the curvature is unpredictable, the only way to reconstruct the path of the bullet in a drawing such as this is to use independent facts to establish the approach and exit trajectories. Without this independent information, the only thing we know for sure is that the approach and exit trajectories cannot lie on a single straight line.

The importance of this discussion of entry and exit wounds on President Kennedy is not indicated by its length. It is included to set the scientific record straight. The actual location of the impact and exit points would make little difference in the effect that the bullet produced in Kennedy's head. Virtually any rifle bullet that penetrates into the skull

96. Neurosurgeon Dr. Michael Carey thinks that he may be falling as a result of temporary paralysis from the spinal damage associated with the neck wound.

97. The obvious requirement for a curved trajectory in the head wound, matching the sketch of figure 52, was not missed by earlier writers. A similar sketch appears in Lattimer's book, *Kennedy and Lincoln,* published in 1980.

will shatter the bones, disrupt the brain, and cause instant death. The major difference would be the site of the "explosion" that relieves the internal pressure.

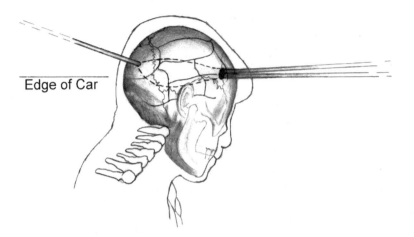

Figure 54. Sketch of the JFK head wound with curved trajectory of the bullet. (Larry M. Sturdivan)

Though the autopsy team was not guilty of mislocating the entry wound to the head, they did make the error of choosing not to take the time to exhaustively document both the head and neck injuries. Proper documentation would have included photographs of the most important details and measurements of the distance of each vital detail from fixed landmarks. Had they considered the scrutiny to which this very non-routine post-mortem examination was certain to be subjected, they most likely would not have cut it short to spare the feelings of the two family members waiting impatiently in the hall outside. Looking back at the event, we find no evidence that either Jackie or Robert Kennedy requested that the autopsy be completed quickly but, under those circumstances, the autopsy team had little time for cool reflection.

And who could have known that other authorities would step in and interfere with the subsequent course of events? Although the formal report might be written up days later, an autopsy report that is likely to become a part of a criminal investigation is never written up without access to any photographs and x-rays taken during the examination—but it was in this case. The photographic material was removed from their possession by the Secret Service when they left Bethesda. The exposed photographic film was taken before being developed. The autopsy team had only briefly examined the x-rays as they searched for the phantom bullet that had entered the President's back at the base of his neck but apparently never exited. The major blunder was in not dissecting that wound to find the exit at the throat.

Only after the autopsy had been terminated did Commander Humes make two phone calls to Dr. Perry at Parkland, a few minutes apart. It was then that he learned of the tracheotomy that had obliterated a missile wound. At this point, he understood why there was no bullet in the body, but no "exit wound" either. This revelation required revision of the draft autopsy report,[98] but the final draft was still completed before the end of the weekend. The official report connected the obvious entry wound in the back, at the base of the neck, to the obliterated exit wound in the suprasternal notch under the collar and tie. If Humes knew about the remarks of the Parkland doctors about an "entry wound in the front of the neck," he was not disturbed by it. He knew that the treating physician often misidentifies the manner and sequence in which wounds are produced. It is sufficient for the emergency room staff to treat the wounds and symptoms as presented. For that job, knowing the sequence in which they were caused may be the subject of curiosity, but is of little or no importance.

It also was not disturbing to Commander Humes that the autopsy team had no success probing the wound at the base of the neck to find it emerging at the throat. He knew human anatomy better than most of his critics do. There are many layers of overlapping muscle in the upper back and their relative position had to have shifted between the time that the President was shot and the time that they were attempting to probe the wound as he was lying on the autopsy table. Even if they had known the position of the President's arm at the time of the shot and attempted to move it into that position, there is no guarantee that they could have gotten all the holes through the layers of tissue to line up. Cold, dead

---

98. Autopsy critics like to make a major point of this revision, but it was very difficult to explain the "missing" bullet until Humes learned about the wound that had been obliterated. Then everything fell into place and the autopsy report could be written with surprising accuracy, considering that the photographic material was not available for reference. Should Humes or one of the others have phoned Parkland while the autopsy was still going on? Probably. But it is very easy to second-guess the autopsy team, years after the event and out of the context of that tension-filled laboratory.

muscles, reputedly still in rigor mortis at the time of the autopsy, would not have contracted like living muscle. The only way that they could have explored the track of the bullet with any certainty was to have dissected it. They chose not to—for the sake of the time it would have taken.

The most frequently cited difference between Parkland and Bethesda reports is the "entrance wound to the throat" error. As Michael Baden, Chairman of the House's Forensic Pathology Panel, told Gerald Posner, "…the treating physicians…are wrong half the time about exit or entrance…. The mistakes in judgments from Parkland are exactly why we have autopsies."[99] Calling it mistakes in judgment may be a bit harsh. It usually results from jumping to conclusions, based on an incomplete set of facts. He is placing no blame on the Parkland surgeons for making errors that had nothing to do with treating the patient. It is not their job.

Among the physicians in that emergency room, there was extensive experience treating emergency trauma. Several had personally observed and treated hundreds of bullet wounds. Dr. Baxter testified, "…we admit and treat, I would estimate, around 500 gunshot wounds per year…" But Dr. Akin also stated, "…most of them are injured with low velocity missiles, smaller caliber—.22 caliber to .38 caliber,…I don't see too many exit wounds." In conversation, Dr. Grossman pointed out that the members of the ER staff who attended the President were very young. He estimates that the average age was little more than 30. The oldest, Kemp Clark, was 38. None could have had experience treating military casualties in WW II or Korea. The few rifle bullet injuries they had seen, if any, were likely all caused by hunting bullets. It is certain that none of them had observed wounding by turn-of-the-century-design military bullets. If they suspected the exit wound was from a rifle bullet (as they should have—from Secret Service sources standing nearby), they would have expected it to be even larger and more ragged than the hole left by handgun bullets. A hollow-point or soft-point hunting bullet would have been deformed into a lump of twisted metal by the time it exited, leaving a gaping, ragged hole. In the majority of cases within their experience, even a fully-jacketed handgun bullet would have yawed to a nearly

---

99. Over the years there have been several studies documenting the misidentification of entrance versus exit wounds by emergency room personnel. Dr. Baden was probably recalling some of these. Two articles on the topic are listed in the Bibliography (see Collins). In brief, their entry/exit differentiation is only a little bit better than a flip of a coin.

sideways position before exiting. These would also create a ragged exit wound. If it does not hit a bone while still at high velocity, the WCC/MC bullet does not deform like a hunting bullet nor yaw as rapidly as a handgun bullet.

Earlier we discussed the instability of a bullet in tissue that causes the yaw to grow. As it yaws, the bullet gains angular momentum. The angular momentum may be thought of as the amount of persistence with which it rotates. A short, light bullet, like a small handgun bullet with a certain amount of angular momentum, may yaw rapidly. A long heavy bullet with the same angular momentum will turn more slowly, but its motion is just as hard to stop. Though it had acquired considerable angular momentum in passing through the President's neck, the WCC/MC bullet was still moving nearly point-first as it exited his throat. Under normal circumstances, the exit wound in the skin of his neck would have been smaller than the ER physicians would have expected it to be, but it would still have had somewhat ragged edges and would have had no semblance of the abrasion collar that surrounds an entry wound.

The typical exit wound is shown in a diagram in figure 55. As the bullet exits, it pushes the flesh and skin ahead of it, ripping its way out through stretched and distorted tissue. This is the reason that the edges are ragged and torn. But the exit wound from President Kennedy's throat was through the shirt and tie immediately beneath a close-fitting collar and knot. You don't think of a few pieces of cloth as having much inertia (resistance to being moved) or strength, but recall the exit of the bullet from Governor Connally's chest. The bullet passed through the layers of cloth in the front of his coat so fast that it did not have time to move before the bullet was gone. In the short time it takes the bullet to penetrate, the inertia of the cloth holds it as though it were clamped in place. Only after the bullet is long gone (relatively speaking) does the momentum deposited by the bullet push out the front of the coat, which then collapses in a movement that is visible to the naked eye. The cloth resists being perforated and gains momentum roughly proportional to its strength.

Whenever the clothing is loose fitting, its presence has little effect on an exit wound through human skin. But when the clothing is held close against the skin, the skin and underlying tissue cannot bulge out as in the typical exit wound. The skin presses tightly against the restraining cloth, also shown in figure 55, which prevents stretching and tearing. It

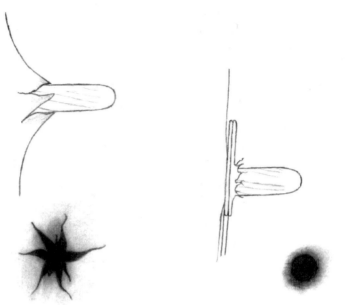

Exit through bare skin   Exit through "shored" skin

Figure 55.   Illustration of bullet exit wounds through skin, unconstrained and constrained by snug clothing. (Larry M. Sturdivan)

can even be pushed so tightly against the cloth that it acquires a bruised, hemorrhagic circle around the exit hole that bears a superficial resemblance to an abrasion collar. Close inspection of this type of wound might (albeit rarely) reveal the pattern of the cloth pressed into the bruised area that will distinguish it from a true abrasion collar. However, none of the physicians mentioned an abrasion collar. If they noticed a bruised ring surrounding the throat wound that looked like one, they obviously did not examine it closely.

Even the exit hole through goat skin in the Biophysics Lab neckshot simulations were not the typical exit wound with radiating tears, even though these simulated exits were not shored up by a close-fitting collar. Several entry and exit wounds from this test are shown in figure 56. Exits are a bit larger than entry wounds, but by no means badly torn and stellate. Had they been constrained, they probably would have been even smaller.

In the drawing that duplicates the autopsy photograph of the tracheostomy in the President's throat with a photo inset of the autopsy picture (figure 57), there are small circular arcs at the top and bottom of the cut. Given the resolution of the original photograph, it is impossible to tell whether this arc is part of the permanent cavity left by the bullet or a hemorrhagic area at the margin of the hole left on the skin by the pressure of the exiting bullet pushing it against the unyielding collar and tie. In either case, it is not the ragged exit wound typically expected from a bullet. It is clean and round, an appearance one would easily mistake as an entry wound.

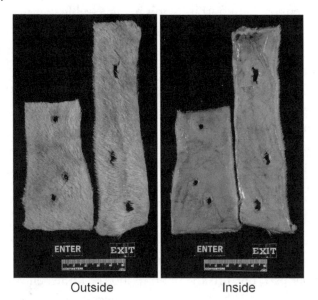

Figure 56. Entrance and exit holes through goat skin from the Biophysics neck-shot simulations. *(Biophysics Division, EA/Dale Myers)*

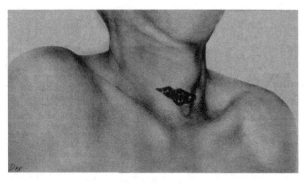

JFK EXHIBIT F-36

Figure 57. Dox drawing from the photograph of the tracheostomy in the president's throat. *(National Archives)*

Autopsy critics quote the report of two FBI agents present at the autopsy, Agents Sibert and O'Neill, which mentions "surgery to the head" of the President. This statement is used to conclude that there were "surgical" alterations of the President's wounds to make it appear that the bullets entered and exited from the opposite directions. It is inconceivable that the autopsy team would either not notice "surgery to the head" of the President or not report it. Nor is it conceivable that the brain could have been removed and replaced (another Lifton claim) without the autopsy team being aware of it. Such a major finding could not have been simply overlooked when they were preparing their report.

What is conceivable is that two FBI bystanders misunderstood some of the conversation of the pathologists around the autopsy table. This was confirmed by the FBI observers when asked about the statement. The routine for removal of the brain from the skull in a post-mortem examination calls for severance of the spinal cord as low as possible. It was not necessary to remove the "skullcap" in this case. All the team had to do was "reflect the scalp backward" by making minimal additional cuts and remove some pieces of bone that were already loosened when the skull shattered. This enlarged the existing hole enough to allow the brain to be removed. After severing blood vessels and connective tissue to free the upper part, one lifts the brain to insert a knife beneath it to sever the cranial nerves and the brainstem's connection with the cord. These procedures were probably the "surgery" mentioned in the FBI report. When the brain is lifted, the cord is pulled upward a short distance into the skull. So when the brain is removed, one obtains a short sample of spinal cord along with it.

Critics manage to transform a prepared section of the cord into something sinister. On the contrary, taking a section for microscopic examination in this area to document any damage to the spinal cord makes perfect sense. The fact that there is no mention of damage to the cord in the supplementary autopsy report is evidence that microscopic damage was not observed. This is consistent with an amount of stretching (shearing) that would have produced a mechanical stimulation of the nerves, but left no visible microscopic damage to the individual axons. It also indicates that the cord was not previously transected (the brain had not been removed before the autopsy).

Conspiracy authors also make good use of the statement that a "missile" was recovered from the head wound during the autopsy. This missile, which they insist is a bullet, is mentioned in a receipt from the Secret Service. By this device, they create both a "missing bullet" and recovered fragments for which there is no receipt. In fact, the term "missile" is used in wound ballistics and forensic pathology to describe any penetrating object. When a bone is struck and shattered by a high velocity projectile, fragments of bone are often propelled through the adjacent tissue. As in the case of John Connally's lung wound, these bone fragments are referred to as "secondary missiles," as opposed to the "primary" missile that propels them. The receipt for the "missile," mentioned in the autopsy report, is simply a receipt for the small lead fragments that were recovered from the brain at autopsy.

The neck wounds shown in the autopsy pictures also correlate perfectly with the other evidence. In many pictures taken along the motorcade route, the President's suit coat is seen to be riding up his back as he waved to the crowd. See figure 58. When the coat is in this position, the holes in his coat and shirt line up with the wound in his back at the base of his neck. Critics use the hole in the coat to prove that the entry

Figure 58. Croft photograph of the presidential limousine, showing the position of the president's coat shortly before the second shot (first hit). *(National Archives/John Hunt)*

wound on the back was lower than the autopsy photographs show it to be. It hardly needs to be stated that using a piece of movable clothing to dispute the location of a wound is a bad approach.

The x-rays show a faint, but perceptible, shadow of a wound track running from the entry location shown in the autopsy photos to the exit point at the suprasternal notch where his tie was knotted over the President's collar. Both his tie and collar were damaged. The entry wound indicated by the measurements listed on the autopsy sheet is consistent with the autopsy photographs. The entry was located just above the transverse process of the first thoracic vertebra (a slim finger of bone sticking sideways from the vertebra). When the House Forensic Pathology Panel examined the President's neck x-rays, they determined that the soft tissue adjacent to this process was slightly damaged. The bullet did not strike either the transverse process of the thoracic vertebra or the body of the cervical vertebra. Had it contacted either, the nose of the bullet would have been dented and the x-rays would show the bone to have been damaged.

Contrary to the accusation that they mislocated the President's entry wounds, the observations of Humes, Boswell, and Finck, in both the report and WC testimony, are in remarkably accurate agreement with the autopsy photographs that they were not allowed to consult. The autopsy was not perfect, but it was not the botched job that the critics claim it was. It did supply the information critical to documenting the case. Of particular value were the location of the entry wounds, the photographs and x-rays, critical observations documented in the report, and—perhaps the most important—the small fragments recovered from the President's head wound.

Unfortunately, their speculations based on those observations and on second-hand reports of Connally's wounds were not quite so accurate. Identifying the large defect in the side of Kennedy's head as a bullet exit, a garbled account of break-up and tumbling bullets, jumping to conclusions about CE 399 not being able to cause Connally's wounds or depositing fragments in his wrist or thigh continue to provide conspiracy writers with ammunition. Had they discussed the Biophysics Lab tests with the wound ballistics experts, some of these erroneous WC speculations, and the errors in the Clay Shaw testimony by Finck, could have been avoided. In fact, this discussion would have been very helpful to the Biophysics Lab team as well, both before and after the experimental testing.

This points out a flaw that the Warren Commission investigation shares with the HSCA investigation some 14 years later. In both cases, the full-time staff, who were really conducting the investigation, carefully kept the experts isolated from each other. The reason for this in a typical "legal" investigation is to keep cross-contamination from coloring expert opinion, a flaw that might be exploited by the defense in the trial. In these investigations there was obviously not going to be a trial and, thus, no real justification for preventing the experts from talking to each other. One suspects that the real reason for keeping the experts from communicating with each other was to preserve the power of the staff members. The staff is the only body privy to all the information, so they can direct the investigation as they wish and pick and choose the information that contributes to making the case that they want to make. The downside is that information known to one group of experts that others would find helpful is never communicated. The only people who have all the information at their disposal are a group of lawyers who do not have the technical background that would allow them to understand all that the scientific data imply.

CHAPTER ELEVEN

A Puff of Smoke

> [The sound of the shots] "came from the left and in front of us, toward the wooden fence, and there was a puff of smoke that came underneath the trees on the embankment."
>
> —*James L. Simmons*[100]

Because of the infamous fog in London, the burning of soft coal was banned many years ago. It was found that the "fog" was actually a product of the smoke from soft-coal fires. The atmospheric conditions that occur frequently in that area cause microscopic water droplets to condense around the fine particles created by burning coal. Instead of rising, the way we imagine a smoke column behaving, the smoke and water "fog" hangs in the low spots and is not dissipated until the atmospheric conditions change or a wind sweeps it away. The burning of soft coal was not banned from the English countryside, so the phenomenon may still be seen in rural villages under the proper conditions. Figure 59 is a picture of the village of King's Somborne, located in rural Hampshire, southwest of London. This picture was taken on a winter day when the atmospheric conditions were right for a coal-fired "London fog."

Smoke

Mark Lane started the "puffs of smoke" story when he read the Warren Commission affidavit of Austin L. Miller who said, "I saw something which I thought was smoke or steam coming from a group of trees north of Elm off the railroad tracks." Lane interviewed several of the railroad employees and found seven among them who would admit to having seen "smoke" among the trees behind the fence. Ordinarily we would discount the appearance

---

100. From an interview filmed and tape recorded by Mark Lane in Mesquite, Texas, on March 28, 1966. Quoted in *Rush to Judgment*.

of smoke from a rifle unless the assassin was firing a black powder "blunderbuss." Modern smokeless propellant usually lives up to its name. The combustion products of so-called smokeless powder includes few particulates that may act as condensation nuclei. Under the same atmospheric conditions that produce the London fog, though, these particulates may induce small droplets of water to condense around themselves, like the coal smoke in the picture of King's Somborne. Under these conditions—that might have existed in Dallas on the day of the assassination—a faint cloud of water droplets will form in front of the gun muzzle, creating a momentary impression of "smoke." Even under ideal conditions, this cloud is very short-lived. Compared to the combustion products of many coal stoves burning for many hours, the amount of particulates from a gunshot is minute. The droplets will dissipate and evaporate immediately, even in nearly still air. They would vanish in a small fraction of a second in a breeze such as the one blowing in Dealey Plaza that day.

Movies of the test firings done for the acoustic studies commissioned

Figure 59.   Picture of the village of King's Somborne in rural England, with "London fog" from soft coal fires. *(Larry M. Sturdivan)*

by the HSCA in 1978 show a few shots from the Mannlicher-Carcano which have a wisp of "smoke" near the muzzle in a single frame following the shot. Tellingly, the only evidence was in the movies. None of the eyewitnesses present that day report seeing smoke from a gunbarrel.

The existence of smoke behind the fence near the railroad overpass has always been controversial, because of Miller's statement that it might be "steam." Indeed, there was a steam pipe in the area near the railroad tracks, according to testimony to the WC by the ubiquitous Deputy Constable Seymour Weitzman. Immediately after the gunfire ceased, he heard someone say that the shots had come from the "wall" [beside the railroad overpass]. He told the Commission, "I immediately scaled the wall....My hands grabbed steampipes. I burned them." At this point we acknowledge Jim Marrs, the JFK-assassination writer who repeats every scrap of evidence that anyone has advanced in support of the existence of a conspiracy. In his book *Crossfire,* he draws to our attention a movie made by NBC photographer Dave Weigman, who had been riding in a car at the back of the motorcade. In Marrs words,

> Hearing shots, Weigman started filming even before the firing stopped. He then jumped out of the convertible and ran up the Grassy Knoll with his camera still operating. Because of all this motion, his blurred and jerky film was overlooked as assassination evidence until recently. However, in one clear frame, which depicts the presidential limousine just entering the Triple Underpass, a puff of smoke is clearly visible hanging in front of trees on the knoll—exactly where Holland and the other railroad workers claimed to have seen it.

But the presidential limousine did not go under the underpass until several seconds after the shooting stopped. It took Weigman that amount of time to leave his car and run across the Plaza. This is much too long for the "smoke" from a rifle to have hung around the location. It is also at a time when Senator Yarborough and Mrs. Cabell said that they could smell gunpowder in their cars in the middle of the motorcade.[101] Apparently the impossibility of the "smoke" both staying on the grassy knoll and drifting back to the middle of the motorcade did not occur to

---

101. Conspiracy writers also use these statements to support the existence of grassy-knoll gunmen. They claim that it is much more likely that the odor of gunpowder would have drifted to the back of the motorcade from near ground level than from the sixth floor of a building. But the picture of King's Somborne shows that "smoke" from combustion products often settles into the low spots on a humid day. It had only stopped raining in Dallas shortly before the motorcade began. In addition, the cars in which the Cabells and Yarborough were riding were more nearly downwind of the Depository than the grassy knoll, if the wind swirling around tall buildings can be said to have a single direction.

Marrs. Weigman's picture could not possibly show the puff of "smoke or steam" seen during the shooting by the railroad workers, but it could show another puff of "steam" from a leak or a pressure-regulating vent in Weitzman's steam pipe. Of course, in the many conspiracy scenarios, not all the gunmen are near the steampipes. But if you have ever seen wisps of condensed water vapor venting from a steampipe, you realize that the water droplets can be whipped many yards away from the vent by a breeze before they dissipate and evaporate. There was such a breeze blowing in Dealey Plaza that day. On the other hand—in the view of some—the smoke on Weigman's movie could just be some light reflecting off of some out-of-focus leaves on a tree. In either case, there is no reason to believe that anyone saw "smoke" from a firearm at that location.

Weitzman's response to the shouts of people who heard the sound of gunfire from the fence behind the knoll was not unique. In still pictures taken after the last shot, Patrolman Bobby Hargis, one of the four presidential motorcycle escorts, is shown running up the grassy knoll. Conspiracy advocates often claim that he ran there because he heard gunfire from that location and went looking for an assassin behind the fence.

What he said in his sworn testimony to the Warren Commission was, "Well, at the time it sounded like the shots were right next to me. There was not any way in the world I could tell where they were coming from, but at the time there was something in my head that said that they probably could have been coming from the railroad overpass, because I thought since I had got splattered, with blood—I was just a little back and left of...Mrs. Kennedy...."

In other words, he thought the blood splatters would follow the bullet. Looking to the opposite side of the President from the blood splatters that hit him, it seemed to Hargis that the bullet must have come from the right end of the railroad overpass. The questioning continued a few lines later.

Mr. Stern: "And did you run up the incline on your side of Elm Street?" [the grassy knoll]

Mr. Hargis: "Yes sir; I ran to the light post, and I ran up to this kind of a little wall, brick wall up there to see if I could get a better look on the bridge [railroad overpass], and, of course I was looking all around that place by that time...."

Mr. Stern: "Did you get behind the picket fence that runs from the overpass to the concrete wall?"

Mr. Hargis: "No."

Mr. Stern: "On the north side of Elm Street?"

Mr. Hargis: "No, no; I don't remember any picket fence."

Not only did he not run up the grassy knoll to look for assassins behind the fence, as often claimed, he did not even remember that there was a fence there. Although he only ran up the knoll to get a better look at the overpass, pictures taken a short while later show many police and civilians on the hill. Interestingly enough, those same pictures show Jean Hill still standing or sitting beside her friend Mary Moorman on the south side of the street, the opposite side from the grassy knoll. Jean Hill is the lady who told Jim Marrs in 1989 that she had rushed across the street, dodging the last cars in the motorcade, and ran up the grassy knoll in time to see a gunman leave the parking lot carrying a rifle. That story is quite different from what she told the police on the day of the assassination and to the Warren Commission some months later. In her sworn testimony, she specifically stated that she saw no gun and the man she pursued gave her no reason to believe he had done anything wrong other than the fact that he was running, not from the parking lot, but across the grass in front of the book Depository.

When he arrived at the parking lot behind the fence, Seymour Weitzman found that a railroad yardman was already there. When he asked him if he had seen anything unusual, Weitzman testified, "He said he thought he saw somebody throw something through a bush."[102] Every square inch of the area, including the area under the bushes, was searched, but nothing was found: no rifles, no cartridge cases, not even a matchstick. Since they have no physical evidence that a gunman was there, the conspiracy writers make the most of the only thing they have: the footprints. They find it very mysterious that an observer would stand behind the fence to watch the presidential motorcade when they could be on the grass of the knoll or even on the sidewalk. Of course, they do not find it at all mysterious

---

102. It was in the search for this object thrown through the bushes that Weitzman found the fragment of skull near the curb at the site of the fatal shot.

that one of their star witnesses, J. C. Price, chose to watch the motorcade from the roof of a building on the other side of Dealey Plaza, several times farther from the motorcade than the mysterious footprints were.

Price was the witness who signed an affidavit on the day of the assassination which stated that he saw a man leave the area behind the fence after the shooting holding something in his hand. When grilled by Mark Lane, he admitted the object in the man's hand "…could have been a gun." Marrs repeats the Lane story of a man hurrying from the lot with a gun in hand on page 39, and criticizes the WC for never having questioned Price.[103] Not surprisingly, both men leave out Price's first impression: that the object in the man's hand was a hat. By the time we reach page 478 of *Crossfire*, Price's story has grown into one of "…seeing a man with a rifle running behind the wooden picket fence on top of the Grassy Knoll." It is conceivable that Price was far enough away that he could not distinguish a hat from a handgun—but if he could not distinguish it from a rifle, one would wonder about the value of his observation. Both Lane and Marrs quote from Price's affidavit taken on the day of the assassination: "…there was a volley of shots, I think five and then much later…another one." What they do not say is that the text they omitted in the place of the final ellipsis consists of the words "maybe as much as five minutes later."

Conspiracy researchers do not confine their search to overlooked NBC movies and observations of remote witnesses. They also examine in minute detail any photograph that was taken in Dealey Plaza near the time of the shooting. While many find assassins behind trees, bushes, and the fence in these pictures, the HSCA's expert photography panel did not. They carefully examined these controversial pictures and found that the shadowy gunmen figures were just that—shadows. In one case, the shadows of the "man" and the "gun" were found by the House Photo Panel to be separated by several feet.

---

103. This is one of the most frequent complaints leveled at the WC by critics and one of those with the least validity. The WC could not possibly interview everybody who was in Dealey Plaza that day. Whenever the staff interview, police interview, or affidavit was sufficient or indicated nothing new was to be gained, the witnesses were not called. This does not mean that the contents of those interviews or affidavits were ignored or considered invalid by the WC or its staff. When the HSCA interviewed Billy Lovelady to determine if he was the person seen in the Altgens photograph standing on the steps of the Depository, the sworn testimony was again taken by the HSCA staff, not by the members of the House of Representatives.

Conspiracy researchers discovered another witness, Gordon Arnold, when he was interviewed by a Dallas reporter in 1978. Arnold, a GI home on leave in November 1963, stated that he was watching the motorcade from behind the fence and that he was sure he heard the gunshots coming from his immediate area. Frightened, he fell to the ground until the shooting stopped. Arnold relates another phony-CIA-identification and policeman-confiscating-his-camera story with some crying and kicking as embellishment. Significantly, he did not say that he saw a man with a gun. If he were at that location, it would not be surprising that he heard gunshots coming from a direction other than from the Depository. They could have been either shock waves from the supersonic bullets or the muzzle blast reflected from the concrete overpass or nearby buildings.

If Arnold was actually there on the day of the assassination, he could have been the person J. C. Price saw, GI cap in hand, hurrying out of the parking lot. It could, indeed, have been his "mysterious" footprints that constitute the only physical evidence indicating that somebody was behind the fence at the time the motorcade passed, gunman or not. Posner doubts he was there because he does not appear to be where he said he was in pictures taken at the time of the assassination. But the maker of the footprints or the person Price saw (likely one and the same) does not appear in any of the pictures either. We know that the footprints were fresh. The morning's rain would have partially or completely washed out any old footprints. Given the evidence of the fresh footprints, it is obvious that somebody was there that morning, though there is no evidence of more than one person. Whether that individual was still there during the assassination and whether he was, in fact, Gordon Arnold is open to question. In either case, we have no reason to believe that the person who left footprints was any different from the hundreds of others who were in or around Dealey Plaza to see the presidential motorcade.

The acoustic evidence presented during the HSCA hearings was discredited by independent experts and modern reconstruction of the position of all motorcycles. Earwitness accounts of shots coming from the grassy knoll are easily explained by echoes and misleading shock waves from bullets. The puffs of "smoke" were actually wisps of condensed steam. The recent stories of witnesses who claim that they saw gunmen behind the fence were found not to be credible. Those who were in the best position to see that area at the time of the shooting—including, perhaps, Gordon Arnold—did not see anybody with a gun. The many purported pictures of "gunmen" on the grassy knoll were discredited by the HSCA photo panel. Although Abraham Zapruder was standing near the grassy knoll, he acknowledged that he could not tell where the gunfire was coming from. Dr. David Green told the HSCA that, when standing near Zapruder's position, "A shot from the knoll usually sounds like a shot from the knoll." In addition, Dr. Hartmann, who stood on the same pedestal that Zapruder was standing on while shots were fired from the grassy knoll stated; "I would have expected the witness to be more definite that there was something to the right [the knoll] if there had been a shot from there."

In spite of these problems, there seems to be an attitude of "where there's smoke, there's gunfire" in the minds of conspiracy theorists. It is an article of faith that there was a man firing a weapon from the fence behind the grassy knoll. Just because the acoustic evidence, the only scientific evidence they had, was shown to be invalid does not mean that the gunman was not there; it just means that the "proof" has not been found yet. On the other hand, the opinion of experts casts doubt on the existence of a second gunman, but it does not prove there was no shot from the knoll. Unlike most cases of trying to prove a negative, in this case there is proof that there were no gunshots fired from the trees, behind the fence, or anywhere on or behind the grassy knoll at the time of the assassination. The proof comes from Dr. William Hartmann's "jiggle" analysis.

Sound and Jiggle

The studies Louis Alvarez did for Bell and Howell were mentioned in chapter three. He conducted this investigation after he noticed an insuppressible 3-cycle-per-second "jitter" pattern in his own amateur movies, tracking a moving animal across the African plain. Alvarez, however, misinterprets this jitter as an internal neuromuscular oscillation. Actually, an "internal neuromuscular oscillation" is usually a symptom of a malady like Parkinson's disease. The jitter Alvarez discovered is not totally internal in origin. It has an external component: the visual feedback from the scene in the viewfinder. As the photographer pans to follow the subject, the camera will move off-target a bit because of imperfect angular matching or unanticipated change of direction or speed by the subject. The visual system feeds the signal to the brain, which detects a mismatch and sends a signal for a correction to the muscles involved in the tracking movement. As this correction is made, it results in a slightly larger than average blur on a frame or two. If the adjustment is a slight over-correction or there is another change that results in imperfect tracking, it will result in another deviation that must be corrected. Alvarez found that this cycle—sensory input/mental processing/muscular movement—takes about a third of a second and sets up a feedback loop that results in the three-per-second "jitter" cycle. This tracking-error cycle has nothing to do with the startle reaction that he sought. He discovered it in completely normal, startle-free movies that he made himself.

Alvarez extrapolated his internal jitter mistake into a "neuromuscular oscillation" that would result from a startle reaction to a loud noise. That is, he assumed that a startle would result in a series of large peaks. But there is no sensory feedback to produce a "cycle" from a single loud noise like a gunshot. In normal people, the rule is "one stimulus—one reflex reaction." In your next physical exam, note how an involuntary reflex works. When the doctor taps your knee, your foot does not bounce for a while at three bounces per second; it jerks once and returns to its previous position. Alvarez correctly identified a three-per-second jitter due to normal panning error, but a startle is characterized by a single jump that results in a large blur in a single frame or, occasionally, in two adjacent frames. The latter is caused by the startle reaction being centered between frames, so that the first frame gets the beginning of the startle-induced movement and the second records the end of it.

The presence of a highly blurred frame on the film does not prove the presence of a startle, acoustic or otherwise. There are many reasons for unsteadiness in the pictures taken by a hand-held camera. A visually-produced startle such as the sudden appearance of an unexpected object in the viewfinder, difficulty tracking a moving object past an obstruction, or a momentary loss of balance can all cause large smears. Yet the absence of a jiggle does prove the absence of a nearby gunshot. The startle reflex is just what the name implies: an involuntary muscular reflex—like the knee-jerk reflex. If it exceeds a person's startle threshold, it cannot be suppressed.[104]

Alvarez' article discusses the fact that cameramen from CBS duplicated, for their four-part special in June of 1967, the startle reaction

104. More detail on the startle reflex is included in Appendix E.

that he expected to appear in Zapruder's movie. They placed the cameramen off the side of a firing range at a distance equal to the distance Zapruder was from the President's car at the final shot. When a rifle was fired down the range, the bullet passed the point where the car would have been. He quotes from Walter Cronkite's narrative. "The film taken by these cameramen showed the effect of the shots, despite instructions to hold steady. Even in steadier hands, motion was always noticeable. This frame shows highlight dots around the car's windshield. In reaction to a shot, the dots changed to crescents. And in the following frame they became streaks, comparable to streaks found in some frames from Mr. Zapruder's film." Notice that Mr. Cronkite did not say "following frames." He referred to frame as singular.

In a private conversation in 2000, Dr. Hartmann described an informal experiment he conducted during the 1978 acoustic tests. As he stood at various places in Dealey Plaza during the firing tests, he would run a pencil across a blank piece of paper. When the gunshot was fired, his pencil mark would show a jagged line from a startle reaction. During the conversation, he made a representative drawing of that pattern. This drawing is reproduced as figure 60. The next time you are startled by a loud noise, try to suppress it. By the time you realize that you have been startled, the reflex has already happened. After repeated exposure, the magnitude of the reaction diminishes, but it never completely disappears.[105]

During the House hearings, Dr. Hartmann discussed the updated version of the Alvarez "jiggle analysis" of the Zapruder film that he and colleague Frank Scott completed. Hartmann and Scott measured indicators of camera motion that are different from Alvarez' measure of the angular acceleration between sequential frames. Hartmann plotted a measure of the "smear" of small images, such as points of light reflected from the shiny surface of the car, in the space of a single frame. The plot is reproduced as figure 61. Scott made measurements of the displacement of the camera between frames. All three types of measure are quantitative indications of the motion of the camera caused by the startle reaction or

---

105. The day I reported to work at the Aberdeen Proving Ground, my new supervisor was showing me the ropes when a loud explosion nearly caused me to jump out of my chair. "What was that!" I said. "What was what?" he replied. "That noise!" "Oh, that's just an experiment in one of the test ranges. You'll get used to it." A few weeks later, I had my first off-post visitor. We were talking about an upcoming test between our two labs when suddenly he almost jumped out of his chair. "What was that!" he said. "What was what?" I replied.

other twitch in the otherwise smooth panning.

Alvarez presumed that the number of large peaks that started at frame 318 were due to Zapruder's nervous system being "set into oscillation" by the shock wave of the bullet—a "startle" reaction. Hartmann followed his lead and looked for three or more series of jiggles. In letters to the HSCA and in his final report, he identified two "series," one following frame 318, another in frames in the 190s. He also identified the large blur at frames 158/159 as a possible startle from a shot, though it was not part of a series of large smears. He never found a smear or a series that he could identify as the "fourth shot" found by the acoustic experts. The HSCA's staff evidently presumed that not all bullets would pro-

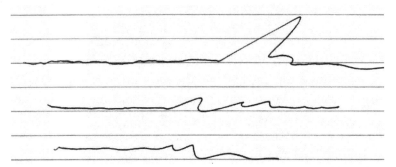

Figure 60.   Dr. William Hartmann's sketch of startle reactions in pencil lines drawn at the time of rifle shots in Dealy Plaza during the reenactment for the acoustic tests. *(William Hartmann/L. M. Sturdivan)*

duce a startle reaction. They used the acoustic analysis to place two more gunshots—one earlier than the series Hartmann found in the 190s and another between that and the final series. Both of these, they concluded, were missed shots.

The timing of the final shot was quite easy due to the explosive spray from the President's head in Zapruder frame 313. As the spray was quite extensive in this frame, it was assumed that the bullet actually struck nearer the preceding frame, at 312. Exactly six frames (one-third of a second) later, a very large blur is seen in the Zapruder film, at frame 318. This very clear sequence provides our best estimate of Zapruder's startle delay.[106]

A statistical analysis of Hartmann's blur data is in Appendix E. It

---

106. It is no coincidence that the one-third second delay in the startle reaction is the same as the normal one-third-of-a-second cycle in the normal "panning-error" cycle discovered by Alvarez. The same sensory/processing/movement sequence is involved in both.

shows that Zapruder's film did have the three-cycle-per-second "jitter" that Alvarez found to be characteristic of human panning corrections. It also shows that the size of the correction blurs in his normal, uneventful photography provides a measure of the statistical significance of the large blurs that are thought to signify particular events. The analysis shows that the series of large blurs in Zapruder's film following the assassination (beginning about frame 330) are not at the rate characteristic of panning corrections, but are more likely to be evidence of his emotional reaction after he realized that he had just seen the President's head explode from a gunshot.

Then how about the series identified by Alvarez and Hartmann in the 190s? Is that evidence of a "neuromuscular oscillation" as a result of a startle from the second shot? It does have the characteristic three-cycle-per-second rate postulated by Alvarez. We also notice in Hartmann's chart, figure 61, that the road sign begins to intrude into the frame (and Zapruder's viewfinder) in frames in the early 180s. By frame 191, the sign has obscured the car back to the windshield. Could these strong peaks be a result of genuine difficulties in his tracking the limousine and its passengers as it passed behind the road sign?

It was noted that there was about a six-frame delay between the noisy stimulus and the blurred frame from Zapruder's acoustic startle reaction (a shot at frame 312 and the large blur at 318). Thus, a shot at 190, as proposed by the HSCA, could not have produced the series of strong peaks starting one frame later, at 191. A shot stimulating a peak at 191 would have had to reach the car about frame 185. As we saw in chapter seven, the shot through his neck, resulting in the President's awkward, elbows-raised posture, must have elicited a reaction very quickly, probably in half the time of Zapruder's six-frame startle delay. If there were a shot at 185, John Kennedy should have been reacting before 191—but he is not. Although the last clear frame before he is obscured is 193, there is a relatively clear frame at 200 and the President is not completely hidden by the sign until about frame 212. Nowhere in this interval is there visible reaction from a shot. The Acoustic Panel's second shot, on the other hand, was set at 196 (which does not coincide with the timing from Hartmann's jiggle analysis, as claimed in the HSCA final report). This relieves the problem of Kennedy's reaction not being seen by frame 193, but starts the "neuromuscular oscillation" five frames before the shot. Since the "series" begins before either proposed shot could have

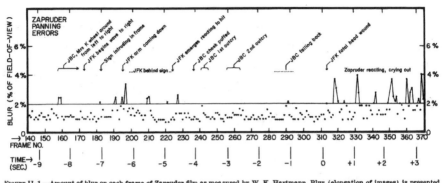

FIGURE II-1.—Amount of blur on each frame of Zapruder film as measured by W. K. Hartmann. Blur (elongation of images) is presented in terms of percentage of width of a whole frame. Large blurs represent jerking of camera, suggesting a startle reaction.

Figure 61. "Jiggle Plot" from the Zapruder movie, prepared by William Hartmann for the HSCA, extending the pioneering effort by Louis Alvarez. *(National Archives)*

stimulated it, this series of large blurs must have been caused by something else. The most likely explanation is the obvious one: the blurs resulted from tracking problems produced by the road sign.

The HSCA also contracted the Jet Propulsion Laboratory (JPL) of Pasadena, California, to do analyses of the photographic evidence. A letter on file at the National Archives, dated August 28, 1978, from Robert Selzer of JPL says: "The sharp camera movement from Z226-Z229 is ascribed to post-sign camera adjustment in the report. Would someone who believes or theorizes that Connally was hit around frame Z234 agree Z226-Z229 was not a shot sound event?" In other words, the large peak at Z227 and camera movement indicated by other measures in this region were far enough after the sign-tracking problem that JPL was questioning whether it was part of the jitter cycle "adjustment" or whether there was a gunshot in this interval. Interestingly, this blur at frame 227 was the one identified in 1967 by Charles Wycoff—of Edgerton, Germeshausen, and Grier (EG&G)—who was working with CBS in their documentary on the assassination. He noted the large blur at 318 and concluded that there would be a five-frame delay between the shock wave of the shot and Zapruder's startle. Thus, he fixed the time of the second shot at frame 222. CBS and EG&G did not note the likely effect of the tracking problem of the road sign and suggested that the blur at 190 might have been the startle from the first shot. Like Alvarez, they did not have the early frames to study, so they could not find the blurs that

Hartmann mentioned at frames 158/159.

Based on Robert Smith's suit bulge, FAA concluded that the second shot coincided with frame 224. But while a bullet could pass through his coat, through his arm, and into his thigh in a small fraction of a frame interval, the front of a suit coat does not move as fast as a bullet. If it did, the bulge would not be seen in the Zapruder film either. If you tap a piece of cloth as heavy as the front of a suit coat, you will see that it takes an appreciable fraction of a second to reach its maximum deflection and return to its original position. Although there was considerable momentum deposited in Connally's coat as the bullet penetrated, there had to have been considerable delay between the penetration and the peak of the bulge.

In the early 1990s, Dr. John Lattimer and colleagues used an M-C carbine identical to Oswald's and ammunition from the same lot Oswald owned to conduct tests that simulated the shot through Kennedy's neck and Connally's thorax, wrist, and thigh. The results, printed in the *Journal of the American College of Surgeons,* showed a suit bulge similar to Connally's. In these tests, the suit bulge peaked in about a tenth of a second after the passage of the bullet. This translates to about two frames of the Zapruder movie. So we need to look for a peak that might indicate a "startle" shortly after frame 224. Sure enough, there is the peak at 227, the one noted by JPL and EG&G. If this peak resulted from a startle, it would indicate that a shot was fired about five or six frames earlier, near frame 221 or 222. This is just two or three frames before the bulge reached its peak at 224.

The pieces of evidence, Zapruder's startle at 227, the suit bulge at 224, the President's hand movement between 223 and 224, his involuntary posturing reaction beginning at 224, and Connally's reactions beginning immediately thereafter, are all consistent with a shot that reached the car and injured the two men about frame 221 to 222.

But if Connally is correct in his consistent stand that he heard a first shot some seconds before he knew he was hit by the second shot, where is Zapruder's startle from the first shot? The only large peak before the tracking problems with the road sign is the double peak at frames 158/159. This peak would indicate the passage of a bullet near frames 152/153, one that prompted John Connally and Jackie Kennedy to swivel rapidly to the right. Connally begins to move at frame 162, less than one-quarter of a second after Zapruder flinches; Mrs. Kennedy a few frames later. The House Photo Panel determined that

Connally turned 90° to look over his right shoulder in less than one-third of a second.

Another person is also seen in the Zapruder film to be reacting to that first shot. Rosemary Willis, the young daughter of photographer Phil Willis, was running along at the front of the limousine on the opposite side of the street from Zapruder. She is looking back over her right shoulder in the direction of the limousine or the Secret Service car. At frame 165, Rosemary rapidly begins to slow her running steps and comes to a complete stop before frame 190, still looking over her right shoulder as the limousine passes by. In a newspaper interview a few years later she said "In that first split second, I thought it was a fire-cracker. But within maybe one-tenth of a second, I knew that it was a gunshot. And though I don't remember stopping and turning, I'm sure I did. I think I probably turned to look toward the noise, toward the book Depository."[107] Her hesitancy in identifying whether she stopped to look over her right shoulder is understandable, as she was already looking over that shoulder as she stopped. She just continued to look in the direction from which the gunshot seemed to come as she slowed to a stop and the limousine passed out of her view.

In the scientific literature that documents the startle reflex, there is some indication that the vigor of the startle "jump" is proportional to the volume of the stimulus and is weaker if just above the "startle threshold." But a shot from the grassy knoll would have been very loud at Zapruder's position.[108] Dr. John Lattimer and his sons, Gary and Jon, conducted experiments with a Mannlicher-Carcano rifle that they reported in the April 1972 *Bulletin of the New York Academy of Medicine.* They note, "The intensity of the recoil and the noise of the shot were approximately similar to those of the popular 30-30 cartridge used extensively by American riflemen. If one stood even a little in front of the rifle muzzle, without ear coverings, however, the reports were so loud as to be nearly intolerable. We were impressed by the fact that [if] such a rifle had been discharged a few feet to the right rear of photographer Abraham Zapruder (as from the "grassy knoll," as alleged by some), Mr. Zapruder would have been acutely aware of a deafening explosion with each shot."

Both the rifle report and the shock from the supersonic bullet

---

107. Interview by *Dallas Times Herald* reporter, Marcia Smith-Durk, published June 3, 1979.

108. Dr. Hartmann reported that all shots were very loud in the 1978 acoustic tests, whether the rifle was fired from the sniper's nest or the grassy knoll.

would have been much louder at Zapruder's position than the first two shots from the Depository, both of which exceeded his startle threshold. But frame 296, the time at which the shot from the grassy knoll was supposed to have occurred, according to the acoustic study, is followed by a long, jiggle-free span.[109] Not only is there no blurred frame six frames later, at 302, there was no startle reflex anywhere in the interval between frames 227 and 318. These two peaks, the one at 158/159, and the series containing the road-sign difficulties were determined by two separate statistical tests to be significantly higher than Zapruder's normal jiggle peaks (in Appendix E).

Timing Inconsistencies

What if the HSCA just got the timing wrong? Perhaps there was a shot hidden in the large peaks for which there are other explanations. For instance, the shot might coincide with one of the jiggles caused by tracking adjustments as the limo was passing behind the road sign. It would be impossible to distinguish the contribution from a startle versus the contribution from a large adjustment in panning. It is not unlikely that the startle blur would occur within one frame's distance from the normal cycle. After all, the startle peak at frame 227 falls right in phase with the existing cycle. But a knoll shot during this interval could hardly go unnoticed. Dale Myers reconstruction of the events in his documentary *The Secrets of a Homicide: The JFK Assassination* includes the view from the vantage point of the grassy knoll shooter standing behind the fence to Zapruder's right. During the period of large tracking-error peaks in Zapruder's film, frames 190 to 210, any shot at the President would almost certainly have hit somebody. The field included the President, a couple on a park bench on the pergola, near Zapruder, who obscured Mr. Kennedy during a portion of that interval, and the large crowd on the sidewalk at the inside corner of Houston and Elm who provided a backdrop for the occupants of the limousine throughout that period.

A miss at frame 196, the time that the HSCA said that one oc-

---

109. The small blip at frame 291 cannot indicate a gunshot at frame 296, because the reflex has to follow the shot. The statistical analysis of Appendix E shows that the peak at 291 not only falls in place in Zapruder's normal jiggle pattern, its magnitude is not enough larger than other adjustment peaks to be statistically significant.

curred, would have been easier to have gone unnoticed, as it would have gone into the grass nearly devoid of spectators. This shot, however, was not only precluded by the lack of a startle, but also frequently blocked as the car passed behind several trees. The open spots between tree trunks would have given only a momentary glimpse in which to aim and fire. Even without the missing startle from Zapruder, it was nearly an impossible shot.

Eyewitness (and earwitness) accounts lead to the conclusion that another missed shot hidden among the emotionally produced jiggles following the lethal shot is even less likely. The car was accelerating in this interval, enhancing the obscuring effect of the trees. Furthermore, virtually everybody who saw the gunshot to the President's head described it as the final shot, whether they heard one shot or several.

Dr. Wecht's "near simultaneous" shot from the knoll that could have entered the explosive hole in Kennedy's head was discussed in chapter eight, where it was shown to be incompatible with the photographic evidence from the autopsy. A simultaneous shot, however, cannot be disproved by the startle analysis, as two shots with a very short separation between them would cause only one startle blur.

The acoustic experts concluded that shots occurred at frames 166, 196, 296, and 312. Not only is the shot from the grassy knoll at 296 rendered impossible by the startle analysis, their first shot from the Depository, at 166, is after Mrs. Kennedy and Mr. Connally have begun to swivel back to look over their left shoulders. The large blurs from startle reactions that should be seen about six frames after their proposed first two shots—at or near frames 172 and 202—do not exist. Frame 166 is also the moment that the Warren Commission determined that the President would disappear behind the leaves of the oak tree (as seen from the sniper's nest, where they said this first shot came from). The only HSCA shot that corresponds to a startle is the last, and that is only because it is the one used to fix the time scale in the first place.

Robert Blakey's explanation for the first shot occurring after Connally's turn was nearly complete was that it was merely a time-scale difference between the Zapruder film and the Dictaphone belt (see chapter three). Yet this would give nearly a one-second discrepancy from the first to last shot. A difference of a few percent between the two might be within expected accuracy of the reconstructed times, but this would be an error of nearly 10 percent between the timing of the visual and sound recordings. Correcting for this improbably large error, on the other hand, would push their second shot even further back in time, perhaps near 190. This avoids the interference of the oak tree but increases the discrepancy between the shot and the reactions of the two men.

Dale Myers painstaking reconstruction in his documentary of the motorcade around and through Dealey Plaza show that there was no motorcycle, McLain's or any other, near the positions identified with the Acoustic Panel's four shots at the time they were thought to have been recorded on the Dictaphone disk. This adds further evidence that the HSCA's conclusion regarding the number and timing of shots has no scientific basis.

In summary, there are startle reactions at frames 158/159, 227, and 318 corresponding to shots reaching the car, or narrowly missing it, at or near Zapruder frames 152/153, 221/222, and 312. Figure 62 shows Hartmann's peaks plotted alongside the peaks from the analysis by Frank Scott and Alvarez's peaks from his original article. Scott plotted the between-frame movement of Zapruder's camera: the change in position of the camera on two sequential frames. Alvarez transformed the position data into an acceleration of the camera. Like Hartmann's, Scott's analysis identifies all three startle peaks. Alvarez could not find the peak at frames 158/189 because he did not have access to those early frames. His analysis is equivocal on the 227 peak also, though distinct on the peak from the final shot at 318. None of the three measures shows a startle peak in

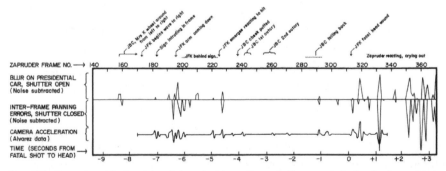

FIGURE II-5.—A comparison of the three independent records of largest blurs or tracking errors, in the Zapruder film, as derived by W. K. Hartmann (top, above line), Frank Scott (top, below line), and L. Alvarez (bottom). Magnitude of blur or panning error is indicated by length of curve upward or downward along direction of vertical axis. Frame numbers and times in seconds are given at top and bottom along horizontal axis.

Figure 62.   Hartmann's, Scotts', and Alvarez' "jiggle" peaks plotted on the same graph. *(National Archives)*

the interval corresponding to the HSCA's grassy-knoll shot.

The time between the first shot, which missed, and the second, that hit both men, was about 3.8 seconds. The time between the second and third shot, the one that killed the President, was about 4.9 seconds. Both intervals are considerably longer than the minimum time of 2.5 seconds, established by the Warren Commission, for an experienced shooter to get off sequential shots from Oswald's Mannlicher-Carcano rifle. This timing sequence leaves ample time for the sixth-floor shooter to reestablish an aim point for the next shot.

Why the assassin's first shot missed, not only his target, but the entire limousine, may forever remain a mystery. The shot near frame 152 is well clear of the oak tree. A competent and experienced gunman, capable of making the following two shots, would not have taken a shot if his view were severely obstructed by the window frame or another object. Possible factors contributing to the miss are:

1) The relative motion of the limousine at that angle was greater than it was for the later shots. At the third shot, the car was moving almost directly away and slightly downhill.

2) The shot was taken less than a second before the car would pass behind the tree. Was it rushed?

3) The steepness of the angle might have precluded using the stacked boxes as a "bench rest" for this shot. Was the gun being supported on the side of the window and slipped down just before the trigger was pulled?

4) Finally, "buck fever"—described by hunters as "freezing" just before the shot and shooting just after the target has bolted. Tellingly, buck fever usually happens on the first appearance of a suitable target, and is less frequent on subsequent opportunities, if any.

In any case, the first shot was at an angle much too steep for the bullet to have ricocheted from wherever it hit. It would have disintegrated on impact with the street or fragmented on impact with the soil, leaving the resulting bullet fragments embedded too deeply beneath the grass of the plaza to ever be found and recovered. The limousine was nearly in the center of the street at the time of the first shot. A miss by the margin that would have allowed the bullet to hit the sod in the center of Dealy Plaza would be truly incredible. The street impact is much more probable. It is unlikely, however, that any of the fragments from this splattered bullet would have traveled far enough to scratch James Tague's cheek.

The HSCA's claim that there was a shot from the grassy knoll not only lacks credible evidence in its support, but also its existence is precluded by the several pieces of mutually supportive evidence that we do have: Barber's identification of cross talk, McLain's denial, Myers' reconstruction of the motorcycle positions, and the lack of a startle blur on Zapruder's film. Recent attempts to resurrect the acoustic evidence by means of a recording needle jumping back to record over the previous track a minute later are futile in the absence of a cycle carrying a microphone to detect the sound.

CHAPTER TWELVE
The Conspiracy Myth: "I'm Just a Patsy"

"No, sir, I didn't kill anybody. I'm just a patsy."
—*Lee Harvey Oswald*[110]

In the last several chapters we covered the science that provides the underpinnings for the investigation of the Kennedy assassination, the Tippit murder, and the Connally wounding. At the same time, we debunked a number of the more credible myths that originated in the misunderstanding of some of the evidence in the case: the magic bullet, bullets throwing Kennedy's body (but not Connally's!) in the car, the shot from the grassy knoll, and so on. Now it is time to pull all the science together to answer these questions: Did Oswald fire all the shots that caused injury in Dealey Plaza on November 22, 1963? Did he have help? The first is amenable to scientific proof; the second is not. As many have pointed out, in the allegation of conspiracy, the burden of proof necessarily rests on the conspiracy advocate. Merely standing by and expressing no opinion on the topic, except as refutation of the advocate's case for conspiracy, on the other hand, is unsatisfactory to an author and unlikely to please the reader. In the second half of this chapter, we will discuss the evidence we have, the absence of evidence that should exist in the presence of a conspiracy, and the limits those two factors place on the conspiracy that might have been. First, however, we get to the actual shooting.

Oswald's Involvement in the Shootings

The flood of allegations that Assistant FBI Director Belmont complained about in his memo of November 27, 1963, has continued, unabated to the present. Fortunately, for the sake of the scientific investigation, some early misinterpretations and fabrica-

---

110. Shouted to reporters in response to a question while being moved from one place to another in Dallas Police Headquarters on the afternoon of November 23, 1963.

tions of the conspiracy buffs quickly became part of the "JFK folklore" and most stories soon evolved to support those myths. For instance, Charles Harrelson confessed to being one of the assassins while disguised as one of the "three tramps." This and similar three-tramp stories were debunked when the names of the real tramps were unearthed by Mary LaFontaine early in 1992. Other false confessions and false accusations, too numerous to mention, have been similarly discredited in the last 40 years, often by researchers who have incorporated it into their own conspiracy book.

Other seemingly credible evidence, offered by serious people trying to be helpful, such as Julia Ann Mercer's green truck, were dismissed through hours of investigative work by the police (the green truck was a real air-conditioning truck and the real air-conditioning workmen were not carrying a "gun case" up the hill). Some eyewitness testimony printed in the Warren Report has not been so satisfactorily resolved, though most is difficult to "mold" into a conspiracy story. There is nothing sinister in this. Hardly any criminal investigation of any complexity is resolved without unexplained "loose ends." In fact, the enormous effort put forth in the Kennedy investigation leaves us with an unusual situation: Nearly all the loose ends are in the notoriously unreliable eyewitness testimony.

In spite of the Warren investigation—some would say because of it—the conspiracy idea came to surround the Kennedy assassination like no other political assassination ever had before. The conspiracy-minded HSCA investigation merely added fuel to the fire. The idea of a Kennedy conspiracy is now so pervasive in books, movies, and television that it has probably become a permanent fixture in the American culture, like Roswell aliens, flying saucers, and Elvis sightings. The person who sets out to eradicate those myths entirely is taking on a fool's errand. The best that can be hoped is to bring a rational perspective to the question for the sake of those who are open-minded and objective.

We can reconstruct most of the events surrounding the assassination using only the physical evidence and laws of nature. A small amount of reliable contemporary witness testimony, as well as some scientific interpretation, is helpful in knitting the physical evidence together. The massive amount of hearsay, speculation, and allegation, used liberally by the conspiracy writers, but which is inconsistent with this coherent body of reliable evidence must, out of necessity, be ignored. We can note, however, that its refutation is inherent in the reconstruction of the actual events.

Several conspiracy writers have attempted to discredit the physical evidence in its entirety, because to exonerate Oswald in the shooting it is necessary to do so. None of us are so innocent as to believe that no criminal has ever planted or forged evidence to try to "frame" someone else, or that no police official has ever faked or planted evidence in an attempt to obtain a conviction. Those who claim that virtually all the physical evidence in the Kennedy case was fraudulent, however, are either extremely naive themselves or believe that the reader is. Take the discussion on faking photographs in chapter ten, for instance. The detail of the difficulty inherent in photographic forgery serves well as an illustration because, of all types of physical evidence in the Kennedy case, photographs would have been the *easiest* to fake.

Aside from the difficulty of forging photographs and surgically altering wounds to fool experienced pathologists, there is proof that none of the forensic evidence was faked. Consider the entirety of the physical evidence and how it fits perfectly together. The testimony of two groups of photographic experts regarding the authenticity of the "backyard photographs" of Oswald and his murder weapons was reinforced by the surfacing of another copy of one of these in the possessions of his friend George de Mohrenschildt. Moreover, this photograph had Oswald's signature on it. The images from the Zapruder film of the final shot with its heart-wrenching explosion of the President's head matches perfectly with the autopsy photographs and x-rays. The gaping hole and rupture marks are in exactly the same place. The forward movement of Kennedy's head between Zapruder frames 312 and 313 agree with the finding of a cratered entrance wound of the back of his skull mentioned in the autopsy report. Even the magnitude of the motion agrees with the amount of momentum deposited in the Edgewood Arsenal skull shots simulated by using the Oswald rifle and identical ammunition. The neuromuscular spasm that moved the President backward was documented in animals and in a prize-winning photograph of a similar human tragedy long before the assassination took place.

The small fragments recovered from the President's head wound were traced by neutron activation analysis to the bullet fragment found in the front of the limousine. This bullet, in turn, was proven to have been fired from Oswald's rifle, found on the sixth floor of the Depository, consistent with an entry from the back. The extent of fragmentation of the skull, seen in the x-rays, matches that seen in the simulated skull shots, conducted with the Oswald rifle months later (shown in figure 38). The rupturing of the President's skull adjacent to the track of the bullet is very similar to that seen in the experimental skull shots. In the simulations, some of the skull fragments were torn loose from the elastic 'scalp' as it hinged open. The violent ripping and hinging motion sent skull fragments in all directions, completely independent from the direction of the bullet that had caused it. In the assassination, skull fragments were recovered from locations outside of the car as well as in the back seat.

The jiggle analysis of Zapruder's movie agrees perfectly with the observation of the reaction of the occupants of the car and their testimony regarding those actions.[111] For instance, Governor Connally's movements, his turning in response to the first shot, the bulge in his suit coat, and the flutter of his hat are in perfect accord with Zapruder's startle reactions recorded on the film as clearly as the more obvious images, as they happened. Mrs. Kennedy's and Rosemary Willis's reactions to that first bullet match the governor's, well within expected differences in voluntary reactions to a strong stimulus.

The engraving from Oswald's rifle is on CE 399, while fragments from its core were removed from the governor's wrist, a fact proven by the chance characteristics of the alloy used in the cores of the bullets and a neutron activation analysis that was beyond the state of technology at the time anybody could have been forging or planting evidence. A retrospective analysis of the data from the FBI's first aborted NAA attempt produced results that agree with the data from an improved technique done 13 years later. When one of these bullets struck Connally's rib, the extent of its deformation is totally in accord with physical theory, and very similar to the deformation of an identical bullet which produced a similar wound in a goat's ribcage. Even the slight difference in the

---

111. Some have tried to discredit the Zapruder film by alleging alterations that left features out of synch, such as the blink rate of the lights on the Secret Service followup car, or "impossibly" rapid movement of people whose images appear there. Why would they overlook these obvious images but go to the trouble to reestablish the three-cycle-per-second "jitter" discovered by Alvarez and seen in Hartmann's plot? How could they even know that they should? The irregular blink pattern, on the other hand, has a perfectly innocent explanation. It is called "aliasing," the interaction of rates of occurrence of something and the independent rate of sampling. Aliasing is what makes the wagon wheels seem to turn backward in Western movies. In this case, the framing rate of Zapruder's camera and the blink rate are aliased. The framing rate changed slightly as the camera's spring wound down and the blinks might have had slight irregularities as well. The combination should have produced erratic effects.

amount of deformation to these two bullets is accounted for by the difference in the amount of soft tissue penetrated, and the resulting velocity lost, before striking rib. The trajectory of the bullet that caused the wounds to both men point toward the upper floors of the Texas School Book Depository, while the fragments recovered from both men's wounds independently point to the bullets fired from the rifle found on the same floor of that building. The cartridge cases found at the window were discharged within that rifle.

The President's reaction to the first hit, characteristic of an involuntary postural reaction, is conclusive evidence of damage to his spinal cord at the level of the last cervical vertebra. A reconstruction of the bullet's path from the entry wound to the exit at the tracheotomy incision, both shown in autopsy photographs, narrowly misses the spine at precisely that level; at a distance such that the compression of the soft tissue would cause the requisite amount of damage. The x-ray of the President's neck shows damage adjacent to the lateral process of the first thoracic vertebra, which the reconstructed track misses by a hair's breadth. It also shows a shadow of the wound track that leads to the tracheostomy in his suprasternal notch. After considering the evidence they did not see, such as the bullet wound in the back at the base of the President's neck, and the minor contradictions in their individual reports, the observations of the Parkland physicians are surprisingly consistent with the autopsy findings (though some of their initial interpretations, based on incomplete knowledge of the facts, were not).

The simulations at the Biophysics Laboratory produced data that were in complete agreement with the other physical evidence, in spite of the fact that the researchers were not allowed to see the autopsy photographs and in spite of the prior doubts expressed by the lab supervisors that the WCC/MC bullets could have inflicted both of the President's wounds (the moderate through-and-through wound to his neck and the massive head wound) in sequential shots. But the unexpected results were in perfect accord with physical theory and the unseen photographic material. Along this same line, Failure Analysis Associates not only independently confirmed the HSCA's expert reconstruction of a single-bullet trajectory through the two men, they found a curvature in the trajectory through Connally's trunk that they could not correctly explain, but which also was required by physical law. Dale Myers independently reconstructed a nearly identical path.

While one of the pieces of physical evidence could conceivably have been faked by an expert, there is no possibility that an expert, or team of super-experts, could have fabricated the perfectly coordinated whole. This brings to mind the recurrent theme in most conspiracy books. All the officials alternate between the role of "Keystone Kops," with the inability to recognize the implications of the most elementary evidence and "evil geniuses," with superhuman abilities to fake physical evidence, that is in complete agreement with all the other faked evidence. It is as near a certainty as anything involved in this case that, individually or collectively, they were neither. All of them—Secret Service, FBI, police, postal employees, Warren Commissioners, laboratory workers, and others involved in the investigation—were ordinary human beings. Like the rest of us, they were capable of making mistakes but, within their areas of expertise, they certainly possessed far more skill and experience than their critics.

The one bit of "scientific" evidence that is glaringly at odds with all the above is a finding of a shot from the vicinity of the grassy knoll by the HSCA's acoustic experts. At the time that this additional shot was to have taken place, a startle reaction is conspicuously absent from Zapruder's film, even though the weapon and passing bullet would have been much closer to Zapruder's ear than the bullets fired from the Mannlicher-Carcano rifle in the corner of the Depository. Finally, the anachronistic presence of voices repeating dialog that was recorded on the other police channel almost a minute after the assassination and the absence of crowd noises, no racing motorcycle engine, and the motorcycle's siren missing from this tape betray the recording—not as forged—but merely misidentified. Myers' finding that there was no motorcycle, McLain's or anybody else's, at the position of the microphones at the time the Acoustic Panel says the shots were fired, is just icing on the cake.

The totality of reliable physical evidence, supported by eyewitness accounts of his doing what the physical evidence shows he did, makes the case against Lee Harvey Oswald an open and shut case. He murdered John Kennedy and Officer Tippit and gravely wounded John Connally. The Lane myth of "Oswald as Patsy" and all similar conspiracy myths merit no serious consideration. Only one question remains.

Did he have help?

The question of conspiracy rests on whether Oswald did what he is known to have done completely on his own initiative. There cannot be a scientific disproof of conspiracy. An event that does not happen leaves no evidence to be used in the proof.[112]

History is not very encouraging to those who allege conspiracy. Most attempted presidential assassinations, successful or not, were carried out by single individuals, acting alone. Even the attempt on Harry Truman by Puerto Rican separatists was carried out with all the conspirators on the spot and all captured immediately after the attempt. There was no evidence of any other individual being involved, never mind the vast network of conspirators required by most JFK conspiracy theories.

We can, of course, examine the credibility of the one "official" conspiracy theory: the HSCA report. How well did they make the case? Faced with the mass of credible physical evidence just reviewed, they had no choice but to acknowledge the participation (at least) of Oswald in the conspiracy that Robert Blakey, the Mafia-chaser from the Kennedy administration and chief of the investigatory staff, wanted to pursue. The investigation by Robert Blakey and the HSCA staff was directed toward building a case against the mob. Nevertheless, the only scientific evidence of a conspiracy that the HSCA found in over two years of thorough investigation was the acoustic analysis of impulses from a Dictaphone belt and some contemporary witnesses who heard the sounds of gunshots from the direction of the grassy knoll or saw some "puffs of smoke" behind the wooden fence. The HSCA did not find the witnesses to be credible who, years later, "remembered" that they had seen gunmen behind the fence. Nor did they find pictures of "gunmen" lurking in the trees or bushes near the grassy knoll.

In spite of their best efforts, the HSCA and staff were unable to establish any meaningful connection between Oswald and the Mafia and were only able to establish the most tenuous connection between Ruby and the mob. Ruby knew McWillie, who worked for the Mafia, but was not a member of the Mafia. He made some phone calls to an associate of Hoffa, but Ruby said they were in connection with his union troubles and the HSCA found no evidence that they were not. In any case, they were made before the presidential trip to Dallas was planned, so they

---

112. The absence of a startle on the Zapruder film is the counterexample that is so rare as to be almost unique.

were, at best, evidence only of some contact with the mob. Ruby, with his tenuous connection with the Mafia and no experience as a "hit-man," is the least likely recruit imaginable for the Mafia to contract for a "hit" on Oswald. In any case, the hit could not have been planned for Dallas before the Dallas trip was planned and, if the hit were not planned for Dallas, there would have been no conceivable reason for involving Ruby. Those phone calls, however, were the last provable contact between Ruby and La Cosa Nostra. Any actual planning meetings that might have taken place were never unearthed.

To call the assassination of the President of the United States the "hit of the century" for the Mafia would be an understatement. It would be more likely the "Mafia hit of all time." Even less of a case can be made for Oswald to have been recruited for this hit than can be made for re-cruiting Ruby. The HSCA's expert consultant on organized crime, Ralph Salerno, attempted to satisfy his House employers by giving examples of Mafia hits contracted to outsiders who were considered expendable. In his best example, the hit men were experienced killers who were nabbed by the police before the hit was even attempted. In another example, a pesky reporter was successfully blinded by acid, but again the hit men were soon caught. After they were caught, the outside hit men promptly "spilled their guts"—an act of betrayal that would have been unlikely for an inside team. In a third example, the hit man was himself killed on the spot.

These non-traditional hits generally turned out to be disasters, either thwarted by the police before the attempt could be made or resulting in some of the Mafia middle men going down with the killers. The success rate in his examples of non-traditional Mafia "hits" would not give a group of conspirators a great deal of confidence in imitating them. They would be far more likely to stick to the traditional methods that have resulted in successes, like the elimination of Hoffa. (Note that we do not know much about the most successful of mob hits. That is part of the reason for their success.)

Then let us consider how well Oswald fits Salerno's mold as the outside hit man. The only "experience" Oswald had was an attempt on the life of General Walker, an assassination attempt that the HSCA makes no effort to pin on the Mafia and one that the Mafia could hardly have even been aware of. Even if they had known, they would not have been encouraged by the failed attempt. In fact, the shot at Walker is a much better piece of evidence for the lone assassin case. For this reason, the critics usually either ignore the Walker attempt or dismiss it as a Warren Commission fabrication. But the only gap in the case found by the HSCA for Oswald being the gunman in the Walker case was the inability of the ballistic experts to match the recovered bullet to Oswald's rifle "to the exclusion of all other weapons." The fact that it was a WCC/MC bullet "compatible" with having been fired from the Oswald rifle, combined with Marina's compelling testimony and the other physical evidence, complete the case against Oswald—and against a conspiracy to kill General Walker.

It is more likely that Marina was the only person who knew of that attempt. So as far as the hypothetical group of conspirators knew, Oswald was a complete novice. Likewise, the killing of Tippitt is almost certainly just what it seems to be: a "poor dumb cop" who happened on the assassin by accident and got killed because he did not seriously think that he could randomly encounter the escaping gunman. This is a point in favor of the police officer's being cautious every time a stop is made, but not a point in support of the existence of a conspiracy. In spite of his best attempt, Salerno makes no case for Oswald being a "hit man" for anybody, much less the Mafia.

Since nonevents leave no evidence, perhaps we might speculate a bit on the evidence that should have been found if there were a conspiracy. We can be sure that the Cosa Nostra is not the only group that is capable of learning from their successes and failures over its centuries of experience in eliminating enemies, rivals, and disloyal members from their own ranks. Any group of conspirators that could pull off the assassination without leaving a trace of physical evidence that points to another person besides the designated "patsy" must rival the abilities of the Mafia. Thus, we can be sure that any "hit" of this magnitude would have some of the characteristics Ralph Salerno discovered in the typical Mafia killing.

Mr. Salerno's description of the successful Mafia hit included a nontraceable chain of influence between the "authorizer" and the hit team. The team included the primary killer, a backup, a getaway car, and an "intercept" car driven by a person with no police record to crash into a police vehicle to foil pursuit. Not all these features appeared in every mob hit nor would they necessarily appear in a hit made by a group other than the Cosa Nostra, but some of these features have been present in every successful mob hit, traditional or not.

So what is missing if Oswald did have help? The backup assassin could remain invisible, as Oswald succeeded in accomplishing the job within nine seconds of his first shot. But where was the getaway car? Even if we assume that Oswald somehow learned at the last minute that his "associate" in the getaway car was out to eliminate him and somehow avoided him in his escape, his subsequent behavior makes no sense. First of all, where would the team look for him? It is not likely that they would attempt to search every bus and taxi in Dallas or assume he would suddenly learn how to drive and acquire a car on his own. The best chance they would have is to go to his rooming house in hopes of ambushing him there. Oswald would have been smart enough to figure this out, so that is the last place he would go. But what actually happened? Oswald went home, calmly changed jackets, picked up his handgun, and walked out completely undisturbed.

If a group could make a nationally known celebrity such as Hoffa vanish without a trace or a government agency could assassinate a head of state like Allende (as the CIA is alleged to have done), then is is inconceivable that that same group could not manage to eliminate a waif like Oswald who, before his arrest in the Texas Theatre, was known by only a handful of family, coworkers, and casual acquaintances. The "nobody" who was, in various conspiracy stories, so easily manipulated that he essentially framed himself suddenly became untouchable by those who manipulated him. Of course, he was not clever enough to avoid being stopped by a policeman who was randomly driving the streets of his assigned area in hopes of spotting a fleeing assassin. Again, we get a whiff of the Keystone Kop/evil genius dichotomy.

Unable to eliminate him on the scene and too stupid to look for him at home, the conspirators' only recourse is to send a novice hit man into the police station (twice) to kill him in front of dozens of well-armed law enforcement officers. Ruby, on the other hand, though "worried sick" about the assignment, is very casual about carrying it out. Instead of arriving at the publicly announced time of the move, he casually strolls down the ramp to the basement of the police station an hour late. In the usual scenario, the writer is forced to conclude that the conspirators have enough influence with Chief Curry to force him to wait until Ruby is there before bringing Oswald down to the location chosen for the hit. So Ruby deliberately keeps them waiting nearly half an hour while he leisurely drives downtown, then remembers that an employee might be evicted for non-payment of rent and makes a side trip to Western Union to wire her the money, killing another half-hour. The evidence of sophistication and competence in the assumed co-conspirators is notably missing.

Ruby's public statements, trial testimony, and WC testimony reflect several reasons for killing Oswald, including sparing Mrs. Kennedy the pain of returning to Dallas to testify (his most frequent reason). In truth, Ruby's distorted view of reality probably led him to believe that he would become a hero by eliminating the assassin. He must have been surprised to learn that killing Lee Oswald was not considered heroic, but merely the deranged act of another "nut case."

A high-level conspiracy like the CIA and Mafia attempt on the life of Castro involves conspirators who are very good at their job. They involve only the absolute minimum of trusted professionals and use very simple plans that are as foolproof as possible. Each person that is involved must be an indispensable link in the chain that is to work if the operation is to be successful. Real conspiracies to commit murder do not have "casts of thousands," or even a dozen. Excess baggage only means another point of vulnerability—of failing to do the job or being found out. One can argue that the attempt against Castro only failed because the last link in the chain lost his nerve at the last minute. We also note that he was the only link (of very few) who was not CIA or Mafia. The fatal weakness of the plan was that they had to rely on a close associate of Castro—the "outside hit man"—to deliver the poison pills. As such, this is another lesson in the pitfalls of abandoning the tried-and-true methods and relying on those who are not "inside" professionals.

So we are left with a notable absence of credible physical evidence pointing to a co-conspirator coupled with a lack of evidence that should have been there if a co-conspirator had existed. Instead, the only reliable, scientific evidence points to two "lone nuts:" the second acting alone to kill the first in the mistaken belief that he would become a hero by doing so.

But what motive did Oswald have to kill John Kennedy, if, indeed, an irrational killer needs a motive for what he does? Few people ask what motivated John Hinkley, Jr. to shoot, and nearly kill, Ronald Reagan, in 1981. Much the same goes for Charles Guiteau (President James Abram Garfield, 1881), Leon Czolgosz (President William McKinley, 1901),

Sirhan Sirhan (Senator Robert Kennedy, 1968), Squeaky Fromme and Sara Jane Moore (attempts on President Gerald Ford, 1975) and the rest of a long list of successful and unsuccessful assassins. John Wilkes Booth is probably the only successful presidential assassin with a clearly defined motive that is almost universally accepted.

Taking a cue from the conspiracy theorist, we can construct a credible explanation, based on minimal data. Investigations by Epstein, Posner, McMillan, and Mailer find Oswald to be a sincere ideological Marxist, though his knowledge of the subject was—like most Lee Oswald undertakings—superficial. He was also a person who felt compelled to be important. Marina Oswald undoubtedly knew Lee as well as any person could. When asked what she thought his motive might have been, she told the Warren Commission, "I can conclude that he wanted in any way, whether good or bad, to do something that would make him outstanding, that he would be known in history." His try at international fame as a Marine defector to the Soviet Union fell flat. The Soviets found him more of an embarrassment than an asset. He knew nothing that the KGB did not know in greater detail, and sooner, than he did. His return to the United States was an admission of failure and a blow to his ego. His attempt to associate with the national Marxist community by starting the New Orleans chapter of the Fair Play for Cuba Committee resulted in little recognition and no recruits. His arming himself and attempting to defect to Cuba was thwarted, first by an uncooperative wife and then by Cuban and Soviet bureaucrats. Thus, he could not gain recognition as the only Marine to join Fidel's army in what he imagined would be their battle against capitalism. Even his attempt to assassinate the outspoken right-wing leader, General Walker, was defeated by a chance deflection from the window glass.

Although he did try to avoid capture, killing a second victim in the attempt, he left a string of clues that would unerringly point to him as the assassin. It is hard to avoid the conclusion that it was deliberate. Using an alias to order the weapons, but having them shipped to his own post office box would serve to delay, but not conceal the discovery that they were his. He gave a picture of himself sporting those weapons to one of the few people who could be considered a friend, with "killer of fascists" written in Cyrillic on the back. It is clear that, if captured, he wanted there to be no doubt that he was responsible for the assassination.

Why else would he carry a forged ID with his alias, Alek Hidell, printed on it? Although he never expressed a dislike of John Kennedy, and he almost certainly would have preferred any of his earlier attempts to achieve notoriety, his compulsion to be important remains the only likely motive for the crime. Perhaps, early that morning of November 22, 1963, he realized—quite correctly—that this would be his only chance to transform Lee Harvey Oswald into a household name.

APPENDIX A

Rumors Dispelled by the Warren Commission

Below are rephrased and shortened summaries of some rumors and speculations about the JFK assassination and the Warren Commission's related conclusions.

Rumor: Lee Harvey Oswald is seen in a picture standing on the steps in front of the Texas School Book Depository Building at the time of the shooting.

WC: The man in the picture is Billy Lovelady. The identification was made by Lovelady and several of his fellow workers in the Depository.

Rumor: A man was seen running from the Depository toward the railroad overpass.

WC: Jean Hill said she saw the running man immediately after the shooting stopped and described him to police shortly thereafter. Pictures of that area taken at that time do not show anyone present, running or not. No other witnesses came forth to corroborate her statement.

Rumor: A motorcycle policeman ran up the "grassy embankment" to pursue a "couple" fleeing from an "unguarded" railroad overpass from which the fatal shot was fired and a rifle cartridge was found.

WC: Clyde A. Haygood was identified from photographs as the policeman in question. Haygood testified that he did not see anyone running. At 12:37 Haygood reported that the shots had come from the Texas School Book Depository building.

Rumor: Several bullets were found: one on the JFK stretcher at Parkland Hospital and another by Deputy Sheriff E. R. Walthers in the grass of Dealey Plaza.

WC: After the assassination, two large fragments, weighing 44.6 grains and 21.0 grains, were found in the limousine, along with several small fragments of lead. A nearly whole bullet was found after it rolled off the stretcher used by Governor Connally. No other bullets were found. Though he searched that area on the day of the shooting and again two days later, Walthers denied that he found a bullet or that he told anybody that he found a bullet.

Rumor: There was a bullet hole in the windshield of the presidential limousine.
WC: There was an abrasion and a small amount of lead on the inside of the windshield and a small pattern of cracks on the outside at that point, but no hole through the windshield.

Rumor: There was an "entry" wound in the president's throat.
WC: Doctors at Parkland hospital initially thought that the wound in the throat could have been either an entry or exit wound, without doing a close examination with the intent of determining which it was. After the autopsy became available, they agreed that it was an exit wound.

Rumor: JFK was shot when the limousine was on Houston Street approaching the Texas School Book Depository building.
WC: Motion pictures taken at the time show that the President was first struck from the rear after the car had turned on to Elm Street.

Rumor: The motorcade route was changed after the map was printed in spite of the fact that the logical route would have led directly from Main to the Stemmons Freeway ramp. Oswald could not have known about the motorcade before the day of the assassination.
WC: The motorcade route was decided by November 18 and published in both Dallas papers on November 19. It was not changed thereafter. The normal, and only legal, entry to the Stemmons ramp from Main is via Houston and Elm. A direct entry from Main would have caused a near stop as the car went over the concrete barrier or made a complicated s-turn beyond the barrier.

Rumor: The package carried by Lee Harvey Oswald actually contained curtain rods.

WC: Mrs. Johnson, his landlady, said that Lee's room had venetian blinds, curtains, and curtain rods. Oswald had said nothing to his wife or Mrs. Paine about curtain rods. Mrs. Paine's curtain rods were still in her garage when the police arrived after the shooting and none were found in the Depository. Lee was carrying only a soft drink when last seen in the building, approaching the exit. The empty package was found at the scene of the shooting.

Rumor: Lee Harvey Oswald was a poor shot and could not have fired three bullets in the 5.5 seconds in which the shooting took place.

WC: Experts determined it was possible to fire three shots within 5.5 seconds. Lee Oswald had qualified as a sharpshooter and marksman with an M-1 rifle in the Marine Corps. Marina testified that he had practiced operating the bolt of the rifle at their home in New Orleans. The Warren Commission concluded that Oswald had the capability to commit the assassination.

Rumor: The rifle used in the assassination was a Mauser. The authorities said that the rifle they found on the sixth floor had the name stamped on it and could not, therefore, have been misidentified.

WC: The rifle was found by Deputy Sheriff Eugene Boone and Deputy Constable Seymour Weitzman, the original source of the speculation that it was a Mauser. They did not handle the weapon and could barely see it in its original location. The manufacturer's name is not on the rifle, only the inscription "made in Italy." Captain Fritz and Lieutenant Day, the first to handle it, properly identified it.

Rumor: The ammunition available for the Mannlicher-Carcano rifle was old WWII bullets that were unreliable.

WC: The ammunition used was made recently by the Western Cartridge Company and was fired in Oswald's Mannlicher-Carcano over 100 times in testing without a misfire.

Rumor: The presidential limousine slowed or stopped after the first shot. Or, the presidential limousine was moving 12 to 20 miles per hour during the shooting.

WC: During the time that the shots struck the president, the car was moving at an average speed of 11.2 miles per hour. As it was going down a slight incline and directly away from the Depository, experts said it was an easy shot.

Rumor: Robert Hughes' 8mm movie shows the silhouettes of two men at the sixth-floor window of the Depository 10 minutes before the shooting.

WC: Examination of the film by the FBI and the U.S. Navy Photographic Interpretation Center shows that the second "figure" is a shadow cast by the cartons near the window.

Rumor: The FBI denied that Oswald's palmprint was found on the rifle recovered from the sixth floor of the book Depository.

WC: The FBI confirmed that the palmprint lifted by the Dallas police from that rifle was Oswald's. They deny that any FBI agent made any such statement to the press.

Rumor: Pictures of Lee Harvey Oswald holding the murder weapons were "doctored" or "faked." The pictures were composites with Lee Harvey Oswald's face pasted on somebody else's body.

WC: *Life, Newsweek,* and the *New York Times* notified the Warren Commission that they had retouched the photographs and had inadvertently altered the appearance of the rifle. Marina testified that she took the pictures in question and experts state that the original prints are not a composite.

Rumor: Lee Oswald spent the morning with coworkers right up to 12:15, a mere 15 minutes before the shooting.

WC: Coworkers testified that they did not spend the morning with him. He was last seen by Charles Givens about 11:55 am on the sixth floor.

Rumor: The remains of a chicken lunch on the sixth floor were left by an accomplice of Oswald who may have hidden out there overnight.

WC: The chicken lunch had been eaten shortly after noon by Bonnie Ray Williams, who went to the fifth floor shortly thereafter.

Rumor: There was too little time for Lee Harvey Oswald to have gone from the sniper's nest to the lunchroom by the time he was seen there by Truly and Baker.

WC: A series of time tests by WC investigators, Roy Truly, and Patrolman M. L. Baker shows that it was possible for Oswald to have placed the rifle behind the box and descended to the second floor before being seen by the two men entering the lunchroom.

Rumor: Police were sealing off the building by the time Oswald had arrived at the second floor.

WC: The police may have begun to take position at some exits to the building as early as 12:33 when he was last seen walking toward an exit, but it is unlikely that the building was completely sealed off before 12:37.

Rumor: Description of Lee Oswald at 12:36 was too accurate to have come from eyewitnesses. Or, the broadcast description was not accurate enough to prompt Tippit to stop Oswald.

WC: The description was broadcast at 12:45 and was similar to that of Oswald, but it lacked important specifics such as hair and eye color. There is no way to be certain that Tippit recognized Oswald from the broadcast description. The Dallas Police Department radio log at 1:29 p.m. shows that the police radio dispatcher noted a similarity between the president's assassin and Tippit's slayer. It is likely that Tippit stopped Oswald because of the broadcast description.

Rumor: The log for William Whaley's cab that Oswald took from the Greyhound Terminal shows them departing at 12:30, a time at which Oswald was accused of firing the shots from the sixth floor of the Depository.

WC: The log entry does show 12:30, but Whaley testified that he was not accurate in logging times. He usually logged at 15 minute intervals and sometimes did not make log entries until three or four trips later. The bus transfer in Oswald's possession at the time of his arrest was stamped 12:36 p.m. He probably entered the cab at about 12:47 or 12:48 p.m.

Rumor: Oswald did not have time for all of the movements imputed to him between his departure from the Texas School Book Depository and his encounter with Tippit.

WC: The Commission reconstructed his movements, timing the taxicab ride at 5.5 minutes, the walk from the 700 Block of Beckley, where he left the cab, to his apartment at 1026 N. Beckley at 5.75 minutes. This put him at his apartment before his 1:00 p.m. encounter with Mrs. Roberts, ample time to walk less than a mile to 10th and Patton by 1:15.

Rumor: Mrs. Helen Markham was the only witness to the killing of Tippit. She put the time at just after 1:06 and described the killer as about 30, short, stocky, with bushy hair, and wearing a white coat. She said that she identified Oswald in the lineup because of his clothing rather than his appearance.

WC: There were two other witnesses to the killing: William Scoggins, a taxi driver parked at the corner of 10th and Patton, and Domingo Benavides, who used Tippit's car radio to notify the police dispatcher of the shooting at 1:16 p.m. Barbara and Virginia Davis saw a man with a pistol in hand walk across their lawn immediately after hearing the gunshots. All of these people, except Benavides, subsequently picked Oswald out of a lineup as the slayer. In addition, six more witnesses identified Oswald as the man they saw in flight after the murder of Tippit: Ted Calloway and Sam Guinyard, from a lineup, Warren Reynolds, Pat Patterson, and Harold Russell, from pictures, and Mary Brock who saw Oswald walking at a fast pace through a parking lot in which Oswald's discarded jacket was later found. Mrs. Markham denies that she ever described the killer as short, stocky, and bushy-haired. She stated in her testimony that she identified Oswald "mostly from his face." Oswald was not wearing the same clothing in the lineup as he was when captured at the Texas Theatre.

Rumor: Lee Oswald, Jack Ruby, and J. D. Tippit lived near each other and were mutual acquaintances. Lee Oswald was on his way to Jack Ruby's apartment when stopped by Tippit.

WC: Oswald's room was 1.3 miles from Ruby's apartment. Tippit's residence was about 7 miles away from the other two. Investigation has revealed no evidence that Oswald and Tippit were acquainted, nor had mutual acquaintances. All assertions that Oswald was seen in the company of Ruby or anyone else from the Carousel Club have been investigated. None merits any credence. There is no credible evidence that Oswald knew Ruby or where he lived. Ruby was acquainted with another Dallas policeman, G. M. Tippit, but not the one who was killed.

Rumor: Tippit was not supposed to be in the patrol car alone, was not supposed to be in Oak Cliff, and violated procedure when he made a stop without notifying headquarters by radio.

WC: Dallas police confirm that about 80 percent of day shift patrolmen worked alone, the radio log shows that Tippit was directed to go and remain in Oak Cliff after the assassination, and there was no regulation or requirement to radio in when stopping to question a suspect.

Rumor: Mrs. Johnson stated that Oswald could not have hidden a revolver in his room.

WC: Mrs. Johnson testified that he "never brought that rifle in my house.... He could have had the pistol, I don't know, because they found the scabbard." The holster [scabbard] was found by the police in their search.

Rumor: Oswald was a spy for the Soviet Union or CIA or FBI.

WC: There is no evidence that Oswald had any working relation with the Soviet government or any intelligence service. Any value he might have had as a Marine electronics technician would have

disappeared when he defected. While Marguerite Oswald frequently expressed the opinion that Lee was an agent, her testimony was that "I cannot prove Lee is an agent." The Directors
of the FBI and CIA testified that Oswald was never employed by
either agency in any capacity.

Rumor: Marguerite Oswald was shown a photograph of Jack Ruby by an
FBI agent the night before Ruby killed her son.

WC: On the night of November 23, 1963, Special Agent Bardwell
Odum of the FBI showed Mrs. Oswald a picture of a man to
determine whether the man was known to her. Mrs. Oswald
stated subsequently that the picture was that of Jack Ruby. The
WC examined the photograph and determined that it was not a
picture of Jack Ruby.

Rumor: The headquarters detachment of the U.S. Army, under orders
from Secretary McNamara's office, began to rehearse for the funeral more than a week before the assassination.

WC: That assertion is based on an interview with Captain Richard
Cloy by the Jackson, Mississippi, *Clarion-Ledger,* February 21,
1964. Cloy is quoted as saying, "we…had just finished a funeral
rehearsal because there was grave concern for President Hoover's
health. But we never expected that our practice was preparing us
for President Kennedy."

APPENDIX B
Retardation and Deformation of Bullets

Construction of a Military Bullet

Military bullets, like the Mannlicher-Carcano, have a solid, "closed" nose. Most bullets made in the United States are of two parts: a gilding metal jacket and a lead core. Gilding metal is a type of brass, an alloy of copper and zinc. The hollow jacket is stamped from a metal "cup" by a series of hydraulic presses. The completed jacket of a military bullet is closed at the front by either a pointed or a parabolic "nose" that results in the desired aerodynamic characteristics. The nose smoothly transitions to a cylindrical body, left open at the base. The jacket is then filled with a core of lead with a diameter slightly smaller than the cavity in the jacket. The density of the lead core gives the bullet its weight while its pliability minimizes the wear to the gun barrel. This core is usually hardened with a small percentage of antimony. One final hydraulic press sets the core firmly into the jacket. The core is locked in place by crimping the end of the jacket over the base of the core at the edges and running a circumferential crimp (called the cannelure) around the outside of the jacket. The cannelure puts a slight indentation into the core material, locking the core and the jacket together.

The finished product may be seen in the photographs of figure 16. The lead-and-antimony alloy is usually left exposed at the base of a military bullet. In contrast, the jacket of a hunting bullet usually has a closed base and an open point, exposing the lead core at the tip. The exposed lead may have a deep indentation (hollow-point) or be rounded into an aerodynamic shape (soft point). The lead never touches the rifle barrel, in either the military or hunting bullet, only the jacket does. The jacket holds the bullet's shape as it is accelerated down the gun barrel by the propellant gas, "lubricates" its passage down the barrel to minimize friction and maximize velocity, and prevents the barrel from being fouled by lead deposits.

Stability of the Bullet

Bullets are designed to be stable in flight. The bullet is stabilized by spin, like a gyroscope or toy top. The gyroscopic stability maintains the bullet in a nose-first position as it travels through the air. The bullet is spun by means of a set of spiral grooves cut into the inside surface of the gun barrel. The raised sections between the grooves are called lands. This alternating set of lands and grooves is called rifling, from which the rifle derives its name. When the bullet moves from the firing chamber, it is gripped by the lands, pressing corresponding grooves into the gilding metal jacket. As the bullet moves from the firing chamber into the barrel, the lead core "gives" beneath the jacket so that the bullet is custom molded to fit the configuration of the barrel. This provides a tight gas seal to ensure a high, consistent velocity. A bullet made of solid bronze, steel, or other hard metal would quickly wear down the lands, but would not deform to fill the grooves, allowing gas to leak by and lowering the muzzle velocity.

The spiral angle of the rifling is usually constant from end to end. So the spin increases in lock step with the linear velocity as the bullet is rapidly accelerated through the barrel by the hot, high-pressure gas produced by the burning propellant (still informally called gunpowder). Like the toy top, the bullet is spun around its "axis of symmetry." The axis of symmetry, also referred to as the "long axis", is an imaginary line from the bullet's tip through the center of its base.

When its line of flight is not aligned with its long axis, the bullet is said to be yawing. The angle between the long axis and the line of flight is called the yaw angle, drawn in figure 16. In normal aerodynamic flight, after it emerges from the "bubble" of propellant gas in front of the muzzle of the rifle, the bullet's yaw quickly diminishes to a level between zero and five degrees. The normal, in-flight yaw of the Mannlicher-Carcano bullet in air is near zero. In a denser material, such as flesh or water, the story is different. Flesh or other soft tissue has about the same density as water—about 800 times the density of air. As the bullet enters the dense material, it loses its gyroscopic stability and its yaw quickly grows, like the "wobble" of a toy top running down. If the depth of penetration through tissue is sufficient, the bullet will flip completely over through a backward orientation, then its angular momentum will carry it on toward point-first again. Given enough penetration distance, it will usually return toward a backward position.

Once the bullet is immersed in a medium as dense as tissue, its spin has little effect on the growth of yaw. Some writers refer to the yaw growth in dense media as "tumbling"—a term that is somewhat misleading. The HSCA drawing of an impact by a badly yawed bullet in figure 28 illustrates the usual impression one gets. The word tumbling, whether in air or in tissue, gives the impression that the bullet rotates many times, end-over-end, as it penetrates, but the bullet actually seldom makes a complete 360° turn before exiting a target the size of a human body. Most bullets will never make the full circle, no matter how deeply they penetrate. If it stops in the target, the undeformed bullet almost always comes to rest pointed backward. Similarly, the bullet that was yawed by passing through the president's neck did not describe the motion shown in the picture. The yaw of that bullet grew from some very small angle when it exited the president's throat to an angle between 30° and 60° when it hit the governor's back (depending on what the actual size of the wound was).

Some rifle bullets yaw in dense materials faster than others. Long heavy bullets with a short, parabolic nose like the Mannlicher-Carcano yaw relatively slowly, and generally do not complete a full turn before returning toward a base-first penetration. Short, light bullets with a long, pointed nose, like the 5.56 mm (.223 caliber) M193 bullets used in Viet Nam and its replacement, a standard NATO round of the same caliber, will yaw more rapidly. That is, they will reach a given angle of yaw in a shorter penetration distance and, if they do not deform, generally rotate to about 270° before settling toward a base-first penetration. Since the bullet has lower drag when traveling point first than when moving sideways, those bullets which yaw slowly will penetrate more deeply into tissue, other things being equal, than those which yaw rapidly. Its slow yaw growth, combined with its relatively large mass, is the reason for the great penetrating ability of the Mannlicher-Carcano bullet.

First we will consider the loss of velocity in a bullet's stable mode —in air. Then we will consider its behavior in its path through tissue, a medium dense enough to cause all bullets to be unstable.

Retardation (Velocity Loss) in Air

The aerodynamic drag law can be used to calculate the loss of velocity with range in normal flight through air. The drag force on the bullet is:

$$F = \tfrac{1}{2}\, C_D \rho A V^2 \tag{1}$$

where:

F = Force (= Mass times acceleration)
C_D = Air Drag Coefficient of the Bullet (depends on bullet shape)
ρ = Density of air (grams/cubic centimeter)
A = Mean Presented Area (square centimeters)
V = Velocity (centimeters/second)[1]

If C_D, ρ, and A are considered constant, equation 1 may be solved for the velocity at any range:

$$V_X = V_0 \exp\left(-\tfrac{1}{2} C_D \rho \tfrac{A}{M} X\right) \tag{2}$$

where exp denotes exponentiation of e, the base of the natural logarithms, and

M = Mass (in grams)
X = Range (in centimeters)
V_0 = Muzzle velocity (in whatever system you want to use: e.g., feet/second, centimeters/second)
V_X = Velocity (in whatever system is used for muzzle velocity)

C_D, the drag coefficient, is not actually constant, even for a given bullet shape, but varies with mach number (the velocity of the bullet divided by the speed of sound). Quantities in the exponential must be in consistent units. As the exponent in equation 2 is a dimensionless term, however, one may choose different units for the velocities in equation 2. The velocity at range X will be in the same units as muzzle velocity.

The Biophysics Lab took samples of unfired Mannlicher-Carcano bullets from the lot the FBI said was used in the assassination. The means

---

1. Equations 1 and 2 are expressed in the cgs system of units, but any consistent set of units would do just as well.

of the sample physical constants they found are:

> Mass: 10.45 grams (about 161 grains or 161/7000 pounds)
> Length: 3.029 centimeters (about 1.19 inches)
> Diameter: 0.667 centimeter (about 0.263 inches)
> Mean Presented Area, A (point first): 0.349 square centimeter
> Mean Presented Area, A (sideways): 2.02 square centimeters

Even though the drag coefficient varies with Mach number, the M-C bullet remained supersonic throughout the distances between the sniper's nest and the president for both shots, so that the value given below yields reasonable approximations at ranges of interest. The density of air also varies with altitude, relative humidity, and atmospheric pressure, but is reasonably well approximated as 800 times less dense than water or tissue. For approximate values, use:

> $C_D = 1.0$
> $\rho = 1/800$ grams per cubic centimeter

Average muzzle velocity of the WCC cartridges used:
$V_0 = 2160$ feet per second (65,800 centimeters per second)[2]

Approximate ranges of interest:
JFK neck shot: $X = 188$ feet (5,700 centimeters)
JFK head shot: $X = 265$ feet (8,100 centimeters)

Table B1. Velocities Measured for the Biophysics Division Simulations.

Simulation	Range	Measured Velocities	Mean Velocity
Neck	180 feet (~55 m)	1940, 1862, 1910	1904 feet/sec (580 m/s)
Wrist	210 feet (~64 m)	(five shots)	1858 feet/sec (566 m/s)
Chest 1	210 feet	1855, 1880, 1881	1872 feet/sec (561 m/s)
Chest 2	210 feet	1906 to 1945	1929 feet/sec* (588 m/s)
Skull	270 feet (~82 m)	1790, 1833, 1854	1826 feet/sec (557 m/s)

* Environmental temperature was warmer on the second day, resulting in higher initial velocities.

---

2. Units are first given in whatever units were used in the original measurement.

Retardation in Tissue

A bullet's velocity decreases rapidly when penetrating tissue. At high velocity, the "drag" force that slows it is roughly proportional to the density of the material being penetrated and the presented area of the projectile. If everything else were held constant while the density of the substance being penetrated was doubled, then the drag force would double. The same is true of presented area: To double the presented area is to double the decelerating force. The drag force, however, is proportional to the square of the velocity. This means that if the velocity is doubled, the drag force is quadrupled. This dependence of drag on the density, presented area, and, most especially, the velocity is expressed in the aerodynamic drag law (equation (1) above). Sir Isaac Newton first proposed this law in the seventeenth century. This law is used to calculate the velocity of the bullet as a function of the distance traveled down-range in air.

The aerodynamic drag law is not suitable for bullets penetrating tissue. For tissue retardation, we need a better approximation that properly accounts for the greatly increased "skin drag" which results from the bullet's being immersed in tissue, as well as its changing orientation as it yaws. The tissue retardation law we will use is a generalized version of the retardation law posed by M. H. Resal over a hundred years ago (reference B1). The equation does not account for the strength of the tissue, nor how that strength varies with the deformation rate. These effects are important at lower velocities, but can be neglected at high velocities and will be neglected herein. For better approximations, see the articles by Peters and associates (references B4 and B5).

However, the reason for the high drag of the bullet moving sideways is the "presented area" of the bullet and its blunter shape when moving other than point first. The presented area is the area you would see if the bullet were coming directly at you. If the bullet were in normal flight, that area would be a circle with a diameter the same as the bullet's (looking directly at the nose). If the bullet were yawed to 90 degrees—traveling sideways—the area would be the profile of the bullet. These two presented areas are the minimum and maximum presented areas of the bullet, as shown in figure 16. As the bullet's yaw grows after penetration, the presented area changes smoothly and continuously from one to the other.

The force equation is:

$$F = C_I \rho AV^2 + C_V \frac{A\mu V}{b} \tag{3}$$

The velocity in tissue is given by:

$$V_X = (V_0 + \frac{C_V\mu/b}{C_I\rho}) \exp(-\tfrac{1}{2} C_D \rho \frac{A}{M} X) \tag{4}$$

where

C_I = The inertial drag coefficient (comparable to half the drag coefficient of equation 1)

C_V = The viscous drag coefficient

μ = Viscosity of tissue (grams/centimeter^{2}second)

b = Thickness of the layer of liquefied tissue surrounding the penetrating projectile

Other variables are the same as defined earlier.

In tissue, we do not have to worry about supersonic versus subsonic drag coefficients. All bullets are subsonic in tissue, which has a velocity of sound around 1500 meters/second (nearly 5,000 feet/sec). This is a velocity higher than that of the fastest bullets. So both drag coefficients may be considered to be constants. The ratio μ/b may also be considered constant and combined with the viscous drag coefficient, creating a single quantity, $C_V\mu/b$. The values of this and the inertial coefficient have not been determined for bullets, as they have many different shapes and the coefficients would not remain constant as the bullets yaw within the tissue. We can, however, use the coefficients for shapes we do have to approximate the tissue retardation of the Mannlicher-Carcano bullet. When moving sideways, the M-C resembles a cylinder moving sideways. The M-C bullet has parabolic nose. When the bullet is moving point-first, the proper value of C_I for its parabolic shape would be slightly lower than that of a sphere.

Drag Coefficients for Spheres and Cylinders in Tissue:

$C_V\mu/b = 3000$
C_I: sphere = 0.10, cylinder = 0.175

The relevant densities are:

Water: 1 gram/cubic centimeter (g/cc)
Soft Tissue: 1.05 g/cc
Bone: ~2 g/cc

The Biophysics Lab tests were conducted in Maryland in April/
May of 1964. Considering that it was warmer in Dallas on the day of the
shooting than it was during these tests, the average initial velocity from
the sniper's window was probably a bit higher in Dallas. A reasonable
estimate would be about 660 meters/second. A corresponding estimate
of the striking velocity on the president's neck would be about 615 me-
ters/second, with an error of plus or minus 10 meters/second.

For the penetration of the president's neck, the bullet passed nearly
point-first all the way. The researchers at the Biophysics Lab estimated
that the distance through the president's neck would have been between
13.5 and 14.5 centimeters. In their tests, using gelatin, horse meat, and
goat meat as simulants, they measured exit velocities without getting
entrance velocities to avoid disturbing the bullet and to facilitate aiming. Comparing those exits to independently determined residual velocities at that distance (see Table B1), they estimated that the bullet would
have lost between 106 and 134 feet per second velocity in penetrating
the president's neck. Using 13.5 cm for X, 1.05 grams/cubic centimeter
for the density of soft tissue, and substituting the other appropriate values in equation 3 yields a velocity loss of about 54 meters/second. This
would result in a striking velocity on Connally's back of about 560 me-
ters/second with a larger estimated error of perhaps ±15 meters/second.
Although the WCC/MC bullet has less drag than a sphere of the same
diameter when traveling point-first, it is only important for the neck
wound. When the bullet struck Connally's back it was badly yawed, having both an increased presented area and drag coefficients more akin to
those of a cylinder.

As the yaw of the bullet would have been over 20° to have caused
the elongated entry wound, the coefficients for a cylinder and an intermediate presented area, A, should be used for further velocity loss estimates. It is estimated that the path through the governor's chest was 25
to 30 centimeters, including about 10 centimeter of bone (twice as dense
as muscle). If it is assumed that the middle third was rib, the bullet would
have had a velocity that decreased from about 440 meters/second to 244

meters/second as it penetrated rib and would have had an exit velocity of about 150 meters/second from his chest, all with a probable error of ±30 meters/second. The bullet started at an appreciable yaw and exited going nearly backward.

The striking velocity on the wrist was virtually the same as the exit velocity from the chest. The path length through the wrist was 6 to 8 cm including perhaps 3 centimeters of bone. Here we can shrink the estimated error somewhat, as we know that it barely managed to exit the wrist. From independent tests, we can determine that to barely penetrate skin covered with light clothing (the Governor's thigh) the bullet, traveling nearly backward, would have had a velocity of about 40 meters/second ±6 meters/second (reference B2). A projectile generally either stops within the body or has an exit velocity a bit greater than this. The probability that the bullet, moving backward, would penetrate bone (Reference B3) independently confirms the reasonableness of a striking velocity of 150 meters/second on the radius bone in the wrist.

We have already noted that soft tissue is 800 times denser than air. Bone, in turn, is roughly twice as dense as soft tissue. Thus, the deceleration of the bullet is enormously increased in tissue over the drag it experiences in air. It is this drag force that damages soft tissue and bone. You might say that the tissue is pushing against the bullet to slow it and at the same time the bullet exerts the same force against the tissue, tearing soft tissue and breaking bones. Bone, having twice the density of soft tissue, also produces twice the 'inertial' drag force. Its greater strength causes a further increase in drag, especially at lower velocity. If the drag force is great enough, it will even damage the bullet. Bullet damage is more likely in bone.

It is obvious that bone is harder than soft tissue and perhaps a little less obvious that fully jacketed bullets are harder than bone. One measure of the "hardness" of a solid material is its "yield strength," the pressure that it takes to permanently deform the material. Pressure is measured in terms of force/unit area. In a malleable material, such as most metals, increasing pressure will produce elastic deformation up to its yield strength. Release the pressure and it would return to its original shape. At or above its yield strength, the material will undergo plastic deformation and will be permanently bent or dented.

The yield strength of the gilding metal jacket of the Mannlicher-

Carcano bullet is approximately four times greater than the 'yield strength' of bone—that is, it would take about four times the amount of pressure to put a permanent dent in the bullet than it would to chip or crack a bone.[3] Whatever the density and strength of the material the bullet penetrates, however, there is a velocity high enough to permanently deform it. With sufficient velocity, the drag pressure will exceed the yield strength of the bullet.

Yield strengths of some relevant materials are:

Bone: $9.75 \cdot 10^8$ dynes/centimeters^2
Gilding Metal: $3.8 \cdot 10^9$ dynes/centimeters^2

(The yield strength of soft tissue varies greatly, from skin and muscle to internal organs to fat, but all are orders of magnitude lower than the above.)

Dividing both sides of equation (3) by A gives an expression for the force/unit area—that is, pressure anywhere along the path of penetration. But bullets are not solid gilding metal. They have a jacket of gilding metal surrounding a lead core that, of course, is not as strong. Bones are not solid either; they have a hard crust and a cancellous (sponge-like, but rigid) center, filled with marrow and blood. So the above yield strengths cannot yield precise deformation pressures with which to compare pressure calculated from the penetration law. Thinner jackets will have lower deformation velocities than thicker ones. Calculation of the yield strength of hard shells filled with a material of different density and yield strength are exceedingly complex. But the M-C bullet has a relatively thick jacket, so one can calculate rough approximations from the above information.

The pressure at which the heavy gilding metal jacket of the M-C bullet will begin to deform corresponds to a velocity of about 520 meters/second, if the bullet is traveling point first. If the bullet is moving sideways the drag coefficient is greater (cylinder vs. sphere) so the pressure is higher at the same velocity. This lowers the deformation velocity to roughly 425 meters/second. The higher the velocity at which the bullet strikes bone, the higher the pressure and the longer the deforming

---

3. Brittle materials like bone do not incur plastic deformation. They resist deformation up to a certain pressure, then will chip or crack. The term 'yield strength' is not quite accurate in this case. It would probably be more appropriately called the 'fracture strength' of bone.

pressure will last. Therefore, the amount of deformation in the bullet increases rapidly as the velocity rises from these thresholds. When the deformation results in rupture of the jacket, the deformation increases rapidly, as the yield strength of lead is much less than that of gilding metal and not much higher than that of bone. The actual yield strength of the lead core depends on the amount of antimony present in the alloy (see Appendix E) and the amount of work hardening the lead is subjected to in the manufacturing process.

The above comments lead to the following conclusions:

• Bones produce more than twice as much pressure—to retard or deform a bullet—as soft tissue does at the same velocity. (Doubling the density only doubles the drag force.)

• Velocity is more important than density or material strength in producing deformation. (Doubling the velocity quadruples the force.)

• Because the yield strength of gilding metal is nearly four times that of bone, a bullet can smash a bone without exceeding its own yield strength. That is, the bullet will not deform.

• There is some velocity high enough that bone will deform a bullet. At about 1.4 times that velocity, soft tissue will also deform the bullet. This is because velocity is squared in the term that is dominant at higher velocities. (The square root of 2 is about 1.4.)

As Newton observed in his first law: Nature dictates that an object in motion will continue moving in a straight line unless acted on by an outside force. Bullets are no exception. Contrary to the apocryphal stories in the medical literature, the bullet or fragment that still has enough velocity to produce significant penetration does not "bounce" off a bone or a tissue interface at a large angle, then proceed to injure another distant part of the anatomy. The change in direction is usually a gradual one caused by the lift force on a yawing or deforming bullet.

One can use the definitions of force and acceleration and the above yield strength to determine that a bullet cannot be abruptly deflected and remain intact. A direction change is an indication of acceleration (distance over time-squared). The force is directly proportional to the acceleration. If a WCC/MC bullet undergoes a direction change of, say, 30° in the length of a gelatin block (about 38 centimeters or 15 inches), it will not be deformed. If it undergoes the same direction change within its own length (about 3 centimeters), the force would be increased by the inverse square of the ratio of the times it took to effect the change in direction. At roughly constant velocity, it would take over 10 times as long to go 38 centimeters as to go 3 centimeters. Thus, the force (and the pressure) would increase by over 100 times. This is a pressure so high above the yield strength of the gilding metal jacket that it would cause catastrophic failure of the bullet. For this reason, a true ricochet must impact at a very small angle to the surface from which it ricochets, to dramatically lower the acceleration it undergoes. Even then, the ricocheted bullet is usually badly deformed.

The exception is when the projectile is moving below the velocity necessary to exceed the yield strength of the bone. If a bullet has too little remaining energy to penetrate bone, it might bounce off at a sharp angle, but would only penetrate a short distance in soft tissue before stopping. The bullet that penetrated John Connally's body wall traveled at relatively high velocity all the way through and remained in grazing contact with the rib for 10 centimeters, badly fracturing the bone. Then, the curvature of the bullet's trajectory and the curvature of the rib, which determined the curvature of his thorax, took its path away from the rib and out through his chest wall.

References

B1. L.M. Sturdivan. A Mathematical Model of Penetration of Chunky Projectiles in a Gelatin Tissue Simulant, Chemical Systems Laboratory Technical Report ARCSL-TR-78055, Aberdeen Proving Ground, MD. August 1978.

B2. J.H. Lewis, P.H. Coon, V.R. Clare, and L.M. Sturdivan. An Empirical Model to Estimate the Probability of Skin Penetration by Various Projectiles, Chemical Systems Laboratory Technical Report ARCSL-TR-78004, Aberdeen Proving Ground, MD. April 1978.

B3. L.M. Sturdivan and R. Bexon. A Mathematical Model of the Probability of Perforation of the Human Skull by a Ballistic Projectile, Chemical Systems Laboratory Technical Report ARCSL-TR-81001, Aberdeen Proving Ground, MD. April 1981.

B4. C.E. Peters. A Mathematical-Physical Model of Wound Ballistics, *Journal of Trauma* (China) 6(2) Supplement, 303-318. 1990.

B5. C. E. Peters, C.L. Sebourn, H. L. Crowder. Wound Ballistics of Unstable Projectiles. Part I: Projectile yaw growth and retardation, *Journal of Trauma,* 40(3) Supplement, S10-15. 1996.

APPENDIX C
Statistical Analysis of Data from Neutron Activation Analysis

(The statistical calculations and plots were made using Minitab™ Statistical Software.)

To understand the unique properties of the four lots of bullets made by Western Cartridge Company for use in the 6.5mm Mannlicher-Carcano rifle (abbreviated hereafter as WCC/MC), one has to know a little bit about how bullet cores are made. Most bullets are made to a specification that requires a hardened lead core. All natural lead ores contain trace amounts of other metals, including silver, antimony, copper, arsenic, etc. In refined lead, the amount of these other metals is not large enough to significantly alter the physical properties from that of pure lead. The lead (chemical symbol Pb) is hardened by adding a specified percentage (usually a few percent) of antimony (Sb) to the natural alloy of nearly pure lead. To obtain a uniform hardness, the batch of alloy must be thoroughly mixed before it is formed into cores and inserted into the jacket to make the bullet. The Pb/Sb mix is melted, mixed, and cast into very large ingots.

Cores are made by extruding the alloy through a die by a large hydraulic press. (The die is a very hard steel plate with a hole or holes of the right diameter drilled through it.) Whether hardened or not, the cores are still informally referred to as 'lead.' The extruded rods of lead are sliced off as they emerge at precisely the length required for the weight of each core, then formed at the tip end to fit the jacket. The thorough mixing results in cores that are very uniform, so one cannot ordinarily distinguish among bullets from a single batch by analyzing the alloy for amounts of trace metals. Different batches of alloy, however, will contain different levels of trace elements. Generally, a 'lot' is a production run that may or may not have anything to do with changes in the materials of manufacture, so there may be more than one ingot used in a lot or there may be more than one lot with cores made from the same ingot.

The specification for MC bullets required unhardened lead. The distribution of Sb in 'pure' lead follows the typical bell-shaped 'normal' curve, with a very small mean concentration and a small variance (a narrow span of concentrations). When Western made four lots of WCC/MC bullets for the U.S. Department of Defense in the 1950s, they evidently mixed pieces of hardened lead, left over from production runs of a different bullet, with a larger quantity of 'pure' lead to make the cores. This process would yield 'unhardened' lead cores, containing higher levels of Sb than would be found in lead refined from natural ores. As the lead was melted, the chunks of hard lead would produce pockets with high Sb content within the lower-Sb alloy that would not disappear without very thorough mixing. Instead of the usual bell-shaped curve, the distribution of Sb in the incompletely mixed alloy would describe a bimodal (two-humped) curve, with the height of each peak proportional to the fraction of hardened and unhardened alloy in the mix. If that molten batch had subsequently been thoroughly mixed, it would have produced an alloy with a uniform concentration of Sb: that is, the two peaks would have merged into one sharp peak at an intermediate concentration. But mixing requires time and money, so evidently the ingots were only mixed to dilute the high-antimony pockets sufficiently to ascertain meeting the specification.

At intermediate stages of mixing, the smaller peak of higher Sb alloy would move toward and merge with the larger peak of unhardened alloy, being diluted as it merged. After the two peaks merged to form a single peak, the diffuse pockets of higher concentration of Sb would cause the distribution to be skewed from the bell-curve shape, with a heavier tail on the higher concentration side of the peak. In a distribution skewed this way, the mean concentration would be higher than the median.[1] In this case, the log of the concentration is often more symmetric, thus, bet-

---

1. The mean is the usual numerical average. The median is the central value, with half the sample higher and half lower. Both are used as measures of the 'center' of the population. The values in the tail of the distribution are used to generate measures of the spread of the data. Measures often used are the variance, the average of squared deviations from the mean, or the standard deviation, the square root of the variance (aka, the root mean square error). Population with more samples on one side of the 'central' value than the the the other are called "skewed." Extreme skewness invalidates the usual statistical test results. The statistician likes to work with 'symmetric' populations (i.e., those that have low skewness).

ter approximated by the usual normal, or Gaussian, distribution assumed in the standard statistical analysis. In other words, the true distribution would be closer to lognormal.

Why were the recovered and test samples so close?

This section is intended to provide insight into the process that created test samples that were near the samples recovered from the bodies of the two men and why the variance in Sb concentration within the core of a single bullet is irrelevant to the statistical problem. The explanation is for information only and is not necessary to justify how the available data came to exist. The data stand on their own, with two homogenous groups falling into the only physical grouping that makes sense.

The 'magic' bullet, CE 399, requires no explanation for why the recovered fragment and intact bullet were so similar. The lead recovered from Connally's wrist had to come from the bulge of lead at the base of the bullet. All test samples were taken from that same location, so all were necessarily nearby lead alloy and not representative of the variance throughout the bullet. The broken bullet fragment found in the car after exiting from Kennedy's head is a bit more complicated.

One has to look closely at how those fragments were formed to see the local source of the lead they contain. As the bullet penetrated the skull, it was badly deformed. The nose was flattened and pushed sideways as it entered because of the angle it made with the skull. The rear portion of the bullet, however, had tremendous inertia that tended to make it go straight ahead. These opposing forces crimp the bullet, creating a tremendous internal pressure as the lead is squeezed within the bending jacket. When the jacket ruptured some distance beyond the entry point, a small spray of lead fragments squirted out of the crack. Like the breaking of a fluid-filled container (visualize rupturing a grapefruit section with a spoon), this spray relieves the enormous internal pressure, so that the spray of small fragments stops immediately. Under the continued retarding pressure from the tissue, the bullet continues to break apart as the split in the jacket widens and extends around the bullet. Few, if any, small fragments are dislodged within soft tissue, though some might be scraped off on the harder skull bone as it exits.

As the jacket splits laterally, the lead inside is stretched, like pulled taffy. Eventually, the jacket may split in two, with the pieces of jacket enclosing the lead and pulling it in two as they part. In either case, the exposed surface is not far from that lead that was shed in the rupture spray. Samples for Neutron Activation Analysis (NAA) analysis were taken from that exposed surface, not from the lead deep within the jacket. The larger recovered fragment, recovered from the front of the head, next to the skull, may have been scraped off the exposed surface as the bullet fragments exited the skull. This, of course, was also close to the source of the "spray" fragments. While these samples might have a larger variance than those from the base of CE 399, it would be much smaller than Guinn's quarter-bullet variance is.

The Distribution of Antimony in the Cores of the Four Lots of WCC/MC Bullets

Vincent Guinn's NAA data for characterizing lead from random samples of WCC/MC bullets appears in Appendix D of reference C1. He obtained his random sample of lead cores from the open base of 14 bullets randomly drawn from the four existing lots of WCC/MC ammunition. Two bullets were drawn from Lot 6000 and four bullets each from Lots 6001–6003. The antimony content of those 14 samples appears in Table C1. The 'weight' of the sample is actually its mass, but Guinn's original term is kept for clarity.

The original table also contains the silver, copper, and sodium content of these samples. These are of some minor interest in the investigation, but will not be used in the analysis that follows. The major variation in the concentration of 'trace' elements within these rounds is in the antimony. The concentration is given in parts/million (ppm) or one microgram of the element per gram of the alloy.

Table C1. Antimony Content of Random WCC/MC Bullets

Lot	Lot Number	Weight (mg)	Antimony (ppm)	Log Antimony Concentration
6000A	1	51.2	173	5.15329
6000B	1	45.6	261	5.56452
6001A	2	47.8	158	5.06260
6001B	2	57.9	732	6.59578
6001C	2	58.5	1218	7.10497
6001D	2	47.2	161	5.08140
6002A	3	51.8	385	5.95324
6002B	3	47.2	949	6.85541
6002C	3	55.3	24	3.17805
6002D	3	51.3	121	4.79579
6003A	4	54.3	730	6.59304
6003B	4	44.6	80	4.38203
6003C	4	44.7	464	6.13988
6003D	4	44.0	240	5.48064

Abbreviations are: mg = milligrams, ppm = parts per million

From the wide variety of levels of antimony content within the bullet lots, it appears that there are no significant differences among the four lots. Assuming, for the moment, that this is true, we can look at the means, standard deviations, and so on, of the antimony levels of all 14 samples. These few points are not sufficient to determine whether the intermediate mix was still bimodal or had merged into a skewed distribution with a single peak. The means and medians of the raw Sb measurement and the natural logarithm (Ln) of that measure appear in Table C2.[2] In the raw measure, the mean is much larger than the median, as expected for a skewed distribution. The insignificant difference between mean and median in the log measure is only one indication that the

---

2. The mean is the average Sb, or Ln Sb content. The median is the central value, with half higher and half lower. The standard deviation is (sigma represents summation over the 14 samples):

$$\text{Standard Deviation} = \sqrt{\frac{\sum(\text{sampleSb} - \text{mean Sb})^2}{14}}$$

distribution is nearer lognormal. A better illustration of the difference appears in figures C1 and C2. These figures are so-called normal plots, or n-plots of the data. The n-plot shows the 14 concentrations, ranked from lowest to highest, plotted against what is called the standard normal variate from the Gaussian distribution. If the data were perfectly normally distributed, the plotted points would make a perfectly straight line. The skewness of the raw data is readily seen in the nonlinearity of the points (the tight curvature at the left end of the data), in figure C1. A statistical measure of the lack of normality called the Anderson-Darling (A-D) test is printed on the figure. The p-value is the lowest test probability for which a statistical test is valid. As the usual test of significance is for 0.05, a p-value of 0.05 or higher is desired for any statistical tests—the higher the better. If the data formed a perfectly straight line on the n-plot, the A-D p-value would be 1.0. The very low A-D p-statistic of 0.03 in figure C1 indicates that the data are far from a normal distribution, so much so that it cannot be used for any useful statistical test. All tests will be conducted on the logarithms of the antimony levels.

Table C2. Comparison of Means and Medians for Antimony Content, Raw and Log Values

Variable	No.	Mean	Median	St. Dev.	Minimum	Maximum
Sb	14	406.9	250.5	371.2	24.0	1218.0
Ln Sb	14	5.567	5.523	1.074	3.178	7.108

Normal Probability Plot

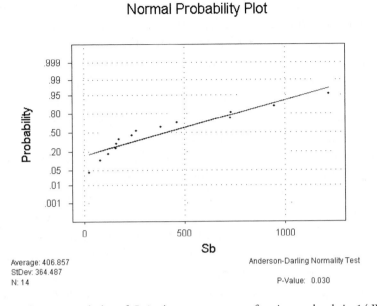

Average: 406.857
StDev: 364.487
N: 14

Anderson-Darling Normality Test

P-Value: 0.030

Figure C1. Normal plot of Guinn's measurements of antimony levels in 14 WCC/MC bullets.

Normal Probability Plot

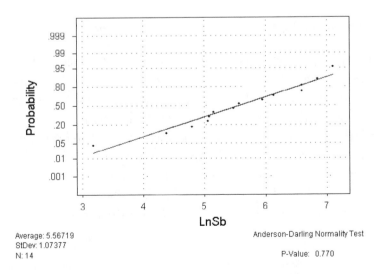

Average: 5.56719
StDev: 1.07377
N: 14

Anderson-Darling Normality Test

P-Value: 0.770

Figure C2. Normal Plot of Guinn's 14 antimony measurements on the natural log scale.

For the natural logs of the same antimony concentrations, the mean and median are 5.567 and 5.523 (which are equivalent to a geometric mean of 261.6 and median of 250.4 ppm). The increased linearity in the n-plot of the log values in Figure C2 is evident and the A-D p-value increases to a respectable 0.77. There is no indication in the shape of the line that the distribution is still bimodal, but there could still be a slight 'bump' on the upper tail. In any case, the distribution is well approximated by the lognormal distribution of figure C2.

The point above the line on the right indicates that the upper tail is truncated, and the point above the line on the left indicates that the lower tail is heavier than "normal." Both of these are understandable when one considers the way that different concentrations of antimony in the original constituents move toward the mean with increased mixing. The larger quantity of low-antimony lead in the mix can leave relatively larger pockets of low-concentration, 'natural' alloy, while the smaller pockets of high-antimony alloy form a secondary peak that shifts downward and flattens with mixing, but retains something of its shape as it merges into a unimodal, skewed distribution. This leaves the upper tail truncated. The significance of these observations is that we need to stay away from the extreme tails of this distribution when conducting statistical tests.

A Test of Lot-to-lot Differences of Antimony Concentration

Our earlier assumption that there was no lot-to-lot difference in the antimony content was checked by a General Linear Models (GLM) statistical analysis of the data in table C1, using lot number as a factor and weight of the sample as a covariate.[3] Table C3 summarizes the output of the statistical test. The important results are expressed in the p (for probability) values. A p-value greater than 0.05 (that is, the chance of observing these differences in a random sample would be one in twenty) is not usually considered statistically significant. The p-values in table C3 indicate that there is no significant lot-to-lot difference (a p of 0.669 means that two out of every

---

3. The GLM is similar to the more-familiar Analysis of Variance test with unequal sample sizes. In table C3, the terms are defined as follows: Seq SS = Sequential sum of squares; Adj SS = Adjusted sum of squares; Adj MS = Adjusted mean squares; F = the F-statistic upon which the test is based. For details, consult a standard statistics text under Analysis of Variance.

three random samples would have lot-to-lot differences as high or higher than this one). The weight (of the individual samples) is also not statistically significant. This means that there are no differences caused by some samples being very small and others being relatively large.

Table C3.   General Linear Models: Analysis of Variance for LnSb, using Adjusted Sum of Squares for Tests

Source	DF	Seq SS	Adj SS	Adj MS	F	P
Weight	1	1.542	2.296	2.296	1.81	0.211
Lot No.	3	2.041	2.041	0.680	0.54	0.669
Error	9	11.406	11.406	1.267		
Total	13	14.989				

A Test of the Probability that a "Planted" Bullet Would Match a Recovered Fragment

Guinn's data appear in table I, Appendix B of reference C1. His measurements are more accurate than the FBI's analysis done 15 years earlier, primarily because of new detectors that better discriminated the signals from the various trace elements and a technique that eliminated the systematic error that caused the FBI to label their analysis inconclusive. Guinn's antimony data are reproduced in table C4. Data on content of metals other than Sb are omitted.

CE 399 is the stretcher bullet. CE 842 is the fragment recovered from Connally's wrist. CE 567 is the bullet fragment with portions of jacket and core found in the front of the limousine. CE 843 consists of the two small fragments recovered from the front of Kennedy's skull, grouped together for Guinn's analysis. CE 840 is one of the fragments recovered from the carpet in the rear passenger compartment of the car.

First we will consider the probability that one or two of the recovered samples were 'planted' by a conspirator to implicate Oswald.

Table C4.   Calculation of the Standard Normal Variate, x, and Cumulative Distribution, P, from Guinn's NAA of Recovered Bullet and Fragments in the Kennedy and Connally Shootings

CE #	FBI #	Sb (ppm)	LnSb	x	P
399	Q1	833	6.7250	1.0782	0.8595
842	Q9	797	6.6809	1.0371	0.8501
567	Q2	602	6.4003	0.7758	0.7811
843	Q4, 5	621	6.4313	0.8148	0.7894
840(1)	q14(1)	638	6.4583	0.8299	0.7967
840(2)	Q14(2)	647	6.4723	0.8430	0.8003
840(m)	Q14(m)	642.5	6.4653	0.8364	0.7985

To conduct statistical tests on the samples in evidence, we need an estimate of the mean and variance of the antimony concentration in the general population. These may be estimated by the average and standard deviation of the 14 points of table C1. On the log scale, the population mean is estimated to be 5.567 and the population standard deviation 1.074. The standard normal variate, which we call x in table C4, is calculated by subtracting the population mean from the Sb concentration in the sample and dividing the difference by the population standard deviation. The standard normal variates are used to calculate the cumulative probability distribution, P, up to the point x. This is equivalent to the probability that the given sample is larger than the fraction of the population represented by P. Though the recovered bullets and fragments have cores that are above the geometric mean of antimony concentration, they are on the flat part of this curve, well below the outlying point on the upper right of Figure C2. Thus, we are avoiding the tails of the distribution where P would be doubtful.

Differences in the P-values in table C4 may be used to define how "close" two samples are to each other, as the difference is a measure of what proportion of the population lie between the two levels. For instance, the difference between CE 399 and CE 842 is 0.0094, indicating that less than 1 percent of the population lies between these two concentrations. Two different determinations were made of CE 840, so the difference between determinations one and two, 0.0036, gives us a measure of the lowest detectable difference in antimony concentration, about one-third of 1 percent. The mean of the two determinations is indicated by (m).

The point of these calculations is that not all conspiracy scenarios justify assuming that the samples are drawn from five independent WCC/MC bullets. Some conspiracy scenarios frankly admit that Oswald was a probable shooter, but that only one of the five samples being derived from a different source would prove a conspiracy. The other four could be the very non-random samples the Warren Commission, the HSCA, and many others claim they were. How likely is it, then, that the one random sample would match one group or the other?

Consider the scenario that someone "planted" CE 399 in Parkland to frame Oswald for the crime. This would only work, of course, if they somehow gained possession of a bullet that had been fired from Oswald's rifle (and ignores the fact that CE 567 also has engraving from the Oswald rifle on it). Then we need to estimate the probability that a randomly selected bullet would have an antimony concentration at its base that was as close as the Sb concentration of CE 399 is to that of CE 842. But the difference in the P-value of the two, in Table C4, only gives us about half the desired probability estimate. The concentration could actually be lower than that of CE 842 and still be as close to CE 842 as CE 399 is. So we need to consider the standard normal variate in the interval as far below as CE 399 is above. Subtracting the difference from that of CE 842 gives us a standard normal variate, $x = 0.9960$ with a corresponding cumulative probability of p of 0.8403. Thus, the total interval width is the difference $0.8595 - 0.8403 = 0.0192$, or about 1.9 percent. A sample from the base of a random bullet from any box of WCC/MC ammunition would have less than a 2 percent probability of being as close to the recovered fragments from John Connally's wrist as CE 399 is.

Random matches to members of Group 2 are a bit more involved as well as more difficult to use in constructing a conspiracy scenario. Table C5 has the relevant calculations. As before, we need to calculate a standard normal variate as far above CE 843 as CE 840 is below.

Table C5.   Cumulative Probability from the Gaussian Distribution

Antimony Concentration from:	x	P
CE 843	0.8048	0.7894
"Other side" of CE 840 (from CE 843)	0.8680	0.8073
Mean of CE 840 and CE 843	0.8206	0.7941
"Other side" of the above (from CE 567)	0.8654	0.8066
Mean of Group 1 (CE 842 and CE 399)	1.0576	0.8548
Mean of Group 2 (head & car fragments)	0.8057	0.7897
"Other side" of Group 2	0.5538	0.7101

The row labeled "Other side" of CE 840 has the relevant x-value and the corresponding P. The difference is: 0.8073 - 0.7894 = 0.0179. The unconvincing argument that somebody planted fragments in the upholstery that would match the head fragments has little probability (about 1.8 percent), and even less credibility.

Planting a bullet fragment with engraving from the Oswald rifle (that is, CE 567) that would match the other two samples makes more sense, in spite of the difficulty of obtaining such a fragment to plant. If we calculate a standard normal variate that is as far above the mean of CE 840 and CE 843 as CE 567 (the engraved fragment) is below, we get the x and P values listed on the fourth line of Table C5: P = 0.8066. Subtracting the P-value for CE 567 listed in Table C4 (0.8066 - 0.7758 = 0.0308) leaves about 3 percent probability of this close a match by chance alone.

To successfully 'frame' Oswald for two shots made by another person would have required planting both CE 399 and CE 567, the bullet and fragment that both had the engraving from the Oswald rifle. The probability that these two plants would match the fragments recovered from the two men is the product of the two separate probabilities, 0.0308 x 0.0192 = 0.00059—that is, the probability is less than six in ten thousand.

With only one determination of each concentration, we cannot calculate the probability that five random samples from the WCC/MC population would fall into the two groups proposed by the Warren Commission as having come from two separate shots—that is, CE 399 and CE 842 in the single bullet shot and the other three associated with the Kennedy head shot. This corresponds to the assumption that all five samples originated from a different source, such as five different bullets being used in the shooting. We will return to this calculation later.

How Unusual was Guinn's "Unusual"?

Guinn noted that all the fragments and bullets have an antimony concentration above the geometric mean for the population. So how probable is the random selection of two bullets that the Warren Commission concluded caused all the injuries to the two men? For this we need to select one group as the "reference" and calculate how probable it is that a random sample would be as close as the other is to it. The two different calculations, with two different reference groups, give slightly different results. Let us use the fragments from JFK's head and car as the reference (call it Group 2), as almost everybody would agree that this shot is the fatal shot that was shown so dramatically in the Zapruder film. It is also very likely that some of the remnants of this bullet would be found in the car.

The x-value of the last entry in table C5 is the same distance from the x-value of Group 2 as the x-value of Group 1 is, but on the lower side. The difference spanned in the P-variable is (0.8548 - 0.7101 = 0.1447) about 14.5 percent probability of selecting two bullets that would fall this near to one another. Thus, about one in seven pairs of bullets from a box of WCC/MC ammunition would have antimony concentrations this close. There is nothing particularly relevant about this calculation except to note that events with probabilities of 14 percent, while unusual, are not considered particularly rare, whereas those with probabilities of 2 percent to 3 percent are unusual enough to be considered statistically significant.

How "Close" were Guinn's Samples to the Alloy in the Recovered Samples

We note that the fragments deposited in Connally's wrist are thought to have come from the base of CE 399, as were the samples taken, first by the FBI and later by Guinn, for analysis. Thus, they both came from nearby sources and, indeed, the difference in these two samples is about 4 percent of their average concentration. The fragments deposited in JFK's head and the small lead fragments found in the car were thought to have come from the bullet represented by the large fragment containing engraving (Group 2). Not surprisingly, the range of concentrations in samples in Group 2 is about 6.7 percent, a bit higher than the range in

Group 1, but still much narrower than the range Guinn found throughout the cores of WCC/MC bullets he analyzed at widely separated locations. This is because the small fragments all come from the lead surface exposed at the crack in the bullet jacket. As this surface was stretched when the bullet was torn in two, the sample taken from the surface of the recovered large fragment was still relatively near the origin of the small fragments, not representative of the whole-bullet variance found by Guinn.

A Test of the Probability of "Accidental" Grouping of the Five Recovered Samples

Dr. Guinn mentioned in his HSCA testimony that the FBI had conducted NAA on the recovered bullet and bullet fragments listed in Table C1. They did not give these results to the Warren Commission, as they had judged them to be inconclusive. In four different runs, they got four different sets of results. While the different fragments had the same relative levels of trace elements, the magnitudes of the quantities varied widely between runs. Guinn identified this problem as a systematic error. The results of all four of the FBI's NAA runs are in the files of the National Archives. The reader can find them on Professor Kenneth Rahn's website (Reference C2). The results of run 4 are listed in table C6. There were from three to five samples from each fragment subjected to analysis.

As there were multiple samples from each fragment, these data may be submitted to a statistical analysis to determine the probability that random samples would fall into the two groups that the Warren Commission concluded they belonged. That is, they identified CE 399 with CE 842, the fragment from the governor's wrist and the remaining three fragments with the bullet that hit the president's head. We see that these concentrations of Sb are different than the concentrations in Guinn's data. The FBI's other three runs on the same samples show even larger differences, due to whatever caused the systematic error (detector drift, variations in exposure times, or whatever).

Table C6.   Data from FBI Neutron Activation Analysis, Run 4 (Source: National Archives)

Group	FBI #	CE #	Sample No.	Weight (mg)	Log Weight	Antimony (ppm)	Log Antimony
1	Q1	399	1	7.16	1.96851	643	6.46614
1	Q1		2	4.20	1.43508	636	6.45520
1	Q1		3	1.79	0.58222	750	6.62007
1	Q1		4	1.24	0.21511	749	6.61874
1	Q1		5	1.16	0.14842	749	6.61874
1	Q9	842	1	1.92	0.65233	690	6.53669
1	Q9		2	2.07	0.72755	662	6.49527
1	Q9		3	1.34	0.29267	677	6.51767
2	Q2	567	1	39.75	3.68261	521	6.25575
2	Q2		2	21.60	3.07269	521	6.25575
2	Q2		3	3.84	1.34547	578	6.35957
2	Q2		4	3.68	1.30291	515	6.24417
2	Q4,5	843	1	3.22	1.16938	555	6.31897
2	Q4,5		2	6.85	1.92425	552	6.31355
2	Q4,5		3	21.15	3.05164	532	6.27664
2	Q4,5		4	0.825	-0.19237	606	6.40688
2	Q14	840	1	10.65	2.36556	543	6.29711
2	Q14		2	9.70	2.27213	582	6.36647
2	Q14		3	5.78	1.75440	546	6.30262
2	Q14		4	3.77	1.32708	552	6.31355
2	Q14		5	2.85	1.04732	587	6.37502

Table C7.   Comparison of Means and Medians for Antimony Content, FBI Run 4

Variable	No.	Mean	Median	St. Dev.	Minimum	Maximum
Sb	21	607	582	79.1	515	750
Ln Sb	21	6.4007	6.3665	0.1263	6.2442	6.6201

As before, we analyze the log concentration, which is closer to the normal distribution that is implied in standard statistical tests. The comparison of means and medians in table C7 shows that the 21 points in the FBI data of table C6 are similar to the Guinn data on 14 random bullets. Again the mean and median are much closer on the log scale.

Because of unequal sample size, a General Linear Models (GLM) analysis is again used. The design of the model is quite simple: There are two groups with two and three specimens per group and three to five measurements on each specimen. Measurements are nested within specimens and specimens are nested within groups. Thus, the assumption of any interaction terms is inappropriate. The only unusual feature is a covariate, the weight of the sample.

The influence of weight of the sample on the measured content of antimony is one possible contributor to the systematic error in the FBI's NAA analysis. The GLM analysis in table C8 isolates this effect and removes its influence. First, one can get a visual comparison of the different levels of significance of weight in the two analyses by looking at plots of the data on raw and log scales in figures C3 and C4. But the definitive result is in the summary of the GLM analysis. In this analysis, the five recovered samples are grouped as the WC concluded—that is, CE 399 bullet with Connally wrist fragment and fragments from JFK head with fragments found in the car.

Table C8.   General Linear Model (Warren Grouping, Natural Logs of Antimony and Weight)

a. Factor Definition

Factor:	Type:	Levels:	Values:
Group	fixed	2	1,2
Specimen (Group)	fixed	5	Q1,Q9 (Gp 1), Q14, Q2, Q4, 5 (Gp 2)

b. Analysis of Variance for LnSb, using Adjusted Sum of Squares for Tests

Source	DF	Seq SS	Adj SS	Adj MS	F	P
LnWt	1	0.168372	0.025542	0.025542	13.25	0.002
Group	1	0.115222	0.098973	0.098973	51.34	0.000
Specimen (Group)	3	0.006763	0.006763	0.002254	1.17	0.354
Error	15	0.028917	0.028917	0.001928		
Total	20	0.319274				

The term Specimen(Group) merely indicates that the three to five specimens are nested within the member of the group. As in ANOVA, the P indicates the probability that the factor would be found to have this mean square (Adj MS) by chance alone. There is no significant difference in specimen, as indicated by the fact that this level of specimen differences would occur 35 percent of the time from random chance. The p value is rounded to three significant figures, as no analysis is accurate beyond this level. The 0.000 figure for Group means that this grouping would occur fewer than five times in ten thousand random data sets of this size. It is actually fewer than one in ten thousand, if the actual number associated with this f-value is considered. In practical terms, this means that there is almost no chance that this set of five samples came from five different bullets, as alleged in some conspiracy stories.

To show that the results do not depend on using the lognormal distribution for analysis, the GLM result was repeated with the raw values (not transformed by taking logarithms). The results are given in table C9. Again the Group factor is very highly significant, as indicated by P = 0.000, though the f statistic is a bit smaller. In this analysis, the significance of the weight covariate is lost, in spite of its highly visible presence in Figure C3, and on the natural log scale in Figure C4. Again the difference of specimens from each bullet or fragment is not found significant.

Table C9. General Linear Model (Warren Grouping, Raw Values of Antimony and Weight)

a. Factor Definition

Factor:	Type:	Levels:	Values:
Group	fixed	2	1,2
Specimen (Group)	fixed	5	Q1,Q9 (Gp 1), Q14, Q2, Q4, 5 (Gp 2)

b. Analysis of Variance for Sb, using Adjusted SS for Tests

Source	DF	Seq SS	Adj SS	Adj MS	F	P
Weight	1	361630	3199	3199	2.52	0.133
Group	1	67657	59058	59058	46.49	0.000
Specimen (Group)	3	2172	2172	724	0.57	0.643
Error	15	19055	19055	1270		
Total	20	125047				

There are a total of ten different ways that a group of five samples could be grouped into one set of two and a second set of three. The above analysis only considers the probability of finding any two groups that would have Sb concentrations as close as these are. To show that other groupings do not show the significance of the meaningful group, another GLM analysis was run with the group that is the second-most-compatible of the two groups—that is, CE 399 with fragments from JFK head and those from rear floorboard carpet and the bullet fragment from seat cushion (piece of jacket and core together) with Connally wrist fragments. The results are in table C10.

Table C10. General Linear Model (Alternate Grouping, Natural Logs of Antimony and Weight)

a. Factor Definition

Factor:	Type:	Levels:	Values:
Group	fixed	2	1, 2
Specimen (Group)	fixed	5	Q1, Q14 (Gp 1), Q9, Q2, Q4, 5 (Gp 2)

b. Analysis of Variance for LnSb, using Adjusted SS for Tests

Source	DF	Seq SS	Adj SS	Adj MS	F	P
Weight	1	0.168372	0.025542	0.025542	13.25	0.002
Group	1	0.000531	0.000073	0.000073	0.04	0.849
Specimen (Group)	3	0.121454	0.121454	0.040485	21.00	0.000
Error	15	0.028917	0.028917	0.001928		
Total	20	0.319274				

The analysis of variance for the alternate grouping, in table C10, shows that the alternate group variable is completely insignificant. All the difference is accounted by the weight of the sample and the specimen from which it came—that is, the specimens within each group are very highly significantly different. Analyses on the other possible groupings are similar. If any of the nine non-Warren groupings had been observed, it would not have supported the Warren Commission's determination that CE 399 had deposited the fragment in Connally's wrist and that the fragments found in the car were associated with the fragment from

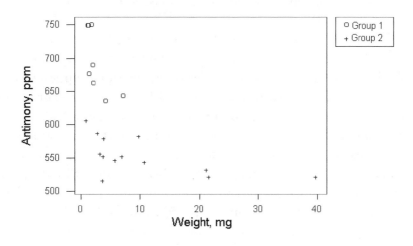

Figure C3. Raw values of antimony concentration as a function of sample weight

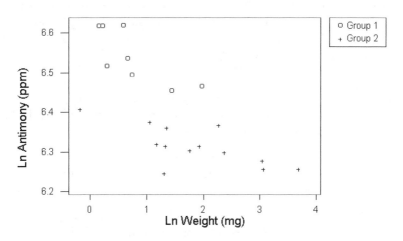

Figure C4. Antimony concentration versus weight on natural log scales

Kennedy's head. Thus, the fact that the highly significant group was the meaningful one out of the ten possible further reduces the probability by a factor of ten. Thus, the one in ten thousand odds become one in a hundred thousand.

These probability measurements represent the least possible restriction on the initial assumptions. They are the best that a co-conspirator could do if he had complete knowledge of the type ammunition Oswald was using and attempted to duplicate it as best he could. Thus, these probabilities are the starting point from which one can calculate other probabilities under other reasonable scenarios. If we further assume that the conspirator did not know or did not care that Oswald was using a Mannlicher-Carcano rifle, and picked another rifle along with the physical characteristics that go with its ammunition, the probability of that core matching the cores randomly selected from the WCC/MC bullets is another one or two orders of magnitude lower. This lowers the odds to a one-in-a-million chance of a match being this close, on the basis of the NAA alone.

This appendix is a summary of the results published in references C3 and C4.

References

C1. Vincent Guinn's Neutron Activation Analysis published in the House Select Committee on Assassinations Hearings Volume I, JFK Exhibit F-331, pages 506 to 552. Data were taken from Appendix B, Table I, p. 538 and Appendix D, Table II-A, p. 547.

C2. Professor Kenneth Rahn, Center for Atmospheric Chemistry Studies, Graduate School of Oceanography, University of Rhode Island, Narangansett, RI. Web address: http://karws.gso.uri.edu/JFK/scientific_topics/NAA/NAA_and_assination.html

C3. K. A. Rahn and L. M. Sturdivan. Neutron activation and the JFK assassination, Part I. Data and Interpretation. Journal of Radioanalytical and Nuclear Chemistry, Vol. 262, No. 1 (2004), 205-213.

C4. L. M. Sturdivan and K. A. Rahn. Neutron activation and the JFK assassination, Part II. Extended benefits. Journal of Radioanalytical and Nuclear Chemistry, Vol. 262, No. 1 (2004), 215-222.

APPENDIX D
Conservation of Momentum and Energy

Basic to the understanding of classical physics is the understanding of the quantities involved and the equations that relate them. For instance, the product of speed and time yield a distance. Travel 45 miles/hour for two hours and you will have traveled 90 miles. Distance is a quantity that is distinctly different from either speed or time. If we represent speed, time, and distance by the letters S, T, and D, the equation that relates them is:

$$D = S \times T$$

Alternatively, we could indicate a product by putting characters side by side, as ST.

Two physical concepts that were first expressed by Isaac Newton about 350 years ago: the conservation of energy and momentum. Let us define mass as the property that gives an object weight. (In outer space, where objects are "weightless," they still have the same mass that they had on Earth.) Momentum is defined as the product of the mass and velocity. Velocity is similar to speed, but has a direction associated with it. Quantities that have direction are called vectors. Speed could be thought of as the magnitude of the vector velocity.

Alternatively, momentum may be defined as a product of force and time where force is also a vector. The two expressions yield the same quantity. Like "distance" in the first paragraph, energy and momentum are entities distinct from mass and velocity from which they are derived. If momentum is represented by P, mass is represented by M, and velocity by V, then

$$P = MV$$

Momentum, unlike energy, is conserved as a vector. For example, a billiard ball may strike another billiard ball of the same mass squarely, transferring all its momentum. In this case, the second ball rolls off with the same velocity (speed and direction) that the first ball had, yet the first ball stands still at the point of the collision. In this case, the transfer of momentum is complete. For a second example, let us presume that the pool ball is hit by a piece of clay which sticks to the ball after the collision. If the clay has a mass M1, a velocity V1, and momentum P, while the ball has a mass M2, the conservation of momentum is expressed by the equation:

$$P = M1 \times V1 = (M1 + M2) \times V2$$

That is, the combined mass of the clay and ball will move at a velocity V2 that makes the momentum of the combination equal to the original momentum P. It will also be moving in precisely the same direction that the clay originally was. If this direction is considered positive, then momentum in the exactly opposite direction would be negative. Positive and negative vectors of the same magnitude cancel each other (add to zero).

Energy is a quantity whose physical definition is very close to its common meaning ("I haven't got the energy to spade the garden today"). The physicist defines energy as "the capacity to do work," but then he has to define "work." Let's take a shortcut that isn't quite as exact, but is more intuitive. Energy is the stuff that allows us to move things, heat the teapot, react chemicals, or blow things up. All of these, mechanical energy, heat energy, chemical energy, and so on. may be converted to each other—but always with a little loss to more basic forms of energy, such as heat (the law of "entropy"). Nevertheless, when the conversion is finished, and we add up all the different forms of energy, including heat energy, we end up with the total amount of energy that we started with. Thus, energy is conserved.

We say that energy is conserved as a "scalar" quantity. That is, it may be measured on a scale of units, like quarts of water or kilowatts of electricity. A scalar quantity cannot be canceled or negated by adding negative values of the quantity (negative quarts, for instance). So we say that a scalar is non-directional.

If energy is represented by E and other quantities are as above, then the equation for kinetic energy, the energy associated with motion, is:

$$E = \tfrac{1}{2} MV^2 = \tfrac{1}{2} MV \times V$$

In words, kinetic energy is one-half the mass times the square of the velocity.

Let us illustrate the difference between kinetic energy (the scalar) and momentum (the vector) with a relevant example. Since illustrative examples do not have to be easy to do, but only easy to understand, let us conduct it in outer space where we can suspend a rifle without the necessity of wires or strings and we can conceptually fire it without worrying about whether the bullet punches a hole in something, such as the side of the spaceship. A rifle hanging motionless in space has no momentum with respect to our spaceship. If we neglect the momentum of the propellant gas that follows the bullet out the muzzle when it is fired,[1] the momentum of the bullet must be equaled by a momentum imparted to the gun in the opposite direction. Consider the momentum of one to be positive and the other negative, since they are in the opposite direction. Then their sum is equal to zero, conserving momentum. If the bullet has a mass of 10 grams and a velocity of 1000 meters per second, and the gun has a mass of 5 kilograms (5000 grams), the velocity of the gun would be 2 meters/second in the opposite direction. They each have a product (mass times velocity) of 10 kilogram-meters per second, or kms, of momentum.[2] The energy of the two is quite different. The product of half the mass of the bullet times the square of its velocity yields 5,000 kilogram-(meters per second) squared, or kmss, but only 10 kmss for the gun. That is, even considering the momentum of the propellant gasses, over 99.5 percent of the kinetic energy goes with the bullet.

Now let us consider what happens when a bullet hits a person. The WCC/MC bullet at a range of about 60 meters has a residual velocity of about 560 meters/second and weighs about 10.45 grams (0.01045 kilograms). The bullet's momentum is

$$P = 0.01045 \times 560 = 5.852 \text{ kms}$$

---

1. In reality, the momentum of these gasses is not negligible. They have a momentum that is roughly comparable to the momentum of the bullet. So the momentum received by the gun is larger than that of the bullet.

2. The scientific reader's indulgence is requested in allowing us to use unconventional units of momentum and energy for the sake of simplifying the calculations, here and later.

If a human head weighs 4 kilograms (more or less), and the total momentum of the bullet were transferred to the head, it would move at a velocity

$$V = P/M = 5.852/4 = 1.463 \text{ meters per second.}$$

A movement of the head of about a meter and a half per second is the velocity of a vigorous nod. Actually, the tests at Edgewood Arsenal showed that the bullet lost about half its velocity, and a minute part of its mass (that is, about half its momentum), in the simulated skull shots. At impact, President Kennedy's head would begin to move at a velocity of less than a meter/second.[3] But his head was not free to move very far at such a velocity, as it was tied to a body that weighed an order of magnitude more. By the time the momentum was transferred to Kennedy's 80 kg (177-pound) body, the 5.852 kms of momentum would move him at about 8 centimeters/second (about 3 inches/second). Let us consider just how much velocity that is. As a person stands, he does not remain perfectly rigid like a light pole. He sways from side-to-side as he keeps his balance. Three inches/second is comparable to the velocity the human body reaches just maintaining balance. It certainly is not something that throws a person violently into the back seat of a car at the "80 to 100 feet per second" that Crenshaw calculates for the President's movement into the back of the car seat.

The above shows that any reasonable bullet will not throw a person in any direction. We must look for another explanation for Kennedy's backward movement in the car.

---

3. This is the magnitude of the forward velocity of Kennedy's head, seen for a frame or two in the enhanced Zapruder film, immediately after the shot that exploded his skull. After that he begins his violent backward movement that is considered in the main text.

APPENDIX E

"Startle" and "Jiggle" Analysis

The Biology of a Startle

A startle reflex may be caused by a number of sensory input events: a loud noise, a sudden bright flash of light, the sight of a snake or spider nearby, or even an unexpected gust of wind or sudden encounter with a strong, foul odor. The most common, and the one of concern here is the acoustical startle. There is an abundance of published material explaining the physiology and neural mechanism of the startle, dating back for several decades. An excellent summary is given in the Introduction of a book by Ronald C. Simons (reference E1).

A startle is a rapid tensing of the muscles, perhaps in preparation for a quicker flight or fight reaction in response to a perceived threat. The startle has nothing to do with the higher intellectual center of the brain. In reference E2, author Peter Brown reports that "the startle reflex exists in anencephalic [human] infants." Brown et al., in reference E3, also note that it occurs undiminished in deceberate animals. The startle reflex is created in the caudal brainstem. The brainstem is often referred to as the "reptile brain" that also controls respiration, heart rate, and basic emotions such as fear.

No matter what stimulates it, the startle starts with a very rapid eye blink, followed immediately by a tensing of the muscles of the face and neck, then the muscles of the upper trunk and arms. Last, and not always, is a less strong reaction in the muscles of the lower trunk and legs. The intrinsic muscles of the hands and feet react more slowly—slower than the length of the efferent neural pathways would indicate.

The response time, the onset of the muscular response, is usually short but is quite variable. Simons documents the mean time for the muscular action of six subjects. The delay between the stimulus (loud noise) and the onset of the eye blink was about

0.084 seconds (sec). In an additional 0.072 sec the muscles of the eyelid were at maximum tension. The maximal response lasted only 0.044 sec before another 0.072 sec of relaxation, for a total duration of less than 0.30 sec. The onset of tensing the muscles of the upper trunk averaged about 0.12 sec. Time to maximum tension consumed another 0.11 sec But the maximum contraction lasted nearly 0.67 sec, for a total duration of nearly one second. P. Brown and colleagues give a slightly shorter time for the beginning of muscular response for the biceps and triceps (arm muscles) of about 0.07 sec in 12 subjects.

People are subjected to varying levels of noise all the time without experiencing a startle reaction. The volume threshold that differentiates startling noise from ordinary noise is quite variable, depending on the individual, the environment, expectation or lack of it, the mood of the person (cautious and fearful versus calm and confident), and so on. P. Gogan randomly varied the magnitude of the acoustic stimulus within the tests of eight laboratory volunteers (reference E4). The tests were conducted in an anechoic chamber with a very quiet background of 20 decibels (db) of ambient noise. He observed consistent startle responses with 32 db stimuli. The strength of the startle, as described by the volunteers and seen on electroencephalograms and electromyograms (brain and muscle responses) were greater with 66 db inputs and greatest for 92 db noises. He found no simple method of relating the magnitude of the sound to the strength of the response, but (in my opinion) there is almost certainly a saturation effect. That is, the strength of the startle approaches a plateau with increasing volume. After the maximal startle reaction is reached, there would be no further increase with louder stimuli.

All references discuss the aspects of sensitization and habituation in the startle response. If a person is very anxious or fearful, he may become sensitized to a startle stimulus. That is, his threshold decreases and the strength of the startle increases with repeated exposure. On the other hand, repeated startles with no associated danger will raise the threshold and decrease the magnitude of the muscular response. The decrease in sensitivity is also very dependent on the context. The habituation to a frequent stimulus in one environment may not decrease sensitivity in another place and time.

The evidence of Abraham Zapruder's startle, the blurred frame on his movie, occurs about 0.33 sec after the bullet reached the car, several feet away. This delay includes a few milliseconds for the shock wave to reach him, the time of beginning of a muscular response, the rise time to maximal muscular tension, the time for the camera's inertia to be overcome, and the time for creation of a smeared image on the film.

The rather long duration of the whole startle indicates that the orientation reflex immediately returns the camera to its pre-startle position. In fact, it is the muscles of the forearm that move the fingers and the intrinsic muscles of the hand at the base the thumb that work in concert to complete the grip. This means that tension reaches a maximum in the fingers a slight bit before it does in the thumb. If there were no delay between the onset of the startle-engendered tension in the muscles of the arm and hand there might not be a jiggling of the camera at all. In any case, the tensing of the muscles that lasts nearly a second does not suppress or change the period of the three-per-second jitter cycle that Alvarez discovered in the hand-held camera. This is seen in the analysis of Zapruder's jiggle pattern.

Statistical Analysis of the Jiggle

In 1978, the HSCA asked Dr. William Hartmann to measure the blurs in the Zapruder film to repeat Professor Louis Alvarez' search for the "neuromuscular oscillation" from a startle reaction to gunshots. Hartmann used the original film for the measurements with the exception of those few frames destroyed by CBS when they spliced the film during their period of ownership. For these frames, Hartmann used a first generation copy made by the FBI before the film was sold to CBS. He made the measurements from smears in points of light reflected from the chrome work on the limousine. He used the image of the film projected, a frame at a time, on the wall. The magnitude of the blur was expressed as a percentage of the width of the full frame. He evidently measured blurs to the nearest 0.1 percent. Any greater precision would probably be lost in the measurement error—and would be entirely unnecessary. His plotted data are reproduced in figure 60 of the main text. A larger-scale version of the plot is also included below as figure E1 to make the features easier to see.

As a check on our expectations, let us determine if we can find the normal tracking-error cycle in the "quiet" portions of the Zapruder film. Note that we cannot expect to see a peak in the blur plot at every sixth frame. The human nervous system is not a metronome, so the next peak might appear in 5 frames or 7 frames—or, if the photographer does not perceive any error in tracking (the external feedback), then a "correction" peak is unnecessary and will be missing altogether. If there is a very smooth tracking period that needs no corrections, the cycle might break off and restart a few frames later, as the feedback loop reestablishes itself. Finally, though the startle is a single jump, that large deviation from smooth tracking will tend to "reset" the cycle.

Ignoring Hartmann's arbitrary line at 2 percent, we can, indeed, see the three-cycle-per-second tracking error in those "normal" blur measurements. For instance, the large peak at frames 158/159 resets the cycle. It is followed by smaller peaks at frames 165, 171, 177, and 182. They vary in size because the magnitude of the correction varies in accordance to the perceived need. The correction peak at frame 182 is fairly large, while the peak at 165 is almost indistinguishable from the average blur. But look at the intervals: 6, 6, 6, and 5 frames apart. Another series is seen at frames 291, 296, and 302. If we look forward and back, there is a peak 12 frames earlier at 279 and 11 frames later at 313. The peaks that might have appeared near frames 285 and 308 are missing. Look at the strong series of blurs in frames in the 190s, identified by Hartmann as indicative of a gunshot. There we find peaks (not all above 2 percent) at frames 191, 197, 204, 209/210, 221, and 227. The intervals are: 6, 7, 6, 11, and 6, indicating that there is a peak missing near 215.

Now look at the large series that first caught Alvarez' eye and made him think that there might be evidence of a startle from bullet shock waves in the Zapruder film in the first place—the series of large blurs following the head shot at frame 312. We note that there are very large blurs at 318, 331, 342, 351, 360, 363, and 369. In the first part of this interval, the three-cycle-per-second period between relative peaks appears. Six frames after the shot, the startle peak appears at frame 318. The small peak at 324 and the peak at 331 are at intervals of six and seven frames later. But after this the three-per-second pattern completely breaks down. If we assume that the 363 peak is part of the much larger peak at frame 360, then the intervals following frame 331 are 11, 9, 9, and 9 frames. A nine-frame interval indicates a two-cycles-per-second pattern. Evidently, the peaks after 331 are a result of Zapruder's emotional outburst after he realized that he just saw the president's head explode. It certainly does not resemble his normal tracking error cycle of three-per-second. The "series" of jiggles that Alvarez saw in the later stages of the Zapruder film is not at three-cycles-per-second and is not a sign of a nervous system set "oscillating" by the startle from a shot. It is the result of the reaction labeled "Zapruder reacting, crying out" in Hartmann's plot.

In chapter eleven, the three startles from gunshots are separated from the blurs resulting from Zapruder's difficulties tracking the limousine past the road sign and the emotional outburst after the assassination. The blurs at frames 158/159, 227, and 318 are startles from the shock waves of bullets that reached the car about six frames earlier at frames 152/153, 221, and 312.

Neglecting those peaks during the emotional outburst following the final shot that killed the president, Hartmann measured 190 points, one each for frames 141 to 330. Zapruder's three-cycle-per-second adjustment peaks are discernable throughout this region, yielding 26 relative adjustment peaks listed in table E1. In the table the Ln stands for the natural logarithm of the relative peaks in the adjacent column. The table includes some very large peaks associated with Zapruder's difficulty tracking the limousine as it moved behind the road sign.

Table E1. Relative Peaks from Hartmann's Blur Measurements from the Zapruder Film

Frame	Peak (%)	Ln Peak		Frame (cont'd)	Peak (%)	Ln Peak
143	1.5	0.405		227	2.6**	0.956
148	1.4	0.336		233	1.3	0.262
154	1.7	0.531		241	1.9	0.642
158/9	2.4**	0.875		263	1.6	0.470
165	1.2	0.182		265	1.5	0.405
171	1.5	0.405		271	1.2	0.182
177	1.4	0.336		279	1.6	0.470
182	2.1	0.742		291	2.1	0.742
191	2.5*	0.916		296	1.7	0.531
197	3.4*	1.224		302	1.5	0.405
204	1.6*	0.470		313	2.0	0.693
210	2.5*	0.916		318	3.7**	1.308
221	2.1*	0.742		324	2.2	0.788

*Peaks associated with tracking past the road sign.
** Peaks associated with startle reactions from rifle fire.

If the large peaks attributed to road sign intrusion and the three peaks from Zapruder's startle reaction are eliminated, then 18 peaks remain. These are the 18 points without asterisks in table E1. These will be assumed to characterize Abraham Zapruder's normal tracking-adjustment peaks in normal panning to photograph an object moving across a motionless background. A normal plot, or n-plot, of these 18 peaks is shown in figure E2. This figure is a so-called normal plot, or n-plot of the data. The n-plot shows the 18 normal peaks (on the log scale), ranked from lowest to highest, plotted against what is called the standard normal variate from the Gaussian distribution. If the data were perfectly normally distributed, the plotted points would make a perfectly straight line. The figure also has the average and standard deviation of these 18 points. These serve as estimates of the mean and standard deviation of the peaks in Zapruder's normal "jitter" cycle. Notice that the data plotted are on the log scale. This plot has better Anderson-Darling (A-D) normality statistics than a similar plot using raw blur percentages. The implication of this is that the magnitude of Zapruder's peak adjustment follows a normal proportion rather than normally distributed absolute movement. In other words, within his normal, unobstructed panning movement, the adjustment blur that is twice as large as average is about as likely as one that is half as large.

The wavy line that the points describe about the straight line that would represent a perfectly normal distribution of peaks is present in both the raw and log values, but is much more pronounced in the raw measure. This deviation from a straight line accounts for the less-than-ideal p-value of 0.40. Any p-value much larger than the test statistic to be used (usually 5 percent or 0.05), however, yields an acceptable approximation; the larger the P, the better the approximation. We note that Hartmann's 2 percent threshold was an arbitrary one that he picked to eliminate the normal panning adjustment peaks. Using the properties of the fitted normal curve of figure E2, however, we can establish an alternate threshold based on the normal statistical variation. Using the customary level of significance would require that we find a level that would contain 95 percent of Zapruder's adjustment peaks. Approximately one out of twenty peaks in Zapruder's normal panning cycle would exceed that threshold.

From tables of the normal distribution, we find that the 95 percent point is 1.645 standard deviations above the mean. Using the average and standard deviation from figure E2 yields 0.78209 for the log of this value. Taking the antilog yields a threshold of 2.186 percent—just a bit higher than Hartmann's arbitrary threshold. With this as a test statistic, we find that all three startles exceed the threshold and would be termed significant. In fact, the lowest peak, at frames 158/159 exceeds 98 percent of this population, while the startles at frames 227 and 318 are both well above 99 percent.

Relative peaks at 182 and 291, which were above Hartmann's threshold, are not significant. One of the 18, the peak at frame 324, is almost identical to the statistical threshold (2.2 vs 2.186). This is not far off of the one in twenty that is expected, which tends to verify the accuracy of the test. To determine how well such a test will discriminate startle peaks from normal panning peaks, we can rerun the statistical analysis with 19 points made by including the lowest 'startle' point, 2.4 percent, with the other 18. This 19-point sample is plotted in figure E3. This group has an average of 0.495, a standard deviation of 0.204 and an A-D p-value of 0.415. The 95 percent threshold is calculated to be 0.8306 (2.295 percent). By this test, all three startles are still significant, but the point at frame 324 is not. The lowest startle peak is more than a tenth of a percent above this very liberal threshold that includes it as a data point.

By all measures, tracking past the road sign is a significantly troublesome task for Zapruder. The test is appropriate for this series, as the series has the characteristic three-peaks-per-second of the normal human panning-adjustment cycle. While the peaks marking Zapruder's emotional outburst at the end of the motorcade series have their own significance, they are not at the characteristic period of a normal panning adjustment cycle. The above statistical test cannot be applied to them.

In summary, after eliminating the road-sign tracking errors, there are only three peaks left, indicating Zapruder's startles that correspond to the three shots from the Texas School Book Depository. The peaks at frames 158/159, 227, and 318 indicate shots near frames 153, 221, and 312.

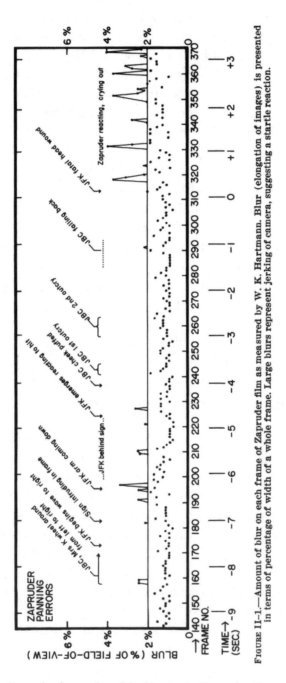

FIGURE II-1.—Amount of blur on each frame of Zapruder film as measured by W. K. Hartmann. Blur (elongation of images) is presented in terms of percentage of width of a whole frame. Large blurs represent jerking of camera, suggesting a startle reaction.

Figure E1. Frame-by-frame plot of the blur in the Zapruder file, as a percent of the whole frame. Prepared by Dr. William Harmann for the House Select Committee on Assassinations.

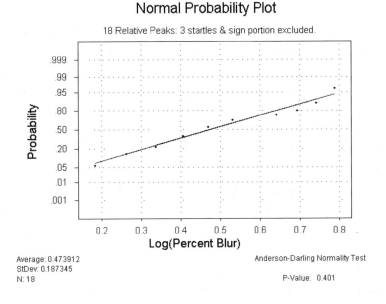

Figure E2. Normal plot of Zapruder's normal tracking adjustment peaks

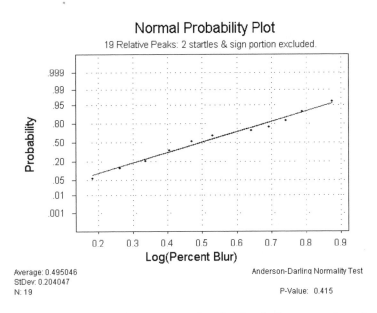

Figure E3. Normal plot of the 18 normal peaks plus the lowest startle peak

References

E1. Ronald C. Simons, "BOO! Culture, Experience, and the Startle Reflex." Oxford University Press, New York & Oxford. 1996.

E2. Peter Brown, Physiology of Startle Phenomena. "Advances in Neurology," Vol. 67, Chapter 19, pp 273 – 287. Lippincott-Raven Publishers, Philadelphia. 1995.

E3. P. Brown, J.C. Rothwell, P.D. Thompson, T.C. Britton, B.L. Day, and C.D. Marsden. "New Observations on the Normal Auditory Startle Reflex in Man." *Brain,* 114: 1891 – 1902. 1991.

E4. P. Gogan, The Startle and Orienting Reactions in Man. A Study of Their Characteristics and Habituation. *Brain Research,* 18: 117 – 135. 1970.

E5. Louis Alvarez, A physicist examines the Kennedy assassination film. *American Journal of Physics,* vol. 44, no. 9. 1976.

E6. William Hartmann, testimony published in the House Select Committee on Assassinations (HSCA) Hearings Volume 2, U.S. Government Printing Office, Washington, D.C. 1978.

BIBLIOGRAPHY AND SOURCES:

Government Reports:

House Select Committee on Assassinations, Hearings, Volumes I through IX, U.S. Government Printing Office, Washington, D.C., 1978.

House Select Committee on Assassinations, Final Report, U.S. Government Printing Office, Washington, D.C., 1979.

Olivier, Alfred G. and Dziemian, Arthur J. *Wound Ballistics of 6.5-mm Mannlicher-Carcano Ammunition,* US Army Edgewood Arsenal Chemical Research and Development Laboratories Technical Report CRDLR 3264. March 1965.

The Warren Report: The Official Report of the Assassination of President John F. Kennedy, Associated Press edition (abridged, with added photographs), 1964.

The Report of the Warren Commission, Final Report plus 26 volumes of testimony and exhibits. US Government Printing Office, Washington, D.C., 1964.

The Wound Data and Munitions Effectiveness Team–Vietnam Study. Data stored in the Uniformed Services University of the Health Sciences, Bethesda, MD. Access limited to research on approved projects.

Books and Articles (for web articles, see Individual References) :

Non-conspiracy:

Alvarez, Louis, "A Physicist Examines the Kennedy Assassination Film," *American Journal of Physics,* Vol. 4, No. 9, 1976.

Artwohl, Robert R., "JFK's Assassination: Conspiracy, Forensic Science, and Common Sense" *Journal of the American Medical Association: JAMA,* Vol. 267, No. 20, pp 2804-2807.

Baden, Michael, *Unnatural Death,* Ivy Books, Ballantine Books. Random House, New York, NY, 1990.

Bishop, Jim, *The Day Kennedy Was Shot.* Gramercy Books edition, Random House, New York, NY, 1968.

Canal, John, *Silencing the Lone Assassin.* Paragon House, St. Paul, 2000.

Collins, Kim A. and Patrick E. Lantz, "Interpretation of Fatal, Multiple, and Exiting Gunshot Wounds by Trauma Specialists," *Journal of Forensic Sciences,* Vol. 39, No. 1, 94-99. January, 1994. Also see the Medical News and Perspectives Column: Teri Randall, "Clinicians' Forensic Interpretations of Fatal Gunshot Wounds Often Miss the Mark." *JAMA,* Vol. 269, No. 16, pp 2058 – 2061. April 28, 1993.

Gray, Henry, *Gray's Anatomy,* numerous reprints of the 1901 original are available in libraries and bookstores; e.g., Bounty Books, New York, NY, 1977.

Guinn, Vincent P. and John Nichols, "Neutron Activation Analysis of Bullet-Lead Specimens: The President Kennedy Assassination," *Transactions of the American Nuclear Society,* Vol. 28, 92-93, 1978.

Journal of the American Medical Association (JAMA) interviews: See name under Individual References (p. 315).

Lattimer, John K. and Jon Lattimer, "The Kennedy-Connally Single Bullet Theory: A Feasibility Study," *International Surgery,* Vol. 50, No. 6, 524-532. Dec 1968.

Lattimer, John K., Gary Lattimer, and Jon Lattimer, "Could Oswald Have Shot President Kennedy? Further Ballistic Studies," *Bulletin of the New York Academy of Medicine,* Second Series, Vol.48, No. 3, 513-524. Apr 1972.

Lattimer, John K., *Kennedy and Lincoln: Medical & Ballistic Comparisons of Their Assassinations.* Harcourt Brace Janovich, New York, NY, 1980.

Lattimer, John K., "Additional Data on the Shooting of President Kennedy," *Journal of the American Medical Association,* Vol. 269, No. 12, 1544-1547, March 24/31, 1993.

Lattimer, John K., Angus Laidlaw, Paul Heneghan, and Eric J. Haubner, "Experimental Duplication of the Important Physical Evidence of the Lapel Bulge of the Jacket Worn by Governor Connally when Bullet 399 Went Through Him," *Journal of the American College of Surgeons,* Vol. 178, 517-522, May, 1994.

Levy, Michael L., Daniel Sullivan, Roderick Faccio, and Robert G. Grossman, "A Neuro-forensic Analysis of the Wounds of President John F. Kennedy:

Part 2—A Study of the Available Evidence, Eye-witness Correlations, Analysis and Conclusions," *Neurosurgery*, Vol. 54, No. 6, June 2004.

Mailer, Norman, *Oswald's Tale: an American Mystery*. Random House, New York, NY, 1995.

Manchester, William, *The Death of a President*. Harper and Row, New York, NY, 1963.

McMillan, Priscilla Johnson, *Marina and Lee*. Harper and Row, New York, NY, 1977.

O'Donnell, Kenneth P. and David F. Powers (with Joe McCarthy), *Johnny We Hardly Knew Ye: Memories of John Fitzgerald Kennedy*, Pocket Books edition, New York, NY, 1973.

Posner, Gerald, *Case Closed: Lee Harvey Oswald and the Assassination of JFK*. Anchor Book edition, Bantam Doubleday, New York, NY, 1994.

Rahn, Kenneth A., and Larry Sturdivan, "Neutron activation and the JFK Assassination: Part I. Data and Interpretation," *Journal of Radiological and Nuclear Chemistry*, Vol. 262, No. 1, 205-213, 2004.

Schlesinger, Arthur M. Jr., *A Thousand Days: John F. Kennedy in the White House*, Fawcett Crest edition, New York, NY, 1967.

Sturdivan Larry, and Kenneth A. Rahn, "Neutron activation and the JFK Assassination: Part II. Extended Benefits," *Journal of Radiological and Nuclear Chemistry*, Vol. 262, No. 1, 215-222, 2004.

Sullivan, Daniel, Roderick Faccio, Michael Levy, and Robert Grossman, "The Assassination of President John F. Kennedy: A Neuroforensic Analysis—Part 1: A Neurosurgeon's Previously Undocumented Eyewitness Account of the Events of November 22, 1963." *Neurosurgery*, Vol. 53, No. 5, 1019-1027, November 2003.

Conspiracy:

Anson, Robert Sam, *They've Killed the President!" The Search for the Murderers of John F. Kennedy*. Bantam Books, New York, NY, 1975.

Blakey, G. Robert and Richard Billings, *The Plot to Kill the President*. Times Books, New York, NY, 1981. Reissued as *Fatal Hour: The Assassination of President Kennedy by Organized Crime*. Berkley Books, New York, NY, 1992.

Crenshaw, Charles A. (with Jens Hansen and J. Gary Shaw), *JFK: Conspiracy of Silence*. Signet Books, Penguin Group, New York, NY, 1992.

Epstein, Edward Jay, *Inquest: the Warren Commission and the Establishment of Truth*. Bantam Books, New York, NY, 1966. (Original by Viking Press, 1966).

Epstein, Edward Jay, *Legend: the Secret World of Lee Harvey Oswald*. Reader's Digest Press, McGraw-Hill, New York, NY, 1978.

Fensterwald, Bernard Jr. (compiled by Michael Ewing), *Assassination of JFK by Coincidence or Conspiracy?* Zebra Books, Kensington Publishing Corp., New York, NY, 1977.

Fetzer, James H., (editor), *Assassination Science: Experts Speak Out on the Death of JFK*. Catfeet Press, Peru, IL, 1998

Fox, Sylvan, *The Unanswered Questions about President Kennedy's Assassination*. Award Books, New York, NY, (revised) 1975.

Garrison, Jim, *On the Trail of the Assassins*. Warner Books edition, New York, NY, 1988.

Groden, Robert J. and Harrison Edward Livingstone, *High Treason*. Berkley Books edition, New York, NY, 1990.

Hayman, Leroy, *The Assassinations of John & Robert Kennedy*. Scholastic Book Services, New York NY, 1976.

Hurt, Henry, *Reasonable Doubt*. Henry Holt and Company, Owl Book Edition, New York, NY, 1987.

La Fontaine, Ray and Mary, *Oswald Talked: the New Evidence in the JFK Assassination*. Pelican Publishing, Gretna, LA, 1996.

Lane, Mark, *Rush to Judgment*. Fawcett Crest edition, New York, NY, 1967.

Lifton, David S., *Best Evidence*. Signet Books, Penguin Group, New York, NY, 1992.

Marrs, Jim, *Crossfire: the Plot that Killed Kennedy*. Carroll & Graf paperback edition, New York, NY, 1989.

McDonald, Hugh C. (as told to Geoffrey Bocca), *Appointment In Dallas: The Final Solution of the Assassination of JFK,* Zebra Books, Hugh McDonald Publishing Corp., New York, NY, 1975.

Menninger, Bonar (& Howard Donahue), *Mortal Error*. St. Martin's Press, New York, NY, 1992.

Oglesby, Carl, *The JFK Assassination: The facts and the Theories*. Signet Books, Penguin Group, New York, NY, 1992.

Thomas, D.B., "Echo Correlation Analysis and the Acoustic Evidence in the Kennedy Assassination Revisited," *Science and Justice,* Vol. 41, No. 1, 21-32, 2001.

Zirbel, Craig I., *The Texas Connection.* Warner Books edition, New York, NY, 1991.

Individual References:

Abbreviations: HSCA – House Select Committee on Assassinations, testimony or report. WC – Warren Commission, testimony or exhibit; Aff. – affidavit or official signed statement. Volume and page follow. E.g., WC XX, 1-20. DP – Dealey Plaza. DPD – Dallas Police Department. TSBD – Texas School Book Depository. JAMA – Journal of the American Medical Association.

Akin, Gene C., Parkland ER anesthiologist: WC VI, 63-68.

Aleman, Jose, Mafia Associate: HSCA V, 301-324.

Anderson, Jack, Columnist for Washington Post: HSCA V, 365 (Reprint of column: JFK Exhibit F-409).

Arce, Danny, DP witness: WC VI, 363-367.

Aschkenasy, Ernest, Queens College, New York City, HSCA Acoustic Expert: HSCA V, 555-615.

Baden, Michael, Spokesman for the Forensic Pathology Panel at the HSCA public hearings: HSCA I, 180-323. Interview with G. Posner; *Case Closed,* p 337.

Baker, Marrion L., DPD motorcycle policeman, DP witness: WC III, 241-270. WC Aff. VII, 592. WC Statement, XXVI, 679.

Barber, Steve, acoustic study debunker: Personal commnications; numerous, 2003, 2004. Web articles: "Acoustic Evidence of Conspiracy?" http://mcadams.posc.mu.edu/acoustic.htm "The Acoustic Evidence: A Personal Memoir" http://mcadams.posc.mu.edu/barber.htm "Double Decker" http://www.fjk-online/doubled.htm

Barger, James E., Chief Scientist, BB&N, HSCA Acoustic Panel: HSCA II, 17-105; V, 645-690. Report: "Study of the Acoustics Evidence Related to the Assassination of President John F. Kennedy," HSCA VIII, 1-185.

Bates, John, senior firearms examiner, NY State Police Laboratory, Albany: HSCA I, 444-489.

Baxter, Charles R, Parkland Physician (JFK).: WC VI, 39-45. Report reprinted in Texas State Journal of Medicine, V. 60, 61-74, Jan 1964. Interview in JAMA, V. 267, No. 20, pp 2804-2807.

Beavers, William R., WC psychiatrist who interviewed Ruby: WC XIV, 570-579.

Benavides, Domingo, witness to Tippit killing: WC VI, 444-454.

Bennett, Glen, Secret Service Agent, SS Followup car: WC statement XXIV, 541-542 (Exhibit 2112)

Blakey, Robert, HSCA Chief of Staff: HSCA, All volumes. Particularly, HSCA Final Report.

Bledsoe, Mary, Oswald's former landlady, Dallas: WC VI, 400-427.

Boone, Eugene, Dallas County Deputy Sheriff, TSBD search: WC III, 290-295.

Boswell, J. Thornton, JFK Autopsy team, Bethesda: WC II, 376-377. Interview in JAMA, V. 267, No. 20, pp 2794-2803.

Bowers, Lee, Union Terminal railroad tower man, DP witness from tower: WC VI, 284-289. Lane interview: Rush to Judgment, pp 23-24.

Boyers, Chester H., Officer in Charge, autopsy lab, Bethesda Naval Hospital: HSCA Aff. Dec 4, 1978, in files of National Archives, College Park. Statement given to John Canal, Dec 2003.

Brennan, Howard, DP witness: WC III, 140-161, 184-186, 211. WC Aff. XI, 206-207.

Brewer, Johnny Calvin, shoe store manager, Texas Theatre witness: WC VII, 1-8.

Cadigan, James C., WC handwriting expert: (paper bag) WC IV, 89-100; (handwriting) VII, 418-438.

Callaway, Ted, witness to LHO fleeing Tippit scene: WC III, 351-357.

Canal, John, JFK Author: Personal communications: numerous throughout 2003 and 2004.

Canning, Thomas, NASA engineer, HSCA Photo Panel: HSCA II, 154-203, (trajectory analysis) VI 32-62.

Carrico, James, Parkland Physician, JFK: WC III, 357-366; VI, 1-7. Report reprinted in Texas State Journal of Medicine, V. 60, 61-74, Jan 1964. Interview in JAMA, V. 267, No. 20, 2804-2807, May 27, 1992.

Champagne, Donald, firearms & tool mark examiner, Fl. Dept. Criminal Law Enforcement, Talahassee: HSCA I, 444-489.

Clark, Kemp, Director of Neurological Surgery, Parkland: WC VI, 18-30; ltr. to Adm. Burkley XXI, 150-152. Report reprinted in Texas State Journal of Medicine, V. 60, 61-74, Jan 1964.

Cole, Alwyn, WC handwriting expert: WC IV, 358-403; XV, 703-709.

Connally, John, Governor of Texas: WC IV, 129-146. HSCA I, 11-60.

Connally, Nelly, John's wife: WC IV, 146-149. HSCA I, 11-60.

Corbett, Francis, Itek Corporation, Lexington, MA. Study for HSCA, "John Kennedy Assassination Film Analysis," undated, in files of National Archives, College Park.

Craig, Roger, Dallas County Deputy Sheriff: WC VI, 260-273. WC Aff. XIX, 524; XXIII, 817; XXIV, 23.

Cunningham, Cortlandt, FBI firearms & tool mark examiner: WC II, 251-253; III, 451-496.

Curry, Jesse, Dallas Chief of Police: WC IV, 150-202; XII, 25-42; XV, 124-133; WC Aff. XV, 641.

Davis, Virginia, Tippit witness: WC VI, 454-468.

Day, J. Carl, Lieutenant, Identification Bureau, DPD: WC IV, 249-278. WC Aff. VII, 401-402.

de Mohrenschildt, George, Dallas friend of Lee and Marina Oswald: WC IX, 166-284. HSCA, XII, 49-68. Book (unpublished): reprinted in HSCA XII, 70-315.

Dziemian, Arthur, Director, Biophysics Laboratory, Edgewood Arsenal, MD: WC V, 90-94. (Also see government reports, under Olivier).

Euins, Amos Lee, DP witness: WC II, 201-210. WC Aff. XVI, 963 (Exhibit 367); also XIV, 4 (Exhibit 1978).

Finck, Pierre, Lt. Col., Armed Forces Institute of Pathology, Autopsy Team, Bethesda: WC II, 377-384. Interview in JAMA, V. 268, No. 13, pp 1748-1754.

Frazier, Buell Wesley, gave Oswald rides to TSBD: WC II, 210-245.

Frazier, Robert A., FBI firearms & toolmark examiner: WC III, 390-441; V, 58-74, 165-174.

Fritz, J. William, Chief, Homicide Bureau, DPD: WC IV, 202-249; XV, 145-153.

Garinther, Georges, Human Engineering Laboratory, Aberdeen Proving Ground, MD: Personal communications Aug. 1978. Sketches to HSCA staff 1978. Personal communication (phone call) January 9, 2002.

Green, David, Chairman, National Research Council Committee on Hearing, Bioacoustics, and Biomechanics, HSCA Hearing Panel: HSCA II, 111-128.

Greer, William, Secret Service Agent, driver of Presidential limousine: WC II, 112-132.

Gregory, Charles, Parkland Physician, JBC: WC IV, 117-129; VI, 95-104. Report reprinted in Texas State Journal of Medicine, V. 60, 61-74, Jan 1964.

Groden, Robert, HSCA Photo Panel: HSCA I, 62-140.

Grossman, Robert, Parkland physician, JFK, head entry witness: Personal communications, Aug & Dec 2003, Sep 19, 2004. AARB Interview March 21, 1997, on web at www.aarclibrary.org/publib/jfk/arrb/master_med_set/md185_0004a.htm See articles under Sullivan and Levy in Bibliography.

Guinn, Vincent, HSCA Neutron Activation Analysis expert: HSCA I, 491-567. See articles under Guinn, Rahn, and Sturdivan, in Bibliography.

Hargis, Bobby W., DPD Motorcycle Officer: WC VI, 293-296.

Harkness, D. V., Sergeant, DPD, in front of TSBD: WC VI, 308-315.

Hartmann, William, HSCA Photo Panel, "jiggle" analysis: HSCA II, 4-16, 130-137, (panning error/blur analysis) VI, 19-30, (comparison with acoustics) VI, 30-31. Letters to the HSCA dated August 11 and October 19, 1978, in the National Archives, College Park, file. Personal communication in meeting of November 27, 2000, Tucson, Arizona. Personal communication throughout 2003 and 2004.

Herndon, Bell P. polygraph operator for the FBI (Ruby's polygraph): WC XIV, 579-598.

Hill, Clinton J. Secret Service Agent, followup car (ran forward): WC II, 132-144.

Hill, Jean Lollis, DPD witness: WC VI, 205-223. Marrs' *Crossfire,* pp 38 & 323. Lane's *Rush to Judgment,* pp 222 & 242-3.

Holland, S. M., Union Terminal railroad employee, DP "smoke" witness: WC VI, 239-248, Aff. XIX, 480, XX, 163 (same one). Lane references "Interview of Holland by Mark Lane, filmed and tape-recorded in Irving Tex., 3/21/66." Lane's *Rush to Judgment,* pp 25-6, 28, 31, 243.

Holmes, Harry D., U.S. Post Office Inspector: WC VII, 289-308, 525-530.

Hosty, James, Dallas FBI Special Agent assigned to Lee Oswald: WC IV, 440-476.

Humes, James J. Pathologist in charge of JFK Autopsy: WC II, 347-376. HSCA I, 323-332. Interview in JAMA, V. 267, No. 20, pp 2794-2803.

Jarman, James, DP witness in TSBD: WC III, 198-211.

Jenkins, Marion T. Parkland physician, JFK: WC VI, 45-51. Report reprinted in Texas State Journal of Medicine, V. 60, 61-74, Jan 1964. Interview in JAMA, V. 267, No. 20, pp 2804-2807.

Jimison, R.J., Orderly at Parkland Hospital, JBC Operating Room: WC VI, 125-128.

Johnson, Claudia (Lady Bird), Lyndon's wife: WC Aff. V, 564-567.

Johnson, Gladys J. (Mrs. Arthur C.), Lee Oswald's landlady: WC X, 292-301

Johnson, Lyndon, Vice-President: WC Aff. V, 561-564.

Jones, Ronald Coy, Parkland physician, JFK: WC VI, 51-56.

Kellerman, Roy H., Secret Service, Assistant Special Agent in Charge of the White House: WC II, 61-112.

Kennedy Jacqueline, First Lady: WC V, 178-181.

Kounas, Delores, McGraw-Hill, third floor of TSBD, DP witness: WC Aff. XXII, 846.

Lane, Mark, Conspiracy author, former lawyer for the Oswalds: WC II, 32-61.

Lawson, Winston, Secret Service Agent, in lead car: WC IV, 317-358.

Light, Frederick, Biophysics Division supervisor: WC V, 94-97.

Lovelady, Billy, DP witness from steps of TSBD: WC VI, 336-341. WC Exhibit No. 2003.

Lutz, Monty, firearms & tool mark analyst, Wisconsin Regional Crime Lab, New Berlin: HSCA I, 444-489.

Mack, Gary, Curator, Sixth Floor Museum, Dallas: Personal meeting October, 1997. Personal communications in 2003 and 2004.

Markham, Helen, Tippit murder witness: WC III, 305-322, 340-342; VII, 499-506.

Mason, Richard, Medical Examiner, San Jose, CA: Personal meeting, May 6/7, 2003. Personal communications May/June 2003.

McCamy, Calvin, Spokesman, HSCA Photo Panel: HSCA, II, 142-154.

McClelland, Robert, Parkland physician, JFK : WC VI, 30-39. Report reprinted in Texas State Journal of Medicine, V. 60, 61-74, Jan 1964. Interview in JAMA, V. 267, No. 20, pp 2804-2807.

McDonald, M. N., DPD Patrolman, arrest in Texas Theatre: WC III, 295-304.

McLain, H. B., DPD motorcycle policeman, implicated by HSCA as the one with a stuck microphone button: HSCA V, 617-641. Statement in Web article by Dallas County Sheriff, J. C. Bowles: http://www.jfk-online. com/acousticarc.html (Dave Reitzes' website.)

McNally, Joseph P., HSCA handwriting expert: HSCA II, 372-387; IV, 254-259; V 254-361. Report, "The Examination of the Handwriting and Fingerprint Evidence," HSCA VIII, 223-249; Exhibits, VIII, 251-389.

McWillie, Lewis, Mafia employee, acquaintance of Jack Ruby: (testimony) HSCA V, 2-239; (deposition) V, 15-150; (FBI Interview) V, 152-159.

Mercer, Julia Ann, DP "green truck" witness: WC Aff. XIX, 483-484.

Miller, Austin, Railroad employee, DP "smoke" witness: WC VI, 223-227.

Mooney, Luke, Deputy Sheriff, TSBD search: WC III, 281-290.

Myers, Dale, www.jfkfiles.com.

Newman, William Eugene, DP witness: WC Aff. XXII, 843. Sheriff's Dept. Affidavit reprinted HSCA V, 508-509. Marrs' interview in Crossfire, p 70.

Newquist, Andrew, special agent and firearm and tool mark examiner, Iowa bureau of Criminal Investigation: HSCA I, 444-489.

Nicol, Joseph D., Superintendent, Bureau of Criminal Identification and Investigation, Illinois: WC III, 451-515.

Norman, Harold, DP witness in TSBD: WC III, 186-198.

Nosenko, Yuri, Soviet defector, claimed knowledge of Oswald in USSR: HSCA XII, 477-527.

Olivier, Alfred G., Branch Chief, Biophysics Laboratory, Edgewood Arsenal, MD, supervisor of WC tests: WC V, 74-90. CBS TV interview, 1967, based on government report referenced above. Personal communication, September 30, 1996.

Oswald, Marina, wife of Lee: WC I, 1-126; V, 387-408, 410-420, 588-620; XI, 275-301. As Marina O. Porter: HSCA II, 206-319. Depositions (Sep 20, 1977 and Aug 9, 1978): XII, 319-434.

Oswald, Marguerite, mother of Lee: WC I, 126-264.

Paine, Ruth, friend of Marina Oswald (Marina and baby staying with her): WC II, 430-517; III, 1-140; IX, 331-434; XI, 389-398. WC Aff. XI, 153-155.

Perry, Malcolm, Parkland physician, JBC: WC III, 366-390; VI, 7-18. Report reprinted in Texas State Journal of Medicine, V. 60, 61-74, Jan 1964. Interview in JAMA, V. 267, No. 20, pp 2804-2807.

Postal, Julia, ticket taker at Texas Theatre: WC VII, 8-14.

Price, Jesse C., DP witness: WC Aff. in Decker exhibit 5828, XIX, 492. Lane references "Interview of Price by Mark Lane, filmed and tape-recorded in Dallas, 3/27/66." in Lane's *Rush to Judgment,* pp 24-5, 28.

Rachley, Virgie (as Virgie Baker), DP witness: WC VII, 507-515.

Ramsey, Norman, Harvard University acoustics expert, Chairman of the National Academy of Sciences review of the Acoustics study: Report on web at Dave Reitzes' site: http://www.jfk-online.com/nas01.html

Randle, Linnie Mae, Wesley Frazier's sister: WC II, 245-251.

Reid, Mrs. Robert A., DP witness: WC III, 270-281.

Roberts, Earlene, housekeeper/manager of Oswald's rooming house: WC VI, 434-444. WC Aff. VII, 439.

Ruby, Jack, Dallas nightclub owner, killer of Oswald: WC V, 181-213. WC polygraph XIV, 504-570.

Salerno, Ralph, HSCA Mafia expert: HSCA V, 378-471. HSCA Report IX, 1-60.

Scoggins, William, Dallas taxi driver, Tippit murder witness: WC III, 322-340.

Selzer, Robert, Jet Propulsion Lab, consultant to HSCA: letter, dated August 28, 1978, to HSCA, in file of National Archives, College Park (folder 10675).

Shaw, Robert R., Parkland physician, JBC: WC VI, 83-95; (with J. Connally) WC IV, 101-117. Report reprinted in Texas State Journal of Medicine, V. 60, 61-74, Jan 1964.

Shelly, William, DP witness: WC VI, 327-334; VII, 390-393.

Shires, George Thomas, Parkland physician, JBC: WC VI, 104-113. Report reprinted in Texas State Journal of Medicine, V. 60, 61-74, Jan 1964.

Simmons, Ronald, Ballistic Research Laboratory, Aberdeen Proving Ground, MD: WC III, 441-451.

Smith, Joe Marshall, DPD patrolman, in DP: WC VII, 531-539.

Sorrels, Forrest, Secret Service Agent, in lead car: WC VII, 332-360; XIII, 55-83. WC Aff. VII, 592.

Stringer, John: Statement given to John Canal Dec 30, 2003.

Sturdivan, Larry, Edgewood Arsenal representative to HSCA: HSCA I, 383-427.

Tague, James, DP witness, scratch on cheek: WC VII, 552-558.

Tatum, Jack Ray, Tippit murder witness: Posner's *Case Closed*, pp 276-277

Tomlinson, Darrell C., senior engineer at Parkland, found "stretcher" bullet, CE 399: WC VI, 128-134.

Trafficante, Santos, high-ranking member of the Mafia: HSCA 5, 362-375.

Truly, Roy, supervisor, TSBD: WC III, 212-241; VII, 380-386.

Walthers, Eddy Raymond, Deputy Sheriff: WC VII, 544-552.

Wecht, Cyril, Medical Examiner, Alleghany County (Pittsburgh), PA : HSCA I, 332-373.

Weiss, Mark, Professor, Queens College, New York City, HSCA Acoustic expert: HSCA V, 555-615.

Weitzman, Seymour, Deputy Constable, Dallas, TSBD investigation: WC VII, 105-109. WC Aff. II, 46.

Whaley, William, Dallas taxi driver, gave ride to Oswald: WC II, 253-262, 292-294; VI, 428-434.

Whitten, Les, Columnist for Washington Post: HSCA V, 365 (Reprint of column: JFK Exhibit F-409).

Williams, Bonnie Ray, DP witness from TSBD: WC III, 161-186.

Yarborough, Ralph, Texas US Senator, in VP car: WC Aff. VII, 439-440.

Youngblood, Rufus, Secret Service Agent, VP car: WC II, 144-155.

Zapruder, Abraham, Dallas dressmaker, photographer of assassination movie: WC VII, 569-576.

Zoppi, Tony, entertainment reporter, Dallas Morning News, acquaintance of Ruby: HSCA Interview V, 169-173.

INDEX